FREEDOM AND WELFARE

FREEDOM AND WELFARE

SOCIAL PATTERNS

IN

THE NORTHERN COUNTRIES OF EUROPE

EDITED BY

GEORGE R. NELSON

DENMARK

ASSISTED BY

AUNE MÄKINEN-OLLINEN

FINLAND

SVERRIR THORBJÖRNSSON

ICELAND

KAARE SALVESEN

NORWAY

GÖRAN TEGNER

SWEDEN

GREENWOOD PRESS, PUBLISHERS
WESTPORT, CONNECTICUT

Originally published in 1953
by the Ministries of Social Affairs
of Denmark, Finland, Iceland, Norway, Sweden

First Greenwood Reprinting 1970

SBN 8371-2903-6

PRINTED IN UNITED STATES OF AMERICA

FOREWORD

by the Northern Ministers of Social Affairs

The Northern countries, Denmark, Finland, Iceland, Norway, and Sweden, constitute five independent states. They form no political or economic union of any sort. Still, they are often looked upon as a collective entity.

Their peoples are related to each other by a number of firm bonds: Geographical proximity, common history and cultural ties, including the similarity of tongues. They cherish the friendship which unites them and are rather proud of having achieved in their corner of the world the ability to live at peace with each other on a basis of mutual respect and recognition of each other's rights.

Within the international community the Northern peoples undoubtedly feel like, and give the impression of being a more or less distinct family group. They may thus themselves be to blame, if the result has sometimes been an oversimplified picture, standing in the way of a realistic appraisal of existing conditions in this region and of the numerous and important national distinctions actually found. But especially in the social field differences are less essential than in several other domains. In their approach to a number of vital problems of community

1

living the five countries show a basic similarity at the same time that this approach presents certain aspects peculiarly characteristic of these peoples. The present volume is the by-product of one of the many programmes of Northern co-operation. Since the early 1920's the Ministers of Social Affairs of the five countries have met periodically to discuss problems of mutual interest and possibilities for collaboration and co-ordination. At the 1947-meeting, held in Stockholm, it was decided, upon the suggestion of the Icelandic Minister of Social Affairs, to sponsor the preparation and publication, in the English language, of a brief yet comprehensive survey of the ways and means by which the five countries have striven within recent decades to deal with some of the basic problems pertaining to the economic and social welfare of their peoples.

All five Northern countries are parliamentary democracies and it is as free democracies dedicated to the basic humanitarian rights that they have worked and are working today to promote the welfare of their peoples. They do not claim to have found any final solution to the many and intricate social and economic problems with which our industrialized age is beset. It is hoped, though, that this account of the experience gained by the Northern countries in dealing with a number of these problems will be accepted as a modest contribution to the cause of promoting mutual knowledge and understanding among the peoples of the world.

The preparation of the present publication has been entrusted to an editorial committee consisting of George R. Nelson, Danish

II

Ministry of Labour and Social Affairs, editor in chief; Aune Mäkinen-Ollinen, Finnish Ministry of Social Affairs; Kaare Salvesen, Norwegian Ministry of Social Affairs; Göran Tegner, Swedish Ministry of Social Affairs, with Ernst Michanek, of the same Ministry, as alternate; and Sverrir Thorbjörnsson, Icelandic Ministry of Social Affairs. Full responsibility for the form and contents of the book rests with this committee.

August 1953.

Denmark

Finland

Iceland

Norway

Sweden

Editor's Preface

The purpose of the present publication is a limited one. It aims to provide the interested foreigner with a bird's eye view of selected social patterns in the Northern countries as a whole. The emphasis being upon the five countries as a closely interrelated group, it has been felt natural – and preferable to a presentation in national monographs – to prepare the survey by subject, each chapter highlighting the broad lines of action pursued by these countries in dealing with the various problems under consideration.

Inevitably this approach has meant the omission of many important national details at the same time that shortage of space has made for a general brevity of exposition. It follows that the book should be considered an introduction to, rather than an exhaustive handbook on, the subjects dealt with. The expert interested in details is referred to the literature indicated in the bibliography appended to the text.

In its work the editorial committee has been guided by two main practical considerations: First, that the presentation given should be as accurate as in any way possible and, second, that at the same time it should follow a uniform and consistent line of exposition. Accordingly, the working method adopted has been for each of the participating countries to furnish the documentation required and for the editor in chief to utilize the data thus provided for the writing of a common text in the English language.

In undertaking this task the editor in chief has received valuable assistance from a number of experts among whom Mr. Einer Engberg and Mr. Vagn Rud Nielsen, both of the Danish Ministry of Housing, and Mr. Clemens Pedersen, of the Central Co-operative Committee of Denmark, merit particular mention. Moreover, the editor in chief wishes to express his warm appreciation of the untiring effort contributed by his assistant, Mr. Hans R. v. Bülow.

V

The texts prepared have subsequently been circulated to experts in each of the countries concerned for review and comment. The editorial committee hereby acknowledges its heavy debt of gratitude for the constructive criticism and valuable suggestions thus obtained. The final wording has then been hammered out during five meetings of the editorial committee, held in each of the Northern capitals. The committee retains sole responsibility for any factual errors as well as for all opinions expressed in the volume.

In general, the presentation includes developments up to 31 July 1953 although the latest statistical data usually refer only to 1951 or 1952.

GEORGE R. NELSON

VI

Contents

II. LABOUR

IX

V. HOUSING

XI

XII

NOTE

Due to the difficulties inherent in the translation of monetary values from one country to another, no attempt is made to undertake any international comparison involving the use of rates of exchange among different currencies. Monetary values are consequently given in the currency of the country concerned.

At the time of going into print the official exchange rates were the following:

100 Danish kroner	=	14.50 Dollars or	5 £ 3 sh. 4 d.
100 Finmarks	=	0.44 Dollars or	0 £ 3 sh. 1 ¹/₂ d.
100 Icelandic krónur	=	6.15 Dollars or	2 £ 3 sh. 11 d.
100 Norwegian kroner	=	14.05 Dollars or	5 £ 0 sh. 9 d.
100 Swedish kronor	=	19.38 Dollars or	6 £ 17 sh. 9 d.

It may be added, that there would appear to be a consensus of opinion that the general buying power of the Danish, Norwegian, and Swedish currencies is about double the value indicated by the official rates of exchange as against U.S. dollars.

CHAPTER I

THE NORTHERN COUNTRIES

The Lands

The Northern countries are situated between 54° and 71° northern latitudes. Extending beyond the polar circle, they form the northernmost civilization in the world. Oslo, Stockholm, and Helsinki, the capitals of Norway, Sweden, and Finland, are all placed approximately on the 60th parallel, i. e. in the same latitude as southern Greenland, the northern part of Hudson Bay, South Alaska, and the northern part of the peninsula of Kamchatka in Asia. Reykjavik, the capital of Iceland, lies even 4 degrees farther to the north, while Copenhagen in Denmark is as many degrees south of the parallel.

The geographic location of these countries has unquestionably been a major factor in their close association, but at the same time it accounts for certain differences of interests and outlook. Omitting Iceland, the four remaining countries form a close group, the territory of which extends 1,200 miles from the Danish-German frontier in the south to Cape North, the northernmost point of Norway. In the west it is washed by the North Sea and the Atlantic, and in the east it is bounded by the Finnish-Russian frontier. Three of the countries – Finland, Norway, and Sweden – form parts of a continuous territory, with the Danish isles and the peninsula of Jutland in the immediate neighbourhood at the entrance to the Baltic. Iceland, on the other hand, is situated in the North Atlantic, farther away from the other countries than the British Isles.

The sea which links all five countries together has become their second element. Taking advantage of long and accessible coast lines, the Northern peoples have always used the sea as the easiest lane of inter-communication, as the connecting link with the outer world, and as a dependable source of wealth.

The Danish kingdom includes the rocky Faroe Islands, located north of the Shetlands in the Atlantic. Also Greenland, situated

I

between Iceland and northern Canada, and the world's largest island, is part of Denmark; the greater part of Greenland is glaciated. The arctic Svalbard island group is regarded as a part of the Kingdom of Norway, and certain antarctic territories are Norwegian possessions.

Traditionally, the Northern countries are considered minor members of the world community. This does not, however, hold true in relation to their aggregate territorial size. Together they occupy a land area of approximately 450,000 square miles or the equivalent of the United Kingdom, France, and Spain put together. Finland, Norway, and Sweden each cover an area of well over 100,000 square miles, while Iceland is no larger than Kentucky in the USA, and Denmark covers little more than half the area of Scotland.

Their climate is by no means as "arctic" as their latitudes might seem to indicate. Thanks to the Gulf stream and the predominant south-westerly winds from the Atlantic the region is favoured with winters which, although cold enough, are warmer than those prevailing elsewhere along similar latitudes. The average temperature in January roughly equals that of Central Europe and of those regions in the United States which are situated along the 45th degree (e. g. the Great Lakes, Vancouver, etc.). The summers are, of course, not very warm, but even such a northerly spot as Haparanda in Sweden – located in the same latitude as Fairbanks in Alaska – enjoys July temperatures averaging 60° F. As a result, the cultivation of barley, potatoes, clover, and timothy grass is possible even far north of the Arctic Circle. Precipitation is everywhere sufficient to permit agriculture and the growth of timber. The largest rainfall occurs on the western mountain slopes of the Scandinavian peninsula and many rivers, rich in hydro-electric power, therefore take their origin in this region. The long and dark winter nights are counterbalanced by the bright summer evenings, causing the strongest rhythm in the successive changes of season known by any highly developed civilization in the world.

. . . to the beech forests of Denmark where shafts of light play between the tree trunks and the firth glistens in the background . . .

3

4   *... to Norway's mountains and valleys, where the rapids surge restlessly forward ...*

. . . to the red cottages and white birches of Sweden . . .

The whole region was glaciated during the ice periods – the last of these ending only some 15,000 years ago. With the notable exception of volcanic Iceland, the countries are consequently almost everywhere covered by moraines. The glacial soils are, of course, of very different quality, being fertile in Denmark and Skåne (Scania), but rather stony in most parts of Sweden, Norway, and Finland.

While Denmark has practically no natural resources except its assiduously tilled soil, her neighbours are better equipped. The forests which cover a quarter of the surface area of Norway, more than half of Sweden, and almost three-quarters of Finland play a fundamental role in the economies of these countries and probably constitute their greatest single natural source of wealth. Formerly utilized mainly as a reservoir of sawn timber, the forests today furnish raw materials for the modern forest industries producing a variety of essential commodities for the world market. Sweden has a further advantage in possessing rich deposits of iron ore which form a basis for her highly developed steel and engineering industry. Considerably smaller deposits are found, too, in Finland and Norway.

Apart from the coal deposits of Svalbard, all five countries are practically devoid of hard fuel and mineral oils (petroleum) but, here again with the exception of Denmark, this shortage is partly compensated for by the abundant hydro-electric power derived from the numerous rivers and waterfalls. As yet these resources, the development of which requires large amounts of capital, have been only partly harnessed. Even so, Norway had already before the Second World War attained the largest use *per capita* of hydro-electric power in the world. Iceland, with extensive unused water resources, has been able to benefit from her many hot springs; Reykjavik, the capital, is heated by the almost boiling water from such springs, pumped into the town by an elaborate network of pipelines. Denmark, on the other hand, must rely almost entirely on imported fuel for heating and power, although a certain amount of hydro-electric power is transmitted from Sweden.

Finally, the sea has always provided the Northern peoples with an abundance of fish. The famous Lofoten fishing grounds off the northern coast of Norway have yielded their fish harvests for centuries and today deliver enormous quantities for the world market. And the great fishing banks near Iceland have proved of vital importance to that country as the mainstay of her industrial life and export trade.

...all the way to Iceland's geysirs and fields of lava. Here is the famous Thingvellir where the Icelanders held their annual parliament and dispensed justice for almost nine hundred years, starting way back in 930 A.D.

The Peoples

The Northern countries are but thinly populated, totalling only some 18.9 million inhabitants, or 42 to the square mile – as against almost 50 in the United States and 530 in the United Kingdom. But, as the following figures for 1952 illustrate, this overall average covers wide differences from country to country.

[1] *Exclusive of the Faroe Islands, with about 30,000 inhabitants of Scandinavian extraction, and Greenland, with about 20,000 inhabitants of Eskimo origin.*

POPULATION AND POPULATION DENSITY

	Inhabitants	Per sq. mile
Sweden	7,102,000	45
Denmark[1]	4,319,000	261
Finland	4,068,000	34
Norway	3,307,000	28
Iceland	145,000	4

Denmark, with her intensely cultivated territory, is the only relatively densely populated area among the group, the other countries falling far behind, with Iceland as the extreme case. Their low average, however, covers sharp regional differences. The northern parts of Finland, Norway, and Sweden are composed of vast and almost empty expanses, most of the inhabitants living along the coasts, in central Sweden, and on the fertile plains of Scania where the density of population approaches that of Denmark.

In all five countries the past century has witnessed more than a doubling of their population, due mainly to the reduction of the overall mortality rate from over 20 to roughly 10 per 1,000 inhabitants; simultaneously the birth-rate has, however, fallen off considerably.

With progressive industrialization there has been an ever increasing urbanization of the population. While a century ago only about 10–20 per cent lived in towns and urban settlements, this proportion has today risen to 50–70 per cent in all of the countries under review, except Finland, where the rural population is still in the majority.

The Danes, Norwegians, and Swedes have inhabited their present territories since prehistoric times while the Icelanders – emigrants from Norway – first started to colonize their remote island around the end of the 9th century. The foreign visitor will meet many tall, blond, blue-eyed men and women in these countries, forming as they

The lonely, tranquil vista of one of the deep Norwegian fjords contrasts sharply with...

...the fertile landscapes of Denmark and southern Sweden, where small-holdings spring in clusters and a neighbour is never far away.

do the centre of the so-called Nordic stock of the European races. The Finns are typically even more blond, but more squarely built than their Nordic cousins; they belong to the east Baltic race. An ethnographically very interesting small minority of people in the north of Sweden, Norway, and Finland are the Lapps; with their triangular faces, short statures, brown hair and eyes they form a race of their own.

Danes, Norwegians, Icelanders, and Swedes all speak north-teutonic languages, related to the German and Anglo-Saxon tongues and derived from a common language, which was still spoken about 1000 A. D. These languages have since developed along slightly different paths but Danes, Swedes, and Norwegians still understand each other without much difficulty. Icelanders, because of their isolated geographical position, have retained a more conservative language which is not easily understood by the other Northern peoples, but many educated Icelanders command one or two of the other Northern tongues. Thus, the languages contribute to the formation of a cultural unity in the Northern countries.

The Finns speak a language which is not related to any of the great European language groups, but it is somewhat akin to the Hungarian tongue. In prehistoric times, however, the Finnish coastal provinces were colonized by the Swedes – the Swedish-speaking group still comprising some 10 per cent of the population of Finland. Moreover, Finland belonged to the Kingdom of Sweden for many hundred years up to 1809, and today forms part of the Northern sphere of culture. The Lapps speak an ancient Finnish tongue.

Another important unifying factor has been that of religion. Since just before or after the year 1000 A. D. the Northern countries have been Christian. In the 16th century they all seceded from the Roman Catholic Church and embraced Lutheranism, which to this day remains the creed to which the great majority of the peoples adhere.

All in all, community of "race", language, and religion unquestionably plays a major part among the factors which bind the Northern peoples together. However, the strength of these forces should not be overestimated. Especially would it be fallacious to draw the conclusion that a closer study would necessarily reveal close similarities in customs, tastes, temperament, etc. Tell any representative of these peoples that there is no apparent difference between them, and the reaction will not be long in forthcoming.

Some Historical Facts

Although the common history of the Northern countries is often counted as a unifying factor, it would probably be wise to approach this subject with some caution. The tale which this history recounts is by no means one of close and harmonious association alone, but also one of wars and alternate domination.

The peoples of the Northern countries made their first entry upon the scene of world history around 700–800 A. D. when the Viking boats began to make their appearance on the beaches of Western and Northern Europe. The age of the Vikings, which culminated shortly after 1000 A. D., was one of powerful expansion engendered by overpopulation in the home countries and stimulated by the political weakness of the neighbouring communities. The Viking ventures were a mixture of raids, foreign trade, and colonization. While emigrants from western Scandinavia settled in England,

The Northern Vikings once reached the far corners of the earth. The 75-foot Viking ship shown above was found in 1880 at Gokstad, Norway. It was built sometime between 900 and 1000 A.D.

11

Scotland, Ireland, and Normandy, the Swedish Vikings pushed forward into Eastern Europe and established themselves in the towns of Kiew and Novgorod, thus laying the foundations of the first Russian State.

The Northern peoples emerged from the Viking era grouped into three major national units: Denmark, Norway-Iceland, and Sweden-Finland, a development which entailed the integration of numerous smaller groupings while at the same time national distinctions, formerly of small significance, assumed increased importance.

Segregation was, however, counteracted by the Roman Catholic Church, which succeeded in converting the Northerners – hitherto believers in the Germanic deities, with Odin and Thor as principal gods – to Christianity. The Northern Church subsequently freed itself from its dependence upon the German Missionary Church and around 1100 founded a separate clerical province with the archbishop of Lund (in southern Sweden, then a Danish province) as supreme ecclesiastical authority. This was an event of major importance in fostering spiritual independence in the North and although the subsequent development of national churches disrupted this supra-national organization, the conception of the Northern countries as a religious entity survived.

During the fourteenth century, the Hanseatic towns of Northern Germany gradually became the dominating power in the Baltic Sea. The difficulties of withstanding the pressure of German political and economic expansion paved the way for the Union of the Northern monarchies which Queen Margaret of Denmark succeeded in establishing towards the end of that century. The basic political idea underlying the Union was to safeguard peace in the North and to uphold the freedom and independence of these countries against the outer world. The Union lasted for half a century and although it finally gave way to the growing Swedish independence movement, it was still considered of such value as to be revived at intermittent intervals towards the end of medieval times. It was only abandoned definitely when international political conditions changed and the Dutch replaced the Germans as the leading sea power in the Baltic.

After the beginning of the modern era in the early 16th century, the Northern countries followed their own course. Their kings broke away from the Catholic Church and founded national Protestant Churches closely associated with the State. On the political plane the following centuries were characterized by struggles for domination of the Baltic between the two great powers of the North, the Danish-Norwegian monarchy, including Iceland, and the Kingdom of Sweden-Finland.

The Northern countries were peopled by farmers who, despite many onslaughts, succeeded – in most of the countries – in retaining their freedom and established rights. Political controversies hardly penetrated to the common people; more often than not the inhabitants of frontier regions agreed among themselves to safeguard each other's lives and property. In some of the countries, the farmers exerted considerable influence upon the local administration of law and succeeded in retaining a fair amount of local self-government. In the last decades of the 18th century, the Danish peasants – whose status had been harshly restricted for several centuries – obtained the same liberties as their Northern brethren, and, with the active support of the State, a powerful class of independent farmers was established. The free peasantry in all Northern countries was ready for new social and political reforms.

During the Napoleonic Wars the old balance of power in the North was shattered. Finland was torn from Sweden and came under the Russian Czar, but throughout the following century managed to preserve her Nordic legal system. Norway, likewise, was separated from Denmark and united with Sweden instead.

Still, the conception of the Northern countries as an entity survived and towards the middle of the 19th century it found new and strong expression in so-called "Scandinavianism". This movement, which emanated primarily from the universities of Denmark, Norway, and Sweden, had for its original purpose to develop cultural contacts between the Northern countries in science and literature. Gradually, however, "Scandinavianism" also became an active political force, advocating military co-operation among the Northern countries in defence of the Danish southern frontier against the threat of German encroachments. The movement ultimately failed in its political ambitions, but it contributed more than anything else to put an end to the hereditary distrust and hostility among the three nations.

Since the beginning of the 19th century, peace has reigned between the Northern countries. Developments on the world political scene, together with the gradual emergence of these countries as five distinct, and individually rather small, national societies, have removed the foundations for the former policy of expansion directed against each

13

other as well as against foreign powers. In its stead has come a growing recognition of the value of co-operation in the field of international relations coupled with a deepening of mutual understanding which has taught these peoples to solve even their most acute disputes by means of peaceful negotiation.

In 1905 the Swedish-Norwegian Union was dissolved and Norway again became an independent monarchy. After the First World War Finland likewise succeeded in achieving full independence as a free republic. Finally, Iceland, which had remained with Denmark – from 1918, however, as an independent state – in 1944 resumed complete sovereignty as a republic. The present state of affairs, with five autonomous and equal states, is thus actually of recent date. It only remains to mention that the Danish Faroe Islands are – since 1948 – self-governing in all local affairs, and that in Greenland certain matters of purely local interest are decided by the Greenlanders themselves.

The years between the two World Wars witnessed a flourishing of co-operation among the five countries in the fields of cultural and social affairs. The feeling of political and spiritual kinship was further deepened by the hardships brought upon several of the countries by the Second World War. It has, however, proved extremely difficult to translate these friendly relations into a joint stand on the main issues of foreign policy. While the countries of Northern Europe were, with the partial exception of Finland, left untouched by the First World War, the Second World War broke the peace also in this region of the world. In 1940 Denmark and Norway were attacked and occupied by German troops, while Finland, on her side, fought two wars with her eastern neighbour, Soviet Russia. Iceland and Sweden alone were not directly involved in military operations, although British and American forces were stationed in the former country. Within recent years Denmark, Iceland, and Norway have joined the North Atlantic Treaty, while Sweden has clung to her traditional policy of armed neutrality and Finland has followed a policy dictated by her position on the borderline of Soviet Russia. These developments would seem to imply that closer co-ordination in foreign policy among the Northern countries has been deferred to a distant future.

Thus, the close similarity between the Northern countries is not reflected by any identity in the foreign policies pursued, but by the basic likeness of political structures, institutions, and outlook in general. A significant recent manifestation of this indisputable feeling of solidarity is the Northern Council established by decision of the Parliaments of Denmark, Iceland, Norway, and Sweden. This consultative body, which held its first meeting in February 1953, is composed of parliamentarians and of government representatives from the participating countries and has for its purpose to consider and submit recommendations on questions pertaining to intra-Northern co-operation. Although not a formal member, Finland may join such deliberations at her own discretion, in which case her representatives will participate on equal terms with those of the other countries.

Industrial Structure

Keeping in mind their differences with respect to topography and natural resources, it is hardly surprising that there should be considerable divergences also between the industrial structures of the Northern countries. This holds true of all five members of the group but especially of Denmark, Norway, and Sweden on one hand, and Finland and Iceland on the other. While the former three countries have all attained a fair degree of industrialization, the latter two countries have been somewhat later in their economic development, a fact which is still discernible in the greater role played by rural industries within their present economy. One feature, however, is common to all five countries: In order to maintain their standards of living they are all heavily dependent upon a large-scale exchange of goods and services with other parts of the world.

The industrial revolution took its beginning in Northern Europe around 1860–1870 – rather late, that is, in comparison with the major industrial nations; in Finland and Iceland, moreover, it was only well into the present century that industrialization began to make appreciable headway. Here, as elsewhere, it brought radical changes in the structure of the communities. Although the five countries show considerable differences in the degree of their structural adjustment, the main trend has everywhere been the same, agriculture inevitably yielding in comparative importance to the rapidly expanding manufacturing industry and commerce. Within three generations, that part of the population which makes its living mainly from agriculture has in Denmark, Norway, and Sweden declined from 75–80 per cent to only about 20–30 per cent, while the groups employed in industry, commerce, and transport have soared from a modest 10–15 per cent to somewhere in the neighbourhood of 60 per cent. In Finland and Iceland agriculture still outranks industry and commerce, although by a narrowing margin.

In the earlier phases of industrialization manufacturing and basic construction expanded at the expense of farming, but in more recent decades commerce, transport, administration, and other urban service occupations have shown the highest rate of development. Even so, industrialization has proceeded apace, since there has been a steady change-over from handicraft production to industrial manufacturing proper. During the period 1930–1950 the volume of industrial production almost doubled in Denmark and Norway, while it increased by roughly 150 per cent in Finland, Iceland, and Sweden. The Northern countries, however, have been fortunate in escaping the concentration of industry in large and sooty urban agglomerations, like those found in some industrial countries. To be sure, numerous industrial plants are situated in or near the capitals and major cities, but on the whole Northern industry is characterized by its high degree of decentralization. This applies not only to sectors where the emphasis is upon craftsmanship, for heavy industries are very frequently situated in relatively small towns and urban settlements.

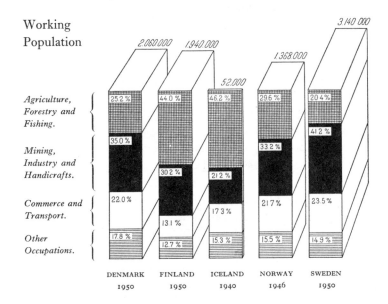

Working Population

Agriculture, Forestry and Fishing.

Mining, Industry and Handicrafts.

Commerce and Transport.

Other Occupations.

	DENMARK 1950	FINLAND 1950	ICELAND 1940	NORWAY 1946	SWEDEN 1950
	2.060.000	1.940.000	52.000	1.368.000	3.140.000
Agriculture, Forestry and Fishing	25.2 %	44.0 %	46.2 %	29.6 %	20.4 %
Mining, Industry and Handicrafts	35.0 %	30.2 %	21.2 %	33.2 %	41.2 %
Commerce and Transport	22.0 %	13.1 %	17.3 %	21.7 %	23.5 %
Other Occupations	17.8 %	12.7 %	15.3 %	15.5 %	14.9 %

Sweden is today the most highly industrialized of the Northern countries. Reliant upon large forest resources and rich deposits of high-grade iron ore, its industry has developed a manufacturing potential of very considerable magnitude. Besides large-scale exports of wood, pulp, and paper, the far-famed Swedish iron ore and steel products are marketed all over the world. In 1950 about 41 per cent of Sweden's working population were employed in mining, industry, and handicrafts, 20 per cent in agriculture, fisheries, and forestry, and 23 per cent in commerce, shipping, and transport.

Denmark is generally known as a large supplier to the world market of agricultural products, and agriculture and the dependent food industries still account for about three-fifths of the country's total exports. But manufacturing – based largely upon imported raw materials – has developed rapidly within recent decades. Today industry and handicrafts have assumed first place in providing employment for 35 per cent of the working population (in 1950) as against 25 per cent in agriculture, forestry and fisheries; 22 per cent being engaged in commerce, shipping, and transport.

Norway is often characterized by her high dependency upon the sea, the earnings of her large merchant marine paying for a major part of necessary imports, and the extensive fisheries playing an essential role in her economy. In 1946 about 22 per cent of the working population were engaged in commerce, shipping, and communications and almost 6 per cent in fisheries. However, industrialization has made rapid progress within the present century, with processed forest products taking a leading place in Norwegian exports. Industry and handicrafts now employ more than 33 per cent of the working population; the percentage for agriculture and forestry being about 23.

Finland's economy rests primarily upon her forests which serve as the natural basis for most of her manufacturing industry and provide her main exports: Sawn timber, pulp, and wood products. Two-fifths of the working population are engaged in agriculture and forestry, frequently pursuing both occupations in combination. Industrialization only began to assume sizable proportions after 1918, when the country attained independence. In 1950 30 per cent were employed in industry and handicrafts.

Iceland is the outstanding fishing nation among the Northern countries. In 1940 almost one-fifth of her working population was engaged in fishing, and fish provide the bulk of the country's exports. One fourth of the working population was employed in agriculture, and well over 20 per cent in industry and handicrafts; recent years have seen an increased development of plants for the freezing, canning, and processing of fish and fish products.

While the preceding paragraphs have emphasized the outstanding characteristics of each of the five national economies, a survey of their main segments may serve to bring out a more rounded picture of actual conditions.

AGRICULTURE

Although eclipsed by manufacturing in several of the Northern countries today, agriculture everywhere remains a major industry. Denmark, however, is the only country producing a net surplus of agricultural commodities for export, while none of the other four countries is fully self-supporting. All five nations rely upon considerable imports of fodder and oil cakes to maintain production on their intensively cultivated soil; also fertilizers are imported, except by Norway which is a net exporter in this field.

Due to climatic and geological conditions the agricultural land is relatively small, amounting to less than 10 per cent of the total area. In Iceland less than one-half of one per cent of the area is under cultivation, in Norway 3 per cent, and in Finland and Sweden 7 and 9 per cent, respectively; Denmark is the outstanding exception with no less than 64 per cent under the plough. In Finland, Norway, and Sweden the farmlands are situated mainly on the territories with marine clays and sands, i. e. along the coasts, in the Oslo basin, and in central Sweden. The latter two districts together with the fertile morainic clays of Scania form the most important agricultural areas north of Denmark.

Except in sheep-raising Iceland, farming is intensive and modern, and generally in the hands of families working their own small farms. In Denmark almost half the farms are holdings of less than 25 acres; the corresponding proportion in Finland and Sweden is about three-fourths, and in Norway it is more than nine-tenths. Nowhere does more than one-fifth of the total agricultural area fall to farms of more than 125 acres; in Norway, indeed, the figure dwindles to less than three per cent.

Another characteristic feature is that today the large majority of farms are owner-operated: 94 per cent of all holdings in Denmark,

The history of the Northern countries has always been in large part a history of their farmers. Many of them have risen to become outstanding public leaders. Here we see the former Danish Prime Minister, Mr. Erik Eriksen, gathering in the harvest on his own 40-acre farm.

19

and 80–90 per cent in Norway and Sweden. In large measure this is due to a deliberate long-term government policy aiming to preserve and promote a class of independent farmers, the traditions of which reach back into early historical times. The means employed to that end are varied and include sales of government lands; strengthening of the position of tenants as against estate owners, particularly with respect to the purchase of land hitherto under leasehold tenure; financial assistance for the establishment of new farms, whether by reclamation of virgin soil or by division of former estates; and legal restrictions upon the right to purchase agricultural holdings. The development of an efficient system of agricultural credit has served as an important supplement to these measures. In Iceland and Finland ownership by farmers of their holdings is somewhat less dominating, but still applies to somewhere between 60 and 70 per cent of all farms.

Somewhat less than half the total cultivated area is in hay or rotated green crops, while grains cover more than one-third of the area, with oats as the most important crop followed by barley, wheat, and rye in the order named; root crops account for about 10 per cent of the area. Utilization of the agricultural land, however, varies between the individual countries. In Denmark grain and root crops are considerably more prominent than in the other countries, while the opposite holds true as regards hay which in Iceland, as the extreme case, rises to no less than 95 per cent of the area in agricultural use.

Animal husbandry and dairy farming dominate Northern agriculture. If, in spite of the considerable acreage devoted to cereals, grain still has to be imported, this is due simply to the fact that by far the greater part of domestic grain production is fed to cattle. Livestock totals 18 million (thus almost equalling the aggregate population) and includes 8 million heads of cattle, 5 million pigs, and 3 million sheep, with Denmark taking the lead closely followed by Sweden. Butter, bacon, eggs, cheese, and meat are today the main processed products, of which Denmark exports large quantities, while the other countries are approximately self-supporting, small surpluses alternating with small deficits. The processing and distribution of agricultural products is mostly in the hands of specialized co-operative organizations which incorporate a large majority of farmers among their members.

Once the fish start coming in, the Norwegian fishermen gather by the thousands off the Lofoten Islands where for a few short weeks the main theme is fish, fish, and fish again.

FISHERIES

The fishing banks of the North Sea and the North Atlantic, particularly south of Iceland and off the western coast of Norway, are among the richest in the world and provide the chief grounds for the extensive sea fisheries of the Northern countries. Their importance is illustrated by the facts that Norway alone has a fisheries production exceeding that of the United Kingdom and that the five countries together catch more fish than any other nation except Japan, the USA, and the USSR. Originally undertaken in the form of coastal

21

fishing from small open boats, as a supplementary occupation to agriculture, fishing has developed enormously during the last few generations and is today largely carried out by fleets of motorized vessels which frequently seek out the fish hundreds of miles from their home ports. Fishermen's co-operatives are of some importance, especially in Norway where they serve as the main marketing agents. Herring and cod form the main share of the catch. Hundreds of thousands of tons are exported annually, fresh, salted, or frozen.

Whaling, in its modern form, was developed by the Norwegians who account for nearly 50 per cent of the annual world catch. Today mainly undertaken from the great "floating factories" plying the Antarctic waters, whaling annually yields 150,000 to 200,000 tons of whale oil, most of which is exported.

FORESTRY

While Denmark possesses only minor forest resources and Iceland none at all, the other three countries are extremely rich in timber. The forested areas of Finland and Sweden each cover around 55 million acres and those of Norway almost 20 million acres. More than nine-tenths of the total wooded area is covered by softwood forests. Exploitation of this abundant wealth is greatly facilitated by the many rivers (älvs) which provide easy and cheap floatways to the mills on the coast.

A considerable proportion of the forest acreage – in Norway more than two-thirds and in the other countries about one-half – is owned (usually in rather small plots) by farmers and small-holders, the remainder being public or company-owned. The cutting of the timber is largely undertaken by the farmers in the winter season. In recent years total cuttings have averaged 2,800–3,200 million cubic feet.

INDUSTRIES AND CRAFTS

Industry in the Northern countries depends mostly upon the raw materials derived from their own farms and forests, mines, and waterfalls. But, to a certain extent, and particularly in Denmark, manufacturing has also been built upon imports of raw materials. By far the larger share of industrial production is for the domestic market, but in certain lines the Northern countries figure prominently as suppliers to the world market.

Every year some 180,000,000 logs churn their way down the Swedish streams toward the sawmills on the coast.

23

The industry of Finland is over-whelmingly based upon her endless forests. This machine in the co-operative SOK factory in Vaajakoski turns out $1^1/_4$ million matches per hour.

The *forest industry* occupies a place of primary importance in Finland, Sweden, and Norway. Within recent decades the industrial utilization of forest products has made enormous strides forward. Sawn timber, for domestic construction as well as for export, remains an important product, but emphasis has shifted increasingly towards the manufacturing of more processed goods. Today the production of paper and pulp plays the decisive role in the forest industry. As a result of continuous research new products are being taken up, the production of artificial textile fibres, wall board, and plastics being but a few examples of rapidly expanding branches. Forest products in various forms have long accounted for a large share of the foreign trade of these countries, at present representing some 25 per cent in Norway, about 50 per cent in Sweden, and in Finland no less than 90 per cent of total commodity exports.

Even more rapid expansion has taken place in the *metals and engineering industries*. Sweden takes the lead in this respect, the high-grade iron ore mined from her rich deposits in the central and northern parts of the country going partly for exports in large quantities and partly for domestic processing into high-quality steels and alloys. The mining and metals industries are today the largest Swedish industrial group, providing employment for more than a quarter of all industrial workers. Denmark, although deficient in minerals, has still succeeded in building up a metals and engineering industry which now employs almost 25 per cent of all industrial workers in the processing of imported raw materials; in its initial phases this development was greatly stimulated by the considerable domestic market created by the industrialization of agriculture and the emergence of a relatively large merchant fleet. In Norway the increased supply of cheap electricity obtained by the harnessing of some of the country's vast resources of water power has been a vital stimulus to the quick development of an important chemical, electro-chemical and electro-metallurgical industry. The Finnish engineering industry is largely a product of post-war years when, due to Russian reparation demands, it became necessary to undertake large-scale development in this field, concentrating upon the production of machinery and the building of smaller vessels.

Swedish steel products are world famous. At the Svenska Kullager- fabriken in Gothenburg a worker tests ball and roller bearings for ultimate precision.

25

Manufactured quality products account for an increasing proportion of the output of Northern engineering industries. Swedish ball and roller bearings, telephones, electrical machines and separators, and Danish diesel engines and cement-making machines are but a few examples of products which have become firmly established on the international market. As seafaring nations it is only natural that these countries should have strong traditions in shipbuilding, and that Sweden, Denmark, and 'Norway, in the order named, should long have figured among the ten leading shipbuilding countries.

The *food-processing industry* is of great importance in all five countries. In Denmark dairies and bacon factories form the basis for that country's large agricultural exports. And in Norway and Iceland great progress has been achieved in the processing of fish and fish products, largely destined for foreign markets. Freezing and canning of fish have attained sizeable proportions and numerous large mills extract oil from herrings, drying the remainder into meal, used for animal feeding.

A considerable proportion of the industrial population remains employed in handicrafts which cater almost exclusively for the home markets. One reason for this may be found in the traditional skill of Northern craftsmen, originally developed through the medieval craft gilds; another reason is the great extent to which local markets for commodities and services are limited by personal preferences. In some trades Northern craftsmanship has attained a level which has made Northern products notable export articles. Thus, Danish silverware and china, Swedish glass and furniture, and Finnish ceramics are today known and sold the world over.

The importance of the crafts is reflected by the fact that the large majority of enterprises are of but small or medium size. Although there has been a certain trend towards larger units, as yet only a minority of industrial workers – in Denmark as few as 31 per cent – are employed in establishments with more than 100 workers.

TRADE AND SHIPPING

Domestic trade in all five countries is divided among a large number of undertakings. Thus, Swedish retail shops number about 83,500, or one for every 80 inhabitants, while the corresponding Danish figures are 78,000 and 54. The typical unit is small – Swedish retail businesses average 2.9 employees – and the few department stores

Northern shipyards and shipbuilders are known the world over. The above scene is from the Kockum Yards in Malmö where a new ship leaves the stocks each month.

are situated in the large cities. With increasing urbanization and improved means of transportation, the mixed business of former days, exemplified by the general country shop, has been increasingly supplanted by specialized establishments. The large majority of retail businesses are privately operated; co-operative stores account for about 10 per cent of total turnover in Denmark and Norway, 15 per cent in Sweden, and almost 35 per cent in Finland.

The number of wholesale businesses is, naturally enough, somewhat smaller and the average unit somewhat larger. A considerable share of the turnover is in imported goods. The wholesale trade is largely concentrated in the large cities which are at the same time the main ports. As in retailing, private enterprise dominates the picture, with the co-operative organizations accounting for a limited proportion of the total turnover.

The importance to the prosperity of the Northern peoples of an extensive *foreign trade* can hardly be exaggerated. These countries carry on a considerable trade among themselves, but their combined resources supplement individual shortages only in part. As a group devoid of a large variety of important raw materials, they obtain the necessary means to pay for imports of these by the large-scale exportation partly of certain indigenous raw materials, e.g. timber and iron ore, partly of processed industrial and agricultural goods, and of fish and fish products.

As will be evident already from the preceding sections, the composition of foreign trade varies sharply among the individual countries, the uniting feature being their dependence upon one or a small number of commodities to earn the foreign currency wherewith to pay for a variety of necessary imports. In Iceland exports are almost exclusively (1951: 98 per cent) confined to fish and fish products, while the preponderance of forest products in Finnish exports is only slightly less; in Denmark agricultural products account for about three-fifths and industrial manufactures for the remaining two-fifths of total exports; of the Swedish export trade about one-half is forest goods and more than one-third ore and metals products, while in Norway forest products comprise roughly 25 per cent of total exports, fishery products being second, and ore and metals third in importance.

The Northern countries rank among the leading suppliers to the world market of several important commodities. Following the

About 20 per cent of the Icelandic population are employed in the fisheries and derived industries. Cod and herring are the most important fish caught on the banks off Iceland.

restoration of her agricultural production after the last war, Denmark has now regained her former dominating position as the foremost exporter of bacon and eggs and has even outdistanced the Netherlands as a seller of butter. Sweden is the largest exporter of chemical and mechanical pulp, and together with Finland and Norway, accounts for approximately three-quarters of total world exports of these commodities. Also as an exporter of iron ore Sweden heads the world list, with France coming second.

Imports are somewhat more diversified, but machinery and raw materials are of dominating importance in all five countries. Fuel is another essential item, especially in Denmark, and except in that country imports of food also account for an appreciable share.

Measured by the relative volume of foreign trade, the Northern countries have long ranked among the foremost trading nations in the world. Between 20 and 25 per cent of their national product is marketed abroad, indicating a foreign trade proportionally even larger than that of the United Kingdom. In 1950 imports of the five countries aggregated about 3,100 million U.S.dollars or more than the imports of France, in spite of the fact that the latter country has a population twice as large as that of the Northern countries.

The United Kingdom is the most important trading partner of all five countries both as regards imports and exports. Next come such countries as Germany, the United States, and the Netherlands. Trade among the Northern countries, if taken individually, is of more limited order but, if added up, it still ranks second only to the trade with the United Kingdom.

Northern transportation largely follows the sea lanes. This applies to internal traffic as well as to foreign trade. Sharply reduced by the severe losses suffered during the Second World War, the Northern *merchant fleets* have been rapidly reconstructed – main emphasis being laid upon motor-ships – and today aggregate 11 per cent of the world's tonnage. Norway with a fleet of more than 6 million tons takes third place among the shipping nations. Northern ships carry not only the foreign trade of their own countries but a major proportion of the fleets are permanently in freight service between foreign ports. In this connection it is worth noting that Northern shipowners do not receive any subsidies from public funds. Shipping is an important source of foreign exchange, especially in Norway where net freight earnings pay for more than one-fifth of total imports.

Facsimile from the Grágás (Grey Goose), ancient code of Icelandic law dating from the 12th century. The Grágás included detailed provisions for the care of the poor and the treatment of offenders. The reproduced document was written around 1250.

Government

Also with respect to the spirit and form of their political life the Northern countries show marked similarities. They are, above all, democracies in the West European sense of this word. Their democratic traditions go far back. The Icelandic Althing celebrated its one thousandth anniversary in 1930, and the Swedish Parliament, according to the tradition, dates from 1435 – but with its roots even further back in medieval times. For more than thirty years these countries have been parliamentary democracies, based on the universal suffrage of both women and men (Finland was the first European country where women obtained the franchise). There are numerous differences from country to country with respect to important details, such as the structure of the legislatures, voting age, etc., but viewed against the fundamental likenesses they are of minor significance.

Local government plays an important role in all the Northern countries. Although their origins go back to the earliest historical ages, the foundations of present-day municipal organs date only from the period 1835–1865. During the growth of democracy in the 19th century the local councils served as training schools for future parliamentarians who there learned to handle public affairs. A great many members of the national legislatures still start their political careers in local government.

Within the framework established by national legislation, local councils and municipal authorities carry primary responsibility for important sections of community life, although decisions with important financial implications require approval by the central government.

Social welfare, public housing, health and education, town and country planning, local road services, and public utilities are the main problems dealt with by local authorities and the past fifty years have witnessed a revolutionary expansion in these fields of activity. However, during the same period the increased financial responsibilities assumed by the central governments in these matters have inevitably implied that general directives to municipalities have become more detailed and that supervision by central governments has tightened.

The primary municipalities, some towns excluded, are grouped in counties which are entrusted with major common tasks such as hospital and road services. In each of these counties a Crown-appointed State official acts as the representative of governmental authority.

Firmly established party groups are the backbone of the political system. By contrast with the Anglo-Saxon two-party system there are four to six parties in each of the Northern countries, a difference which is, at any rate in part, attributable to the rule of proportional representation under which the number of parliamentary representatives of each party depends directly upon the total number of votes

*Local self-govern-
ment has a
thousand-year
tradition behind it
in the North. The
village councilmen
used to sit on
these stones in
Stavnsholt, Den-
mark, to discuss
and decide upon
the common weal.*

cast in its favour. It is only within the last decade that any one
party has been able to poll a majority of all votes, and coalition or
minority governments have therefore been the rule. Nevertheless,
the stability of government has been remarkable; during the period
between the wars the average tenure of office was five years in Denmark
and two to three years in the other Northern countries.

The Social Democrats, or Labour Parties, are by far the largest
single party in Denmark, Norway, and Sweden, while in Finland
and (particularly) in Iceland they are of somewhat smaller importance.
They draw their main electoral strength from industrial and agricultural workers, but also have some following among the lower
middle classes, including small-holders. Never very deeply anchored
in Marxist doctrine, these parties have pursued a consistent reformist
line. Within the last twenty years most Danish, Norwegian, and Swedish governments have been controlled by the Social Democrats,
although often with the support of other groups. Since 1945 Labour
has held the parliamentary majority both in Norway and Sweden.

The parties to the right of Labour mainly include the Farmers,
the Liberals, and the Conservatives (actual party names vary somewhat), which have usually constituted a majority in Parliaments.
To this should be added a Georgist Party in Denmark, a Swedish
People's Party in Finland (recruited from the Swedish-speaking
minority), and a Christian-Democratic Party in Norway.

33

The Farmers' parties find their electorate mainly among independent farmers with medium-size holdings although they are also supported by some of the small farmers. Both in Norway and Sweden in the 'thirties the parties have participated in cabinets dominated by the Social Democrats. The Danish Farmers' Party (Moderate Liberals) has been the leading opposition party to the Social Democrats.

The Liberals, who in Denmark, Norway, and Sweden derive their votes partly from some of the farmers, partly from the urban middle classes – particularly the intelligentsia – have suffered a gradual decline in parliamentary representation within the last generation, although the Swedish party has experienced a renaissance in recent years and today figures as the leading opposition party.

The Conservatives, who were a dominating political power until the turn of the century, today stand considerably reduced in numerical importance. The party receives most of its votes from the middle classes, including particularly independent businessmen and tradesmen, but also many salaried employees. Except in Iceland it has for the last generation been in opposition most of the time.

As for the parties at present in power, they are different, or differently combined, in all five countries. Norway has been under Labour rule ever since 1935. The same so far applies to Sweden, although in 1951 the Farmers' Party was offered, and accepted, a number of cabinet posts; the result being a strengthening of the slender Social Democratic majority in the Riksdag. In Finland a somewhat similar constellation, established in 1950, was replaced in July 1953 by a minority government comprising the Farmers' Party and the small Swedish People's Party. In Denmark the Moderate Liberals and the Conservatives took office in 1950 as a minority government, usually supported by the Liberal Party (Social Liberals); however, in October 1953 they were succeeded by a Social Democratic minority government. Finally, from 1950 the Icelandic cabinet has been formed by a strong majority coalition composed of Farmers (Progressives) and Conservatives.

Communist parties are found in all five countries. In Denmark, Norway, and Sweden they are fairly unimportant, their share of total votes at the last elections being four to six per cent. In Finland and Iceland, on the other hand, they account for more than 15 per cent of all votes cast, a fact which is reflected in the lesser strength of the Social Democrats in these countries.

Popular Movements

The parliamentary system of party government outlined above is the most prominent single manifestation of the democratic way of life of the Northern peoples. For an adequate understanding of their remarkably stable progress within the last generations, and of the basic likeness which this development presents between the countries, it is, however, equally if not indeed more important to appreciate the degree to which the democratic form of collaboration has permeated the whole social fabric of these nations. All five peoples are organization-minded to an exceptional degree and the relatively smooth working of political democracy must be viewed against the background not only of their highly organized political parties, but also of their thriving organizational life in general.

The large number of non-governmental organizations, devoted to a wide range of interests and almost invariably operated according to democratic procedures, reach practically all population groups and have been a vital factor by serving as training schools in practical democracy. The term "popular movements" or "folk movements" has been coined to denote those groups of organizations which represent a number of broad causes – religious, humanitarian, cultural, social, economic, or political in character.

By and large, the era of modern popular movements dates from just before the middle of the 19th century when, especially in Denmark, Norway, and Sweden, a strong religious upsurge resulted in the formation of numerous new groups – inside as well as outside the Protestant State Churches. Almost simultaneously the adult education movement took its beginning; in this connection special mention should be made of the folk high schools which, particularly in Denmark and Sweden, came to play a very considerable part in the cultural awakening of the rural population that took place during the second half of the century. This was also the time when the temperance organizations began to make important headway.

The following decades witnessed the development and subsequent consolidation into powerful economic combinations of rural and urban co-operatives, of trade unions and employers' associations, and of numerous organizations of businessmen from the various sectors of economic life; it also witnessed the formation of voluntary health insurance societies and unemployment insurance societies as well as the emergence of the political labour movement and of the feminist movement. Finally, recent decades have seen the expansion of cultural organizations into mass movements, often sponsored by the political parties; but even these large organizations have been outranked by the enormous growth of the sports movement.

Viewed against the immense weight carried by these manifold organizations, the urge to promote one cause or another by joint efforts becomes a fundamental characteristic of key importance to an understanding of the social patterns prevailing in the Northern countries. Nevertheless, it is worth noting that most of the movements mentioned are not national in origin, but have usually been imported from abroad and adapted to national conditions; it is a natural consequence that international relations still form an integral and highly valued part of their activities. Another feature may perhaps best be expressed by a paradox: The popular movements have proved solid pillars of social progress and social stability, but their motivating force has, in most cases, been one of opposition to the existing state of affairs. Originally the popular movements meant a strengthening of political liberalism; later, upon the introduction of universal suffrage, they have first and foremost paved the way for the peaceful revolution which in the course of two generations has changed the whole social structure of the Northern communities, and which finds its primary political expression in the rise to power of the Labour parties.

The great organizations contain not only elements of change but also of stability. Love of order and aversion to anarchy have proved highly stabilizing factors in these countries. It is realistic to add that this "conservative" aspect has not only always been of great importance within certain organizations, mainly in the business sector, but has tended to assume increasing importance also with other organizations as a result of their gradual consolidation.

The great organizations of labour, agriculture, industry, and commerce have grown into power centres which exercise considerable influence over the programmes and activities of the political parties. They are frequently relied upon to contribute their expert knowledge to the formulation and implementation of government policies. Also, the existence of these movements with their highly developed organizational machinery has made possible a decentralization of functions in several fields. Of particular importance in this connection are the vast labour market organizations which in all five countries regulate labour relations, largely without any public intervention, and the agricultural co-operatives which have on several occasions been charged with the responsibility of implementing government measures on behalf of agriculture.

But, while emphasizing the valuable contributions rendered by these organizations, it would appear relevant to note also the considerable political pressure which Parliaments may find themselves subjected to by interests thus organized. This trend – noticeable also in other countries with strong organizations – may be more or less inevitable, but has in some quarters given rise to fears that parliamentary democracy may be endangered by modern "corporativism". Such misgivings may, perhaps, appear unduly gloomy in the light of Northern experience up to the present time, but few observers will deny that the relations between organized economic interests and the constitutional institutions of democratic government present a problem of considerable importance.

The role played by popular movements in paving the way for political democracy has already been pointed out. But also after the introduction of democratic government they remain of vital significance in bringing democracy into the everyday life of the common citizen, not only by their educational work, but also by the creation of innumerable opportunities for active participation in their work.

Welfare Planning by Consent

The Middle Way is a term frequently used to characterize the course steered by the five Northern communities, equally far from the laissez-faire ideal envisaged by the liberal age and the regimentation practised by modern dictatorships. It may be argued that in its extreme brevity this characterization grossly oversimplifies the issues, but few will deny that it contains an important element of truth.

The Northern countries are, first of all, democracies which in large measure share a common background and ideology. Class differences are small compared with many other countries and there is a distinct leaning towards tolerance and compromise. On this basis, these peoples have in recent times attempted to build a new social structure, providing more equal opportunities for all and better utilization of available resources, with an improved standard of living and a wider scope of social security as the main goals. Industrialization has led to improved material well-being, but has also given rise to a host of acute problems of adjustment, among which the increased insecurity of the individual has been one of the most important. And the principal means of approach has been the joining of efforts, whether through central and local governments or through non-governmental organizations. This emphasis upon co-operation as a vital factor in Northern community life also brings out the peculiar combination of individualism and social solidarity which would appear to be an outstanding feature of Northern mentality. The Northern peoples are realists, and in their "social engineering" they have never followed any one general formula. Planning has been carried out on a strictly pragmatic basis, drawing upon past experience but freely adapting it to changed circumstances. This approach may be lacking in drama, but it has proved well suited to the psychology of these nations and has yielded practical results.

Joint action has given the average Northerner improved opportunities for leading a useful and satisfactory life although involving restraints upon the individual, especially in the economic sphere. At the same time the increased responsibilities gradually assumed by the public authorities have involved a very considerable increase in taxation, present-day government budgets in the Northern countries accounting for one-quarter or more of the national income. Economic and social policies are today no longer separate entities. Social policy has broadened its scope to include numerous fields far beyond its former boundaries and economic policy as a whole is based on social welfare considerations. If the traditional distinction is still maintained in the following paragraphs, this is justified by reasons of expediency in presentation rather than by any presumption of a corresponding clear line of division in practical life.

THE ECONOMIC FIELD

Planning and controls are nothing new in the economic life of the Northern countries. When, especially in the 17th century, mercantilist ideas dominated the actions of statesmen, the rulers of Denmark-Norway and Sweden-Finland strove to establish national manufacturing industries along lines taken over from and with skilled labour imported from more developed countries like France and Holland. The factories thus established were either government-owned or government-controlled in one way or another; these developments, together with the extensive Crown properties of arable land and forests, gave to the State a dominant position in the economic life of the Northern countries in those days. Moreover, the gilds, established in medieval times, for centuries controlled the economic and social life of the small urban communities. Such apparently modern innovations as price and quality controls and allocations of markets were only a few of the regulations by means of which the system was enforced.

Improved communications and the subsequent expansion of international trade did away with the greater part of the industries founded during the mercantilist era. In the middle of the 19th century their last remnants were swept away. When the gilds, long declining, were deprived of their statutory power, one of the main obstacles to industrial development was eliminated. Liberalist ideals became dominant

39

and State controls dwindled to a minimum in these first years of the industrial revolution in the Northern countries. The last decades of the 19th century, however, already saw the beginning of a new trend towards increased governmental and organizational regulation of economic forces.

Most public utilities are owned and operated by the central or local governments. This holds true not only of postal, telephone, and telegraph services, but also of the large majority of power stations, gas- and waterworks. The State took the initiative in building the first railways and the national railway systems are now predominantly in public hands. In Finland, Iceland, Norway, and Sweden the public controls a large part of water resources and hydro-electric power production. The radio networks are everywhere State-owned and -operated, although programmes are free of interference by political authorities. They are also free of any advertizing activities.

The assumption by the community of responsibility in these spheres has rarely touched off any major political disagreement. There has been no basis for serious controversy over the issue of nationalization. In most cases it appeared obvious that only the public had the necessary resources to start and develop such major undertakings in a satisfactory way. In brief, the overriding consideration has been one of expediency.

Public ownership and operation of the large majority of utilities, such as railways, gasworks, and postal and telegraph services, was an accepted fact in all the Northern countries from the beginning of the present century, and developments since then have but emphasized this fact. Peacetime government intervention in the general economic mechanism, however, took its real beginning only in the period between the two world wars, and particularly in the critical years of the early 'thirties. In combating the depression, characterized – as in so many other countries – by balance-of-payment difficulties, agricultural and industrial crises, and high levels of unemployment, the authorities gradually acquired the technique of how to control the functioning of the whole economic system without public ownership of productive resources.

If it is possible to speak of any single aim for public intervention during this period, it was, of course, to reverse the trend of depression in general. But this should not be taken to imply that from the outset there was a co-ordinated economic policy directed towards this aim.

In practice, intervention took the form of numerous separate measures for the benefit of large or small population groups, such as farmers, fishermen, unemployed, etc., who were affected by the depression.

By way of general characterization it may be said that monetary and fiscal policies as well as direct interventionist measures, such as public works, subsidies, production controls, etc., were relied upon. But the objectives of monetary policies changed according to the situation; thus, in the period 1932–1934 Denmark attempted to pursue an expansive policy, but had to abandon this line in 1935, largely because of balance-of-payment difficulties. And, with the possible exception of Sweden, fiscal policies, specifically deficit financing, were in the beginning hardly the result of any premeditated plan; deficits were viewed rather as the unwelcome and inevitable result of declining tax returns and increasing public expenditures for unemployment benefits, subsidies, etc. Due to their high sensitivity to changes in the international business cycle, the Northern countries were, moreover, during the whole of this period obliged to keep a watchful eye upon their balance of payments, with the result that more or less comprehensive import regulations had to be resorted to. This applied especially to Denmark and Iceland where exchange controls were introduced already in 1932. Originally intended as temporary measures, they were retained in subsequent years for two reasons: First, to counterbalance the expansive policies pursued, particularly during the initial period; second, to protect the new industrial enterprises which were established as a by-product of import restrictions.

All of these measures were undertaken in societies where important sectors of economic life were already more or less regulated by strong economic organizations. Workers' and employers' organizations determined labour-management relations in the major part of the labour market and especially decided the general level of industrial wages, thus exercising a strong influence upon the general price level. Large sectors of industry and commerce were organized in powerful associations. The agricultural co-operatives were dominant in the processing and marketing of farm products, and consumers' co-operatives played an important role in the retail trade.

As already stated, there was no preconceived general plan of government intervention; it was essentially a number of critical situations in different fields of the national economy which impelled

41

governments to attempt solutions to problems that were quite obviously beyond the powers of the individual organizations. The assumption of principal responsibility by the public authorities, however, brought very little change in the pattern of organizational life. There was greatly increased direct intervention, but the organizations not only retained their independent status as spokesmen for the interests of their members but were largely relied upon to implement controls. Outstanding examples were the Norwegian and Swedish measures for the consolidation of agriculture, where farmers' organizations, including the co-operatives, played leading roles; throughout the network of measures the interested parties were represented on the large number of boards and committees which were in immediate charge. The fact that the authorities leaned upon the organizations as channels of communication and control thus actually led to a considerable strengthening of organizational influence within the various sectors of economic life. Although this result was hardly intended, there can be no doubt that it facilitated the smooth operation of the many emergency regulations.

Public intervention in the 'thirties signified a considerable forward step in the general trend of growing controls, by authorities and organizations alike, over the working of economic forces. But although several of the schemes introduced went far beyond the mere adjustment to altered conditions and served as vehicles for obtaining important economic advances also of a permanent character, government action during this period was still primarily preoccupied with warding off the effects of economic crises. This was true also of the far more rigorous and comprehensive controls imposed in all five countries at the outbreak of the Second World War, when – although under widely different conditions in the various countries – practically all important sectors of economic life were everywhere placed under tight regulation. It is only in post-war years, under the double impact of changed political outlook and urgent needs of reconstruction and development, that serious attempts at long-term planning have been undertaken.

At the end of hostilities in 1945, the general situation showed sharp contrasts between the five countries. While Denmark, Iceland, and Sweden had been fortunate in preserving their economy basically unimpaired, although production facilities were worn out and stocks depleted, Finland and Norway had suffered heavily. In addition to her grave losses of manpower and the widespread devastations, the Finnish nation ceded valuable areas in the east, the population of which had to be resettled in the remaining diminished territory; furthermore, the country was under obligation to pay large reparations to Soviet Russia. In Norway the national resources had, to a much higher degree than in Denmark, been drained by the enemy. The northern areas had been totally laid waste by the retreating German troops, and half the merchant fleet had been sunk; all told, one-fifth of the national wealth had been destroyed.

Basically, post-war economic policies in the five countries have pursued identical ends: Reconstruction and further development of production machinery with a view to the restoration and improvement of pre-war living standards. Obviously, full utilization of all productive resources – particularly manpower – was a principal means in this connection. At the same time full employment was – here as in other countries – considered an essential social goal in itself. An important feature was also the effort to re-establish equilibrium in foreign payments, particularly in relation to the Dollar Area.

Although the aims pursued by economic policies were thus by and large the same, it is only natural that the differences in background outlined above should have resulted in considerable differences also in the character and scope of reconstruction and planning measures.

Norway has been the Northern country which has gone furthest in the direction of governmental economic planning. Shortly after the liberation the four major parties formulated a Joint Programme laying down the main objectives of reconstruction efforts in all important fields – economic, social, military, etc. With this as a starting point, a succession of annual Economic Surveys mapped out not only changes in the state of the national economy and its prospects, but also an integrated programme of action for each year and each sector of activity. The main goal was the restoration of productive capacity to, and beyond, pre-war levels by the full utilization of all available resources. In order to accomplish this within as brief a period as possible, emphasis was consistently placed upon the rapid expansion of investment, while consumption was held at less than its pre-war volume. The means employed included budgetary surplus policies, credit control, import and export licensing, allocation of materials and manpower to industrial enterprises, wage and price controls, etc. At the same time a more equal distribution of

43

incomes was achieved by increasedly progressive taxation, on one hand, and by considerable food-subsidies and expanded social welfare schemes, on the other, a policy which of course entailed certain difficulties in realizing the objective of curtailing consumption. Plans were necessarily concerned with broad categories and thus lacking in exactitude; they were, moreover, dependent on numerous assumptions, among which those relating to conditions abroad were particularly difficult to assess correctly. But even if implementation showed considerable discrepancies from the blueprint, there can be no doubt that planned direction of the economy was an essential factor in the rapid restoration of national production.

Government planning in the other countries during the immediate post-war period contained most of the elements found in Norway but was generally far less sweeping. In Finland all efforts were bent to the solving of the threefold task of reconstruction: 1) to repair the heavy war-damages; 2) to resettle the dispossessed population of the ceded areas; and 3) to expand industry so as to ensure prompt delivery of reparations to Soviet Russia. Large loans granted by the USA in 1945 gave the Finnish nation valuable assistance in undertaking this heavy programme. Annual Economic Surveys were prepared in Denmark and Sweden as a guide to economic policy, but it is probably correct to say that they constituted broad statements of policy rather than detailed plans. Danish government measures centered upon the restoration of agricultural productive capacity which had declined materially during the five years when foreign supplies of feeding-stuffs and fertilizers were cut off, and upon the modernization of industrial equipment; also the rebuilding of the merchant marine occupied an important place. Sweden, which entered the post-war era with her production apparatus intact, was, on the other hand, able from the outset to concentrate upon the further development of her already considerable industrial potential.

The European Recovery Programme in which all the Northern countries, except Finland, participated, has in several respects exerted major influence upon the planning procedures of the four countries. The common goal was to obtain as soon as possible a satisfactory and stable level of economic activity without extraordinary foreign assistance. One of the most important means to this end – and in itself a further aim – was to promote economic co-operation among the European countries and to remove as many as possible of the obstacles to intra-European trade which had mushroomed during the 'thirties and 'forties. The Organization for European Economic Co-operation (OEEC) was established in 1948 to co-ordinate the conflicting aims of the various member countries, and thus reconcile the divergent assumptions on which national plans were based. Each country was asked to submit a plan outlining its reconstruction programme for the years 1948–52. These plans were subsequently scrutinized by the OEEC and a deliberate attempt was thus made to have the plans of the participating countries – which in the case of the Northern countries were largely a projection of plans for the early post-war years – conform more closely to the general pattern of European reconstruction and development plans. Main emphasis was placed upon the continued expansion of productive capacity as the most important single means of attaining viability, without outside assistance, by 1952.

The participation in the OEEC and the stress laid by that body on liberalization of trade have accelerated the trend towards removal of quantitative controls on foreign trade and exchange operations and, indirectly, also stimulated the efforts to abolish direct domestic controls and regulations. This, in turn, has necessitated increased reliance on the "older" instruments of economic policy, i. e. general fiscal policy and – during the last few years to an increasing extent – also monetary policy.

The Northern peoples today live under a "mixed" economic system. While still essentially based upon private enterprise, governments have everywhere assumed general direction of the national economy – the scope and methods of government control varying somewhat from country to country. Governmental authorities and agencies undertake a variety of essential economic activities in the utilities field, and have also to a certain extent – especially in Norway and Sweden – entered basic industries. Nationalization, however, has not been carried as far as for instance in the United Kingdom, and, although at times sharply debated, it has, in fact, hardly ever figured as a primary issue. In the central control over fiscal, monetary and foreign exchange policies as well as in the regulation of imports and exports, prices, distribution of materials, etc., governments have found instruments adequate to channel economic developments in the desired direction, even while leaving the large majority of enterprises in private hands. In one important field public influence is, however, very limited: Except in Finland, the labour market organizations are in a position to determine the wage level independently and thus to exercise decisive influence over the general price level, a fact which undoubtedly constitutes a latent inflationary element in the economies of the Northern countries. More specifically, this implies the possibility that a government standing strongly for monetary stability may have to face trade unions demanding inflationary wage increases or – an even more difficult situation – labour market organizations agreeing to introduce such increases.

THE SOCIAL FIELD

Present-day social welfare systems in the Northern countries are the product of developments over many centuries. As in many other countries, social policy has not followed any pre-conceived integrated plan, but has emerged as the result of numerous piecemeal reforms undertaken at various times and based upon varying conceptions. Despite sweeping reforms during the last two or three generations, present provisions consequently still bear innumerable marks, more or less discernible, of their historic antecedents.

In Northern Europe, as in many other countries, general poor relief, locally administered, has formed the nucleus of subsequent social policy developments. In one important respect, however, the Northern countries went beyond the pattern of social welfare customary in older times. Central and local governments very early sponsored a programme of public medicine and public hospitals. The Swedish public health system dates back as far as 1681 and during the following century public hospitals were erected in most of the countries. The result has been that in all five countries the hospital system has become predominantly public and available to the whole population free or at very modest charges. Of equal significance is the fact that for more than a hundred years the educational system has been based upon public and free elementary schools.

The advent of industrialism signified a new epoch, although industrialization in Northern Europe never assumed the sweeping proportions nor entailed such grave consequences for the working class as in several other countries. The wage earner, dependent for his support solely upon wages, became the typical figure of the new era. Even in agriculture the pressure of population resulted in an increasing number of landless workers.

Laissez-faire ideology with its emphasis upon the right and responsibility of each individual to manage for himself without public interference, whether restrictive or protective, could not fail to exercise a profound influence also within the field of social welfare. One manifestation of this was the general tightening of poor relief provisions which took place simultaneously with the extension of the popular vote and the abolition of traditional economic restrictions in several of the Northern countries shortly after the middle of the 19th century.

The need for organized Society to play a more active role in the social field was soon recognized. Since the industrial upsurge was the principal underlying factor, the attention of the general public naturally came to be focussed on the protection of industrial workers. Starting in Sweden in the 1850's, and shortly afterwards followed up in the other countries, the legislative foundations were laid for the protection of factory workers. Similarly, the accelerated growth of towns during this period gave rise to the enactment of legislation laying down minimum standards for housing construction with respect to space and sanitation.

As for the poor-law provisions, there grew a wider understanding of the necessity for differentiated treatment of those in need; some causes of distress were so obviously beyond the power of the individuals affected that a uniform application of the strict rules for relief eligibility, involving humiliating conditions such as placement in poor-houses and loss of the franchise, could hardly be justified. Under the slogan "Help for Self-help" there was, furthermore, growing pressure for State support to the voluntary organizations established to protect the ordinary man against the hazards of sickness and unemployment.

Characteristically, there existed a high degree of unanimity among political parties on these issues. The rise of Socialism and the incipient political organization of workers in the years after 1870 obviously provided a most important stimulus. The first advances were, however, due to the Liberal and Conservative parties then in power. When confronted with the effects of economic developments, the Liberals, comprising city intellectuals and small and medium farmers, found it quite consistent with their conviction – never very doctrinaire in these countries anyway – for the State to intervene, especially since the large farming community stood to benefit. The Conservatives too, although perhaps moved by slightly different reasons, took a somewhat similar attitude. The growing Social Democratic parties have always played a leading role in the great expansion of social welfare programmes which started towards the end of the 19th century. But, although there has frequently been sharp disagreement over specific issues and over the timing of various reforms, it is, on the whole, correct to say that the line of development has been one of practically unbroken progress, regardless of changing party colour of governments.

Viewing the Northern countries as a whole, the first great period of legislative reforms may be said to date from shortly before the turn of the century, when a beginning was made in establishing the large social insurance schemes. From the outset it has been a distinctive feature of these schemes that they have generally aimed to cover the whole population, not merely certain limited groups. Subsequent decades witnessed the gradual expansion of social insurance with varying degrees of public support, until practically all of the more common hazards of human life have been covered. That the erection of these comprehensive structures of social security has included also the liberalization and differentiation of public assistance provisions, goes without saying.

The early 1930's are generally considered to have marked the beginning of the second epoch of modern social reform in the Northern countries, an epoch which – following the setbacks suffered during the Second World War – is still in progress. Efforts have been directed along two main lines. In the first place, social security structures have been built out, in some cases by the inclusion of programmes hitherto missing, in others by extending the coverage of existing schemes. Sweeping improvements have been introduced, entailing not only more liberal provisions but also a better co-ordination of existing statutes. In the second place, this period has witnessed the spectacular, if as yet incomplete, efforts made in the development of entirely new fields. Perhaps most important of all, the first decisive steps were taken in the formulation of a national labour market policy, centering upon the full and productive employment of all persons able and willing to work. And at the same time a beginning has been made in establishing massive programmes of family welfare, social housing construction, and prophylactic health, centering upon the improvement of living conditions of families with children.

To a large extent this immense expansion in the scope of social policy must be viewed as a response to the challenge posed by the economic depression in the beginning of the 'thirties. Another important factor was the disturbing trend in the birth rate, which declined steadily from the turn of the century and reached a minimum shortly after 1930. The threat of ultimate depopulation inspired a national surge of interest in the finding of ways and means to check or reverse the tide. And although the rise in births recorded in the following years has to some extent allayed these fears, the stimulus thus given has resulted in a lasting re-orientation of social thinking and action.

The large-scale development of social welfare programmes has entailed a corresponding expansion in their financial implications. In all the Northern countries social expenditures are today approaching or have already passed 10 per cent of the national income; they everywhere rank first or second in central and local government outlays.

With these developments social policy has gone far beyond its traditional boundaries. Formerly based upon the rendering of relief to those in distress, it has increasingly come to center upon efforts for the prevention of such distress: Instead of treating mainly the symptoms of economic insecurity it now attempts directly to attack the causes of poverty. In so doing, social policy is gradually being transformed into a policy of social planning, linked to economic policy by the striving towards a common goal.

A Glimpse at Standards of Living

"When I married in 1904, my daily wages during the winter season would buy me a big rye loaf and a pound of margarine. Today I am able to buy a rye loaf, a wheat loaf, two pounds of butter, two pounds of margarine, two pounds of bacon, four pounds of sugar, and twenty pounds of potatoes." Thus spoke an old Danish agricultural worker when recently asked for his views on the changing times.

In all its simplicity this statement may be considered to reflect quite faithfully the acknowledged fact that, during the last fifty years, the working classes in the five Northern countries have improved their living conditions very considerably. When it comes to measuring the amount of improvement, however, difficulties are immediately encountered. The "standard of living" is, as a matter of fact, nothing that can be combined and expressed in such simple figures as would permit a quantitative comparison. The mixing up of food, housing, clothing, etc., into one single figure will always be arbitrary and the valuation of different commodities and benefits will always vary as between different persons, countries, and periods.

It must also be kept in mind that a comparison which is restricted to part of the consumption only may be quite misleading. In order to yield useful results a standard-of-living comparison must include all "benefits", i.e. not only those paid for, but also public amenities, working conditions, social services, etc. It should further be remembered that averages may conceal considerable differences between different layers of the population.

However tempting it may be, we must consequently avoid presenting general figures showing the over-all improvement of the standard of living during recent decades. Instead, a few data will be presented on certain aspects of consumption and outlay, in order to throw at least some light on the changes which have taken place in the standards of living in the Northern countries, their present level, and their relation to a few other countries.

PROGRESS IN STANDARDS OF LIVING
Consumption

The total consumption of *food,* as measured in calories has, after a continuous increase, not risen during the last decades. This is easily explained: Practically no people nowadays get food which is not sufficient from the quantitative point of view; moreover, the increased number of machines has reduced hard labour and consequently the number of people needing large quantities of food.

Radical changes have taken place in the composition of the diet – the general trend being a substitution of finer products for coarser foods. Significant examples are sugar and milk, the consumption of which shows a spectacular increase – in Denmark up to more than six times the amount consumed a hundred years ago – while at the same time the consumption of bread and flour has declined considerably. In Sweden the *per capita* consumption of sugar more than tripled from 1890 to 1950. The consumption of such former luxuries as tea and coffee has increased twofold or threefold during the last fifty years or so. While long-term developments have gone in the direction of a marked increase in the importance of animal foods as against the cheaper vegetable foods, recent years have seen a considerable expansion in the consumption of fruit and vegetables.

It is as a rule assumed that the increased consumption of more expensive food components implies an increased nutritional standard. However, it should be remembered that this need not always be so. For instance, some people think that the widespread occurrence of caries in the Northern countries proves that what is generally assumed to be an improved food standard is actually a change for the worse. That an increased consumption of coffee and tea represents an improved standard may be doubted. Conversely, most people will maintain that the long-term decline in the consumption of alcoholic beverages in all the countries must be viewed as an improvement.

Housing standards have followed the general trend of development and gradually such facilities as running water, central heating, private baths, and water closets have come into common usage, the rural districts lagging, however, considerably behind. Also the space available to each individual has increased. Although the large cities include residential sections considered sub-standard today, there are practically no slums in the ordinary sense of the word.

If present housing standards still cannot be considered satisfactory, this is primarily due to the serious housing shortage which arose during the Second World War, in part because of the sharp decline in new construction, in part because of a considerable increase in the marriage rate. In the post-war period the higher real incomes of large population groups combined with strict rent controls have,

51

moreover, resulted in a greatly increased demand for housing accommodation. The construction of new dwellings has not been able to keep pace with the demand thus created.

Family budget studies provide another main source of information from which a general impression of changes in standards of living may be derived. The table given below illustrates developments during the last 35 years in two of the countries under review. The Danish figures refer to working-class families in the capital, while the Swedish figures cover workers and lower-grade public servants living in towns or urban settlements.

LOW-INCOME FAMILY EXPENDITURES BY MAIN ITEMS (per cent)

	Denmark		Sweden	
	1914	1948	1913	1948
Food	48	29	44	29
Housing, heat, and light. . . .	19	13	17	13
Clothing and shoes	12	13	13	14
Personal taxes . . . . ⎱	10	10	4	12
Membership fees. . . . . . . ⎰		6	5	4
Miscellaneous	11	29	17	28
total . . .	100	100	100	100

Developments in Denmark and Sweden have been strikingly parallel. In spite of the fact that statistics indicate a considerable redirection of food consumption towards more expensive foods, its relative importance in the budget has declined considerably. Average expenditures for housing accommodation, heat, and light have also declined relatively, but – at least in part – this is due to the rent controls introduced during and maintained after the Second World War. Personal taxes (mainly income taxes) account for a larger percentage of the budget than before; but on the other hand the families whose budgets are analyzed have been among the principal beneficiaries of the extensive community services which have necessitated the higher taxes. Viewed as a whole the table shows a considerable decline in that share of the budget which is required for bare necessities, thus leaving ampler room for individual preferences with regard to all items listed as miscellaneous. The fact that many former "luxury" items classified under this heading are today considered more or less as necessities can hardly change the general conclusion that this development implies a higher standard of living.

Social Services and Working Conditions

Important elements in the standard of living are dependent not so much upon the direct expenditures of individual families as upon community action.

Since this really is the subject matter of the present publication, no comprehensive evaluation will be presented here. Still, it would seem pertinent to call attention to the considerable improvement in living standards stemming from public health measures (one of the effects of which may be read out of the spectacular victories over diseases), from free educational services (which historically rank among the first social tasks undertaken by the community), and from the whole structure of social security schemes.

General working conditions have improved vastly, due largely to comprehensive labour protection measures. Shorter working hours and the introduction of a three-weeks' annual holiday with pay has not only reduced the "pains and strains" of work but has also greatly increased the opportunities of the individual to enjoy leisure and consumption, in the widest sense of these words. As for job security, the record is mixed, but it may be pointed out that while the inter-war period was marked by considerable unemployment, recent years have shown a consistently high level of employment in most of the Northern countries.

Incomes and Their Distribution

Developments in real income, i. e. money income corrected for price fluctuations by means of some cost-of-living index, are frequently used to illustrate the improvements achieved. Wage statistics and income tax returns make it possible to obtain a general impression of changes through the last half century or so.

Swedish figures indicate that the *real incomes* of fully employed adult male industrial workers have more than doubled during the past fifty years. Available statistics suggest that developments in the other four countries have followed a rather similar course, although there may be differences not only with respect to the exact extent of improvement, but also with respect to the times when progress has been most marked. In some of the countries the rapid rise in incomes may have started somewhat earlier, in some a little later. Thus, a similar Danish analysis covering the years from 1872 to 1921 also indicates a doubling of real incomes during that period but, then, industrialization set in rather earlier in Denmark. On the other hand, progress has probably been more rapid in the other Northern countries after the First World War. All in all, the general estimate may be ventured that Northern wage earners have obtained at least a doubling of their real incomes within the last two generations. Since the average number of persons dependent upon each individual income has declined, the improvement *per capita* has actually been somewhat larger.

Simultaneously with the increase in real incomes a limited process of *income equalization* has taken place. The real incomes of the lowest-paid groups, notably agricultural and other unskilled labourers as well as female workers, have risen more and those of the higher income brackets rather less than the "average" represented by male workers in industry. An impression of the present income distribution may be gained by the following figures, which relate to Sweden.

DISTRIBUTION OF INCOMES (1950).

Income (kronor)	Persons in per cent of total	Income in per cent of total
600 – 2,000.	17.1	4.1
2,000 – 5,000.	35.9	22.0
5,000 –10,000.	36.6	44.4
10,000 –20,000.	8.6	19.6
20,000 –	1.8	9.9
	100.0	100.0

A somewhat similar Danish computation gives an almost identical picture and, roughly speaking, the figures are fairly typical of the Northern countries as a whole. With an average income per taxpayer of 5,400 kronor in Sweden and of 6,500 kroner in Denmark, there is still a considerable distance between the two ends of the scale. But neither the high nor the very low incomes dominate. The main part of the population is in the middle and lower-middle income brackets which also account for the overwhelming share of total income. Moreover, many of the very small incomes fall upon persons without dependents (including young persons still training for an occupation).

The figures cited in the preceding paragraphs relate to income before taxes; consequently they do not give a full picture of the way in which the national product is distributed. Account must also be taken of the methods of progressive taxation adopted – mainly with respect to income taxes – in all the Northern countries. The actual

Easy access to Nature is an incalculable but vital ingredient of Northern living standards. Here is seen a cabin on the banks of one of Finlands many lakes.

extent of income equalization during the last fifty years is thus appreciably larger than the table would seem to indicate. In this connection mention may appropriately be made of a recent Danish survey, according to which the net effect of public levies and disbursals in the year 1949 was a redistribution of some 600 million kroner from persons with annual incomes in excess of 10,000 kroner to persons with incomes below that level; this implies a redistribution of almost one-fifth of the potential maximum – which would mean full equalization of incomes after payment of taxes and receipt of social services.

INTERNATIONAL COMPARISONS

The preceding brief survey is necessarily incomplete but still conveys a rough impression of the improvement in Northern standards of living within the past two or three generations. However, the value of these data as an indicator of the present way of life of these peoples is limited as long as they are not supplemented by some information on the status of the Northern countries against an international background. Below an attempt is therefore made to relate the standard of living of the Northern peoples to that of a few other economically and socially advanced countries. At the same time, the difficulties inevitably inherent in such comparisons render it imperative to view the findings as broad approximations only.

Incomes

By way of introduction some figures computed by the United Nations may be quoted:

Source:
Statistical
Yearbook.
United
Nations,
1951.

	National Income per Capita in U. S. Dollars (1949)
United States	1,453
Canada	870
New Zealand	856
Switzerland	849
Sweden	*780*
United Kingdom	773
Denmark	*689*
Australia	679
Norway	*587*
Belgium	582
Netherlands	502
France	482
Iceland	*476*
Ireland	420
Israel	389
Finland	*348*

It will be seen that the Northern countries rank among the 16 countries with the highest *per capita* income. The scale must, however, be interpreted with great caution, not only because of the inaccuracies arising out of different compilation methods, but also because the official rates of exchange considerably undervaluate the internal buying power of many European currencies. Among the five countries under review here, this applies particularly to Denmark, Norway, and Sweden where the internal buying power of the currencies concerned is estimated at almost twice the value indicated by the rate of exchange against U.S. dollars. In consequence, the *per capita* incomes given above greatly exaggerate the differences in real income between the United States and most European countries. To a certain extent this holds true also of some of the differences found between European countries. Thus, the relatively low ranking of Finland and Iceland is probably due in part to the continued importance of household economy in these countries, the produce of which largely evades statistical compilation.

Still, the order in which the countries appear is probably roughly correct. This would lump Sweden and Denmark with the United Kingdom and several members of the Commonwealth, Norway with some of the other countries of Western Europe, while Finland and Iceland occupy a somewhat lower "level of wealth".

Another approach which concentrates more directly on the standard of living of the broad masses consists in comparing the work time required for specified categories of workers to buy certain commodities internationally consumed. If confined to countries with not too dissimilar consuming habits such comparisons would appear of some value. On the basis of statistics compiled for a wide range of food items it is possible, by a process of "weighting", to establish a comparative index of the buying power, in terms of food, of one hour of industrial work in various countries.

INDEX OF BUYING POWER OF HOURLY INDUSTRIAL WAGES (1950)

	Excluding effect of family allowances	Including effect of family allowances for a two-children family	
United States	100	100	*Source:*
Norway	84	86	*Monthly Labor*
Denmark	73	75	*Review, 1951,*
Sweden	63	69	*no. 2.*
United Kingdom	62	64	
Finland	39	42	
France (Paris)	31	42	

The above table would seem to conform reasonably well to the comparison of national incomes previously given. The extraordinary high figure for Norway is a result of the post-war cheap-food policy pursued in that country. On the other hand, the results cannot be taken as adequate indicators of the relative well-being of wage earners in different countries. The index of purchasing power of earnings in terms of food represents, at best, one piece of evidence concerning relative welfare.

Expenditure and Consumption Comparisons

Again, the relative importance of food expenditure on workers' family budgets might be taken as a yardstick for relative living standards in different countries. The statistics available are, however, not

57

readily comparable, since they refer to different years, different sizes of families and different income levels. But while food outlays in the Scandinavian countries, the United Kingdom and the United States generally represent only a little above or below thirty per cent of workers' family budgets, the comparable percentages for Finland and France are not below fifty. The difference would appear large enough to support the conclusion that the living standards of wage earners are generally somewhat lower in the latter two countries.

At the same time it is interesting to find that the daily calorie consumption *per capita* is almost identical in the five Northern countries, the United Kingdom and the United States, the figures ranging from 3,060 calories in Norway to 3,230 in Iceland. Whatever the difference in standards of living as a whole, the peoples of these seven countries certainly have their needs adequately covered in this respect.

As for housing standards, any international comparison must reckon with the dominating influence of the climate. Dwellings in the Northern regions are generally rather more solid than in countries situated along milder latitudes. With regard to the size of dwellings the situation of Denmark and Norway compares favourably with that found in most other countries, while particularly in Finland the average size of dwellings is rather small.

A few figures pertaining to the "consumption" of certain "durable" goods usually associated with a high standard of living may serve as a supplementary illustration.

NUMBER OF TELEPHONES AND OTHER DURABLE GOODS
PER 1,000 INHABITANTS

	Telephones 1948	Radios 1949	Cars 1951	Motorcycles 1951
Denmark	154	278	27	9
Finland	77	165	7	4
Iceland	110	252	42	3
Norway	127	229	19	7
Sweden	207	302	36	32
United Kingdom . .	97	327	45	14
United States	261	543	262	4

The United States is better equipped with telephones, radios and cars than the United Kingdom and the Northern countries. Within

The bicycle is the "automobile" of the average Dane. Place: Knippelsbro, Copenhagen.
Time: 5 P.M., at the close of a working day.

59

a few years, however, Sweden will have reached a point where practically all households have a telephone, and in all the Northern countries radios are gradually being introduced in all homes. Television, on the other hand, is still only in its infancy in the Northern countries.

As for means of transportation, the generally short distances make cars less essential to the typical family; the outstanding exception being Iceland, which has no railways and must rely on automobiles for all transportation by land. In Denmark the bicycle might be characterized as the "car" of the ordinary family household; practically all Danes own and use this vehicle which is especially suited to meet their daily transportation needs. In Sweden, where distances are considerably greater, light motorcycles are very common. Still, there is no denying that the use of automobiles would be very much larger in the Northern countries, were it not for the relatively high prices – largely a result of severe taxation – compared with the USA.

Social Services and Working Conditions

As a study of the following pages will reveal, any full evaluation of the living standards enjoyed by the Northern peoples will have to take into account the amount of goods and services placed at their disposal free or at low cost by community action. In this respect these nations rank with the socially most advanced countries such as the United Kingdom and New Zealand. One illustration of this is found in the fact that the percentage of national income which is devoted to social expenditures in all these countries is approximately the same, namely around 10. A more comprehensive survey of these aspects of Northern life is given in the subsequent chapters, to which these pages have been intended only as an introduction.

CHAPTER II

LABOUR

The Working Man Before and Now

The standard of living of any community is dependent mainly upon the amount of goods and services which it is able to produce. The labour of the population, moreover, is the basic source of production. Clearly, in any discussion of social patterns in Northern Europe considerable prominence must be accorded to the working life of the peoples. It is equally clear that the main emphasis in this connection rests upon the circumstances of that majority of the population which depends upon wages to provide it with a living. The relations of the wage earner to his work derive their special character from the fact that their significance goes beyond that of a mere economic bargain – the worker selling and the employer buying labour – since perforce they condition the life and general status of the worker in some of their most essential aspects. In the following pages an attempt is consequently made to draw a picture of the setting within which the daily labours of the ordinary working man and woman are performed: Working conditions, labour-management relations, and employment opportunities.

Industrialization, by vastly increasing productivity, provided the basis for greatly improved standards of living. But progress was bought at the price of increased insecurity for the individual. The abolition, around the middle of the nineteenth century, of the medieval gild system which, although it had long been declining, still constituted the main framework of urban economic activity, brought revolutionary changes in the position of the working man. The gild system and the restrictions on the right to pursue any trade which were its legal mainstay, were prohibitive to any rapid progress and constituted a serious limitation upon the freedom of workers as well. It did, however, provide the working man with a degree of security

... *the Swedish lumberjack* ...

. . . the Danish house carpenter . . .

the loss of which was later on profoundly felt. The patriarchal relationship between master and journeymen meant discipline and hard work, but it implied a certain responsibility on the part of the master towards his employees in case of sickness, disablement or old age. Neither did unemployment present any danger worthy of mention, since the whole system was so organized as to secure every master his fair share of available work.

The breakdown of this economic system thoroughly changed the structure of urban life at the same time as industrialization called forth an explosive growth of urban communities. A rapidly growing number of people exchanged their peaceful and secure village life for the strenuous and unhealthy life of the early industrial centres. Still, it must be remembered that industrialization in the Northern countries has never reached the sweeping proportions typical of such countries as England and Germany, and that large scale industrial enterprises have always been relatively few and of limited importance.

Even in agriculture the environment underwent considerable changes. The rapid increase of population, which was not wholly absorbed into the growing cities, and the progressive mechanization of agriculture, which demanded greater economic resources on the part of farmers, combined to multiply the number of landless agricultural workers who came to be a social problem of considerable magnitude. In Denmark this unfavourable development was largely forestalled by the co-operative initiative which enabled even small farmers to partake of the benefits of industrialized agricultural production.

Industrialism thus deprived the working man of the security which he had previously enjoyed while risks were simultaneously seriously aggravated. In addition to sickness, disablement, and old age, came the danger of accidents and diseases due to the ever increasing pace and mechanization of production, and the hazards of unemployment which resulted from the continuing changes in industrial activity and which were later augmented by the economic crises.

In his relations with management the position of the working man was inevitably weakened. While the journeyman of former days usually had the prospect of becoming one day a master himself, the distance between the new industrial worker and his employer widened so as to become, in many cases, practically impassable. Workers were individually in a feeble bargaining position against employers, the result being that wages were lowered, while hours of work were

64

. . . the Finnish timberman . . .

increased. These unhappy effects of industrialism were made even more serious for the working man by the increasing employment of women and children in mass production, entailing a further downward pressure upon wages.

Although the abuses in the early stages of industrialization never reached such extremes as in some other countries, it was still the increasing exploitation of women and children which, as 75 years earlier in England, first called for State intervention in the Northern countries. The first effective labour protection acts were put on the statute books in the 1870's. It is characteristic of this legislation that it was enacted by parliaments which were wholeheartedly attached to Liberalism. Consequently, the measures providing for the protection of women and children were motivated solely by humanitarian considerations and by the recognized necessity to safeguard the future manpower and mothers of the nation. Labour protection legislation soon expanded rapidly and under the impact of changing economic and political conditions the various provisions have, by stages, been revised and combined into comprehensive legislative systems. Although labour and management have had a common interest in the promotion of health measures for workers, this field was recognized to be of such importance to the nation as a whole that Society could not leave it to be settled by the parties among themselves, but had to intervene directly. The enormous expansion in the industrial employment of women has obviously been a major contributing factor in this connection.

The agglomeration of large numbers of workers in the work-places and their massing in urban districts stimulated a growing feeling of solidarity and provided the background for the emergence of modern labour organizations. The trade unions were established to protect the economic interests of workers against employers, primarily by replacing the individual labour contract by collective bargaining and contract. Inspired by the same fundamental feeling of solidarity, the development of trade unions was paralleled by the formation of health insurance societies to guarantee mutual help in case of illness, and of consumers' co-operatives to profit from the benefits of wholesale purchases. The first trade unions were founded in the tobacco, building, and printing trades around 1870-1875, and in the course of little more than two generations they have obtained a strength and status probably unsurpassed in any other country.

. . . the Norwegian seaman . . .

In the years immediately before and after the turn of the century the trade unions were further consolidated by the formation of great federations of trade unions. The increase in trade union strength which followed induced the employers to found their own organizations which became the counterpart of trade unions on the labour market. In the past half century labour relations have been decisively influenced and brought to a high level of development by the interaction of these two sets of organizations, although Society has intervened to some extent to safeguard the interests of the community.

The vacuum resulting from the abolition of the old gild system has thus gradually been filled out by a network of regulations, established by agreements between the parties and by public decrees, which govern every important aspect of the relations of nearly all workers towards their work, their employers, and their fellow workers.

Intimately related to this are the measures which have been taken after the war to renew earlier approaches to the problem of strengthening the interest of labour in the enterprises in which they are employed. The last few years have witnessed the emergence of agreements and legislation introducing Joint Production Committees in all enterprises of a certain size. The Committees, which are advisory only, include representatives of the management, of the technical and other staff, and of the workers themselves. Their prime object is to promote labour welfare and productivity and to provide a means of keeping workers better abreast of the general economic and technical development of their firm, thus diminishing their sense of being mere robots in a great machine.

These steps towards a degree of what has been termed industrial democracy may be considered modest enough in themselves. They are nevertheless a significant indication that today it is generally recognized that productivity is fundamental to a continued rise in standards of living and that the working man not only has an important contribution to make in this respect but is entitled to a more active participation in the affairs of the establishment where he earns his living.

Whereas vagrancy was a more or less wide-spread phenomenon in earlier times, unemployment, in the modern sense of the word, was not a problem of serious public concern prior to the 20th century. Appearing intermittently in the years preceding the First World War, it was only in the 1920's that chronic mass unemployment made its

. . . and the Icelandic fisherman . . .

entry. Its social effects were alarming and measures to counteract unemployment became of paramount importance to all the Northern countries. Society soon recognized its responsibility for alleviating the social consequences of unemployment and also undertook large-scale provision of work for idle hands. During the Second World War changed economic conditions resulted in the all but total elimination of unemployment in most of the countries, and this state of affairs has continued almost unchanged also in post-war years.

Today it is generally acknowledged that it is the duty of the community to take all necessary steps to prevent serious unemployment from arising again, and the maintenance of a high and stable level of employment stands foremost on the programmes of every government in the Northern countries.

The high and stable level of employment which has been experienced by the Northern countries since the beginning of the 1940's has lent added importance to the problem of labour mobility. Already as a result of the consolidation of the labour market a certain rigidity, manifest in the inadequate mobility of manpower, geographically as well as between trades, has made itself increasingly felt. With the changing situation, from surplus to scarcity of labour, the adverse effects of this rigidity have become ever more pronounced. Measures to promote labour market mobility have consequently been the subject of serious deliberation in all the Northern countries as part of the general post-war drive for increased industrial productivity. On the other hand, the fact that employers in several of the Northern countries stand ready to engage young people immediately on their leaving school and provide them with comparatively high wages after a short period, has caused a certain lack of interest in training and a certain over-mobility of the labour market. The shortage of skilled workers has become a problem and, in the interest of furthering productivity and industrial safety, an official propaganda campaign has been undertaken in Sweden, directed against the "Jumping Joes" — workers who change their jobs at unreasonably brief intervals of time. Also there has been growing interest in the planned localization of new industrial enterprises, especially in Sweden, where, in numerous cases, this has proved a useful instrument in overcoming labour shortages.

*

This chapter deals with the working life of the common wage earner. Although primarily concerned with present day conditions the main subjects have been grouped in the following pages in accordance with the historical sequence of their development. First, a presentation is made of the various measures undertaken, generally by legislative provision, to safeguard and promote the safety and health of the labouring masses. Second, a survey is given of the complex structure of worker-employer relations, the pivotal points of which are the determination of wages and labour conditions in general. The borderline between the issues dealt with in these two sections is, it should be noted, inevitably blurred in some cases. Next, it falls natural to describe the most recent outgrowth of labour-management collaboration which goes under the perhaps somewhat ambitious title of Industrial Democracy. Finally, an attempt is made to outline the broad features in the general labour market policy which, with its emphasis upon the full and productive employment of the total labour force, forms the present climax of development in the labour field.

There's serious business behind these smiles – – a main key to skilled performance is on-the-job training for young newcomers.

71

Labour Protection

BASIC TRENDS

In many cases protective measures were introduced voluntarily. Once such measures had proved their effectiveness they were usually incorporated into law to assure their application on a national scale. When framing their labour protection legislation the Northern countries were in the fortunate position to be able to profit by the experience of other countries, such as England and Germany, where the industrial revolution had taken place at an earlier date.

The programmes introduced pursue a double aim: Prevention and cure. As for the latter, efforts have been directed to alleviate as much as possible the situation of victims of work accidents and occupational diseases. Such assistance is primarily provided within the framework of compulsory insurance against employment injuries, which will be dealt with in some detail along with the other social security schemes.

See Chapter VII, Social Security, pp. 437–445.

The main emphasis, however, rests upon prevention. The labour protection legislation surveyed in the following pages aims primarily at protecting the worker against the risks to which he may be exposed in the course of his employment. This principle is applied very broadly, the object being to guard against even remote dangers; and beyond the protection against what may demonstrably be injurious to health, the measures enacted endeavour positively to promote working conditions that may contribute to the preservation of good health. In this connection mention should also be made of the influence exercised by the numerous conventions and recommendations in this field originating with the International Labour Organization, a considerable number of these instruments having been ratified by the Northern countries.

Roughly, labour protection has developed along two main lines, distinguishable already in the early start. What could be called protection proper took its beginning rather early – thus in Denmark already in 1832 – with regulations concerning the utilization of steam engines; more comprehensive legislation, however, was not introduced until in the 1870's. It has since developed into a series of technical and hygienic devices and regulations which today form a comprehensive system of safety measures.

The other line of approach lies in the social field. It was initiated by legislation against exploitation of women and children, a legislation which has since repeatedly been revised and extended in scope. The social measures of protection did not, however, remain limited to certain specially exposed groups. They were gradually extended in two directions: First, the avowed aim of labour protection changed from prevention proper to promotion of a general rise in the health standards of the broad masses, and, secondly, as a consequence of the first, it was broadened in scope so as to comprise the whole of the working population. The most important elements in this drive have been the shortening of working hours and the extension of holidays with pay from a few privileged groups to practically everybody. Obviously, at this stage labour protection has become hardly discernible from other social measures intended to promote a general rise in the standards of living of the working classes.

The high degree of political unity obtaining with respect to the earlier, more limited safety measures has not extended to the more far-reaching social measures advanced and advocated on labour protection grounds in a wider sense. Reduction in hours of work as well as paid holidays were originally opposed from employers' quarters, mainly due to the fear of a general decline in productivity, and were, in fact, attained only as a result of heavy and successful labour pressure. Today, there is probably no dissension in principle concerning the benefits to all parties concerned of either the reduced working hours or the annual holiday – but when it comes to further extensions these matters once again become major political issues.

INDUSTRIAL SAFETY
Occupational Hazards of Modern Production

The struggle against accidents in industry has been going on for a long time and considerable results have been obtained. But although the five countries may compare favourably with many other nations in this respect, occupational hazards still remain an acute issue. A few figures will demonstrate its magnitude. In Sweden, for example, the frequency of employment injuries more than tripled during the period 1918 to 1947, although in fairness it should be added that fatal or severe injuries declined in importance; nearly 1,000 accidents occur daily, an average of 500 persons lose their lives every year as a result of injuries incurred during their work, and more than 3,500 are permanently disabled to a greater or lesser degree. These accidents account for a loss of 15 million working days every year, equivalent to the permanent unemployment of as many as 50,000 hands or 4 per cent of the total number of organized workers. It is conservatively estimated that this terrifying incidence of employment injuries results in a loss of 200 million kronor each year, or nearly 1 per cent of the national income. It might be added that the joint labour-management and public efforts have, in 1951, resulted in a slight decline in accident figures. Similar investigations into the rate of employment injuries in the other Northern countries furnish the same distressing picture. In comparison it may be mentioned that in the USA the total volume of disabling employment injuries in 1950 was estimated at 1,950,000 and the number of fatal injuries at 15,500; this latter figure indicates a mortality rate almost fifty per cent above the Swedish rate.

However illustrative of the seriousness of the matter these statistical data may be, they show only the injury sustained by accidents proper, but do not take into account the consequences of occupational diseases or the general effect upon the health of workers due to unhealthy working conditions. To protect workers from these risks is obviously just as important as the prevention of accidents.

"The Transport Department has worked 164 days straight without any accident resulting in sickdays".

Notice, posted on the bulletin board of a Swedish factory, spurs the competitive urge to improve safety records.

Range of Legislation

The oldest legislation still in force is the Danish Factory Act of 1913 (although it has repeatedly been amended and a bill providing for a thorough revision is pending before Parliament). The corresponding Finnish and Norwegian legislation date from 1930 and 1936, respectively, while the present Swedish Workers' Protection Act dates from 1949. The Icelandic Act on Safety Measures in Workplaces, finally, was adopted only in 1952 and is thus the most recent legislation in this sphere.

The provisions of the *Danish* Factory Act apply in their entirety to factories and similar places of work, and also to industrial enterprises which, although not operated as factories, are still considered as coming within the meaning of the Act. With respect to the latter group, which includes craft enterprises employing six workers or more, it is a condition, however, that several workers are regularly employed exclusively or mainly in a workshop or other permanent work-place; in cases where there is particular danger to life or health, establishments are covered even where only two workers are employed. Agriculture, transportation, and building and construction sites are exempt from the Act, as are generally also establishments where less than six workers are employed; shipping, it should be added, is subject to special legislation. Also enterprises which fall outside the Factory Act in full must, however, comply with the rules governing all stationary machinery, the use of which involves risk to life and health and which is propelled by a power unit. An amendment in 1933 widened the machinery regulations to include other dangerous apparatus than machinery.

The *Icelandic* Safety Act, which builds upon older legislation from 1928 similar to the Danish 1913-provisions, covers all enterprises employing two or more persons or using machinery of one horsepower or more.

In *Finland, Norway*, and *Sweden* the Workers' Protection Acts do not in detail specify the enterprises which are covered by the Acts, but stipulate that they apply to all enterprises where persons are employed at the expense of an employer. This very wide field of coverage is, however, limited by a number of exceptions. These limitations are most important in Norway where, for instance, agriculture and shipping are excluded (left to special acts), and least so in Sweden where even pupils following courses in certain occupational schools, residents of certain institutions, and soldiers who perform civil work while on duty are subject to the provisions of the Act.

Viewing the five Northern countries as a whole, several main common characteristics as to range of coverage are discernible in spite of numerous differences of detail.

However much the coverage of some of the protection acts may gradually have been extended, it is still true that their primary objective is to provide for safe and healthy working conditions in industry, i.e. in all factories and factory-like working places.

The provisions make a general exception for all work performed for an employer by the members of his own family provided that work takes place in the home of the employer or is agricultural in character. This means that many small enterprises and, notably, a large number of small farms which are operated exclusively by family members are not covered by the legislation. A similar exception is made for home work, however industrial in character. This exception is natural since in this case the employer has no influence over working conditions. Domestic workers are not covered by the main laws but have been brought within the coverage of workers' protection by special legislation which, in varying degrees, regulates relations between domestic servant and employer.

Work on board ships is not covered by the general labour protection acts, working conditions in this field being of such special character as to call for separate measures which ensure standards comparable to those laid down by protection provisions for employment on shore. Agriculture is covered in Finland and Sweden and, with respect to dangerous machinery, also in Denmark, but not in Norway where special legislation regulating working conditions in this field was, however, introduced in 1948. Whereas civil servants and other employees in public administration are not included under the acts, workers in government-owned enterprises are protected by the same provisions as privately employed workers.

Contents of Legislation

In all countries primary responsibility for adequate labour protection is unequivocally placed upon the shoulders of the employer. It is his obligation to provide everything that, in view of the nature of the work done and the conditions under which it is performed,

may reasonably be regarded as necessary for the protection of his employees from exposure to the risk of accidents and occupational diseases. Due to national differences in the coverage of provisions this general obligation has a more or less wide range of application. When the provisions are studied it is, however, generally found that their practical importance is almost exclusively confined to establishments covered by the protection laws in all the Northern countries.

But though employers carry the main responsibility, workers are obliged to co-operate by exercising proper caution and respecting existing regulations. They may even be penalized for removing safety devices which they find encumbering to their work.

The detailed regulations in force are only partly codified in the protection acts themselves. These are supplemented either by special government orders or directives issued by subsidiary competent bodies. A complete inventory of these various provisions would be highly technical in contents and not very illuminating. Moreover, it would illustrate only the measures taken with the public as initiator or intermediary. Due to extensive propaganda and to the social-mindedness of both employers and workers, considerable progress in labour protection has been attained, however, without calling for legislative intervention. Many of the provisions are therefore of a minimum character, actual measures often providing for higher standards, while others embody standard practice and render unnecessary any collective agreements on the points covered.

Without entering into details it will suffice to state that the provisions in the first place lay down general minimum standards for the work premises so as to ensure the conditions of work deemed necessary for the preservation of good health. They include specified stipulations as to ceiling height, air space, lighting and temperature, sanitary facilities, canteens, etc.

In the second place, the provisions deal with the prevention of accidents occasioned by dangerous machinery. Safety devices are provided for, manufacturers collaborating with specialists from the Factory Inspectorate or other competent bodies. To ensure that every possible step is taken to render machinery as safe as possible, manufacturers, dealers, and persons installing machines are generally held responsible for compliance with safety requirements.

Safety devices, however, cannot eliminate the human factor which inevitably plays a major part in work accidents. Propaganda on a wide scale is therefore employed, especially against carelessness in the handling of tools. Moreover, in Sweden the law provides that safety delegates be elected by the workers at the places of work. Their duty is to ensure that all possible safety measures are taken.

For the main purpose of centralizing all experience gathered as to the causes of employment injuries every occupational accident must be reported to the authorities who, whenever it is deemed necessary, will conduct investigations on the spot. The experience thus gained has been of major importance for the continued improvement of safety rules and devices.

Factory Inspection

The protection legislation is in all countries supplemented by a centralized system of factory inspection.

In *Denmark* the Inspectorate of Work-places and Factories, with inspectors operating all over the country, supervises all enterprises covered by the Factory Act to ascertain that they are operated in accordance with that act. Furthermore, local authorities are responsible for the inspection of all dangerous machinery in operation outside the said enterprises, while public health medical officers assist in the enforcement of health regulations.

Supreme responsibility rests with the Ministry of Labour and Social Affairs. To assist the Ministry and the Factory Inspectorate, a special Labour Council was established in 1901 as a consultative organ. The Council consists of a chairman appointed by the Crown, a representative of the National Health Service and eight members (including employers and workers nominated by the respective central organizations) who are all appointed by the Minister of Labour and Social Affairs. One of their tasks is to decide whether a given branch or enterprise comes within the purview of the labour protection legislation. It may also tender proposals concerning legislation for the protection of workers and has had considerable influence upon the development of such legislation in Denmark.

In *Sweden,* the body appointed to supervise the enforcement of laws for the protection of employees is called the Workers' Protection Board. This body is also authorized to recommend improvements in technical, hygienic, and social facilities. When important questions are to be discussed, four specially chosen representatives for labour and management may participate in meetings of the Board.

About 100 trained inspectors are assigned to 11 districts to investigate safety conditions on working premises. As to places of work where there is no machinery, the inspectors are assisted by one or more supervisors appointed by the public health committees found in every local district. In addition, special inspectors are available for more hazardous occupations such as mining, lumbering, aviation, and the manufacture and storage of explosives. Both the Workers' Protection Board and the inspection teams employ doctors with special training in occupational hygiene.

See Chapter VI, Health and Rehabilitation, p. 328.

A good washroom is as important as a smoothly running assembly line. This one is from the Göta verken shipyards in Gothenburg, Sweden.

When the worst does happen, there's usually a doctor or nurse on hand to administer first aid.

In *Norway,* the Central Inspectorate of Labour is assisted by statutory Workers' Protection Committees in all local districts, composed of at least 3 members of whom one must be a woman, one a worker, and one a technically qualified person. Due to the considerable distances in that country and the high degree of dispersion of industry, which has entailed the localization of many enterprises in rather isolated regions, these local committees have been of great value in furthering labour protection.

Factory inspection in *Finland* dates back to 1889. The present organization was set up by the Factory Inspection Act of 1927. The country is divided into eight districts with State inspectors in charge. Furthermore, in every municipality which harbours enterprises falling under the labour protection legislation local inspectors handle the supervision of smaller establishments.

In *Iceland* factory inspection was introduced by an act of 1928; its provisions have subsequently been amended and included in the new Act on Safety Measures in Work-places from 1952.

It should be pointed out in general that the functions of inspectors go beyond the mere enforcement of rules and provisions. Equally important are their activities as informal consultants and advisers, their wide experience being thus utilized to the greatest possible extent in collaboration with both employers and workers.

81

Occasionally there's even an athletic field on the factory grounds. Here we see employees of the L. M. Ericsson plant in Stockholm making good use of a recess from work.

·Industrial Welfare

Beyond the requirements of workers' protection statutes many enterprises have since long operated or supported special arrangements and facilities which may be grouped under the common term of "industrial welfare". In recent years such activities have undergone rapid development, and most so perhaps in Sweden. One reason for this is found in the tendency towards nation-wide collective agreements which – in a period of high employment – make it difficult for employers to compete for manpower in any other way than by offering such welfare services. Another contributory factor can undoubtedly be found in the fact that the costs of these services are exempt from taxes so that, in the final analysis, they are partly paid for by the community.

Staff counsellors, employed by the firm involved, have become ever more frequent in large undertakings. Apart from practical tasks with respect to medical services and leisure time activities, their work is increasingly directed towards helping employees to solve their personal problems, difficulties of adjustment, etc. Canteens, staff restaurants, reading and smoking rooms have grown in number (permission to smoke has been given in some fields with favourable results). In Sweden, special rooms providing light-treatments for underground workers and similar categories have been introduced here and there. Day nurseries for children of women workers are found especially in those industries, e. g. the textile industry, where large numbers of women are employed; in some cases the firms employ special nurses to take care of sick mothers and their children.

Industrial employment of married women creates special problems. Many firms set up day nurseries as a service to mothers in their employ. The picture is from the Carlsberg Brewery in Copenhagen.

83

Leisure time facilities, e. g. recreation centres, sports, libraries, hobby activities, and educational courses, are receiving increased financial support from private enterprises, although they are frequently operated by independent bodies of which employees or local authorities are members. Also, holiday homes for employees are becoming more frequent and many enterprises are organizing summer colonies or other summer visits for children of employees.

HOURS OF WORK
The Eight-Hour Day

The normal working time today in all of the Northern countries is on an average 8 hours a day and 48 hours a week (the number of hours denoting effective working time). Almost all wage earners work under regulations stipulating the Eight-Hour Day as the maximum, the major exception being, in some countries, agricultural workers whose working day is traditionally somewhat longer than that of workers in industry and commerce. Even the supplementary provisions concerning work on Sundays, night work, and overtime present a rather uniform picture throughout the five countries.

The Eight-Hour Day was introduced almost simultaneously in four of the Northern countries at the conclusion of the First World War when, partly under the impression of revolutionary movements all over the world, workers were in a very strong position, both in bargaining with the employers and in the political sphere. There was, however, a significant difference in the methods by which this important reform was carried out. In Denmark, where trade unions developed earlier than in her neighbour countries, workers were successful in obtaining the inclusion of the Eight-Hour clause in the general collective agreements between trade unions and the employers' organization (1919). In Finland (1917) and Norway (1919), on the other hand, legislative measures to this end were introduced as part of workers' protection legislation, and in Sweden a special act on working hours was adopted (1918) by the Riksdag. In Iceland the Eight-Hour Day was not generally introduced until 1942 when an agreement to that effect was signed between trade unions and employers. A few trades had, however, already adopted the Eight-Hour Day in the years before the Second World War.

The agreements and the legislation originally introducing the Eight-Hour Day were of somewhat restricted scope, comprising mainly

Sun, light, and air are the watchwords of contemporary Northern architects when building for industry. Employees lounge on the lawn outside the Brødrene Andersen clothing factory in Copenhagen.

industrial workers and excluding such major groups as agriculture, shipping, and employees in shops and offices. Gradually, however, the Eight-Hour Day has found ever-widening application and is today a reality for the large majority of wage earners.

In all countries the subject of working hours comes within the scope of collective agreements between employers and employees. In Finland, Norway, and Sweden Eight-Hour Day legislation now, however, lays down a maximum for daily working hours. In part this has meant a supersession of collective agreements by legislative provisions, in part it has expanded working hours regulation to fields not previously covered by collective agreements. Employers and workers are, however, free to agree upon shorter working hours and have done so in several trades, e. g. mining in Sweden.

The present Finnish Eight-Hour Day legislation which dates from 1946 maintains a distinction which was introduced in 1917. In the main branches of employment, including industry and handicraft, working hours are limited to 47 hours a week, or 48 hours in cases of continuous 3-shift work. In other branches whose special character or

85

dependence on season, weather conditions or transport facilities necessitates a more elastic regulation of working hours, work may be so organized as to keep working hours within a maximum of 141 over a period of three weeks. In Norway and Sweden the general Eight-Hour Day regulations, dating from 1936 and 1930, respectively, are less comprehensive in scope, but have been supplemented by acts dealing with special occupations.

Work on Sundays, Night Work, and Overtime Work

In Denmark, Iceland, and Norway *work on Sundays* is generally prohibited, but exceptions may be granted, particularly where such work is indispensable to the community or where production is carried out by workers operating in shifts. In Finland and Sweden, work on Sundays is not expressly prohibited, but it is stipulated that every worker shall have an uninterrupted weekly period of rest of at least 30 and 24 hours, respectively, preferably on Sundays.

Similarly, the Northern countries have gone further than most other nations in prohibiting or restricting *night work*. In Norway all night work is in principle prohibited but, where it is essential to the carrying out of the work involved, exceptions are permitted by the authorities. Similarly, in Sweden night work is as a rule prohibited although an alternative regulation may read as follows: Employees are entitled by law to a sufficient period of rest at night. Here, too, exceptions are granted in special cases as dictated by the nature of the work or the public interest. Thus employees in certain industries, as well as in hotels, restaurants, transportation, hospitals, etc., are excepted. Likewise, night work is permissible in the event of actual or threatened work stoppages, and may be authorized by the Workers' Protection Board under special circumstances.

Finnish provisions lay down that work between 9 p.m. and 6 a.m. may generally be performed only in three or more shifts, in double shift not later than 11 p.m. In the remaining countries, although there are no general legislative limitations on night work, there is a general tendency toward its progressive limitation. The subject is continually under consideration and in Denmark a comprehensive government investigation into the possible harmful effects of night work is in progress. Special measures introduced to protect women and young workers will be dealt with separately below.

Overtime work is not subject to general regulation in Denmark at present. In the other Northern countries, however, it is regulated by labour protection legislation. Finnish and Norwegian legislation also provides for overtime to be paid at certain minimum rates. At the same time these limitations upon overtime work must, for several of the countries, be viewed against the endeavours by organized labour to distribute available work to as many hands as possible in periods of unemployment. The total effect has been to reduce such work to a minimum; thus, Danish pre-war statistics show that overtime work performed in industry normally amounted to only 1 per cent of the total number of working hours. In 1944, a year of almost full employment, the corresponding figure was 3.3 per cent.

It may be added that the post-war production drive has in recent years caused the problems of overtime work to appear in a changed light. During times of full employment it has been found compatible with labour protection principles to encourage a reasonable extension of paid overtime.

Exceptions to the Eight-Hour Day in Agriculture, etc.

As already mentioned, employees in certain fields of activity, among them particularly agriculture and shipping, are exempt from the general Eight-Hour Day legislation due to special conditions of work which also in other respects render their position different from that of the ordinary employee of industry and commerce.

In *agriculture*, where the work load is subject to seasonal variation and where it is difficult to carry out even daily routine tasks within a fixed uninterrupted working period, the Eight-Hour Day has not yet been fully introduced. In Denmark, where working hours have not been subjected to any general regulation by Parliament, trade union strength has been the decisive factor for the extent to which the Eight-Hour Day has spread. Negotiations between trade unions and the farmers' organizations in the spring of 1952 resulted in the reduction of annual working hours by 50 for organized agricultural workers. Under this agreement working hours are henceforth 54 hours weekly in the period 15 May – 14 November and 48 hours weekly in the period 15 November – 14 May.

The comprehensive Finnish legislation on working hours specifically exempts agriculture and forestry from the Eight-Hour working day provisions. However, legislation calling for regulation of working hours in these fields along lines similar to the Danish arrangement mentioned above is at present in a stage of preparation.

In Norway, according to an act of 1948, working hours in agriculture may not exceed 9 a day, or 50 a week during summer time and 46 in the winter season.

The present Swedish act on agricultural working hours, enacted in 1948 and superseding an act of 1936, limits the maximum number of working hours in any single week to 50 hours from March to October and 45 from November to February, which gives an average of about 48 hours for the whole year.

In *shipping*, also, the special conditions of work have rendered the introduction of a straight Eight-Hour Day somewhat difficult, although by now it has been accepted in principle in all the Northern countries. Again, Denmark is the only country where this issue has been settled without direct legislative action. The length of the working day was for many years a matter of conflict between Danish trade unions and the shipowners, but in 1945 a provisional agreement, since prolonged, introduced 3-shift work on all vessels of more than 500 tons gross; it may be noted, though, that the shipowners only acceded to this agreement under pressure from the government.

In the other countries the problem has been dealt with by appropriate legislation. In Sweden the hours of work for seamen were first limited by a provisional act of 1919. The present Seafarers' Hours of Work Act of 1948 has been framed in accordance with the latest international agreements in this sphere. The Eight-Hour Day now applies to all vessels of more than 500 tons gross. Apart from emergency work, overtime work may only be performed up to 24 hours per week and shall be compensated in accordance with specified rules. According to a Finnish act of 1924 the maximum permissible working time at sea during two successive days is 24 hours when watches are kept, exception being made for ship engineers, greasers, trimmers, and stokers who, in specified circumstances, work shorter hours. Work not divided into watches may not exceed 63 hours per week. In collective agreements stipulations have, however, been laid down which go beyond the requirements of this legislation and which correspond closely to the Swedish provisions outlined above. When in harbour, the Eight-Hour Day applies.

As for Norway, legislation initiated in 1939 and revised in 1949 limits the working hours for seamen to 48 hours a week on ships in foreign trade and to 54 hours in home waters, necessary variations in daily working hours being permissible within these totals. Icelandic provisions are likewise based on the 48-hour week, adjustments in daily working hours being permitted. However, with particular reference to work on board the large trawlers which increasingly dominate the fishing fleet, additional rules call for a minimum of 8–12 hours of rest in every 24 hours.

With respect to *shop employees*, the regulations determining the hours during which shops may be open to the public provide a general framework limiting the hours of work. It may be pertinent to note that the gradual tightening of such regulations has been welcomed not only by employees, but also by a majority of small shop owners who, with their families, participate in the operation of their shops. These provisions are found in all five countries; in addition, Finland, Norway, and Sweden have put legislation on their statute books specifically stipulating the Eight-Hour Day for shop employees, with the clause, however, that hours may be prolonged on certain days provided that the working week does not exceed 48 hours (47 hours in Finland). It may be noted that in recent years there have been increasing demands, especially from women employed outside their home, for an extension of shop hours at least one or two days a week.

The limitation of hours for *domestic workers* must be viewed in the light of the important changes which their overall position has undergone. For the last decade or two the situation in the Northern countries, as in several other countries, has been characterized by a continued exodus from the domestic occupations, viz. nursing, housekeeping, domestic service, etc. For generations this broad group has been the Cinderella of occupations, lacking not only the guarantees for decent working conditions given to other categories of wage earners, but also the ability to press their claims by trade union action. A continued state of full employment has naturally provided a strong stimulus to the tendency to move from domestic service into industry, commerce, and clerical work. Moreover, growing social consciousness of the backward position of domestic workers, coupled with the fact that their services have been offered in a "seller's" market, has resulted in special legislative measures for their protection in recent years. As regards the central issue – regulation of working hours and leisure time – the new enactments also have had for their background a desire to raise the status of the group and thus to stimulate recruitment by laying down standards comparable to those prevailing in other occupations. The working day has been limited in two ways – directly by the laying down of maximum hours and indirectly through provisions aiming at securing certain minimum periods of rest and leisure time. Both in Finland and Norway recent legislation establishes 10 hours as the maximum working time per day. Furthermore, in Finland, Norway, and Sweden work may as a rule not be demanded from the assistant after 7–7.30 p. m., nor in Finland and Norway before 6 and 7 a. m., respectively; cash or time compensation should be given for any overtime worked. Other rules, either customary or legislative, which are essentially the same in all five countries, provide for complete freedom every second Sunday and holidays, and one afternoon off every week.

Further Reduction of Working Hours?

Beginning a generation ago in manufacturing and commerce and gradually spreading to ever more fields, the Eight-Hour Day and the 48-hour working week have for a long time been the dominant pattern. Variations may, however, be found. Thus, within recent years the week-end idea has gained in popularity, the result being that in many, especially large establishments, the employees now work 30 minutes longer on the five weekdays so as to be able to leave work earlier on Saturday afternoon.

Even before the last war there were increasing demands from organized labour for a further shortening of working hours with unchanged take-home pay. In part, these demands were due to the considerable level of unemployment prevailing at that time and to the introduction in some countries, e.g. France and USA, of the 40-hour week. Although after the war full employment has largely been attained, labour has continued to press this claim, though increased leisure is now primarily represented as being in itself an advance in workers' living standards. Until now the heavy demands imposed first by reconstruction programmes and since 1950 by expanding defence programmes in several of the countries have, however, hindered the introduction of such a reform. In a few Swedish trades – especially underground workers – the five-day working week has been introduced. In Sweden, also, the third holiday week may by agreement be converted into free Saturdays in the summer season.

PROTECTION OF WOMEN AND YOUNG PERSONS
Women

Present legislation dealing with the employment of women comprises stipulations *ruling out the employment of women in certain sectors of industrial activity*, prohibiting night work, prescribing certain minimum daily periods of rest, and laying down certain periods of maternity leave.

In Sweden, where mining is an important occupation, women may under no circumstances be employed underground in pits or stone quarries, and the government is empowered to prohibit the employment of women also in other occupations which are deemed injurious to their health. In Finland a woman who has not reached 20 may not be mustered in any sailor capacity, and before she is 21 she may not participate in the loading or unloading of ships in foreign trade. No woman may be employed underground in mines or with painting which involves the use of white lead; the same rule applies in Sweden. In Denmark and Norway there is no legislation barring women from certain occupations, but the Danish Factory Act stipulates that in handling dangerous machinery women workers may not wear long hair and must wear clothes which in safety-value are equal to those of men; similar provisions also apply in Sweden.

91

In both Finland and Sweden *night work* for women in industrial employment is generally prohibited. The Swedish Workers' Protection Act further requires a minimum night rest of 11 hours, this period to include at least seven hours of the period from 10 p.m. to 7 a.m. With regard to seasonal work or in extraordinary circumstances this period may be reduced to 10 hours but only for a maximum period of 60 days every year. In Denmark and Norway, on the other hand, no special restrictions have been placed upon the employment of women, partly due to the opposition of women's organizations, who fear that such measures may weaken the competitive position of women as compared to male workers for whom no such restrictions exist; in Norway, where night work is as a rule prohibited also for men, the whole question is of interest only in connection with the granting of dispensations.

Maternity presents a special aspect of female employment. All the Northern countries comply with the recommendation adopted by the ILO in 1919 and ensuring most employed women four to six weeks leave before confinement and the same period after confinement, the only modification being that in Finland the length of the pre-confinement leave is determined individually.

See also Chapter IV, Family Welfare, p. 245.

Children and Young Persons

Legislation dealing with the employment of children and adolescents considers a person under 15 (in Denmark 14, in Finland, in certain cases, 16) a child, and a person under 18 an adolescent. The age limit for children has generally been set to coincide with the normal age at which elementary school attendance is completed.

Child labour is subject to severe restrictions. A child may only be employed at hours that do not interfere with compulsory school attendance and then only in certain types of work which are not liable to be injurious to its health. These generally include agriculture, forestry, shipping and fishing, domestic work, private house-building, and work for family members.

The *age limit* for employment in industry and commerce (except for light jobs as messengers or errand boys) is 14 years in Finland and Denmark. In Norway the corresponding minimum age is 15 years. Sweden maintains a general age limit of 14 years for employment of children; insofar as children are employed in industry and handicraft the limit is, however, 15 years. In all countries it is a further condition that the child has lawfully left school. Industrial child labour, never of particular importance in the Northern countries, has thus been totally abolished. For certain types of work the minimum employment age is even higher. In Denmark the operation of dangerous machinery (specified in the law) may not be assigned to young persons under 16. In Finland and Sweden adolescents may not be employed as stokers or trimmers, in underground mining or stone quarries or in other dangerous occupations.

To complement these measures steps have been taken to ensure that the individual young person, apart from fulfilling the general conditions of age mentioned above, is actually fit to perform the kind of work which is demanded of him or her. In Sweden no young person under 18 may be employed against the doctor's advice and before engagement a *medical examination* must take place and be repeated at least once a year. In Finland similar provisions are in force. In Denmark the employment of an adolescent in enterprises covered by the Factory Act, or in bakeries, calls for a medical examination within 4 weeks.

Working hours for adolescents are in Denmark limited to the same hours as for their adult colleagues, with a possible addition of half an hour daily to prepare for work or clean up in the evening. In Finland working hours are limited to 6 hours for children and 8 hours for adolescents; overtime work may only be performed in emergency situations. In Norway the weekly maximum is 48 hours of work, including attendance at vocational schools; no overtime is permitted in industry and building construction. In Sweden the corresponding maximum is 10 hours a day or 54 hours a week. The necessary leave to attend schools or courses which are partly or fully financed by the public must be given.

In all of the Northern countries *night work* is generally prohibited, the rule being that adolescents may not be employed during the twelve (eleven) hours after 6 (7) p.m. These provisions have in several of the countries provided the nucleus from which restrictions on night work subsequently spread to include also adult male workers.

See above, p. 86.

Sunday work is prohibited to adolescents in Norway. Danish legislation prescribes a minimum weekly period of rest of at least 24 hours, preferably on Sundays; in this connection it must, however, be noted that Sunday work is ruled out for all persons employed in establishments covered by the Factory Act.

Skiing is the most popular winter sport in the Northern countries. All of them, except Denmark, receive abundant snowfalls each year. This picture is from Norway where skiing is the national sport.

HOLIDAYS WITH PAY
A Legal Right

One of the important improvements obtained by the working population during the last generation has been holidays with pay. The annual holiday may be considered an important means of protecting the health of labour and of enhancing its productivity; it may equally well be considered one of the methods, on a par with wage-increases, by which the living standards of workers are raised. Formerly, this institution was the privilege of more limited groups such as civil servants, senior white-collar workers in private firms, etc. In the years following the First World War a growing number of workers, however, also obtained paid holidays by collective agreement with their employers. And in the 'thirties and 'forties all the Northern countries introduced general legislation assuring almost all wage earners a paid holiday of two or three weeks annually. Although originally employers viewed the idea of a comprehensive scheme of annual holidays for all workers with some hesitation, motivated by fear of reduced production, today both parties on the labour market have come to regard the principle of an annual holiday as a natural state of affairs.

In Norway a beginning was made in 1936 when a nine-day annual holiday was introduced, and in 1947 this was increased to 18 days. The Norwegians were thus the first among the Northern peoples to introduce the statutory three-week annual holiday for wage earners.

The earliest Swedish and Danish legislation in this field, dating from 1938, stipulated an annual holiday of 12 working days for practically all wage earners. In 1951 and 1953, respectively, this was extended to 18 days, tantamount to a three-week annual holiday. Moreover, special Swedish and Norwegian acts provide for a six-week holiday for persons exposed to X-ray and radioactive substances.

Icelandic legislation, enacted in 1943, calls for a two-week annual holiday, but a collective agreement, concluded in 1952, established a minimum holiday of 15 days for all organized workers.

In Finland, where shop assistants and civil servants had been entitled to fairly long holidays since the beginning of 1920, an act of 1922 guaranteed holiday rights to all workers as well, but on a considerably lower scale. The present Workers' Annual Holiday Act of 1946 decrees a holiday of 12 working days, but after five years of employment the holiday is increased to 18 working days; this also applies to workers not turned 17 at the end of the calendar year in question. The holiday benefits of shop and office workers continue to be superior to those of other workers since they are entitled to a minimum of one month's annual leave after 10 years of employment in the same firm.

In all countries the holiday should preferably be taken within a certain period, generally the months from May to September. In Denmark, Norway, and Sweden, where the three-week holiday has been introduced, one week may, however, be taken outside the summer season, a provision which, especially in Norway and Sweden with their colder climates, enables workers to enjoy a week of winter sports; in Denmark one week may, moreover, be granted in single days. The main holiday is to be arranged so as to constitute a full fortnight.

Salaried persons receive their holiday pay in the form of continued salary during the holiday period. Workers are assured of holiday pay commensurate with the length of time of their total employment during the year; in some countries this is done by a system of holiday stamps which are handed to the worker together with his wages. In its original and simplest form this means that with a two-week holiday a fully employed worker receives four per cent of a year's regular wage in holiday pay; with a three-week annual holiday the pay amounts to six per cent. The present Danish and Norwegian legislation, however, fixes the pay at 6.5 per cent of wages. The holiday stamps are subsequently cashed at the post offices at the beginning of the holiday season.

Holiday Facilities

It may be all very well to give wage earners the financial means for taking a holiday, quite another question is that of providing sufficient facilities at a reasonable cost to the greatly increased number of holiday-makers. Traditional modes of enjoying holidays, geared to the paying ability of a much more limited group, are obviously beyond the reach of most "new" holiday-makers. It has therefore become necessary to depart from customary patterns if holidays for the masses are to become a reality.

In framing the leisure and holiday habits of the Northern peoples it has been of great importance that manufacturing industry has never been concentrated in a few large sooty cities; in all five countries most industrial enterprises are situated in the country or in small towns. The population has never lost touch with nature. Immediately outside the residential sections of one-family houses and the many garden allotments which surround the towns and small industrial settlements, forests, parks, and commons are the rule – and only seldom does one find the sign "Keep out". The public is free to roam and enjoy Dame Nature at leisure. Similarly, the beaches and the rocky coastal islands known under the name of "skärgården" are all freely accessible.

In addition, the large cities have developed numerous leisure-time reservations comprising cottages, camping grounds, open-air bathing establishments, etc., which are available to the population free or merely at a quite moderate charge. The interest taken in outdoor life and improved vacation facilities has also been strongly stimulated by the many voluntary organizations, e. g. the Tourist Associations, Skiing Clubs, Scouts, etc., active in these fields in all five countries. A large number of youth hostels, tourist stations, cottages, etc., have been sponsored by these organizations.

Great efforts are made to enable also the low-income groups to enjoy a holiday away from home. These beach bungalows, situated at Middelfart, are owned by the Danish organization "People's Holiday". Here whole families can spend their holidays at a very low rental.

As a direct result of the holiday legislation the trade unions, in some cases acting in concert with the co-operative movements and the labour parties, have in Denmark, Finland, Norway, and Sweden taken the initiative in establishing a new organization with the specific purpose of facilitating sound holiday arrangements for the broad masses of people who are now enabled to take a holiday. Apart from acting in general as advisory tourist bureaus, free of charge, these organizations, which in Denmark and Norway have been given the name "People's Holiday", have taken the initiative, among other activities, in establishing many low-cost hotels and a number of "holiday towns". The latter are located on scenic spots and consist of a common boarding establishment for guests who do not wish to

97

cook for themselves, and a number of small, modestly equipped cottages which are rented at very low prices to families who, without being able to afford ordinary hotel costs, wish to spend their vacation at some special spot in the country. In Iceland, a State Tourist Association undertakes the arrangement of low-cost tours within the country as well as abroad, mainly with a view to promoting holiday-making for the broad population.

See Chapter IV,
Family Welfare,
pp. 265–266.

In this connection mention should also be made of the various benefits extended by all five countries as part of family welfare programmes to mothers and children to facilitate their taking holidays (e. g. free transport, holiday allowances, etc.).

The whole holiday movement is still only in its infancy. Investigations undertaken show that many wage earners (thus in Denmark more than one-fourth) simply stay at home during holidays. To a large extent this may be accounted for by the fact that low-income holiday facilities are as yet manifestly inadequate. In part it may, of course, also be due to the inertia of many, especially older people, who have not since youth been accustomed to holidays away from their homes. With the large-scale expansion of low-cost vacation facilities now under way it will not be many years, however, before the annual holiday away from home will become a regular feature of wage earners' way of living.

Tens of thousands
of Danish families
enjoy their holi-
days with the help
of their bicycles.

98

Labour Relations

Since the sway of the medieval gild system was definitely broken almost a century ago it has been a governing principle in all the Northern countries that employers and wage earners should be free to conclude any contract upon which they might agree with a minimum of government interference. It is also of key importance that the old Anglo-Saxon common law tradition, according to which economic associations – irrespective, in principle, of whether on the employer or wage earner side – were held to be "conspiracies", has not played any decisive role in this region. Unlike some other countries, freedom of association was consequently never in modern times seriously contested, although the growth of trade unions and their struggle for the right of collective bargaining has not been without sharp local conflicts, especially in the agricultural field. These rights are now guaranteed in the national constitutions or in special legislation. The result was that workers' and employers' organizations were formed without arousing the violent opposition which in some countries was met with particularly by labour unions in their early stages. Similarly, the right of unions to bargain on behalf of their members, although originally by no means unchallenged, was generally recognized at a relatively early date.

It is within this general framework that we must evaluate the elaborate labour relations structures which in these five countries, and particularly in Denmark, Norway, and Sweden, have today reached a stage of development probably unsurpassed elsewhere.

By far the larger part of the institutional machinery governing labour relations has emerged as a result of co-operation between the two parties in the labour market. If, therefore, at the present time the contents of most labour contracts are largely predetermined by existing contract patterns, this is predominantly due to regulations established by voluntary agreement between vast organizations of employers and workers themselves. In this connection it is worth noting that the interest in such regulations has by no means been confined to labour, since employers have also increasingly come to realize the value of stable labour relations ensured by agreements negotiated with a responsible organization.

State intervention has played a secondary, although by no means unimportant, role. In the first place legislation has, in some of the countries at any rate, laid down certain basic conditions to be complied with in all labour contracts. This applies particularly to Finland where the Labour Agreements Act of 1922 not only gives a definition of what is to be understood by such agreements but also sets out certain general rules governing their conclusion, form and contents. Special mention might also be made of the unique Norwegian provision, dating from 1936, under which an employee, who has been employed for not less than three consecutive years in the same establishment, after attaining the age of 21 is entitled to cash compensation (maximum one-half of his last annual earnings) if he is dismissed without good reason. Secondly, a considerable amount of labour relations legislation mainly consolidates rules already established by agreement between the organized parties. Thirdly, the vital interest of Society in mitigating the effects of industrial strife has led to the adoption of legislative measures which, without definitely abandoning the principle of non-interference in labour market issues, have rendered a major contribution in facilitating the peaceful settlement of labour disputes. And, finally, in most of the countries legislative provision has been made for a certain regulation of labour contracts falling outside the scope of collective agreements. – On the whole there can be no doubt that labour relations legislation has been especially favourable to workers as the presumed weaker party.

Public servants employed by the State or local authorities constitute a group apart, their status with respect to association and bargaining being governed by special legislative provisions. They are not included in the following presentation which relates to the general labour market.

The five countries of Northern Europe display striking similarities in their methods of approach and the results obtained in grappling with problems of labour relations. This likeness is, however, not surprising in view of the many similarities found also in economic, social, and political trends as well as the intimate relations prevailing between these countries. It may be equally useful to stress the fact that numerous differences, although frequently of degree rather than kind, do exist since they may serve to reveal interesting aspects of labour market problems as interrelated with and influenced by general economic, social, and political institutions.

Viewing the Northern countries as a whole, organized labour relations are found to have been fully developed first in Denmark. Norway and Sweden followed suit somewhat later, but caught up quickly, so that these three countries have now for many years been equally well equipped in this respect. Last to catch up were Finland and Iceland, where progress was for some time hampered by political tensions but in recent years these countries, too, have made rapid strides in the creation of comprehensive labour market institutions.

Generally speaking, government initiative in labour market affairs has varied inversely with the success of employers' and workers' organizations in creating by themselves the organs required to deal adequately with labour market problems. The actual extent of labour relations legislation is, however, only partly an expression of genuine public intervention since in large measure it rests, especially in Denmark, upon statutes previously agreed upon by the two parties of the labour market. In Finland, where organizational developments have been slower, legislation has, on the other hand, to some extent preceded such agreements and may in part be viewed as an attempt to pave the way for the establishment of labour market institutions on a Scandinavian model.

The five Northern countries have not discovered a panacea for the solution of those knotty labour problems that would appear to be an inextricable part of democratic industrial society. But the early realization, by both management and workers, that their own long-term interests, as well as those of the community, were best served by the establishment of orderly procedures for dealing with problems in dispute, has certainly proved a major factor underlying the stable progress of development characteristic of these countries today.

GROWTH OF ORGANIZATIONS
Trade Unions

The trade union movement in the Northern countries reaches back to the last decades of the 19th century, the first trade unions being founded in the capitals of Denmark and Norway just before and after 1870. These early attempts to protect the economic interests of industrial labour through collective action proved unable, however, to withstand the pressure to which they were subjected both by Society and employers. It was not until the middle 1880's that vigorous trade unions sprang up in the towns of Denmark,

Norway, and Sweden, first in the tobacco, printing, and building trades. In Finland and Iceland, with their later industrial development, the first national trade unions did not emerge until the middle 1890's.

Their titles today are : De samvirkende Fagforbund (Denmark) ; Finlands Fackföreningars Centralförbund (Finland) ; Albýðusamband Islands (Iceland) ; Arbeidernes faglige Landsorganisasjon (Norway) ; Landsorganisationen i Sverige, LO (Sweden).

At an early stage collaboration between the individual trade unions resulted in the formation of *central federations* to co-ordinate the activities of organized labour on a national scale. The strength of these federations has been ever increasing, although once or twice they have suffered serious setbacks which temporarily reduced their importance.

In Denmark, Norway, and Sweden where the federations were founded almost simultaneously in 1898–1899 the trend has been one of almost uninterrupted expansion in membership. Thus, the Danish and Norwegian movements have suffered only one serious setback, namely in the slump years following shortly after the First World War. Their Swedish counterpart has similarly experienced only one reversal in the wake of a general strike in 1909.

DEVELOPMENT IN THE MEMBERSHIP OF CENTRAL FEDERATIONS

(*in thousands*)

	1900	1925	1952
Denmark . . .	81	237	671 [1]
Finland	56	50	270 [2]
Iceland	–	5	25 [3]
Norway	5	96	503
Sweden	66	444	1,339 [4]

[1] *Excluding certain other unions with a total membership of 28,000 and the Joint Council of Public Servants' and Salaried Employees' Organizations with about 80,000 members.*

[2] *Excluding about 62,000 members of the Central Federation of Salaried Employees.*

[3] *Excluding about 3,000 members of the Central Union of Public Servants and about 2,000 members of the Organization of Salaried Employees.*

[4] *Excluding about 292,000 members of the Central Federation of Salaried Employees and 20,000 members of Syndicalist unions.*

The steady growth of central federations in these countries has been decisively favoured by the continued stability of political conditions and by the fact that unions, although maintaining intimate relations with the respective labour parties, have generally confined their activities to labour market issues and have kept aloof from direct intervention in politics, such as general strikes for political purposes (which in Denmark and Iceland are considered illegal). This has not prevented many local branches of the Norwegian and Swedish trade unions from affiliating collectively with the national labour parties. Individual members are, however, entitled to reserve their position in this respect.

In the remaining countries developments for a long time followed a somewhat different and more fluctuating line. In Finland the first federation of trade unions was founded in 1907, but its activities were interrupted by the civil war following the achievement of national independence in 1918. The federation then came under Communist leadership, but a split took place in 1929 when the Social-Democratic wing left the organization and founded its own non-political federation consisting of 7 trade unions with a total of 15,000 members. Since then this organization has steadily gained in importance, although in recent years it has been hampered by political differences between the member unions.

In Iceland an abortive attempt to found a central federation was made in 1907, and in the following years the trade union movement was reduced to all but non-existence. In 1916, however, a new central federation was started, but the emergence after 1930 of a Communist party resulted in a splitting of that organization in 1938. It was not until 1940 that the political differences were evened out and the central federation reorganized. In 1952 the federation numbered 25,000 members, representing all organized manual labour in Iceland.

A feature common to all the Northern countries is that a limited number of trade unions have preferred to stay outside the central federations. At the same time, large groups of salaried employees belong to trade unions affiliated with the central federations. These unions, which mainly represent intellectual workers, public servants and other white-collar workers, foremen, etc., have, especially in Finland and Sweden, attained sizable dimensions. (In Denmark, it may be noted, the union of commercial and office workers is affiliated with the Central Federation of Trade Unions). The considerable progress which has been made in the organization of non-manual labour within the last decade or two must obviously be viewed against the continuous expansion, found in many industrialized countries, of administrative personnel, both in private business and in the government sector. This trend, coupled with reduced chances of promotion for the individual, has clearly provided a powerful stimulus for the development of organizations also in this field. Results obtained by the older trade unions have been another contributing factor.

Of particular importance is the Swedish Central Federation of Salaried Employees (TCO) which today boasts more than 290,000 members or about one-fifth of the great federation of trade unions. The largest single group within the TCO is that of white-collar workers employed in manufacturing industry. Although on a smaller scale, counterparts to the Swedish TCO are found in Denmark, Finland, and Norway. In the latter country about 70,000 salaried employees, or one-third of the estimated total in this category, are today organized in the Central Federation of Intellectual Workers. In Denmark the various groups of salaried employees who belong to the professions or who have undergone other advanced training were for many years organized in a number of independent organizations. In 1952, however, a first important step towards co-ordinated action was taken when most of these organizations decided to establish a joint council for the protection of the common economic interests of the affiliated groups; these comprise about 80,000 members, half of whom are public servants.

In Sweden there exists, in addition, a central organization, in competition with the LO, which endeavours to unite all Swedish labour under a Syndicalist banner – as yet, however, with limited success, its total membership being only 20,000.

It is not possible to state exactly the degree of organization which has actually been attained in the Northern countries but, with the possible exception of Finland, it is estimated that not less than 80–95 per cent of all workers employed in industry are organized in trade unions, while agricultural workers and shop and office employees are generally organized to a smaller extent. In recent years the organization of these latter groups has, however, made rapid progress and has accounted for a major part of the continued increase in total union membership.

Industrial employment of women has considerably increased in recent years and so has their membership in trade unions. Thus, women members are today found in 44 out of 46 Swedish national unions and account for nearly one-fifth of the total trade union membership. The corresponding Danish figure is practically the same. As a rule women are admitted to trade unions on equal terms with their male colleagues, the existence in Denmark of a special Women Labourers' Union comprising 25,000 unskilled women workers thus being an exceptional phenomenon.

ORGANIZED WAGE EARNERS IN PER CENT OF
TOTAL POPULATION (1952)

Denmark	19
Finland	11
Iceland	21
Norway	17
Sweden	23

The above figures, which relate organized labour as a whole to total population, ignore differences in occupational structure, but still convey an approximately correct impression of union strength in the various countries. A more exact picture is obtained by comparison with the wage-earning part of the population only; this shows that organized workers and salaried employees account for about 33 per cent of all wage earners in Finland, about 45 per cent in Norway, about 50 per cent in Denmark and Iceland, and about 60 per cent in Sweden. By way of comparison it may be mentioned that the corresponding percentage in the United Kingdom is approximately 45.

Comparisons between the membership of the federations of trade unions and the working population would reveal a general increase in organizational strength during the last 30 years. In comparing the changes which have taken place in the different countries the results should, however, be interpreted with caution since they are influenced not only by the varying degree of organization but also by the varying distribution of the working population according to occupations. The increase has been relatively less important in Denmark where organizations were already well developed in 1920. Furthermore, the important part of the population still attached to agriculture in 1950 in both Denmark and Finland, largely as independent farmers, explains why any comparison between trade union membership and working population tends to show relatively lower percentages for these countries.

Trade unions in the Northern countries are open, in principle, to all persons employed in the trade or industry covered by the union. Freedom of association also includes the right to refrain from joining a union – although in practice any refractory worker encounters quite considerable pressure.

The structural set-up is rather similar in all five countries. The local union branch, covering a single plant or limited geographical area, remains the basic unit. These local branches are then grouped along craft or industrial lines into national unions, which in turn are affiliated with the Central Federation. Supreme authority in the Federation rests with the Congress which meets at regular intervals. Between Congress sessions important matters are referred to a representative council which, in turn, elects an executive board, consisting of from 9 to 15 members, which is in charge of the daily work. The individual national unions are organized along parallel lines.

But although the broad outline of organization may be similar, there are still important differences between the five countries.

Early trade unions, in a sense historically the successors of the old journeymen's gilds, were distinctly of a craft character, being associations of workers who had a common education and skill, combined with a well defined range of employment: Baker, mason, printer, etc. Due to the development of industrial enterprises in relatively isolated districts, craft unions in Finland, Norway, and Sweden have, to an increasing extent, been reorganized into industrial organizations comprising all – skilled as well as unskilled – workers within each separate sector of industry. In Denmark and Iceland, on the other hand, unions have largely retained their original structure.

The early organization of the unskilled and semi-skilled workers in Denmark, due largely to competent and aggressive leadership combined with the small size of the country, favoured the successful development of the General Labourers' Union, founded in 1896. This unique organization, which has reached the impressive membership of 240,000 or about 40 per cent of total membership in the Central Federation, has successfully fought off all encroachments upon its jurisdiction, while similar unions of unskilled workers in the other countries have been largely incorporated into industrial unions.

The division of organized labour into skilled and unskilled workers has greatly influenced the development of the Central Federation of Trade Unions in Denmark. The craft unions, striving for greater centralization of executive powers, have been opposed, not without success, by the Labourers' Union; being a minority, although a strong one, the latter was never too willing to cede powers to the Federation where the system of representation at the Congress favoured the craft unions.

Developments in Norway were totally different: In its formative years the Federation assumed great powers, notably by being almost the exclusive repository of strike funds. In spite of the fact that movements influenced by Syndicalist ideas existed inside the Federation for a long period before and during the First World War, the Norwegian Federation of Labour is perhaps the most centralized organization of its kind in the Northern countries.

In Iceland and Finland the history of the trade union federations is characterized by frequent dissolutions and reorganizations caused by political, rather than purely industrial differences between the member unions. As a consequence, these federations have never reached the same consolidated status and centralization of powers as in the other countries.

With respect to centralization the Swedish Federation of Labour occupies an intermediate position between the Danish and Norwegian federations. From the start its powers were very restricted, the individual unions being of such varying strength that the stronger unions were loath to dissipate their financial resources by support of weaker affiliates. The pressure from some large unions, notably the Metalworkers' Union, to invest the Federation with greater powers, and the new situation which developed upon Labour's rise to political power shifted the balance in favour of greater concentration and resulted in radical constitutional changes in 1941. Henceforth, the Federation was empowered to co-ordinate wage campaigns involving more than one union, and its consent was required to any strike affecting more than 3 per cent of the membership of affiliated unions; disobedience to this rule entailed loss of financial support from the Federation's strike fund.

In 1951 this rule was tightened with the result that now the consent of the Federation is required also for small strikes provided they may be expected to involve difficulties for other trade unions or vital community interests. Simultaneously the LO was empowered to create an agreements board for the purpose of improving co-ordination within the trade union movement with respect to wage agreements. A central research organ is to provide the various unions with data concerning relations between wages in the different groups and concerning the general background for future wage policies.

With their growing consolidation the trade unions have gradually accumulated reserve funds, which in several of the countries have assumed sizable proportions. Thus in Sweden the Central Federation in 1951 disposed of about 41 mill. kronor while the individual trade unions boasted resources of no less than 214 mill. kronor, the amount per member varying widely from union to union; the funds are held in cash or on bank accounts or are invested in government securities, dependent upon the degree of liquidity considered advisable by their holders. The amounts held in reserve by the unions in the other countries are considerably smaller.

It is characteristic of the trade union movement in the Northern countries that, however strong the move towards concentration of powers and co-ordination of action has been, the structure of organizations has remained thoroughly democratic. Although the unions have generally had the good fortune of having both outstanding and stable leadership, boss rule as it is known in some countries has been practically unknown. Recourse to universal vote among members is prescribed in the constitutions as the normal procedure for deciding upon issues of vital significance to the unions.

Employers' Organizations

The trade union movement, represented by the large federations, is matched by powerful employers' organizations. While the unions were established to fortify the weak bargaining position of the individual industrial wage earner as against the employer, the employers' organizations have had for their main purpose to strengthen the hand of the individual employer in dealing with the union.

The first important move towards organized collaboration in the labour market sphere between employers, who were otherwise keen competitors, took place in Denmark with the foundation in 1885 of the Association of Employers in the Metal Industries.

Subsequently, employers' organizations sprang up with every advance of trade unions which tended to weaken the bargaining position of individual employers. Following the foundation of the central federations of trade unions, the employers in their turn found it necessary to organize on a national scale. Only in Iceland did an employers' group, namely the shipowners, organize before any trade union existed, and by so doing gave rise to the first move towards trade unionism in Iceland. In that country we also note an interesting and unique event in the history of labour relations in the Northern countries, the Employers' Association of Printers being founded upon the explicit invitation of the Printers' Union which preferred to negotiate with one body representing all employers. Generally speaking, the powers bestowed upon the *national federations of employers* by the members have depended to an important degree on the strength of the labour unions which they were intended to meet. In the Northern countries there have been only few industrial giants potentially strong enough to meet the trade unions single-handed as has been, and still is, the case in the United States. The large number of small and relatively weak enterprises which stood face to face with strong labour organizations tended to promote the delegation of decisive powers to a central association. In Denmark, Norway, and Sweden the federations of employers have consequently been highly centralized from the start and have commanded a strong esprit de corps among their members. It is interesting to compare this with the far more hesitating attitude toward centralization of powers taken by the trade unions.

Their titles are today: Dansk Arbejdsgiverforening (Denmark); Arbetsgivarnas i Finland Centralförbund (Finland); Vinnuveitendasamband Íslands (Iceland); Norsk Arbeidsgiverforening (Norway); Svenska Arbetsgivareföreningen (Sweden).

In Finland where, until recently, trade unions have been rather weak, the Employers' Association founded in 1907 was limited to investigation of and reporting on current problems, and even after its reorganization in 1918 the Finnish Employers' Association did not by far represent the same concentration of power as its sister organizations in the Scandinavian countries. The rapid development of social legislation in Finland following the attainment of national independence rendered the task of protecting and promoting the joint interests of employers vis-à-vis the State very important, but the aims of the Employers' Association have not been defensive only, since this organization has been active also in fostering the initiative among employers to introduce welfare measures for their workers. – In Iceland, too, it was rather late that employers, hitherto organized by branches, centralized their efforts, the Icelandic Employers' Association being formed only in 1934.

Recent statistics show that in most of the five countries the number of workers employed in enterprises affiliated with the federations of employers is considerably smaller than the total number of organized workers in the federations of trade unions; for example in Denmark the ratio is about one to two and in Norway about one to three. This, however, does not convey an adequate impression of the actual importance of employers' organizations. The federations primarily include among their members the large industrial enterprises and within this group the great majority is organized. Furthermore,

109

several trades have their own independent employers' organizations on a national scale. This is generally the case with agriculture and a large number of crafts while in Sweden, for instance, even lumbering, shipping, and commerce are organized independently of the Employers' Association. In Norway one-third of all organized employers in 1944 were affiliated with independent organizations.

The great importance of employers' organizations is, however, not solely dependent upon the degree of organization, but is to a large extent derived from the fact that all leading establishments are within the central employers' associations, which thus control the key industries of each country. The associations develop the policies guiding all employers and are their obvious spokesmen before legislative and administrative authorities in all issues pertaining to the labour market.

COLLABORATION BETWEEN ORGANIZATIONS
Framework

Both trade unions and employers' associations were originally founded as militant organizations whose chief purpose was to attain a maximum of strength for the unrestricted economic warfare then characteristic of their mutual relations. Gradually, however, former antagonistic attitudes have been replaced by a mutual recognition of the need for acceptance of the other party. In the course of time this has resulted in the creation of ever closer collaboration between the parties, the main effort being today directed at the successful conclusion of agreements. The militant potential has been retained, and even strengthened, but is intended primarily to assure negotiators of a maximum of bargaining power, hostilities being opened only reluctantly as a last resort.

When successful, negotiations between the parties result in the establishment of a collective agreement. This may involve, on one hand, one or more employers or an association of employers and, on the other, one or more trade unions, but not individual workers. A highly significant feature, which contrasts with conditions in some other countries, e.g. the United Kingdom, is that the central organizations may conclude agreements directly with one another and that these agreements are binding upon their individual members. New members are bound by agreements previously concluded, and withdrawal from an organization does not absolve any member from obligations accepted through agreements as long as they remain in force.

The specific contents of any concrete collective agreement may range all the way from the regulation of only a single aspect of the relations between workers and employers to detailed provisions governing all relationships in the labour market sector concerned.

In principle, the parties are free to establish the agreement in accordance with their particular needs and inclinations, this right being, however, subject to certain general limitations.

In Finland, Norway, and Sweden a collective agreement must, to be valid, be drawn up in writing; in Iceland it must in addition contain a clause as to its period of validity. Other limitations as to the contents and form of collective agreements are of a negative character only, being confined to what such agreements may not contain. The principal restrictions belonging to this category have already been dealt with above under Labour Protection, such rules being unalterable even when the contracting parties might wish to depart from them. During wartime or other extraordinary circumstances the freedom of contract of the parties has in some cases been severely curtailed, but under normal conditions further limitations are few and mainly of the kind which may be found in legislation or good practice governing all contracts.

The above limitations and the general provisions as to what falls under the term "collective agreements" and as to their legal effect have been developed both by legislation and by mutual agreement between the central organizations. The latter method predominates in Denmark where the parties themselves at an early date took the initiative in establishing a permanent basis for their future relations. In Norway, Sweden, and Iceland the parties, though having utilized collective agreements for a long time, did not work out for themselves any basic regulations as to the conclusion of such agreements. In these three countries the State introduced, in 1915, 1928, and 1938, respectively, legislation on what was to be understood by a collective agreement and on the legal effects of an agreement already in existence. The background for these provisions was the basic fact that the legislation just mentioned included the establishment of labour courts for the final settlement of purely legal disputes. In Finland similar provisions were enacted in 1924, in this case for the express purpose of promoting the conclusion of agreements between organizations hitherto unwilling to take such steps. The revision in 1946 of this legislation was motivated, as earlier in Norway and Sweden, by the introduction of compulsory arbitration in conflicts arising over the interpretation or alleged breaches of existing agreements.

See below, Instruments of Labour Peace, pp. 120-134.

The rapid development in *Denmark* of employers' and workers' organizations of almost comparable strength relatively early convinced both parties of the fruitlessness of unrelenting struggle and thus paved the way for the acknowledgment by employers of the right of unions to bargain collectively. This early willingness of management to enter into negotiations with trade unions largely explains why the most mature system of collective bargaining in the Northern countries came to be developed in Denmark.

In 1898 a joint committee of trade unions and employers' organizations met to negotiate the terms of a general agreement. Differences between the two parties, however, proved too great and negotiations broke down. The following year a comprehensive and prolonged labour conflict threatened to bring the major part of industrial production to a standstill. Under heavy pressure from public opinion the two parties resumed their efforts to find a peaceful solution of the conflict. Negotiations resulted in the so-called September Agreement of 1899, which not only settled the immediate conflict, but implied far-reaching consequences also to future relations between trade unions and employers.

The September Agreement today still forms the *de facto* constitution of Danish labour relations. Its wording has never been amended although under the impact of changing conditions and conceptions it has quite naturally by interpretation acquired a meaning differing in several respects from what was originally read into the text.

Its provisions established a framework for the furthering of ordered and peaceful labour relations: Mutual recognition of the rights of the parties, uniformity of the rules for terminating agreements, and procedure for handling grievances and for giving advance notice of work stoppages. An outstanding feature of the Agreement was the high degree of authority vested in the organizations. The fundamental significance of the agreement, however, lay in the spirit in which it was conceived, a special paragraph stating: " . . . it is taken for granted that the Federation of Trade Unions will be willing to work with all its might together with the Employers' Association for peaceful, stable, and good working conditions . . .". This statement, issued more than fifty years ago by organized employers and workers, provides perhaps the best key to an understanding of why, in spite of frequent bitter conflicts, it has been possible to establish the comprehensive and reasonably smoothly working machinery at present found in Danish labour relations. Today it would appear to describe with a high degree of validity the general attitude prevailing also in the other Northern countries. In its very brevity this succinct pronouncement might therefore be considered to synthesize a major part of the explanation for the relative success achieved by these countries in labour market organization.

Direct negotiations between the central organizations of labour and management have taken place in *Norway* since 1900. The 1915 Act on Labour Disputes established a number of general regulations concerning collective agreements. This legislative initiative explains in part why it was only in 1935 that the two parties themselves concluded an agreement laying down fundamental principles of collaboration. This so-called "Basic Agreement" embodied the mutual recognition *de jure* of the right to organize for collective bargaining, and provided for (1) regulations governing the appointment and functions of shop stewards; (2) grievance and disputes procedure; (3) referenda of proposed agreements; and (4) rules for the institution of sympathetic actions, obliging the central organizations to negotiate before permitting the implementation of such action. Since 1947 time and motion studies in industry have been based on principles formally accepted by the two central organizations.

In *Sweden*, where developments during the first decades of the present century followed a course largely similar to that in Norway, it was the wish to avoid the necessity of government interference that finally led to a decisive conference between the Central Federation of Trade Unions and the Swedish Employers' Association in 1936 at Saltsjöbaden, a suburb of Stockholm. The result was a document known as the "Saltsjöbaden Agreement" (Basic Agreement) of 1938 which, supplemented by a series of agreements concluded in the following years, today forms the basis of relations between the central organizations of the labour market in Sweden. Among its immediate goals was the limitation of conflicts dangerous to the welfare of the community and to neutral third parties. A bipartite, six-member permanent Labour Market Committee was established to deal with specified questions pertaining to the discharge of workers, labour disputes affecting essential public services, and restrictions upon the right to resort to direct action.

113

The Saltsjöbaden Conference has become a recurring feature of Swedish labour relations and a pivotal point in all subsequent joint efforts of organized employers and workers. In 1942 it sponsored the creation of a Joint Standing Labour Protection Committee, in 1944 it took the initiative in creating a Labour Market Occupational Training Council to promote vocational training; furthermore, in 1946 the Conference agreed upon the introduction of Joint Production Committees and, finally, an agreement in 1948 created a system of Joint Standing Committees on Time and Motion Studies. The most recent expression of this trend is an agreement made in 1952 by which the two parties undertook to recommend to their members that wage increases demanded or accepted be kept within certain general limits. On the whole this recommendation has been followed although neither party has assumed any obligation to continue this centralization of collective bargaining.

Thus, in spite of their late start, Swedish labour market organizations have, in an inspiring spirit of co-operation and with a minimum of dependence upon State intervention, succeeded in creating a framework of collective bargaining more complete, perhaps, than in any of the other Northern countries.

In *Finland*, the Employers' Association, following its reorganization in 1918 and the subsequent introduction in 1924 of a collective agreements' act which was intended to promote orderly and peaceful labour relations, took initial steps to negotiate collective agreements with the trade unions. The employers were, however, somewhat reluctant to deal with organizations which in their opinion were not operated on a purely trade union basis, while internal dissension within the ranks of trade unions jeopardized any serious attempt to come to terms with employers.

Whereas until recently labour relations in Finland were hampered by a mutual feeling of distrust between the parties, the institution of closer co-operation among them by a preliminary agreement in 1940 inaugurated a new phase in Finnish labour market history through the mutual recognition of the right of either party to organize and bargain collectively. This was followed up in 1944 and 1946 by general agreements between the central organizations laying down detailed provisions concerning the rights of the respective parties, negotiation procedures and various methods of collaboration. During subsequent years nation-wide collective agreements have been concluded in all important sectors of industry, in forestry and timber floating, and in agriculture.

Collective agreements have been known in *Iceland* since 1904. Following the formation of the Icelandic Employers' Association, special legislation was adopted in 1938 which decreed the exclusive right of trade unions to conclude such agreements. It is worth noting that – contrary to the other Northern countries – the central organizations do not enjoy this right and are free only to conclude general agreements on behalf of such subsidiary organizations as desire them. The first general agreement was signed only in 1951; it may be added that its provisions are based upon agreements already previously entered upon by some branch organizations.

Collective Agreements in Practice

At the present time it has become the normal thing for industrial labour contracts to be concluded on the basis of collective agreements, which cover an ever increasing part of the labour market. No exact Danish figures are available, but according to recent trade union estimates there are, at the present time, about 4,500 collective agreements covering a total of 490,000 workers; more than two-thirds of all adult industrial labourers now work under collective agreements. In Norway there were, in 1940, 6,200 agreements with a total coverage of almost 400,000 workers. The comparable Swedish figures, for 1950–51, were 20,200 agreements and 1,109,000 workers, implying, for manufacturing industries, a coverage of 85–90 per cent.

These figures do not bring out the degree of concentration actually existing. Agreements may be national, provincial, or local in scope; or they may cover the individual enterprise only. The dominating importance of national agreements is, however, clear from the fact that 50 such agreements in Norway covered a majority of all organized workers, whereas in Sweden 217 agreements covered 638,000 workers, or 57 per cent of all organized workers. Furthermore, many agreements covering only a single establishment are modelled on the lines of some national agreement.

Collective agreements are generally concluded for one or two years. There is a growing tendency for agreements to lapse at the same time of the year, for instance in Denmark on March 1. The preceding weeks of negotiation have come to stand out as recurrent critical periods in labour relations.

It is natural that *wage provisions* should hold a predominant position in all collective agreements. Wages are usually either in the form of hourly rates or piecework rates. It is characteristic of the Northern countries that piecework is normally used whenever technically possible and that it applies even to site work in building construction. In 1949 it was found that in Sweden the ratio of piecework hours to total hours worked in manufacturing and mining was about 68 per cent, while the corresponding Danish figure for industry, handicrafts, and transportation in the same year was 41 per cent (46 for skilled workers). A similar Norwegian inquiry undertaken in 1940 brought forth a percentage of 36 for piecework in that country.

Apart from certain standard rates, piecework pay is largely determined by special negotiation between management and workers' representatives at the places of work. Time rates may either be so-called "normal wages", when a full schedule of occupational wage rates is established, or minimum wages below which no worker in an establishment may be paid. Under the former system all workers within the same industry or trade receive the wage agreed upon; but there will often be various wage steps, graduated according to age, seniority, and skill, and individual workers may receive personal increments. The second system, which is frequently applied where work cannot readily be standardized, should not be confused with the "social" minimum wage decreed in some countries; it simply involves the fixing of a time rate, and actual wages may not be lower than this rate plus such increments as may have been agreed upon by individual bargaining between the employer and workers.

Although containing many and detailed wage provisions, the collective agreements do not yield exhaustive information as to the actual size of the take-home pay of workers. Such information is provided by statistics based upon the pay-rolls of a large number of enterprises and is published regularly in the Statistical Yearbooks of each country.

A novel principle introduced during the inter-war period in Denmark and Norway was that of tying wages to a cost-of-living index. It was first applied with respect to civil service salaries, but subsequently spread to the field of collective agreements. In 1939 Iceland and Sweden followed suit. As for the techniques applied, it is interesting to note that while the Danish and Norwegian method for industrial workers was to pay index wage increments as a flat-rate supplement equal for all workers (women and young workers receiving, however, a smaller amount), the supplements in Sweden were computed as a uniform percentage of basic wages.

In Finland wage adjustment for changes in the costs of living was introduced under somewhat different auspices. When, due to the war, the Finnish government in 1942 assumed control over wages, the general approach was to compensate workers for the war-time rise in prices at an average rate of two-thirds, the lowest paid categories being granted full compensation and the higher paid categories receiving correspondingly smaller compensation. From 1947 onwards the successive programmes of economic stabilization have all contained varying forms of wage regulation according to changes in costs of living. Under the present provisions workers are entitled to a five per cent wage increment for every five per cent rise in prices above a basis fixed in October 1951.

Also in the other four countries the governments took action to prevent the war-time rise in prices from setting off corresponding wage increases, but after the war the automatic regulation for changes in the cost of living was resumed. In Sweden the system was abandoned in 1947, presumably due to the confidence of trade unions in their own ability to secure satisfactory wages without any such arrangement. But in 1952 a new agreement was concluded between the central organizations, providing for the right to open negotiations during the year if the costs of living should pass a certain maximum before the expiration of the contract. In Norway the automatic regulation was replaced in 1950 by a system similar to the one subsequently introduced in Sweden; in 1952 this, too, was abandoned.

With war-time and post-war inflation cost-of-living supplements have become an important element in total earnings. The flat-rate supplement practised in Denmark and (until 1950) Norway has considerably improved the wage position of the lower paid as compared with better paid workers, a development which has been advocated by trade unions under the slogan of a "solidaric wage policy". The Swedish scheme, on the other hand, was more conservative since it operated to preserve wage differentials; this has not precluded the pursuing also in Sweden of a solidaric wage policy by means of proportionally larger wage increases, apart from cost-of-living increments, to the lowest paid groups.

Non-wage provisions of collective agreements do not readily lend themselves to any broad summarization. Both legislation and the basic agreements between the central organizations have to some extent reduced the area of bargaining, but many subjects remain which are not easily adaptable to nation-wide standardization· and which thus, despite a general tendency toward greater uniformity, continue to be dealt with on the industry or plant level. Such subjects include the detailed regulation of hours of work, breaks and holidays, and the promotion on the plant level of labour welfare, industrial safety, etc., and also provisions dealing with the set-up of labour relations machinery inside the individual enterprise.

See above, Labour Protection, pp. 72-98.

Without aiming at a complete list of such subjects, it may still be pertinent to call attention to a few matters of special interest.

A problem which in some countries has given rise to many controversies, the *closed shop*, i.e. an arrangement under which employers may engage only organized workers, has never been much of an issue in the Northern countries. The general acceptance of the principle of freedom to work has certainly prevented tendencies to monopolize the right to work from gaining any major importance, while the high degree of organization has admittedly established a condition of *de facto* closed shop in many branches of industrial activity.

As early as in 1899 the Danish September Agreement affirmed the right of management to determine the labour force to be employed. Though the employers' organization has consistently refused approval of any agreement calling for the closed shop, numerous independent employers – mostly in less fully organized trades – have agreed with the unions to employ organized workers only; according to Danish law the trade unions must in this case be open to all qualified workers. (Also in other cases there is a general assumption that trade unions should be open to all new qualified workers; actually, all unions are open today). In Norway unions have acquiesced in the refusal, dating from 1907, by the Employers' Association to permit agreements embodying the closed shop clause. The related union-shop system, i.e. an arrangement under which the enterprise is open to unorganized workers provided that they join the relevant organization within a certain period has, however, been practised by independent employers in the diluted form of limiting employment to members of the Federation of Labour as a whole. Quite generally it may be stated that neither the closed shop nor the union shop is formally applied to any significant extent in any of the Northern countries. Still, the

118

strength of the organizations results in considerable pressure being brought to bear upon the individual unorganized worker so that the two practices may be said to have quite wide *de facto* application.

Another instrument of union security is the limitation of the number of apprentices trained in each trade. Under the impression of widespread unemployment in the inter-war years, clauses aiming at direct rationing of apprentices were inserted in some collective agreements. Many of these provisions, often establishing a ratio of apprentices to the number of journeymen employed, are still in force, but today are mainly used to ensure that training facilities are not rendered inadequate by the employment of too many apprentices in any single firm.

Seniority provisions aiming at the special protection of older workers with respect to discharge and re-engagement are found in some agreements but generally trade unions have not been anxious to force the use of this principle as a means of distributing available jobs among workers. Although only few agreements stipulate strict seniority it is widely practised by employers, as complete disregard of the length of service might arouse unrest among the employees. On account of the small size of most establishments, employers are usually in a position to balance considerations of equity toward older employees with their interest in retaining the younger and frequently more efficient workers.

Of great importance to the smooth adjustment of daily routine problems are the *shop stewards* provided for by collective agreement.

Although there may be differences of detail, the broad lines are similar in the various countries. Shop stewards are elected by the workers, the number depending upon the size of the establishment. Their general role is to act as "representatives of and spokesmen for the organized employees" vis-à-vis the employer. It is the duty of the steward, together with the employer, to strive to maintain peaceful co-operation at the place of work. He presents the grievances of workers regarding working conditions, working hours, overtime, personnel matters, etc., to the employer for discussion and settlement, and also forms the link through which the employer communicates his wishes to the workers. So as to enable the shop steward to discharge his duties appropriately, the agreements specifically lay down that the employer must consult with him on changes in working rules, operational changes calling for fundamental alterations of working conditions, redundancy of labour, etc., although the steward cannot question the decision of the employer. The shop steward is protected by a certain degree of immunity from dismissal.

There appears to be general agreement as to the satisfactory working of the shop steward system. It has proved a practical means of clearing up the misunderstandings and minor disputes which arise in the daily work on the plant level and has thereby made a considerable contribution to the peaceful operation of collective agreements.

INSTRUMENTS OF LABOUR PEACE

One of the outstanding characteristics of the labour market in the Northern countries is the comprehensive procedural and legal structure built up for the specific purpose of limiting warfare between trade unions and employers to a minimum.

The measures adopted in these highly controversial matters have in some instances been enacted against the strong opposition of organized labour, which feared encroachment upon its right to utilize the strike weapon. In other cases legislation has either been prepared in close co-operation with the respective organizations or rendered superfluous because the parties had already for themselves found a lasting solution to their problem.

Whatever their origin, the instruments developed for the peaceful settlement of labour disputes have generally functioned to the satisfaction of both workers and employers, and may today be considered permanent and integral parts of the institutional set-up in these countries. If a comparison be ventured, it might perhaps be said that Denmark and Sweden are the countries where labour market organizations themselves have made the greatest contribution toward the establishment of this peace-preserving system. In the other three Northern countries, where differences between the two parties have been somewhat sharper and political tensions somewhat greater, the State has played a more prominent role.

In dealing with labour disputes a fundamental distinction is made between those issues which are already regulated by agreements and those where no arrangements bind the parties. Where a collective agreement is in force, the freedom of action of organizations and their members is, for the period of its validity, restricted to legal proceedings. Otherwise, the parties are legally free to apply their traditional weapons of labour warfare, notably the strike and the lockout; in these cases the State normally offers only mediation or voluntary arbitration.

Briefly and quite generally it may be stated that *conflicts of rights*, i.e. disputes which arise over the interpretation or alleged violation of collective agreements already in force, may under no circumstances give rise to stoppages of work.

If, however, a conflict is of the nature of a so-called *"conflict of interests"*, i.e. disagreement on a new right in spheres where no such right is established by contract (which usually means a dispute concerning the substance of a new agreement or of an agreement to replace one which has expired), the parties must, when called upon, endeavour to come to terms with the assistance of a government mediator, but are normally free to reject his proposals and attempt to enforce their claims by means of strike or lockout.

Conflicts of Rights

In *Denmark* the September Agreement of 1899 created a Permanent Court of Arbitration of seven members, of which each of the two parties elected three, while the seventh, serving as chairman, was elected by the Court itself from among the lawyers of the country. The Court of Arbitration, which in 1900 was empowered by law to take valid legal evidence, was intended to handle all disputes that might arise from the obligation, undertaken by both parties, to conclude or approve no arrangement that was contrary to the September Agreement.

In 1908, following a strike which paralyzed the daily press, the Minister of the Interior set up a joint committee of representatives from the central organizations of workers and employers to investigate the possibilities of further improving the system of arbitration and mediation during all labour conflicts. The resulting recommendations by this committee included standard rules (the so-called "Norm") for handling trade disputes and the establishment of a standing arbitration court for labour disputes.

The proposed "Norm" was gradually introduced in most agreements and in 1934 remaining gaps were closed by a law giving it legal status. The "Norm" primarily covers all disputes over the *interpretation* of existing collective agreements. If the parties are not able to agree by direct negotiation, the case is submitted by the plaintiff to his organization, which then sets up a rapidly working *ad hoc* conciliation committee of one representative from each side. Should no agreement be reached, the case goes before the organizations sitting together. If still no solution is agreed upon on this level, the issue is finally referred to a trade arbitration court specially appointed in each case for final and binding settlement. The rules of procedure outlined above, except for the final settlement by an arbitration court, also apply to certain disputes of interests.

See also Conflicts of Interests, p.125.

To deal with *breaches* of collective agreements legislation establishing the Statutory Court of Arbitration was enacted in 1910. It provided that the Court (which replaced the Permanent Court of Arbitration) should consist of an equal number of representatives from each of the two central organizations, with two lawyers elected by the Court to act as chairman and vice-chairman. The Court handles cases of violation of the September Agreement or any other collective agreement between a labour organization and an employers' association or a single establishment. The decisions of the Court are final and legally binding, enforceable if necessary by the imposition of fines. It should be added that fines can also be imposed to indemnify a party for losses sustained as a result of a breach of agreement.

The act contained only few material legal directives, based as it was on the September Agreement and collective agreements subsequently concluded. The Court is to prevent that disputes over rights result in strikes or lockouts, but the establishment of such rights is left entirely to the parties. The high degree of reliance upon the central organizations implicit in this arrangement was a considerable tribute to the status which these organizations had achieved only 10 years after their foundation. It was symptomatic of this attitude that the State also left it to them to appoint the Court and entrusted juridical authority within this particular sphere to that Court. The statutes of the Court have been revised only once, i. e. in 1934, when the juridical element among the judges was strengthened. Since 1910 the Court has handled about 4,500 cases; at the present time it deals with some 150 cases every year, about half of which are brought in by employers, and half by workers' organizations.

By and large, the legal machinery established in the other Northern countries to handle disputes over rights is very similar to that found in Denmark. There is, however, this difference that the Danish distinction between disputes over interpretation and disputes over alleged violations of agreements is not applied in the other countries where the labour courts deal with both categories of disputes.

In *Norway* the Labour Disputes Act of 1915 established a Labour Court to replace and consolidate the private courts of arbitration previously instituted by the organizations. The Court consisted of seven members, two nominated by the central employers' organization and two by the central federation of trade unions. The Act prohibited work stoppages in conflicts of rights and prescribed the imposition of fines for any damage caused by violations of its provisions. As previously mentioned, this Act also gave rules for the establishment of collective agreements, compliance with these rules being prerequisite to the eventual enforcement at court.

Because of the geographical isolation of many industrial districts in Norway, local courts were, in more recent years, created to deal with minor questions, the Labour Court in Oslo acting as court of appeal. The findings of the Labour Court are final, except in questions concerning the jurisdiction of the Court.

From 1916 to 1940 the Court has dealt with some 1,650 complaints of which fifty odd per cent were disposed of by formal judgment, 20 per cent were settled through court mediation, and the remainder were withdrawn before trial. The complaints have been brought in by the two parties at a ratio of about fifty-fifty.

Arbitration in disputes of rights was introduced in *Sweden* in 1920 with the statutory establishment of the Central Board of Arbitration which, from 1920 to 1928, dealt with many complaints concerning the proper interpretation and implication of collective agreements.

In 1928 this organ was replaced by the Labour Court in Stockholm. This Court, tripartite as in the other countries, now consists of eight judges, three of them impartial civil servants, two of them nominated by the employers, two by the workers and one by the salaried employees; whenever salaried employees' organizations are involved in the case before the Court their representative replaces one of the members nominated by the workers.

Apart from decisions on the validity or implications of collective agreements and on alleged contraventions of such agreements, the Court also deals with claims in respect of damage caused by alleged breach of contract and with questions concerning the implications of the legislation concerning collective agreements, freedom of association, the right of bargaining, and retention of employment in case of marriage, pregnancy, or military service. As in the other countries procedure before the Court is oral and its findings final.

123

Procedures for final settlement of conflicts of rights were introduced by law in *Iceland* in 1938. The Permanent Court of Arbitration then instituted consists of five members. The central organizations elect one member each, while one is appointed by the Minister for Social Affairs, and the other two – one of whom acts as chairman – by the Supreme Court. Unlike the other countries, compliance with the decisions of the Court may be enforced by work stoppage. Strikes may not be directed against the State, except in its capacity of employer of persons other than public servants. Procedure before the Court is oral. Its findings may only be appealed to the Supreme Court when the Arbitration Court has rejected a case on jurisdictional grounds.

As indicated above, conditions on the *Finnish* labour market were until recently unfavourable to the creation of a court of arbitration, since such a body presupposes the existence of collective agreements. After 1944, however, when collective agreements were concluded in all important sectors of economic life, the need for a special legal organ to deal with disputes regarding the interpretation and alleged violation of these agreements became obvious. In 1946, in connection with a revision of the earlier legislation on collective agreements, the Finnish Parliament consequently passed a law which instituted a Labour Court on the Swedish model. During its first six years of operation the Labour Court has dealt with 93 cases, 54 of which were submitted to it by employers, and 39 by workers' organizations.

On the whole, the experience of the Northern countries with settlement in court of conflicts over rights has been encouraging. Even in Sweden, where it was originally strongly opposed by the workers, the Labour Court has won increasing respect. This is clearly demonstrated by the fact that out of a total of 2,000 cases dealt with, 1,650 have been brought before the Court by workers' organizations.

This success may be attributed to several factors, one of the most important perhaps being the influence of the highly qualified chairmen appointed to the Labour Courts. Another fundamental factor has been the tripartite composition of the tribunals. Although dissenting opinions occur quite frequently, unanimous decisions are the rule rather than the exception – a fact which obviously lends greatly enhanced authority to the findings of the courts. Nothing would be more fatal to successful functioning than long procedural delays, and the expeditious handling of cases which is a characteristic feature of all the Northern Labour Courts therefore goes far to explain the smooth and effective operation of these organs. Also, the degree of continuity in the decisions of the courts has, in course of time, established a legal tradition which, through interpretation and filling-in of gaps, supplements legislation and today may be considered an integral part of labour law in the Northern countries.

Conflicts of Interests

Issues of disagreement are always first dealt with by direct negotiations between the parties immediately involved and, if no settlement is obtained, then by negotiations between the competent organizations. Recourse to legal procedure in conflicts of rights suggests itself as a natural solution in communities with a highly developed judicial system and, as demonstrated in the preceding section, it has in fact been practised by the Northern countries with no little success. Conflicts of interests, on the other hand, do not lend themselves to similar treatment since they are nonjudicial in character, arising over the establishment of a new legal basis for relations between the parties. In these conflicts it is obviously far more difficult to find a yardstick, acceptable to both parties, by which to arrive at a solution of the issue at stake.

While lending loyal co-operation to compulsory arbitration in conflicts of rights, the organizations of both employers and workers have always maintained as a matter of fundamental principle their right to complete freedom of action in conflicts of interests. Up to the present time, the principle of non-intervention in this sphere has generally been accepted in the five countries under review. This, however, has by no means implied complete passivity on the part of Society, the interest of which in the maintenance of peaceful labour relations is clearly the same regardless of the nature of the conflict. Elaborate systems of government mediation have been instituted to prevent hostilities from breaking out between workers and employers before all possibilities for peaceful settlement have been explored.

In *Denmark* the September Agreement of 1899, by stipulating periods of warning (minimum two weeks) before the commencement of any strike or lockout, aimed to ensure that work stoppages were only brought into effect after mature consideration. The "Norm" of 1908 was a further step in this direction, although of limited importance in conflicts of interests as it is applied only to disputes, nowadays rare, over issues arising in the course of an agreement period and not covered by the agreement. Far more important was the proposal of the Joint Committee of 1908 to appoint a government mediator, which was put on the statute books in 1910 with the establishment of the Conciliation Institution. The Mediation in Labour Conflicts Act has since been amended several times, strengthening the authority of the Institution vis-à-vis the parties by extending its powers and increasing the number of mediators.

The mediator, who is appointed by the Minister for Social Affairs upon the nomination of the Statutory Court of Arbitration, must at all times closely follow developments in labour relations. When a conflict threatens to result in open hostilities the parties are, if he so requests, under obligation to continue negotiations under his auspices. He is empowered to demand that hostilities be postponed for one week during mediatory negotiations, pending his public declaration that they have ended without result.

If the mediator does not succeed in making the parties agree, he may either declare that negotiations have broken down, whereupon the parties regain their freedom of action, or place before them a mediation proposal which each party must either accept or reject.

The decision upon such a proposal is taken by universal balloting among the rank and file of the trade unions and by a general assembly of employers. This democratic procedure is the crucial point in the bargaining process, and it may happen that a compromise, which has been reached after many hours and days of strenuous negotiations, is rejected at the final balloting among members. Since opponents to a proposed agreement are usually the most active in going to the polls, special rules have been adopted so as to prevent a small minority from rejecting a proposal which the majority is willing to accept. A proposal is consequently always considered adopted when less than 25 per cent of the members have cast their votes, quite regardless of the distribution of Ayes and Noes, and a rejection is formally recognized only where a clear majority of voters has demonstrated their unwillingness to accept the proposal. In this connection it is of great significance that the mediator has the right to declare that a proposal covering several trades shall be dealt with as a whole so that all votes for or against are counted together, thus preventing any single group of workers from rejecting a proposed agreement covering several trades.

Official organs have for a long time acted as mediators in labour conflicts in *Finland*, but not until 1925 was any procedure laid down by law. The Mediation Act of 1925 was primarily based on voluntary mediation, the mediator intervening only when called for by one of the parties or when public interests were seriously jeopardized. The powers of the mediator were by no means adequate and a proposed amendment was put before Parliament as early as 1931. It was, however, only in 1946 that new legislation on mediation was passed.

Government Mediators are now appointed for 3 years at a time for each district of mediation. In order to protect the normal course of national life from surprise stoppages of work, no strike or lockout involving more than ten workers may be commenced unless the parties have submitted the issue to the proper mediator and duly warned the opposing party not less than two weeks in advance. In some vital industries these rules apply even when less than 10 workers are involved. Mediation proceeds along the same lines as in Denmark, non-acceptance of a mediation proposal being followed, however, by an invitation to the disputing parties to submit their differences for decision by one or more arbitrators.

Together with the institution, in 1938, of the Permanent Court of Arbitration in *Iceland*, a system of government mediation and rules for trade disputes were introduced. The system does not differ to any important extent from the one in force in Denmark.

In *Norway* the Labour Disputes Act of 1915 provided for government mediation in conflicts of interests, through the appointment of a State Mediator and District Mediators. Trade unions or employers who wish to call a strike or lockout must first notify the State Mediator of their intention, such notice to include detailed information regarding total employment in the industry, the number of workers involved in the dispute, the subject matter at issue, and a progress report on the preceding negotiations. Four working days must lapse after notification before any further step may legally be taken. During this period the mediator shall determine whether the notified stoppage will "prejudice public interests in view of either the nature of the establishment or the extent of the dispute". If his conclusion is in the affirmative, the mediator may suspend the execution of the work stoppage until mediation proceedings have taken place. By a revision of the law in 1934 the mediator was empowered to intervene at any stage in the development of a dispute. This amendment represented an improvement since it made intervention possible before the conflict had reached a stage so critical as to render mediation fruitless.

Ten days from the issue of a work-stoppage injunction either party has the right to demand that mediation shall be terminated, after which time proceedings must be brought to an end within four days, leaving the parties with their full freedom of action. The mediator may at any time reopen mediation proceedings and if a work stoppage continues for a month he is under law required to bring the parties together once more. Such mediation is, however, not accompanied by an order to resume work.

As in the other countries the mediator may at any time formulate a proposal for settlement which each of the parties must either accept or reject.

In 1934 rules for the voting on such proposals, based largely upon the Danish legislation, were enacted, but were partly repealed only one year later as a result of labour pressure; the only provisions retained were those empowering the mediator to decree that proposals involving several trades should be considered a whole. The legislation in question was replaced by a private agreement between the central organizations covering voting procedure both on collective agreements and mediation proposals. The parties thereby pledged themselves to take adequate steps to spread knowledge of the contents of a proposed agreement and to ensure that all those entitled to vote are given the opportunity to vote by secret ballot.

In *Sweden* legislation on mediation was considered as early as 1887 and a first legislative step was taken in 1906 when organs of mediation were put at the disposal of the parties. The Mediation Act in force today dates from 1920 but has been amended several times.

As in Finland, the country is divided into mediation districts, each with a mediator. The Mediation Act was supplemented in 1935 by legislation compelling the party which desires to bring a work stoppage into effect to issue a notice of warning to the opposing party and to the mediator at least seven days in advance. In recent years the number of cases submitted to mediation has risen to around 500 annually, 100 of which have been dealt with by special mediators.

Although there are no uniform rules, a ballot – decisive or consultative – is in many cases arranged among the members of the organizations to determine the fate of agreements proposed.

Government mediation and the compulsory temporary postponement of work stoppages, which is its accessory, was originally opposed by the trade unions who argued that the effectiveness of a strike

Accord in the 11th hour. Scene from a collective bargaining conference in Norway.

to a large extent depended upon its coming unwarned. Today, however, both labour and management find themselves in agreement on the desirability of compulsory government mediation, which has become an integral part of collective bargaining. A main reason for this attitude is undoubtedly found in the realization by both parties that labour stoppages will frequently prove more costly than a peaceful settlement.

In any attempt to explain the success of government mediation the personal qualifications of the individuals entrusted with the exacting task of mediating in labour conflicts must be assigned a role of key importance. Besides profound knowledge of the sphere of labour relations, the mediator requires a fine command of negotiation techniques coupled with a broadness of outlook and patience fundamentally important in difficult conciliation proceedings. The respect which the mediators have gained must largely be ascribed to their possessing these faculties and their utilizing the legislative framework, not as strict regulations to be followed to the letter, but as very general directives within which advice and assistance can be given impartially and freely. Of great psychological importance is the mediator's status as the disinterested third party, in which capacity he may propose a compromise solution without weakening the bargaining position of either party.

An important effect of government mediation is, furthermore, that negotiations between the parties are made a matter of public concern.

129

By raising negotiations from the private to the public level, mediation implies an appeal to the sense of social responsibility of the parties; at the same time the authority of the mediator is increased by the fact that he will frequently be considered as representing public opinion. In this connection it should, however, be emphasized that the question of whether a given solution be "just" from one or another point of view is, strictly speaking, irrelevant to the function of the mediator, his sole concern being to find a solution upon which both parties may agree.

The vital element in government mediation is the conciliator's right to formulate a mediatory proposal. In the hands of the able mediator this constitutes an effective and flexible instrument.

The formulation of a mediation proposal also strengthens the position of the negotiators vis-à-vis their own rank and file. Although the negotiators feel that such a proposal represents the best they can get, it may easily be unpopular among the members. If this is the case, the negotiators are able to put part of the blame on the mediator and justify the acceptance of his proposal by the advisability of avoiding unfavourable public reaction. In practice, it has proved much more difficult to reject such a proposal than a mere tentative agreement arrived at through direct negotiations between the parties.

The authority attributed to the mediatory proposal is also largely due to the fact-finding procedure which always takes place during the negotiations at the mediator's table. Many controversies are thereby freed from some of their emotional elements, which often stand in the way of a reasonable solution. In this connection it may also be mentioned that many disputes have been avoided owing to the fact that both parties have agreed to use the same wage statistics.

Compulsory Arbitration in Conflicts of Interests

Without in any way belittling the important role played by government mediation as developed in the Northern countries, it is necessary to recognize the limitations inherent in this approach. To be successful, mediation is primarily contingent upon the willingness of the parties to come to terms. Where such willingness is lacking, as has often been the case in critical situations, mediation is obviously inadequate to preserve labour peace.

The favourable results of compulsory arbitration in conflicts of rights, and the paramount interest of Society in preventing as far as possible any kind of labour conflict, has from time to time evoked strong sympathies for the extension of arbitration to all labour conflicts. As already mentioned, these sympathies have been shared by neither workers nor employers, who consider freedom of action in conflicts of interests a fundamental right, the loss of which would spell doom to the great labour market organizations in their traditional form. In consequence, it has been only under extraordinary circumstances and with many reservations that they have bowed to compulsory arbitration in such conflicts.

Norway has experimented with compulsory arbitration in conflicts of interests during several periods, while Denmark and Finland have only resorted to this procedure during and immediately after the Second World War. Sweden has so far never practised direct intervention in conflicts of interests (although twice during the last years the threat of such intervention has been successfully used as a means of enforcing peaceful settlement upon the parties).

In Norway, it was in the critical years during and immediately after the First World War – when violent changes in the costs of living engendered serious trouble on the labour market – that compulsory arbitration in wage conflicts was forced upon the parties by law, first from 1916–20 and again from 1922–23. In neither case did the tripartite arbitration courts succeed in satisfying either party and with the expiration of the acts arbitration was dropped without much regret. Compulsory arbitration in such disputes was nevertheless resumed 1927–29, but met with stubborn opposition from the workers who, refusing the more formal than wholehearted request from their leaders to comply with the decisions of the Arbitration Court, in the spring of 1928 started a comprehensive walkout. Arbitration was virtually given up when the chairman of the Court succeeded in bringing about a compromise settlement of the current conflict between the parties.

Toward the end of the Second World War the Norwegian government in London faced the enormous task of rebuilding their country. Upon the recommendation of the leaders of the Central Federation of Trade Unions and the Norwegian Employer's Association the government in 1944 laid down temporary provisions concerning wages and introduced compulsory arbitration in wage conflicts. A Wage

131

Board was established, composed of a chairman and six other members, including two workers' representatives and two employers' representatives. Free negotiations between the parties were retained but work stoppages were prohibited. Originally, this arrangement was intended to remain in force only for one year after the liberation of the country. However, it was repeatedly prolonged for one or two years until the end of 1952. Step by step the provisions were modified to facilitate the gradual return to the customary right to effect work stoppages.

The system succeeded in ensuring Norway of labour peace during a period when it was vital to concentrate all available resources on reconstruction and production and to keep wages within limits compatible with the economic development of the country. The success had for its background the recognition by the main organizations involved of the need to solve their problems without recourse to devastating labour conflicts. Each time the question of prolongation or modification of the system was taken up for debate considerable attention was given to the position of the organizations. It was inevitable that compulsory arbitration should entail a weakening of the ability and will of the parties to solve their conflicts of interests by negotiation and mediation; likewise, that the interest of the individual member and his sense of responsibility towards the established wage rates should be reduced. Consequently, organizational support of the 1945-arrangement dwindled progressively and when, at the end of 1952, the large organizations no longer found themselves able to approve of the system it was allowed to lapse.

As from 1953 a number of permanent Wage Boards, composed of experts, have been established to serve as organs of voluntary arbitration of disputes. It is the hope of the authorities that in critical situations the parties will utilize this new institution instead of resorting to ruinous conflicts.

The difficult economic situation during the 'thirties, particularly the precarious balance-of-payments situation and the resulting necessity of maintaining exports, on several occasions also led the *Danish* government to intervene in threatening labour market conflicts. The method followed was most frequently for Parliament to enact the mediator's proposal, but in other instances legislation was passed prolonging the expired agreements for one year without any changes or referring the dispute to an *ad hoc* arbitration court for final and binding settlement. These interventions were, however, all undertaken on a purely *ad hoc* basis as a last resort to avert the damaging results for the country of a conflict. The occupation of the country by German troops during the Second World War temporarily resulted in first priority being given to measures which could ensure complete unity on the home front. Accordingly, a Labour and Mediation Board was established for the duration – partly in response to a joint recommendation from the two central organizations – and entrusted with the final decision upon issues where unity could not be achieved through negotiation between the parties.

After the war, final responsibility for the settlement of current issues, among them mainly wages, again reverted to the parties. The obvious need for sustained reconstruction efforts, however, has resulted in strong pressure by public opinion for the maintenance of labour market peace. On several occasions, therefore, when major strikes or lockouts seemed imminent, Parliament has, as in the 'thirties, resolved to put the mediation proposal tendered by the government mediator on the statute books, thereby forcing a compromise solution upon the parties and averting open conflict. It will thus be seen that although Denmark has never known any regular compulsory arbitration legislation, the principle of non-intervention in conflicts of interests has been repeatedly set aside in the last two decades.

In *Finland* The Emergency Powers Act, introduced when the country was in a state of war and subsequently repeatedly prolonged, invested the government with sweeping authority to prohibit any stoppage of work which might endanger the smooth functioning of vital services; however, these powers have only been utilized very sparingly and it is doubtful whether, under the stormy political conditions prevailing in Finland after the war, such prohibition would have had any effect other than to discredit the government in the eyes of Labour. Since 1942 the government has, with only one short pause in 1950, retained control over the determination of wages so that strikes launched to support wage claims have in reality been conducted against the government rather than the employers.

In *Sweden* compulsory arbitration has so far been avoided in practice, partly by the setting up of the joint employer-union Labour Market *See p. 113.* Committee. During recent years, however, the placing before Parliament of government proposals for compulsory arbitration or a similar procedure has been effectively used. Thus, in 1947 a group of police

133

officers, and in 1951 nurses in key positions, were confronted with proposals of this kind under which they would have been forced to submit to legal settlement of their disputes with their employer – the public. In the latter case Parliament had, indeed, already assembled in order to discuss and pass an act providing for compulsory arbitration of this specific case when the parties found a solution, with the result that the bill was withdrawn.

As yet it is not possible to predict whether compulsory arbitration in labour conflicts of interests has any future in the Northern countries apart from emergency situations. To some extent the final outcome may, of course, depend on whether the system of government-controlled economy will be further developed or gradually discontinued. In the former case it is unlikely that Society would in the long run refrain from assuming at least some control over wages, the most fundamentally important of all prices. In the latter case it is possible that the general relaxation of controls will be accompanied by a "hands-off policy" in conflicts of interests.

LABOUR DISPUTES

Where a conflict of interests proves impossible of peaceful settlement by the efforts of the parties, supplemented by those of the mediator, and where the general situation is not such as to lead to direct public intervention, the parties are free to resort to their traditional weapons of labour warfare. The most important of these is the work stoppage, effected on the employers' side by the lockout, on the workers' side by the strike. Other means are the blockade whereby workers agree to refuse employment proffered by one or more employers, and the boycott whereby employers agree to withhold employment from one or more workers. Often the various methods will be used in combination.

The imposing edifice of labour peace machinery has by no means eliminated such open hostilities.

It is hardly possible to weigh with any degree of certainty the net influence of this machinery in reducing labour warfare. A few general observations may, however, still be justified. Thus, the elimination, except for a few wildcat strikes, of conflicts of rights represents a major and incontestable contribution toward the reduction of work stoppages; similarly, the frequent organizational strikes characteristic of the early years of trade unionism (and well known in countries like the USA even during the period between the World Wars) have been very rare in Northern Europe for the last half century. Moreover, government mediation has with certainty prevented numerous disputes from developing into open hostilities. It would furthermore be shortsighted to overlook the decisive influence which these elaborate methods have had in making the conflicts proceed in an orderly fashion with a minimum of social and political tension. Of even greater significance, finally, is the fact that while the opportunity for effecting a work stoppage is assumed in every collective bargaining negotiation, the vast majority of all agreements are reached without such recourse.

The character of work stoppages has altered considerably during the last fifty years. While in former times labour conflicts were many and individually rather small, the labour market in recent decades is characterized by relatively few, but very comprehensive conflicts. This tendency is the result of the growth and centralization of power in the great organizations as well as of the tendency for all major negotiations to take place at the same time of year and to be decided as a whole. This is found in all countries, although perhaps to a lesser degree in Sweden than in, for instance, Denmark and Norway, and clearly implies that the bulk of time lost by work stoppages during any given period is accumulated in a few "bad" years.

In their activities both trade unions and employers' organizations have generally confined themselves to a "pure" labour market line, avoiding political issues. As a consequence, political strikes have been rare, except in Finland, and general economic conditions have been the principal, constant determinants for the incidence of work stoppages. As everywhere, unrest on the labour market has in the Northern countries been strongly influenced by rapid and violent changes in the economic climate. Thus, the worst conflicts have generally been registered during periods of business recession, viz. the years after the First World War and the years of depression after 1930, or during periods of rising prices, as in Denmark in 1936 and in all the Northern countries except Norway after the end of hostilities in May 1945.

The differences among the labour markets of the various countries invite caution against any rough generalizing comparisons. Still, it may perhaps be said that during the inter-war period Denmark was most successful in avoiding open labour warfare, the loss of workdays being largely concentrated upon two years: 1925, when a general strike occurred, and 1936, when the employers' refusal to offset rising prices by increasing wages resulted in an extensive conflict. On the other hand, Norway experienced a number of bitter conflicts, especially during the 'twenties, and, taking into account the relative size of the countries, probably recorded the largest loss of working days during the period as a whole.

During the Second World War work stoppages ceased almost completely, also in Sweden, the only one of the five countries to remain untouched by foreign military operations.

Upon the conclusion of the war large-scale conflicts, mainly arising from the workers' demand to be compensated for the increased cost of living, took place in all the countries except Norway. Thus, a protracted and extremely costly strike occurred in 1945 in the Swedish metal industry and the following year saw a rather comprehensive strike in a number of important trades in Denmark. In Norway, however, the new Labour government succeeded in obtaining the agreement of both workers and employers to compulsory government arbitration of wage disputes. The following years, on the other hand, were quiet, the notable exception being Finland where continuing inflation together with political unrest and dissension within the trade union movement resulted in extensive strikes during 1949 and 1950.

WORKING DAYS LOST THROUGH LABOUR DISPUTES
(*in thousands*)

	Denmark	Finland	Norway	Sweden	United Kingdom	USA
1945	66	358	65	11,311	2,835	38,000
1946	1,389	116	79	27	2,158	116,000
1947	467	479	41	125	2,433	34,600
1948	8	244	92	151	1,944	34,100
1949	10	1,195	105	21	1,807	50,500
1950	4	4,644	42	40	1,389	38,800
1951	4	324	36	531	1,694	22,900
1952	4	54	124	79	1,793	59,100

Source : ILO Year Book of Labour Statistics 1951-1952.

The post-war record of the Northern countries may be given some perspective by a comparison with that of the United Kingdom and the United States. The above table shows the number of working days lost through work stoppages in mining, manufacturing, construction, and transport in each of the countries during the years

1945 to 1952. No figures are given for Iceland since the labour shortage until 1950 was so acute that almost any worker involved in one of the minor strikes which occurred immediately obtained other employment. During an extensive walkout in December 1952 there were, however, about 300,000 lost working days.

By themselves, these statistics mainly serve to underscore what has already been mentioned, namely that the bulk of lost time is accumulated in one or two single years, the United Kingdom presenting a notable exception to this rule.

ORGANIZED LABOUR RELATIONS IN PERSPECTIVE

The great organizations and related institutions have radically transformed the labour market of the closing years of the nineteenth century. The void left by the abolition of the gild system has been filled by a highly regulated order of stability.

Although the parties still represent, as they must, opposite sides, constant association has imbued both employers' and workers' representatives with a degree of mutual confidence and respect, which is perhaps the most significant aspect of labour relations in the Northern countries.

The conflicts which do occur traditionally occupy a disproportionate measure of public attention due to their surrounding drama and their accompanying inconveniences, occasionally perhaps even hardships, to the community. Open hostilities, however, play only a limited part in the life of the organizations. By far the larger share of their energies is devoted to the less spectacular but nevertheless essential task of ironing out, by mutual efforts, the numerous differences that are bound to arise at the working premises, no matter how detailed the provisions already agreed upon. Also, the rapid technical development characteristic of our time frequently gives rise to situations unforeseen in the agreements and calling for settlement between the parties. There can be no doubt that these pacific functions, which are discharged without any publicity, constitute the real backbone of their work and entail a far heavier taskload than the periodic, hectic discussions on new agreements and simultaneous preparations for a possible conflict.

It may be argued, as it has been argued, that organization has run riot and that the labour market has become overregulated. It is quite true that developments during the past generation or two have limited the freedom of the individual employer and worker to determine at will their contractual relations. And undoubtedly it is possible to point to instances where regulation seems to have gone too far. On the whole, however, there would appear to be general agreement that the various limitations upon individual freedom in this sphere have been a modest price for the advantages reaped.

These advantages may be summarized in two words: Security and order. When entering upon a contract the worker knows beforehand the general conditions of work as well as the wages he will receive (or, at any rate, the established rules according to which his wages will be computed); and by the same token also the employer stands to benefit materially since he is enabled to undertake his calculations on a firmer basis without risking sudden changes in his labour costs. By guaranteeing labour peace during its term of validity, the collective agreement ensures a degree of stability on the labour market which redounds to the benefit not only of the parties immediately involved, but of Society as a whole. To this must be added the high value, from the point of view of practical democracy, of the direct participation – when voting on new agreements – by the individual worker in the establishment of the conditions under which he is employed.

Wages and working hours remain the pivotal subjects around which the activities of the organizations turn. But today the organizations have grown beyond their original role of central bargaining agencies to take on the character of institutions. Although established for the sole purpose of protecting the economic interests of their members vis-à-vis the opposing party, they have gradually, and in recent years increasingly so, come to stand as spokesmen in general of the two parties before the community at large.

In part this development may be considered a natural consequence of the status which the organizations have attained upon reaching full maturity. But it must also be ascribed to the expanding role of government which has characterized the last decades and which has led to a vast body of new legislative provisions in the economic as well as in the social field.

Proper planning and administration of the comprehensive complex of laws touching upon relations between employers and workers obviously has placed a heavy burden upon legislative and administrative authorities. To an ever increasing extent it has been found expedient to rely upon the expert knowledge and long experience accumulated in the great organizations. In this connection it has clearly been of great importance that the organizations are approximately equal in strength and that there has never been any dispute as to which organ should represent workers or employers. Furthermore, legislation in this sphere has often been based, more or less, upon similar measures previously undertaken by agreement between the parties.

The status attained by the organizations has rendered it natural for government authorities to consult them on major economic or social legislation under preparation. Also the parties are frequently directly represented on government commissions drawing up the various measures. Furthermore, for many years the organizations have shared in the administration of the law, participating in numerous administrative organs. Thus, to mention just a few examples from one country, in Denmark the Labour Council established under the Factory Act and exercising a number of functions in relation to the provisions concerning protection of workers, counts among its ten members no less than six representatives of the two central organizations; according to the Labour Exchange and Unemployment Insurance Act the managing board of a public employment exchange consists, in addition to a neutral chairman, of employers and workers nominated by the organizations; under the Holidays' Act of 1938 it is prescribed that the Act shall not apply within trades where the workers by agreement are assured of holidays at least equivalent to those stipulated by the Act, the organizations being in these cases (which are quite numerous) entrusted with the full administration of the scheme. Many more instances could be mentioned but those cited above would appear sufficient to illustrate the way in which the organizations have been drawn into participation in the administrative machinery of these five countries.

Obviously, this development has implied a deepening and widening of organizational activities at the same time as it has served to foster with the parties an increased sense of social responsibility.

The wider perspective given to their work is also reflected in their attitude towards each other. The smaller organizations of former times concentrated narrowly upon the immediate issues at stake: Money wages and working hours, and were hardly inclined or able to consider their differences against the general background of economic and social conditions and changes therein. At the present time, when the two organized parties have become determining factors for the major part of the labour market, it is mutually recognized that their actions have far-reaching effects upon the national economy. With increased understanding of economic relationships, the workers have come to realize that a boost in money wages may be a dubious advantage if the result is simply to let loose a corresponding increase in prices. Employers, on the other hand, by now recognize that reduced wages may not always be a boon since after all the incomes of the wage earners constitute a major part of total demand. On the whole this changed climate must undoubtedly be considered of no mean importance in promoting more reasonable demands and better understanding on both sides of the labour market.

At the same time as relations between employers and workers have been stabilized in an atmosphere of mutual confidence, increased activity and disquiet is found to prevail among one large and expanding group of wage earners, previously not very organization-minded – namely salaried employees, and particularly public servants.

The former passivity of these categories in the organizational field may have been due to a number of reasons which are frequently difficult to pin down. Salaried employees in private business may have been deterred by their personal or political attachment to the middle classes; and in the case of public servants bonds of tradition coupled with a sense of loyalty toward the public authorities have undoubtedly played a major role in determining prevalent attitudes.

But, with the new balance of power found in our modern society, where distribution of the national income has increasingly come to depend upon agreements between large organizations, a feeling has spread among public servants and other non-manual workers that they are being squeezed between the powerful organizations of skilled and unskilled workers, on one hand, and private employers and their organizations, on the other. This sense of being the forgotten third party may become particularly acute during a period of rising prices, when manual workers and employers alike are usually able to obtain a degree of compensation by negotiated wage-increases and price-increases, respectively.

Salaried employees who wish to abandon their defensive attitude are faced with a cardinal issue – should they join a common front of all wage earners through the trade union movement or should they develop their own organizations. On this point a divergence of interest has been manifest as between the lower and higher echelons of salaried employees. The latter groups have not found their economic interests to be sufficiently protected by the policy of wage-equalization which has been pursued by the trade unions under the name of the "solidaric wage policy". Another problem which has become a subject of heated discussion, especially among public servants, concerns the "instruments of warfare". Is it feasible – and is it legal – for public servants to use the strike, the boycott and other methods which have been utilized by organized workers in the struggle to obtain their present position? No attempt will be made here to answer this knotty question but it would appear safe to say that the problems of non-manual workers – their relations to other groups of wage earners as well as the means to be employed in their efforts to assure themselves of a status that is deemed just – will be the object of increased attention in the years to come, both from the political and from the organizational point of view.

In conclusion, the question may be asked: What are the reasons underlying the success of labour market organizations in Northern Europe? Labour market developments are inextricably intertwined with general economic, social, and political changes in the fabric of the Northern societies, and any attempt to enumerate all relevant circumstances would easily degenerate into a mere summary of national history. Yet, among the numerous conditioning factors it may be ventured to single out a few, which are more or less characteristic of all the five countries and which deserve special mention, even though their significance stretches beyond the sphere of labour market affairs.

Undoubtedly the homogeneous character of these countries and the absence of any serious national and religious antagonisms have been among the most important background factors. Similarly, the lack of any sharp class differences in connection with the predominance of small enterprises even in our day, both in industry and agriculture, have considerably facilitated understanding between employer and worker. To this should be added the deeply rooted understanding of the benefits of teamwork which has provided the basis of orderly progress also in other fields. Credit must finally be given to the leaders both of workers and employers who generally have been socially-minded, responsible, and far-sighted personalities.

141

Industrial Democracy

Labour's demand for a voice in the affairs of management is of long standing. Early Socialists conceived of "Workers' Councils" as a vehicle for assuming control over the means of production, thus establishing the Socialistic community, so to say, from within. The subsequent emergence of political democracy in most European industrialized countries was accompanied by a call for economic and industrial democracy. Roughly, we may perhaps say that the concept of economic democracy aimed mainly at the reduction of prevailing inequalities in the distribution of incomes and property, while industrial democracy was interpreted to mean enhanced influence of wage earners upon the management of the establishment employing them.

During the stormy years following upon the First World War the claims for industrial democracy were met in part by the introduction – by legislation or collective agreement – of "Workers' Committees" in such countries as France, Germany, Great Britain and, among the Northern countries, Norway. Even in Denmark and Sweden proposals to that effect were put forward but quashed by strong opposition. Nowhere was anything but limited success achieved, primarily because the terms of reference laid down for the work of these committees were only vague and gave rise to fruitless procedural conflicts, but also because the only significant domain indisputably left to the committees, viz. that of establishing closer contact between management and labour, was gradually taken over by the shop stewards and by specially trained personnel staff, who in this respect proved superior to the committees in efficiency. In Norway, for instance, deliberations in the workers' committees soon degenerated into general discussions centering on the ability of the enterprises to grant higher wages.

It would presumably be correct to state that in recent decades the claim for direct influence upon management within the individual enterprise has gradually lost in vigour. Perhaps the main explanation for this development may be found in the increasing political influence of the working class, manifest in the rise to governmental power of the Social Democratic (Labour) parties of the Northern countries during the inter-war period. Through fiscal, monetary, and commercial policies, through regulations pertaining to dividends, raw-material supplies, etc., labour has been enabled to assume, within the wider framework of general economic policy, a large measure of control over employers' management of their enterprises. Present-day labour leaders in the Northern countries would undoubtedly hesitate to advocate any direct labour take-over of controls in the individual enterprises, measures to achieve the desired degree of influence being preferably conceived as part of a general regulation of the basic components of the economy, planned and directed by the central governments.

Although the term "Industrial Democracy" may therefore have lost some of its former glamour, it is still held forth as a desirable goal to strive for, but has now acquired a more modest content. Today the concept of Industrial Democracy mainly includes such measures as are intended to establish closer and more harmonious relations between the workers and the establishment where they are employed and to stimulate a more active workers' interest in the affairs of the plant with a view to furthering production. Industrial Democracy in this modern version, which does not encroach upon the traditional prerogatives of the employer within his own business, obviously has for its general background the steady growth and consolidation of the whole structure of labour-management collaboration in these countries. At the same time it has been given a decisive stimulus by the establishment in Great Britain, during the Second World War, of Joint Production Committees in individual enterprises. Although originally instituted mainly in order to promote war production programmes by the combined efforts of workers and employers, these organs have served more or less as a model for the modified form of industrial democracy introduced recently in Northern Europe.

Beginning in 1945 and proceeding at intervals of about one year, the central organizations of workers and employers in Norway, Sweden, and Denmark negotiated general agreements providing for the introduction of Joint Production Committees (the Swedish agreement being, however, like all other so-called Saltsjöbaden Agreements subject to subsequent ratification by the sub-organizations concerned). Finland, on the other hand, has undertaken the establishment of such committees through legislation. Already in 1941 a proposal to this effect was placed before the Riksdag, but due to strong opposition from employers' quarters it was not until 1946, and only with several modifications, that a law calling for the establishment of Joint Production Committees in industrial enterprises was finally enacted.

143

Whereas the Danish and Swedish agreements envisage the establishment of a Joint Production Committee only where this is demanded by either management or employees in an enterprise employing 25 or more workers, the Norwegian agreement is mandatory, providing for such a body to be set up in all enterprises with an average of more than 50 employees. It should be added that in all three countries also smaller plants may, under certain conditions, create Joint Production Committees or comparable bodies. The Finnish provisions are of a similar character since, if the responsible parties neglect to elect members to a committee, the Ministry of Social Affairs is empowered to appoint a Joint Production Committee in any plant operating at a minimum of 120,000 working hours a year (about 50 workers).

The field of activity of the committees is essentially the same in all four countries. The present Norwegian agreement may be quoted as an example: "The Joint Production Committee is an advisory and informatory agency set up to deal with the following matters:

a) Informatory and confidential reports from the management concerning the financial standing of the establishment . . . and plans for the immediate future.

b) Informatory and confidential deliberations on matters relative to the technical operation of the establishment, including major changes in methods of production and the quality of the product. The Committee shall promote efficient production and sound rationalization . . .

c) Proposals and measures intended to promote the safety and well-being of workers and salaried employees . . .

d) Social measures (welfare), and

e) Questions concerning vocational training for employees . . . , including guidance to new workers."

As a special Swedish feature it may be mentioned that the corresponding agreement contains rules for the protection of workers in case of dismissal or lay-off. The employer has to give notice of any such contemplated action a fortnight in advance and the employee has the right to bring up the matter before the Committee; the decision of this body may, moreover, be appealed, in the last instance to the Labour Market Committee established by the central organizations.

Quite briefly and generally the purposes of the Joint Production Committees in all four countries may be summarized as follows: To further production, to promote working conditions and labour welfare,

We're all in the same boat: Members of a joint labour-management committee talk things over on board a Swedish merchant vessel.

and to stimulate the interest of employees in the affairs of their establishment. As will be seen, their functions are strictly limited. On the one hand they do not touch upon the fundamental right of the employer to conduct his business as he sees fit. And, on the other hand, care has been taken not to interfere with the domains already under the jurisdiction of trade unions and employers' associations. The committees are thus incompetent to conclude agreements or deal with matters regarding wages and working hours or disputes on the interpretation of time- or piece-rate agreements or agreements respecting the nature of the work. In Finland alone the committees may participate in mediation of disputes about wages and working hours.

Still, the introduction of these new organs marks a significant step forward in the development of labour-management relations. On the part of workers it signifies a stronger appreciation of the fact that,

145

by and large, the main avenue to higher standards of living today goes through increased production. And on the part of employers it reflects a recognition of the important contribution which an efficient and interested labour force may make to the success of their undertakings. The pressing needs of post-war reconstruction programmes have obviously lent a powerful stimulus to these considerations.

In all five countries committee members vary in number from a minimum of 6 to 17 or more, according to the size of the plant. As a rule three separate groups are represented in the committee: Management, technical and other staff, and workers. In Sweden each of the three parties takes one-third of the seats while in Denmark and Finland the number of representatives nominated by the workers equals the total representation elected by the other two groups, management itself being thus in a minority. In Norway, on the other hand, management is represented by as many members as workers and salaried employees together. The task of presiding over meetings and the office of secretary is to alternate between management and the other two parties.

In order to prevent management from frustrating the work of the committees by electing as their representatives junior staff members, it is expressly laid down that only senior officers, and preferably the manager himself, should join the committee. On the other hand, the workers' representatives, who are elected by universal and secret ballot, must be selected among the most capable and interested employees, a certain seniority in the establishment being a further condition of eligibility. The close connection between the Joint Production Committees and the shop steward institution is particularly manifest in the Danish scheme, which lays down that all stewards are automatically members as representatives of the workers. A distinct separation between their function as shop stewards, on the one hand, and as committee members, on the other, is, however, maintained.

In view of the considerable difficulties of implementation encountered in earlier experiments of this kind, great care has been taken this time to have the committees started on a firm basis. As illustrated by the Norwegian and Swedish agreements cited above, their terms of reference have been made as explicit and clear as possible and a central joint organ has been established to co-ordinate the experience gathered and to deal with matters of interpretation causing disagreement between the parties. The committees are entitled to apply to the central organ for advice on all questions. Further, the organizations of employers and workers have taken upon themselves to provide working material and information on such matters as may profitably be dealt with by the committees. In Sweden this very important "backing up" has been supplemented by the institution of short term courses for committee members, given – *inter alia* – at the Trade Union School at Brunnsvik and at the Yxtaholm School operated by the employers. Also, numerous books and pamphlets have been published in recent years with a view to familiarizing the rank and file with the manifold problems relevant to "factory democracy".

In Denmark, Finland, and Norway, respectively, 900-1,000 Joint Production Committees had been established by the beginning of 1952, while Sweden had reached the largest number, with 3,150 committees covering almost 670,000 organized workers. The present rate of increase is rather small and the limit to expansion has probably almost been reached – except in Denmark where a considerable number of establishments with more than 25 employees have not yet introduced the arrangement.

Joint Production Committees have now been functioning for some years. Available progress reports indicate that, on the whole, the system has been successful in so far as it has provided a continuing forum for informal discussions of a host of practical problems on the plant level. It is only natural, perhaps, that workers should have taken a predominant interest in possible measures to improve working conditions and labour welfare in general, while employers have concentrated on the possibilities of increasing productivity. In most of the countries the former category of questions has occupied the major part of discussions. In many cases it has proved possible to obtain agreement on improvements in working conditions, such as better premises, cafeterias, comfort rooms, etc., while labour demands for special welfare measures such as pensions, special assistance during sickness, vacation facilities, etc., have often met with employer resistance. But also the improving of production methods has been a frequent topic of debate. In Sweden, indeed, these questions have occupied a dominating place in the work of the committees. Out of a total of more than 18,000 proposals for improvements submitted by Swedish workers in 1952 about 12,000 were rationalization proposals of which about 4,900 were adopted, rewards being paid to their originators.

Although it is thus possible to point to numerous beneficial results of the work of the committees, it would probably be correct to state that they have not as yet fulfilled the high hopes entertained at the time of their establishment shortly after the last war. A recent report by the Danish Federation of Trade Unions lists three main difficulties that have hampered the full success of the new institutions, difficulties which all four countries would appear to have encountered in varying degree. In the first place, it is claimed, there is still a lack of understanding of the full significance of Joint Production Committees and of the will to co-operate. Moreover, both parties have often lacked the necessary expert knowledge for dealing adequately with the issues raised. Finally, even when the committees have got off to a successful start insufficient energy has resulted in a slackening of subsequent activities. A special workers' complaint is, furthermore, the alleged unwillingness of employers to present the committees with sufficient data on the financial status of the establishment, the workers fearing that they are not assured a fair share of any benefits accruing from increased production efforts. On the other hand, it is frequently asserted by employers that workers' representatives fail to pass on to the rank and file the information made available to them.

These various difficulties are undoubtedly very real but may, at least in part, be ascribed to lack of experience. With the passing of time it should therefore be possible to overcome them at least partially. The present lack of enthusiasm notwithstanding, it is significant to note that the large majority of organized workers and employers are in full agreement as to the value of the committees as an important means of promoting better relations between the two parties in the interest of both. It is probably still too early to pass judgment on the ultimate contribution which these new organs may be able to make.

While the activities of Joint Production Committees are concerned with the individual plant, Norway has also introduced an interesting arrangement providing for co-operation on the branch level. Under an act of 1947 the government has been authorized to set up advisory Joint Industrial Councils for the various sectors of industry and trade, for the purpose of promoting co-operation within the sectors as well as between them and the competent State organs. The councils, which comprise representatives of management, of workers and salaried employees, and of the State, number from 8 to 11 members.

Their terms of reference include the consideration and the submission of opinions or proposals with respect to such matters as the practical application of the results of research within the industry concerned; rationalization; the allocation of working tasks to the individual enterprises; the setting-up, expansion or discontinuation of enterprises, etc.

Up to the present time such councils have been established in ten industries, including mining, ship-building, textiles, paper, cellulose and wood-pulp, etc. There would appear to be general agreement that, thanks to their comprehensive set-up and the expert knowledge represented by their members, these new organs have proved well adapted to deal with a large number of important questions placed before them. At the same time it is recognized that the Joint Industrial Councils are an entirely new form of organization and that their operation consequently has in many cases had to proceed according to the time-honoured method of trial and error.

This threesome – manager, technician, and foreman – pool their skill and experience in tackling the problems of modern industry.

149

Labour Market Policy

FULL AND PRODUCTIVE EMPLOYMENT
THE GOAL

In the field of labour protection Society acknowledged its primary responsibility at a relatively early stage by the introduction of appropriate legislation. As for labour relations, the main institutions were largely developed by the organized parties themselves, public intervention in this sphere being more or less limited to such measures as would promote orderliness on the labour market and mitigate the effects of disputes upon the community.

The last stage has been for Society to assume major responsibility also for what is, after all, the basic labour issue, namely securing the working man full and productive employment. Somewhat oversimplified it might perhaps be said that the role of the public authorities in relation to labour protection and labour relations is largely defensive, in the sense that legislative intervention has been predominantly prompted by a desire to prevent abuse of the labourer or unnecessary labour strife. On the other hand, the emphasis in present-day employment policy has come to rest primarily upon the offensive: The public takes independent positive action to assist in bringing about a state of affairs where all people willing and able to work, can be productively employed. Clearly, also in this sphere development has been gradual, determined by the interplay of the changing conditions and trends in economic and social thinking.

Insecurity on the labour market is primarily the product of modern industrialism. The predominantly agricultural communities of former days were certainly also subject to economic fluctuations but, in the first place, they were generally of far smaller proportions than those experienced in modern times; in the second place, such unemployment as did arise was largely "disguised" in the sense that while the amount of work to be performed diminished, this resulted only in a temporarily less intensive use of manpower. Although this certainly meant a general decline in living standards, it did not totally deprive any individual of his means of existence. Even in the towns it was only later that unemployment proper was known as an occasional phenomenon. Moreover, emigration provided a highly important safety valve throughout the 19th century and up to the First World War; during this period approximately $2^{1}/_{2}$ million Northerners settled in overseas countries, mainly in the United States of America. Mention should, however, be made of the widespread occurrence in older times of vagrancy; any assistance given to persons out of work was under the harsh provisions of the poor law and vagrants were often dealt with under criminal law.

As the industrial revolution in Northern Europe began around 1860–70, it was only from then on that the setting for the modern unemployment problem was established: An expanding wage-earning class dependent solely upon wages for its living and liable to be thrown out of employment during recurrent business recessions. A significant factor in this connection has been the intensity of Northern participation in international trade; the consequence being an extreme sensitivity to economic trends on the world market.

The 20th century has seen unemployment rise to a position of foremost importance. Several phases in the general employment situation may be distinguished. Before the First World War unemployment, although certainly not without importance, did not loom as a problem of serious public concern. In the inter-war period, however, more or less widespread industrial unemployment came to be a normal phenomenon occupying a role of vital significance in economic and social policy. The depression years around 1931–33 marked the climax with twenty per cent or more of organized workers registered as unemployed in Denmark, Norway, and Sweden. In agriculture, on the other hand, the unemployment problem has not attained anything like the same importance. This is due in part to the preponderance of small independent farmers in these countries; in part to the practice of many agricultural workers (especially in Finland, Norway, and Sweden) to supplement their incomes by working in the forests during the winter season. Finally, since the early 1940's, owing, first, to the special conditions prevailing during the war and, later, to the demands of post-war reconstruction programmes, the labour market has been characterized by full, or almost full employment, and in some of the countries even by shortages of labour.

That the community has a responsibility for the alleviation of hardship due to unemployment has been acknowledged in the Northern countries for several decades. The State began by extending financial support to the unemployed, partly by special unemployment cash allowances, partly by subsidies to the various schemes of unemployment insurance (in some of the countries subsequently trans-

See Chapter VII, Social Security, pp. 412–420.

formed into compulsory systems). During the inter-war period, and especially in the years of world depression, public works were undertaken to provide employment for at least some of those out of work; generally these projects were planned so as not to compete with normal business enterprise and consisted mainly in land reclamation, road-building, and excavation, the wages being lower than those paid for similar work in the open labour market. It was felt that a general lowering of wages would promote employment and that the State should not counteract this adjustment of wages to the new level where private enterprise was considered willing to operate. For the young unemployed special projects, including vocational training courses and instructional work, were instituted. Throughout this phase the main emphasis was upon the social aspect of the problem and it is characteristic that the various measures were considered as components of a more or less ambitious "unemployment policy", the broader issue of the level of employment being considered outside the scope of government action.

In the course of the 1930's increasing attention was, however, focused upon the economic side of the unemployment problem and the general economic policies by which it could be tackled. Especially in Sweden there was a radical change in this direction during these years. Traditional fiscal policies gave way before the modern concept of deficit-financing in times of depression. By loans, subventions, and direct placement of orders, private business enterprise received essential support. Agriculture received comprehensive aid in order to maintain the purchasing power of farmers.

Simultaneously, unemployment insurance schemes and benefits were expanded and improved and public works gradually increased in variety and calibre, persons thus employed now coming to receive normal standard wages. Gradually, emphasis shifted from the original crudely quantitative measures to a qualitative policy taking into consideration not only the total number of unemployed, but also their distribution by geographic location, skills, and sexes (the latter factor increasing in importance with the constantly rising number of women employed in industry and commerce).

Still, in most of the Northern countries, it was only during and after the Second World War that a comprehensive labour market policy along such lines came to be fully developed. The situation had now been reversed, the number of unemployed gradually melting away and labour shortages making their appearance. Labour market authorities increasingly had to concentrate their efforts, not on the relief of unemployment, but upon the proper allocation of available labour to meet the most pressing production needs.

Quite apart from the strains of war, the labour experience of these years amply demonstrated the benefits of full employment from both the social and economic points of view. If full employment was possible during war, why not in peace time?

Against this background, and keeping in mind the disruptive effects of unemployment in pre-war days, it is understandable that upon the conclusion of hostilities there should be in the countries of Northern Europe, as in other parts of the world, a unanimous demand that every possible step should be taken to maintain a high and stable level of employment. This view is abundantly reflected in programmes and activities of all post-war governments in the Northern countries. It is no longer merely a matter of social welfare, of preventing hardship as a result of unemployment. Instead of attacking its symptoms, attention is now concentrated upon the roots of the problem, the full and rational utilization of manpower being recognized as a key factor in the healthy development of economic life and the raising of the standard of living of the population. The maintenance of full and productive employment has thus assumed a central position in general economic and social policy.

This necessarily implies that employment considerations influence decisions on a wide range of measures in various spheres of government planning and action: Foreign trade, fiscal and monetary policies, investment, and housing, etc., which exercise a more or less determining effect upon the general climate of economic life and thus also upon employment. An exhaustive review of these various aspects of economic policy as components of a full-employment policy would lead far beyond the natural bounds of this publication. The present chapter, therefore, will deal only with present-day labour market policy, i. e. measures which are primarily intended to ensure every citizen an opportunity of earning a living in an occupation suited to his capabilities. As such, they occupy a position of basic importance to social-welfare policy in general, rather than comprising a separate field of their own. The working man wants first of all to be sure of having a job; financial or other aid when he is unemployed or otherwise sustains loss of income being a subsidiary issue.

The measures initiated with this end in view include, first of all, the extensive development of employment exchanges for the primary purpose of enabling labour demand and supply to contact with a minimum of friction and waste. Closely connected are the programmes of vocational guidance and vocational training.

These basic components of any comprehensive labour market policy are supplemented by that body of measures which has for its direct aim to ensure a proper balance between jobs and men. For the last generation the main emphasis has been laid upon those measures which involved the immediate provision of employment opportunities, mainly in the form of public works. This also includes the special rehabilitation and employment programmes undertaken on behalf of certain categories considered to be particularly exposed to unemployment, such as young unemployed, handicapped persons, older workers, etc. For the last few years labour shortages, rather than unemployment, have, however, been the main problem in several of the countries here under review. This has not precluded some unemployment from persisting in certain trades or areas due to special conditions; this has particularly been the case in Denmark. The general line of approach has been to maintain or even strengthen the defences against unemployment in readiness for a possible future slump. With respect to distressed trades or areas a more differentiated policy – by means of planned investment, control of construction projects and localization of new enterprises – has aimed at securing a basis for continuous employment. The severe Nordic winter climate has traditionally caused seasonal unemployment, especially in the building industry. During recent years technical improvements have, however, made it possible to carry on many such operations also during the cold season; special State measures have been initiated to exploit these new techniques to reduce winter unemployment.

Under the impression of the prevailing general labour shortages in several countries, increasing attention has lately come to be focused on means of procuring all the men needed to fill the jobs. In these countries the full and productive utilization of all employable labour no longer represents merely a social demand and economic desideratum, but is a necessity if current production needs are to be met. In this connection a new set of problems has been encountered. Already due to the high degree of organization upon the labour market, a certain rigidity had manifested itself, particularly in a rather low geographical and occupational mobility. With the advent of full employment this feature has made itself increasingly felt and a variety of measures have been introduced, especially in Norway and Sweden, in order to reduce rigidity and thus to bring about an improved adjustment of available labour to existing employment opportunities.

The emergence of modern labour market policies has involved a considerable expansion and centralization in the administrative set-up. Whereas major responsibility previously rested with social welfare authorities, the trend has been toward the establishment of specialized organs to deal with all aspects of employment services and programmes, e.g. the Labour Directorate in Norway and the Labour Board in Sweden. These institutions keep a constant watch over labour market developments, including not only the annual review of developments during the preceding period but also a prognosis of the trend during the coming year. They further act as central organs for registration and planning of reserve projects and for area development planning, and are responsible for the allocation of funds and government subsidies for public works. Among their most important tasks is, moreover, the supervision of employment exchange and vocational guidance services and also of the unemployment insurance system. In the other Northern countries formal centralization has not yet gone so far. The various measures are still administered by separate organs within the governmental machinery although obviously they cooperate closely. There are, on the other hand, strong similarities with respect to the local units of organization, the municipal and county authorities playing important roles in all five countries in the promotion of employment conditions within their district.

In all the Northern countries local Employment Boards have been instituted. Their mission is to follow labour market developments on the local level and if necessary to initiate public works to provide employment opportunities for the unemployed. Thus, local authorities in Finland are under obligation to provide employment if necessary for up to one-half of one per cent of the registered population. Only after this first step may State measures be called for, either in the form of State public works or State subsidies to works initiated by local authorities or by private enterprises. In other countries, e. g. Norway, the local bodies are predominantly advisory, the implementation of measures being primarily the responsibility of District Employment Committees or, ultimately, of the Labour Directorate.

EMPLOYMENT EXCHANGES

The public employment service in the Northern countries has a more than 50-year tradition behind it, the first employment exchanges having been started by municipalities during the first years of this century. The present institutions are still governed by local authorities or a combination of local and State authorities, except in Sweden where the employment service is now entirely handled by the State. State subsidies were given almost from the beginning simultaneously with rules for the operation of these services.

In *Denmark* the public employment exchanges developed alongside the employment services established by the unemployment insurance societies, the activities of which in this field early had attained considerable proportions. In the years 1927–1928 the public employment exchange was reorganized, special legislation providing for a nation-wide network of employment exchange offices, one in each county, with additional branch offices as required. These institutions provide employment services directly at the same time as they coordinate the numerically far more important employment services operated by the various unemployment insurance societies within their area. In *Finland*, government directives issued in 1926 provided for special boards to direct the work of local employment offices. Subsequently, grants-in-aid were increased and in 1936 the present Employment Exchange Act was passed. During the war the State established new employment offices and the municipal exchanges were subjected to closer State supervision. An *Icelandic* decree of 1935 made the establishment of employment exchange facilities compulsory in the towns. The *Norwegian* employment exchanges have been under the supervision of a central State inspectorate since 1916. The present system is operated under the responsibility of the Labour Directorate, State-operated county employment offices being supplemented by local employment exchanges in each municipality. State supervision of employment exchanges was introduced in *Sweden* in 1914. A nation-wide employment service was established by law in 1934, with central offices in each county supplemented by local branches.

In post-war years the employment exchange offices have increasingly been used as instruments for the active full-employment policy. This has necessitated a further widening and strengthening of the public employment services.

The tasks of the public employment exchanges are essentially the same in all five countries. Their original and still their main purpose is job placement. At an early date the exchanges were also made control organs for the publicly subsidized unemployment insurance. Gradually the employment exchanges have become of key importance in all labour market questions. Thus, they are required to contribute actively toward establishing a balance between the supply and demand for labour in all fields of employment. To this end the exchanges collect and compute statistical information and prepare surveys and forecasts on the labour market situation. Moreover, especially in Norway and Sweden, the employment offices play an important role in those public activities which are directly connected with full employment policies, e. g. industrial localization, investment-controls, the establishment of investment-plans, the direction of public works for unemployed, etc.

Employment services in the Northern countries likewise follow largely similar principles in their work and in their pattern of organization. The public employment service is organized to cover the entire country, not only geographically but also as regards national economy. The organization is headed by a central government agency for the entire employment service. Regional organs (except in Denmark and Iceland) supervise the employment service within their respective districts. At the base of the pyramid are the local employment offices which vary in size according to their jurisdiction. In some of the Northern countries there are also local agents stationed in smaller districts. Local employment offices number 37 in Denmark, 93 in Finland, 6 in Iceland, 56 in Norway, and 236 in Sweden; to these must be added a large number of local agents in Norway and Sweden. In Denmark the public offices are supplemented by some 3,700 branch offices of the unemployment insurance societies, each of which furnishes employment services to its members. In order to provide the best possible service the employment offices have now selective placement departments, for example on behalf of farmhands, building construction workers, seamen, shop and office employees, etc. Moreover, the exchanges maintain specialized services in various industrial trades.

Special boards, committees or councils are attached to the public employment service. In some cases they make the binding decisions themselves; in others, they act in an advisory capacity only. A common

157

feature, however, is that these organs are composed of labour and management representatives in equal numbers.

Employment exchanges are open to everyone and all services, except individual advertizing, are rendered free of charge. The employment service is neutral and impartial. In general it is optional both for employers and for workers whether or not they avail themselves of the exchange service or accept its proposals. However, in all the Northern countries unemployed persons who wish to qualify for unemployment benefits are under obligation to register as job-seekers with the employment exchanges or – in Denmark – with the unemployment insurance societies. In Norway, moreover, employers generally are required to report vacancies to the local office, and both in Norway and Sweden employers must give advance notice of major staff reductions. Compulsory employment service, requiring employers to hire labour through the exchanges, has been prescribed only infrequently, notably with respect to emergency work programmes. Also, according to the Genoa-Convention ratified by all five countries, the merchant marine may hire seamen only through the appropriate special branch offices of the public employment exchange.

The chief consideration in placing an applicant is his or her qualifications for a particular job, social considerations playing only a secondary role. In Denmark it is further stipulated that among several equally qualified applicants the employment service shall give preference to members of the unemployment insurance societies. In recent years an increasing number of jobs have been filled through the offices of the public employment exchanges. This is especially true in Sweden, where the service now annually places more than a million persons; almost half the placements are, however, of short duration only. On the other hand, it remains a fact that the major part of all placements are still undertaken without the assistance of these institutions. As already indicated, the Danish unemployment insurance societies play a dominant role as placement agencies. They maintain a complete register of all unemployed members and are largely relied upon especially by urban employers in need of skilled manpower. In all the Northern countries the press fulfils an extremely important function as intermediary. In order to save applicants unnecessary expense and trouble which may result from employers advertising anonymously, it has been found expedient, both in Denmark and Norway, to decree that such advertizing must contain information as to the kind of work offered, the training or other qualifications required, and the minimum wage for the job. Private agencies operating employment services on a commercial basis are in general prohibited. However, in several of the Northern countries certain associations conducting such activities on behalf of their members have been permitted to continue, subject to license by the authorities.

"Well, young man, what's your ambition in life?" A vocational counsellor in Denmark gives some advice to a prospective recruit to the labour force.

VOCATIONAL GUIDANCE

In the Northern countries – as in most other highly developed societies – young people have gradually acquired greater freedom in the choice of occupation and training. They are no longer bound so much by family traditions and it is only within certain branches, such as agriculture and fishing, that one may still speak of so-called hereditary occupations. To be sure, occupations which require advanced schooling are also today recruited in a far too one-sided manner from a social point of view. In Sweden, for example, it is estimated that only one-third of the students attending universities or similar institutions come from farmer, artisan and worker homes which represent about four-fifths of the population. However, the social, psychological, and economic factors underlying this lack of proportion are now in process of elimination. By a variety of

159

measures, including liberalized provisions for student loans and scholarships as well as the broadening of the general and vocational school systems, it is attempted to "democratize education". Obviously the improved means of communication and higher standard of living in general play a role in this connection.

At the same time that young people have come to enjoy greater freedom to choose an occupation and a training in line with their own personal desires and aptitudes, the actual choice has become much more complex than it was a couple of generations ago. Under the impact of technical, economic, and social developments, industrial life has grown ever more differentiated and complicated. The old, relatively broad categories have branched out into a multitude of specialized occupations and, in order to satisfy the modern demand for specialists, vocational training (and in part elementary schooling as well) has had to be differentiated and expanded by means of new curricula and courses. In brief, vocational and educational training today is a highly complicated labyrinth – and it is asking too much to expect young people to find their way through this labyrinth without any assistance. In addition, many of them have to wrestle with special difficulties: Personal defects and weaknesses, difficulties of social adjustment, economic problems, and the like – all of which put obstacles in the way of their staking out a suitable career without outside help.

Development

The need for vocational guidance received the attention of State and local authorities at a relatively early stage. In Sweden, for example, the Riksdag discussed this question already in 1906 and mention may be made, *inter alia*, of the attempts made during the first decades of the present century with Youth Placement Agencies attached to the schools in several of the larger cities. When the public employment services grew in scope, they too began to take an interest in this field. The first Northern "Youth Employment Exchange" – a placement service for young people under the age of 18, organized within the framework of the public employment service – was established by the town authorities in Copenhagen in 1917. Vocational guidance was included on the programme of this institution which, during the 1920's, was strengthened by the addition to its staff of expert psychological and medical counsel. In 1927 the psychology department of the Exchange was reorganized as an independent institute having for its task to administer selective tests on behalf of various enterprises and government offices as well as to participate in vocational guidance programmes. This institute was the first of its kind in the Northern countries. Denmark scored another first in 1935 when a special vocational cross-reference file was devised to assist counsellors in their work and young persons in their choice of training and occupation.

Gradually, the other Northern countries also began to set up youth departments at the municipal employment exchanges located in the large cities; during the 1930's, moreover, several noteworthy attempts were made to institute a vocational information service in conjunction with the schools. Here and there, certain initiatives were also taken within the school system, not to mention the efforts which were sponsored privately (for example, by certain voluntary associations). But these measures were mostly sporadic: An occasional pamphlet, a few lectures, etc. – and in most cases the programme of vocational guidance remained on paper.

What was lacking – besides funds and qualified staff – was, above all, a nation-wide programme under central direction. It was evident that, sooner or later, the State would have to take charge of the problem of organization, and within the last decade this has also happened in Denmark, Finland, Norway, and Sweden.

Organization of vocational guidance under State auspices was first introduced in *Sweden* where the development of a national vocational guidance programme is also most advanced at the present time. The first State subsidy was granted already in 1928, and in 1934 the Employment Exchange Act provided further possibilities of expansion. However, the real turning point came only in 1940 when the employment exchanges were taken over by the State and placed under the direction of a central agency (now the Labour Board). As part of a general programme calling for the expansion of public employment services this organ also initiated the organization of youth guidance and placement services covering the whole country.

Special departments for youth placement and vocational guidance were set up in the central employment exchanges of each county (24 in all), as well as in Stockholm; 25 additional large employment exchanges organized their own "branches", while other exchanges were authorized to take on part-time staff for the task (in most cases this was implemented by the appointment of teachers who served as "contact men" between their schools and the exchange). Most of the informatory material required is prepared by the "Vocational Guidance Office" which forms part of the Labour Board and which is also in charge of organization and instruction.

See below,
pp. 163-164.

However, the basic work of organization is not yet completed. One task which still remains is to ensure more consistent effectuation of that part of the programme which provides for the co-operation of the schools.

In *Denmark*, the above-mentioned "Youth Employment Exchange" long remained the only one of its kind. During the 1940's a number of experimental programmes were launched by some of the large cities and a few employment exchange offices, with the support of the Ministry of Labour. However, it was only in March 1953 that, following years of preparation, a nation-wide scheme of vocational guidance was enacted. The programme is based on team-work between the public employment services and the schools, with administrative responsibility placed on the former. Special vocational counsellors will be attached to the various exchanges while central direction is vested in the Labour Directorate.

In *Norway*, too, the placement and counselling services for young people are undergoing rapid development. In principle, these services are being organized on the basis of a proposal, submitted in 1948 by an *ad hoc* advisory committee, according to which twelve "Institutes for Vocational Guidance and Personnel Psychology" are to be set up throughout the country to carry out practical psychological tests and to assist the central authority (the Labour Directorate) in supervising the activities of the local offices for vocational guidance; it is estimated that such offices will be needed for 60–65 localities.

Five institutes and about 15 local offices have already been established but it would appear that the full development of the scheme will require considerable time, mainly due to the shortage of staff. In this connection it should be noted that the local Norwegian employment exchanges are not State-operated. To be sure, vocational guidance programmes enjoy relatively generous State subsidies, but many local authorities still hesitate to shoulder the costs involved.

Developments in *Finland* have likewise been hampered by the lack of a State employment service upon which to build. As yet, only two large towns – Helsinki and Tampere – maintain youth placement and vocational guidance services, organized within the framework of the general employment exchange. For certain formal reasons the Finnish Riksdag in 1951 found itself obliged to reject a previously accepted proposal which provided for a State-operated employment service and an ancillary vocational guidance service. A new bill is now awaited from the government. At the same time, however, a government committee is inquiring into the question of how to fit vocational guidance into the school system. This undertaking has sprung from the fact that in Finland there have long been spokesmen for the idea that primary responsibility for guiding youth in its quest for a vocation should rest with the schools. It is still anyone's guess which of these two alternatives will finally be adopted.

In *Iceland* a 1949 law stipulates the establishment of a vocational guidance service at the earliest possible moment. Activities are, however, still in the preparatory stage. Some counselling work is carried out as part of the activities of public employment exchanges, but no programme for the systematic extension under State auspices of present facilities has as yet been drawn up.

To summarize, it may be stated that recent developments have led to a considerable expansion of vocational guidance programmes. At least in Denmark, Norway, and Sweden the basis has now been established for nation-wide vocational services under State direction. The fact that vocational guidance is linked to the public employment exchanges places it in a position where it may be expected to render valuable assistance to young people who are starting their careers.

At the same time it is recognized that *youth must be contacted before leaving school*, the more so since already in their school years many young persons stand in need of vocational guidance when choosing their courses of study and training. In the Northern countries, as elsewhere, vocational orientation and individual counselling, are consequently given in elementary and secondary schools and today form an important part of the whole programme. This, obviously, requires close co-operation between the various authorities concerned.

Still, opinions differ with regard to the extent to which the school should play a more direct and active role in the work of vocational guidance. That school teachers, having observed the attitudes and capacities of their pupils over a considerable period of time, can make a valuable contribution, goes without saying. In Denmark, however, the part assigned to teachers within the framework of vocational guidance programmes would appear rather limited as yet. Also in Norway vocational guidance in the schools is still mainly the responsibility of vocational counsellors, but the aim is gradually to transfer the work of basic instruction in this field to the schools, although the general directives will be laid down by the counsellors. In Sweden, where a broader programme of instruction has been drawn up, a rational division of labour has been agreed upon. Classroom teachers in the elementary schools are to be responsible for vocational orientation, utilizing material furnished by the State Employment Exchange. In the secondary schools, however, State vocational counsellors are to carry primary responsibility for guidance work. The contemplated "unified school" of the future, which combines elementary and junior secondary grades, will employ special "vocational teachers", whose salaries will be jointly paid by the school system and the State Employment Exchange.

Methods

The actual work of vocational guidance follows very similar principles in all five Northern countries and the methods used are almost the same as those developed in other countries.

In the first place, an attempt is made to furnish a broad vocational information service by means of publications, question hours in the schools, lectures at parents' meetings, and radio-listening groups. Also, the schools make extensive use of educational films and field visits to different enterprises and, on occasion, representatives of various occupations are asked to orient students. This programme is supplemented by so-called practical vocational guidance which is becoming ever more common, particularly in Sweden. Pupils in the final grades of elementary school are given the opportunity to work for a week or so in a workshop where they may acquire first hand knowledge of the occupation in which they have expressed interest.

But, first and last, vocational guidance implies counselling of a more personal character. To an ever increasing extent, young people are turning to vocational counsellors for specialized information or for assistance in their choice of occupation and continued training. Incidentally, many older persons also make use of this service. The documentation required by vocational counsellors in their work – occupational cross-reference files, outlines of training courses, etc. – is chiefly prepared by the central agency.

In his efforts to ascertain the qualifications of a client, the counsellor must mainly rely on his own ability to elicit the necessary information by means of conversation and systematic questioning. Such data are also sought (partly by utilizing special questionnaires and appraisal charts) from teachers, foremen, and other persons who have had an opportunity of judging the behaviour of the client in different working situations.

Quite often the advice of medical experts is needed. *Inter alia*, the opinions of school doctors are considered desirable and co-operation with them is being extended – especially in Sweden, where doctors enrolled in the State-subsidized school health programme are required to arrange for medical vocational counselling.

Psychological and aptitude tests are utilized in all the Northern countries although the ideas entertained as to how testing should be organized and as to the proper scope of testing procedures vary somewhat. The greatest scope for psychological testing has undoubtedly been provided by Norway. When, in 1932, the Oslo Employment Exchange set up a department for youth placement and vocational guidance – the first of its kind in that country – it also established an institute for industrial psychology. Today there are five such institutes in Norway and seven more are in the planning stage. They function as testing centres for the local vocational guidance offices and are staffed with counsellors and trained psychologists. To a certain extent they also operate as ambulant units in the field.

In Finland, the Vocational Training Department of the Ministry for Trade and Industry includes a unit which originally was intended to be in general charge of the organization of vocational guidance. Actually, it has concentrated instead on the work of devising psychological aptitude tests and analyses. The Youth Placement Office in Helsinki, however, comprises also a section for the undertaking of aptitude tests. In Denmark and Sweden the authorities have – at least for the time being – preferred to leave the actual testing to relatively independent institutes for industrial psychology. Denmark has two such institutes: One in Copenhagen, operated by the municipal authorities, the other in one of the large provincial towns in Jutland, under private management. Sweden has two institutes for industrial psychology, attached to the Universities of Stockholm and Gothenburg; a third institute is being established at the University of Uppsala. Whenever the vocational guidance counsellors find that there is need for a more thorough psychological examination, they can refer to an institute of this kind. Subsequently, it is up to the counsellors to exploit the test results in further consultations and to take the practical measures required.

The latter task has been considered an essential part of vocational guidance programmes in the Northern countries. In most cases, it will not be sufficient to assist the individual by appraising his aptitudes or by giving him advice and information. It is equally important to help young people carry out their future plans in keeping with the conclusions reached by consultation and, if possible, to follow their progress along part of the way. Counsellors must therefore closely follow the actual employment situation. They must further maintain good contacts, not only with vocational training institutes, but also with a variety of enterprises and organizations. It is precisely for this reason that the co-ordination of vocational guidance with the public employment exchanges has been considered an issue of great importance in all the Northern countries.

VOCATIONAL TRAINING

In the following pages the term "vocational training" is used to denote such training as ordinarily does not presuppose more than elementary-school education. By and large, the presentation is confined to a survey of training programmes which cover occupations in industry, handicraft, commerce, and home management. Moreover, a brief summary of comparable facilities for agriculture and forestry is included.

At first glance, vocational training in the five Northern countries presents great similarities. The training furnished in vocational schools, i. e. trade schools as well as schools offering commercial, domestic, agricultural, and other training, has everywhere aimed at turning out more qualified workers by giving either basic all-round knowledge – practical and theoretical – of an occupation or advanced training based on rather broad elementary training.

The co-ordination of vocational training and general education has received less attention. Ordinary schools have only in exceptional cases included vocational training in their curricula or co-ordinated their instruction with the training provided by the vocational schools or on the job. And where this has been done, the vocational training given has been elementary and theoretical in character.

On-the-job Training with Supplementary Schooling

In principle, vocational training in the Northern countries has been organized largely after the German and Swiss patterns. This means that most of the practical vocational training takes place on the job while supplementary instruction in theory or combined theory-practice is given in the trade schools.

Trade schools are usually private or maintained by local authorities and are operated largely with funds contributed by the State. The same system prevails in all the Northern countries although the proportion of municipal and private schools varies, as do government appropriations. Generally, supplementary vocational instruction comprises from 6 to 12 hours per week (in Iceland 10 to 18 hours), and centres almost exclusively on subjects directly related to the occupation under study. General education thus plays a very limited role, except in Iceland where it accounts for about one-half of all hours given. Supplementary instruction is usually given in the evening. In all five countries, however, efforts are under way to shift an increasing part of classroom instruction to day-time hours. For certain trades, agreements have been reached with employers whereby one full working day or two half-days per week are set aside for classroom instruction. In Iceland, supplementary vocational instruction is concentrated to a two-month term during the winter.

Obviously, the possibilities for the individual apprentices to supplement their training with classroom instruction depend primarily on whether there is any appropriate school located within manageable distance. In Denmark, with its high density of population and good transportation facilities, the system functions very well. In the other Northern countries, however, distances between settled areas are greater, sometimes so great that it is impossible for young people to attend a school based on part-time instruction.

The efficiency of a training system which is based on teamwork between the trade school and the workplace does not, however, merely depend on the density or accessibility of schools. It depends equally upon the attitudes of employers and authorities toward vocational training. Four of the five Northern countries have regulated broad sectors of vocational training by special apprenticeship laws.

The oldest and most comprehensive legislation in this field is found in *Denmark* where the first apprenticeship law was enacted in 1889 (last revised in 1937). According to this law every artisan, factory-owner, tradesman, gardener or other proprietor who wishes to employ a person under 18 years of age (except as a labourer, messenger or special worker) is under obligation to draw up a written contract. This contract must contain information about the occupation in which the apprentice is to be trained and is subject to approval by the employment exchange (in Copenhagen the Labour Directorate) so as to ensure that it satisfies the requirements of the act and that conditions of work at that particular workshop are suitable for proper training. No one who has not himself received approved training in his occupation is permitted to employ or instruct an apprentice. The apprentice is under obligation to attend supplementary instruction in a trade school, the employer paying the cost of tuition and instructional materials. The apprentice, whose working hours – including classroom instruction – are limited to nine hours a day, is entitled to wages, but they average only about one-tenth of the earnings of skilled workers. Apprentice-training is completed by the compulsory journeyman's examination which takes place before a special commission of experts in the occupation concerned. Generally speaking, the active role played by individual employers and by the labour market organizations is one of the most characteristic features of vocational training in Denmark, many of the trade schools being maintained by private organizations and individuals. It is largely due to this fact that practical industrial training combined with supplementary instruction in technical trade schools has here proved such a satisfactory arrangement that – in spite of intermittent discussion – no great need has been felt for other training systems which might possibly better achieve the desired goal.

In *Finland* the training of apprentices is regulated by legislation enacted in 1923 (revised in 1934). This law, however, covers only manufacturing and handicrafts and applies only to towns of at least 5,000 inhabitants. Its enforcement is supervised by Apprentice Boards appointed by the local authorities. The law contains no clauses regarding the competence of those who are to be in charge of training. Furthermore, the shortage of technical trade schools has prevented many apprentices from receiving supplementary classroom instruction and local enforcement of the law has not always been effective. Still, the prevailing sentiment is in favour of retaining apprenticeship legislation on the statute books and efforts are currently directed toward tightening enforcement and improving economic conditions for both apprentices and their instructors. The possibility of extending legislation to cover occupational categories outside manufacturing and handicrafts is also being discussed.

Iceland has had an apprenticeship law since the turn of the century. This law, which was amended in 1927, applies to manufacturing industry and the handicrafts and corresponds roughly to the Danish provisions. It also specifies the number of apprentices which may be admitted at one time, the scope of their duties, and the qualifications of masters who employ apprentices. For a long time actual employment conditions in Iceland rendered the law virtually invalid but following its renewed revision in 1949 it now appears to be functioning effectively.

Apprenticeship legislation now in force in *Norway* dates only from 1950, and it is therefore too early as yet to evaluate its effectiveness. It covers occupations in the handicrafts, industry, commerce, and clerical work.

In *Sweden* the training of apprentices is regulated solely by voluntary agreements between labour and management. The two parties have for a number of years maintained a joint research and information unit for questions relating to vocational training.

A few figures, relating to the year 1950, may serve to illustrate the extent and efficiency of vocational training courses for industry and handicrafts in each of the Northern countries.

	Population (mill.)	*Enrolment in Vocational Courses for Industry and Handicrafts*
Denmark	4.3	49,000
Finland	4.0	13,000
Iceland	0.15	1,000
Norway	3.3	16,000
Sweden	7.0	30,000–35,000

The country with the most developed apprenticeship legislation – Denmark – has proportionally about twice as many pupils in vocational schools for industry and the handicrafts as any of the other countries. In Denmark, where annually 17,000–19,000 youngsters enter upon an apprenticeship, about one-third of all industrial workers are skilled, in the sense that they have completed four years of training as apprentices. It is also worth noting that, whereas the greater part of practical apprenticeship training in that country is furnished in small masters' workshops, in Sweden it is mostly undertaken by the large enterprises, especially in the engineering industries.

The general educational system – from the elementary school all the way to the universities and colleges – is, on the whole, structured in such a way that the higher institution of learning builds on the lower one. In most of the countries – with Denmark as the main exception – no corresponding division by stages is found with respect to vocational instruction. In recent years, however, the introduction of such a division also in this field has everywhere attracted increasing interest. There is a growing recognition that basic instruction should not aim solely at industrial practice and that young persons should also be given an opportunity for advanced and more theoretical studies in their chosen occupations.

In this connection it should be noted that, in Denmark, apprenticeship training is, in numerous occupations, a prerequisite for continued theoretical schooling, particularly in the metals and building trades. Norwegian developments may be said to have partially proceeded in the opposite direction by the adaptation to some extent of elementary schooling as a preparation for advanced technical training. The same applies in Iceland where admission to trade schools is contingent upon the young person having attended a two-year or three-year secondary school subsequent to his completion of the six-year elementary education. An Icelandic law of 1946 gives trade school graduates a certain priority for jobs in industry and commerce.

Where no systematic division by stages exists there are parallel institutions with comparable educational curricula to serve, on one hand, young persons with a good theoretical background and, on the other hand, young persons with comprehensive practical experience. As examples of the Swedish system of secondary education may be mentioned the technical colleges of university rank and the technical trade institutes.

The preceding pages have centered upon vocational training for industry and the handicrafts but apply in the main also to basic training for commerce. In all the Northern countries this training has, so far, largely taken the form of practical work on the job, supplemented by instruction in a vocational school.

With respect to training for domestic work it is obvious that the relations between school and place of work cannot be regulated by law in the same way as is the case for commerce, industry, and handi-crafts. Training in domestic science and the home arts is largely given by means of courses of briefer duration than, but otherwise similar to, the supplementary vocational school courses for other occupations. A notable feature is the more mature clientele enrolled in home economics courses as compared with training schools for the other occupations which mostly enlist young people who are just out of elementary school and starting upon their careers. This seems natural enough, since most young women acquire a serious interest in the home arts only after having established their own homes. Thus, also in this field the classroom supplements the practical experience imparted to the pupils by their daily tasks.

Full-Time School Training

It has previously been indicated that, with the possible exception of Denmark, the supplementary instruction provided by the voca-tional schools does not reach a large enough number of young people. Consequently, these countries have found themselves ob-liged to devise other forms of instruction as a supplement to those outlined above. Young people are brought together to receive full-time training in a school for longer or shorter periods before they enter upon an occupation. The training given in the vocational school generally includes both practical and theoretical instruction, thus replacing in part the training of apprentices at the work-places. These combined practical-theoretical schools are differently organized in Finland, Norway, and Sweden, the three Northern countries where this type of school has attained its broadest development.

In *Finland*, the so-called preparatory schools for industry, handi-crafts, and home management offer two-year courses with 35 weeks of instruction per year. The curriculum includes eight to nine hours of general education, five to ten hours of occupational theory, and 20–25 hours of work practice per week. These schools have a twofold purpose: First, to provide a theoretical and practical foundation for the pursuit of an occupation and at the same time to educate for civic responsibility; second, to furnish an elementary education which qualifies for admission to advanced schools of vocational training. During the academic year 1948–1949, Finland had 35 preparatory schools with an enrolment of 5,400 students. A counterpart to these institutions is found in the two-year commercial schools which are based upon elementary school education and are attended by about 2,000 students. There are also a few central vocational schools offering more advanced instruction, partly in co-operation with private firms. In contrast to the other Northern countries, the Finnish schools with full-time programmes now enroll more students than schools providing supplementary part-time instruction.

In *Norway*, the preparatory workshop schools usually give courses of six to twelve months' duration, but there are also two-year programmes in the so-called prolonged preparatory schools, and three-year programmes in the so-called complete workshop schools. The preparatory schools aim to teach the pupils enough about tools, materials, and methods of work so that they may undertake their apprenticeships with profit. These schools are more strictly vocational in emphasis than the preparatory trade schools of Finland. Most workshop and preparatory schools are public but a few of them are operated by private industrial enterprises. In the housekeeping field, basic full-time instruction is given in home-making institutes, which offer courses generally lasting five, sometimes ten months. Workshop schools for industry and handicrafts and the home-making institutes each enroll about 3,000 pupils annually.

Basic full-time instruction for commercial occupation is given in two forms: (1) In half-year courses with the same subject matter as the basic two-year evening courses; (2) in one-year courses with a wider choice of subjects.

In *Sweden*, some 2,000 pupils are enrolled on full-time courses which prepare for commercial occupations, and another 2,000 study home economics (this latter figure includes both homemaking institutes and farm housekeeping schools). These schools resemble their counterparts in Norway. Initially, instruction is basic and general; later it is broadened and differentiated, first by practical experience gained on the job and subsequently by means of specialized studies. Elementary commercial courses are usually of one year's duration and are based upon elementary school education. Courses in domestic science last ten or (usually) five months.

Basic full-time instruction for industry and handicrafts differs in Sweden according to whether emphasis is on the industrial or handicraft aspect. Training in workshop schools for industrial jobs usually lasts for a two-year period and graduates are as a rule engaged as third-year apprentices in an industrial enterprise. Training for

172

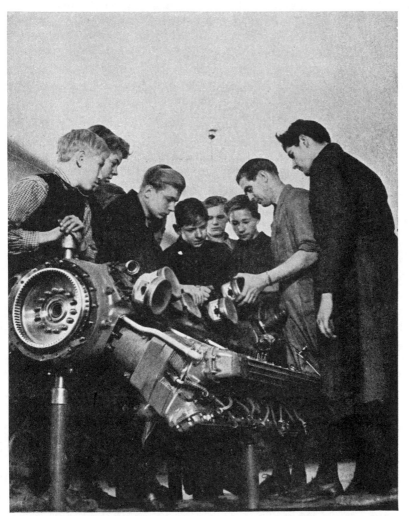

There's nothing like having a look at the real thing. Scene from a Swedish workshop school.

handicraft occupations in the workshop schools extends over a four-year period, usually concluding with a journeyman's examination. This examination may be taken on the school premises, but is not supervised by the school. The Swedish workshop schools, like their Norwegian counterparts, have hitherto been almost completely practical in emphasis and very little in the way of general education has been included in the curricula. Today it is, however, possible to provide for a certain measure of general education and instruction in civics in the full-time vocational training courses.

I73

The Swedish workshop schools, with an annual enrolment of 6,000 pupils, are predominantly operated by the local or county authorities. There are extremely few workshop schools under private management. On the other hand, there are about 60 so-called industrial schools, operated by private firms and functioning along the same lines as the workshop schools; the enrolment in industrial schools is probably in the neighbourhood of 2,000.

There can be no doubt that preparatory vocational training in full-time schools involves considerably greater expense for Society than supplementary part-time instruction. Pupils enrolled in full-time schools are also far fewer than those in part-time courses, except in Finland. However, the number of full-time pupils has increased considerably during recent years. This applies particularly to Finland and Norway where present efforts go in the direction of requiring a certain amount of classroom training as a necessary preliminary to the practising of any occupation. In this context, the relatively heavy proportion of instruction in general subjects found in the preparatory vocational schools of Finland should be recalled; these schools thus form a continuation and development of the elementary school and at the same time prepare pupils for their future occupations.

In all the Northern countries efforts are now being made to give all young people who choose to discontinue their general education a period of vocational training in the classroom to prepare them for gainful employment. The most radical approach is found in Iceland and Sweden.

The Icelandic 1946 School Act stipulates that youngsters who have completed six years of elementary children's education may choose one out of three curricula: First, a two-year youth school with two branches, one of which is mainly theoretical while the other emphasizes work instruction; attendance at this school constitutes the compulsory minimum. Second, a three-year secondary school which admits graduates to senior high schools or vocational schools. And third, a four-year junior high school from which students may pass on to vocational schools or certain posts in public service.

In Sweden the Riksdag has resolved to extend compulsory schooling by one year to a total of nine years, the implementation to take place as soon as adequate facilities and teachers are available. The last year of this nine-year school is to comprise three curricula: The first of these prepares for advanced theoretical studies on the senior secondary-school level; the second furnishes a general course roughly corresponding to that of the present "realskola" (equivalent to British modern school or American junior high school); and the third, while offering some instruction in general subjects and civics, concentrates on giving pupils a preparatory vocational training, wherever possible in co-operation with the trade schools. The new, so-called unified, nine-year school is now operating on an experimental basis in various parts of the country. When it has been fully introduced, vocational training in the classroom will form an important element of the education of a very large number of Swedish school children.

This new type of school has as yet no real counterpart in the other three countries, although the vocational curriculum has much in common with that of the Finnish preparatory trade schools. However, the new Icelandic and Swedish systems are by no means unique phenomena. They should rather be regarded as manifestations of the widespread efforts made in many countries to place vocational training on a par with theoretical instruction in the schools.

Other Training

In addition to these two chief forms of vocational training in the Northern countries – practical training in industry supplemented by school instruction, and preparatory practical-theoretical training confined chiefly to the vocational school – all five countries operate numerous other programmes. Different kinds of advanced training are offered by full- or part-time courses, courses in foremanship, courses in advanced handicrafts, etc. From the point of view of organization and system, these types of training do not differ from those described above.

The Danish handicraft schools furnish an interesting example. These schools have developed as an outgrowth of the folk high schools, which emerged around the middle of the 19th century and have played such an important role in the educational and spiritual advancement of the farming community; they provide concentrated, predominantly theoretical courses of two to five months' duration, as a supplement to practical training. Besides instruction in occupational theory, the courses include a fair amount of general education. Similar courses, though less general in scope, are also found in the other Northern countries. It seems likely that this kind of course, which is well suited for countries where young people can be recruited for part-time courses only with difficulty, will be emulated and developed in all the Northern countries. However, it should not be restricted to training for handicrafts only, but might equally well be applied to other occupational categories.

In many countries the Second World War entailed quite radical changes in the methods of vocational instruction. Intensive and thoroughly rationalized methods have been developed for short-term training, not only of skilled workers and craftsmen but also of other categories of wage earners. Such methods have been introduced to some extent in the Northern countries, especially within the manufacturing industries, but also in the trade schools. In Denmark for example, the trade schools – in addition to their courses for apprentices and journeymen – now also provide supplementary theoretical instruction for semi-skilled operatives and similar categories.

A special problem is posed by the great army of unskilled workers employed in industry and commerce. These large groups would appear to present particular difficulties in Denmark with its strong and rather rigid craft traditions. Far more than in any of the other countries the lack of proper training in a skilled occupation is here a severe handicap in the working life of a labourer.

In order to make up to some extent for the lack of vocational training of such large categories as messengers, work boys, women factory workers, domestic servants, etc., who at the age of 18 usually drift into the ranks of the unskilled workers, the responsible Danish authorities have in recent years sponsored a variety of educational programmes. A large number of local authorities have established free evening schools for young persons out of school. Although primarily devoted to general education, these schools also offer a number of courses directed at vocational improvement. Furthermore, special legislation, adopted in 1942, provides for the operation of young people's schools with a view to imparting some training to young persons outside the skilled professions. The courses given are highly varied: For young men they deal with the work in a certain industry where a number of the pupils are employed, for young women they may aim at domestic training, etc. A potentially far-reaching initiative in this sphere was that taken some years ago when the General Labourers' Union and the Employers' Association together started the first of a network of schools for unskilled workers. These institutions, which receive considerable subsidies from the State, are intended to further a general semi-vocational training for workers who wish to improve their qualifications.

Obviously, also other occupational categories than those described above require vocational training to a greater or smaller extent. Thus, the training required today for employment in agriculture and forestry is quite different and far more comprehensive from what it was only a few decades ago.

Agricultural schools differ from most others in that they mostly train self-employed persons – in this case farmers who cultivate their own land (with or without hired help) – as well as managers and other supervisory personnel of larger holdings. With the increasing mechanization of agriculture there is, however, a growing realization that some vocational training must also be arranged for farm hands who have traditionally received their training exclusively on the job.

Agricultural training in all the Northern countries is chiefly given in residential schools which are usually subsidized by the State and open to both farmers and farm hands at very modest fees. These schools may largely, and especially in Denmark and Sweden, be considered a supplement to the folk high schools previously mentioned. Courses at the Danish schools last from five to nine months and aim at giving pupils a measure of theoretical training adapted to the requirements of practical life. Swedish agricultural schools fall into several categories, some of which give only theoretical instruction (in courses of from five to ten months' duration) to persons who have already had some practical experience, while others give one- or two-year courses which combine practical and theoretical training.

A beginning has also been made in the establishment of specialized training facilities for farm hands. In Denmark a number of agricultural youth schools have been established since 1942 with State support; these schools offer a minimum of between 36 and 45 hours of vocational instruction to young agricultural labourers during the winter season. Similar courses, especially intended for the training of cattle hands, were introduced in Sweden several years ago.

In addition to the more general training provided in the institutions mentioned thus far, there are numerous specialized schools for dairying, horticulture, etc. In Finland, Norway, and Sweden, where lumbering is an important branch of the economy, a large number of forestry schools are in operation.

EMPLOYMENT PROGRAMMES
General Approach

As already indicated, it was the world depression in the early 'thirties and the resulting steep increase of unemployment which, in the Northern countries as elsewhere, necessitated a revision of Society's traditional passive attitude towards the fluctuations in economic activity characteristic of most industrialized communities in our time.

The old and tried measures (relief works and doles) proved inadequate to cope with the situation, but were nevertheless resorted to at the start when nothing better was at hand. In fact, governments and parliaments lacked sufficient expert knowledge as to how the crisis could be properly combated. The findings of Keynes and the "Stockholm Economic School" gradually paved the way for an improved understanding of the multiple relevant factors underlying general economic developments, and especially of the effects upon employment of government economic policy. The theory which was then developed and since has influenced the use of public investments and other provisions by means of which public authorities attempt to promote a high and stable level of economic activity, is probably well-known and may be summarized as follows:

In periods of high activity in the private sector of national economy the State and local authorities should refrain as far as possible from making inroads upon scarce labour resources. Instead, they should establish a reserve of investment projects at such times to facilitate their prompt implementation if and when private activity should tend to slacken, such a policy to go hand in hand with budgetary surpluses in "good" years and deficit financing in "bad" years. Should unemployment arise, a policy conducted along this line will directly provide employment in the fields sponsored by public authorities and in enterprises which deliver the necessary materials, but will have secondary effects as well, since it will assist in maintaining the buying power of private households, to say nothing of the psychological effects upon business of an avowed full employment policy.

In countries like the Northern where public investments form a major proportion of total investment and where the public is already the largest employer in communications, railways, roads and highways, power production, and other public utilities, such a policy would appear particularly effective. Further, it must be noted that, in relation to employment policy, public investments proper are not the only relevant categories. To a very considerable extent construction of housing is today in these countries directly or indirectly financed by the public and may thus readily be brought to conform to general economic policies.

See Chapter V,
Housing,
pp. 293–298.

In all the Northern countries ultimate responsibility for employment policy rests with Parliament. The government is responsible for implementing policy, but the practical tasks have largely been entrusted to more or less independent departments or institutions.

These organs are under the obligation of closely following trends and developments on the labour market and to prepare each year a survey of the situation together with a prognosis for the coming year. In years of labour shortage they shall endeavour to have public works postponed, if this can be done without prejudicial effect, and they have a voice in determining when projects receiving government aid shall come into operation. The existing, temporary regulations concerning building activities have, it may be added, increased their possibilities of directing important sectors of the labour market. Under the auspices of the central organs measures are taken to bring such projects as have temporarily been postponed to a sufficiently advanced stage of administrative and technical preparation so as to enable them to become operative at very short notice. A list of such reserve projects has been set up and is constantly being kept up-to-date, so as to provide at all times accurate information on the scope and variety of the projects at hand.

On account of the anti-inflationary policies pursued after the war public investments have been held back as far as possible so that today projects waiting to be executed have accumulated to a very considerable extent. To take one country as an example, the Swedish investment plans in 1948 represented a total expenditure of 4,100 mill. kronor and, if realized over a period of 2–3 years, would entail a doubling of total normal investments. While a large part of the projects will require unskilled labour (roads, airfields, etc.), other projects will necessitate the use of special materials or will consist in the placement of industrial orders.

In Norway, and to some extent also in Sweden, planning and timing of public works have been only one feature of the general policy concerning public and private investments, which has here assumed particularly sweeping proportions. Employment policy is

179

thus based upon the annual "manpower budget" or manpower programme which is included as a part of the Economic Survey – the nation's economic programme – annually adopted by Parliament. The manpower budget is not only a prognosis for the coming year, indicating the estimated labour force in the various industries and the expected seasonal changes therein, but also a programme to be implemented to the extent that manpower distribution may be controlled. It consequently also sets out the measures contemplated to influence the labour market. These include, first, the regulation of investment – government investments through ordinary State budget appropriations, municipal and private investments through allocations of materials – of labour and, to some extent, of imports. Second, localization of investments by measures to promote the utilization of idle or under-employed manpower where such exists. Third, measures to increase manpower mobility – geographically as well as vocationally – and to promote the recruitment of manpower for important industries. The major investments are regulated according to what serves rationalization and productivity, including direct public investment in key industries.

The guiding principle is not primarily the employment of as many workers as possible, but rather considerations as to what will provide the most valuable employment in future. It is, however, obvious that there are limits to the successful pursuit by each country of an independent policy of stabilization of economic activity at a high level. The high degree of dependence of the Northern countries upon international economic developments creates considerable difficulties in conducting an expansive employment policy of their own. (On the other hand, this very dependence will, of course, if the high general level of economic activity characteristic of the major countries in post-war years is upheld, facilitate the maintenance of full employment also in the countries of Northern Europe). The possibility of a decline in economic activity and a subsequent rise in unemployment must thus be reckoned with. Moreover, there are other causes of unemployment than economic fluctuations of the kind described above, so that the problem of maintaining a high and stable level of employment presents other aspects as well.

As a matter of fact, the Northern countries have, apart from one or two very limited recessions, enjoyed highly favourable general employment conditions in the post-war period, and such unemployment as has occurred must mainly be attributed to these other causes. Except in Denmark, unemployment figures have been negligible (in Norway and Sweden averaging only 2-3 per cent of organized workers) and labour shortages have posed more difficulties than the few small "unemployment pockets" in certain areas or trades. Danish post-war developments have, however, been somewhat different. In spite of a high level of economic activity, unemployment has averaged 8–10 per cent. Differences in unemployment insurance provisions and in statistical methods may play a role in this connection but even so there is hardly any doubt that "real" unemployment in Denmark has been consistently higher than in the other Northern countries. It is somewhat difficult to give a fully satisfactory explanation of this situation, which depends upon numerous, partly interrelated factors. Among these, particular prominence is usually accorded to the continued sharp seasonal variations, especially in construction work; but also the disequilibrium between skilled and unskilled labour in connection with insufficient occupational and geographical mobility is frequently mentioned in this connection. Thus a situation has been possible where, in the face of unemployment in numerous fields, other trades have had to contend with a persistent shortage of labour. Under these circumstances the permanent legislation concerning public emergency relief works, established in the middle 'forties, has been of considerable significance and has provided employment for thousands of workers annually.

Seasonal Unemployment

The geographical location of the Northern countries produces considerable climatic variations between summer and winter, the latter being generally so severe as to render many outdoor activities impossible or, at best, rather difficult. In agriculture, for example, practically all outdoor work is brought to a standstill during the winter months. But for the existence of other opportunities, widespread seasonal unemployment in the agricultural population would be practically unavoidable. In Finland, Norway, and Sweden forestry requires many hands during the winter season and, at any rate in the latter two countries, the problem in recent years has rather been one of providing enough manpower for forestry work which is of primary importance to the national economy. In Denmark, although agricultural employment necessarily declines on account of

181

winter conditions, the large part of farmwork devoted to the raising of livestock provides a somewhat more even distribution of work over the whole year.

All the same, in spite of various kinds of work forming a seasonal counterweight of considerable importance, employment as a whole shows a distinct peak in midsummer and a slump during the winter, notably in the months of January and February. The actual size of such seasonal unemployment depends, of course, upon the severity of the winter. In Denmark unemployment percentages during the six winter months are generally more than twice the summer figures. For comparison it may be mentioned that the corresponding British figures show hardly any variation at all.

It is primarily road and building construction work which is subject to such seasonal fluctuations, the effects of which are felt in a great many trades, notably those supplying raw materials, etc. for that type of work. The hindrances to continued activity during the winter are, however, largely of a nature that may be overcome. Special efforts have been devoted to the finding of methods whereby building and other construction work can proceed under periods of severe frost. Today the major technical problems involved have been solved, but the methods advocated entail some extra costs and the problem of their financing has not yet been satisfactorily dealt with. Also, building tradition is often a further hampering factor. To some extent attempts are being made to concentrate public building construction to the winter months, and in some countries special support is granted to private construction projects which are continued in the cold season.

See also Chapter V, Housing, pp. 322–324.

Structural Unemployment

In the last few years, when unemployment in general has not been much of a problem, special interest has been devoted to the local (both in the geographical and occupational sense) "unemployment pockets" which have persisted even in periods of labour shortage.

Measures to promote geographical mobility of manpower have been introduced in Norway and Sweden in direct connection with employment exchange services through which grants of free travel and special allowances for breadwinners obliged to live away from their homes have been issued. In recent years these countries have devoted particular attention to the transfer of idle manpower during the winter season from agricultural or other activities running low at this time of the year to work in the forests. Also in Denmark the problem of geographical mobility has been a cause of concern. For decades the unemployment insurance societies have issued grants for moving expenses. On account of the housing shortage, labour transfers from one district to another have, however, in recent years been possible only on a limited scale. The state of full employment has led to special difficulties in some areas by further increasing the demand for modern housing. Thus, a vicious circle is created: In order to attract more manpower to localities where there is a shortage, it is necessary, temporarily, to put up with an even greater shortage of labour in order to provide the necessary housing accommodation.

The various courses for re-training (and training of unskilled) and the deliberate long-term efforts to direct young persons into trades where shortage of labour is anticipated will, it is hoped, promote a larger degree of occupational mobility. Some resistance from certain labour groups must, however, be reckoned with. As long as the fear of future unemployment influences trade union policies, self-interest points towards a policy of maintaining traditional, rigid barriers between trades and of limiting access to the skilled occupations to the minimum estimated to be sure of employment; hence, the continued shortage of manpower in certain key trades simultaneous with overcrowding in other parts of the labour market.

Structural unemployment may, however, affect large geographical areas, in which case effective labour mobility would entail complete depopulation of the districts concerned. To meet such a situation, methods of directing industry, especially new industrial enterprises, to the spot where manpower is available have been put into operation. In Norway, for example, where the districts in the far North were almost totally devastated during the war, a special development plan for this region has been put into action so as to establish a permanent basis upon which the population may be assured of their livelihood. In Norway and Sweden efforts have been made to direct industrial enterprises to areas where labour was already at hand, such as districts where one of the sexes lacked adequate employment opportunities. The means employed to that end include pressure from the labour market authorities as well as from the housing authorities in control of new construction; direct negotiations between authorities and enterprises have also frequently proved an effective method.

In both countries a start has been made in the carrying out of economic surveys and analyses of the various provinces as a basis for area-development planning aiming at a more effective utilization of available natural resources and manpower. On the whole the Northern countries have not, it may be added, been faced by the problems of "distressed areas" in the same sweeping proportion as was the case in Great Britain during the period between the wars.

Labour Shortages

In their present form employment programmes in Northern Europe may be considered the response of the countries concerned to the challenge of the 'thirties, their leading motive being: "No more unemployment". In the above presentation emphasis has thus inevitably been on the measures directed against unemployment.

Especially with regard to the more general policies aimed at preventing economic slumps, no evaluation has been attempted. This is natural enough since these policies have not as yet been seriously tested. Due in part to deliberate government action, in part to developments beyond the control of governments, a state of full employment – in certain periods even "overfull" – has prevailed in the whole post-war period. Thus, far from calling measures to prevent unemployment, economic conditions have on the contrary generally been such as to call for sustained anti-inflationary efforts.

There are several reasons for this, but the following probably rank among the more fundamental. During the Second World War the Northern countries, although mostly spared from large-scale devastations, were more or less stripped of stocks and had their industrial equipment worn out, in both cases without any possibility of effectuating normal replacements. Simultaneously, consumption of consumers' goods, notably of such durable articles as clothes, household appliances and the like, was severely reduced while – except in Iceland – construction of housing was sharply cut, in Norway being brought to an almost complete standstill. When the war ended there was consequently an urgent necessity for large investments in stocks and machinery and a considerable pent-up demand for a wide range of consumers' goods. This, combined with a high degree of monetary liquidity, both as regards enterprises and private households, produced a strong pressure upon available resources, a pressure which resulted in a steeply increased demand for manpower.

In all the countries economic recovery programmes were set up, envisaging a gradual return to normal conditions within a period of about five years. A common characteristic of these programmes was the key role occupied by available materials supplies and manpower which set a limit to the pace at which recovery could be achieved. In Finland, this shortage was further increased by the large war indemnities due from that country to the Soviet Union, the payment of which necessitated a radical expansion of the Finnish metal and shipbuilding industries. Payment was completed in August 1952.

The direct effects of war and recovery efforts had by no means run their course when the currency devaluation of September 1949 and the deterioration of international relations (especially pronounced after the outbreak of the Korean conflict in 1950) put a renewed strain upon the economies of the Northern countries. In Denmark, Norway, and Sweden the situation has been further aggravated by increased defence programmes.

A feature which has given rise to preoccupation, especially in Sweden, but which is of importance in the other countries as well, is the demographic development. In the first place, the years of the Second World War and the immediate post-war period witnessed a marked – if largely transitory – increase in the number of births and within a few years all the Northern countries will be faced with the problem of providing adequate vocational training and employment opportunities for these generations of young people which exceed the "normal" number by up to one-third. Far more important from a long-term point of view is, in the second place, the general trend towards a progressive aging of the population. During the next generation the age groups of 50–65 years and above will increase very much in number while simultaneously the younger age groups of 20–50 years will become relatively fewer. The problems which this development involve are further aggravated by the fact that expansion in urban industries, which hitherto has been based upon immigration from agriculture, no longer can rely upon this source to the same extent. The shortage of labour, experienced in general in Finland, Norway and Sweden, and partially in Denmark, is thus not only a result of the immediate economic situation, but is also to some extent due to more deep-seated causes.

The realization in responsible circles of the serious character of this issue has, in the last few years, brought increased attention to the possibilities of utilizing the considerable manpower reserves constituted by the physically and mentally handicapped as well as elderly persons. In Finland and Sweden the problems of labour shortage arose more than ten years ago upon the outbreak of war and vigorous measures had to be taken to safeguard vital industries. Due to the responsiveness of their peoples to appeals for voluntary sacrifices, compulsory measures were largely avoided.

Such voluntary sacrifices can, however, hardly be relied upon in peace time and, since compulsory measures are generally frowned upon, labour shortages have in post-war years presented an intricate problem to the Northern countries.

Employment of Handicapped Persons

A special aspect of employment policy which deserves separate mention is that pertaining to the placing in employment of handicapped persons who, owing to physical or mental defects or social hindrances, find it more difficult than others to obtain and keep employment. Roughly, the causes leading to a person being considered as handicapped in the above sense of the word may be classified in two separate categories. First, such physical or mental abnormities or diseases which, without being totally disabling, reduce the working capacity of the individual or necessitate the use of special equipment and second, social handicaps such as insufficient training, penal record, protracted unemployment, or old age. Even without entering upon a detailed discussion of these various causes (or combinations thereof), it should be stressed that social handicaps in many cases present a barrier to employment opportunities fully as serious as "objective" physical or mental defects.

The fact that during the last few years these problems have been the object of extensive debate, study and action must largely be viewed against the general widening of social policies. However, the scarcity of industrial manpower during the Second World War sparked a new interest in handicapped persons as a latent reserve, an interest which the favourable employment conditions of post-war years have served to maintain. In Finland the many disabled war veterans have represented a further powerful stimulus to this new orientation.

For a long time special schools have existed for those limited groups who on account of blindness, deafness, or other shortcomings were specially handicapped. Increased use has been made of occupational activities as part of physical therapy programmes. This side of the problem has received considerable attention, but viewed as a whole the efforts toward enabling the handicapped to provide for themselves have been insufficient in scope and largely frustrated by the difficulties of providing gainful employment for the persons involved. Obviously, when, as in the 'thirties, a considerable percentage of the normal labour force is unemployed, the chances of the handicapped are deplorably small.

See Chapter VI, Health and Rehabilitation, pp. 359–377.

Much has been done by private organizations to provide work openings for the clearly defined groups of seriously disabled such as the blind, the deaf and dumb, etc., and whole industries especially equipped for such persons have been established and have proved their ability to compete in the open market. But, however much these efforts at establishing schemes of sheltered employment are welcomed, they are today recognized as insufficient. There is an increasing understanding of the need for a comprehensive approach to this problem, aiming towards the full utilization on the normal labour market of all the numerous groups previously characterized as "second-rate manpower". If successful, such a policy will, in the first place, lend a new feeling of self-confidence to those who previously had no hope of being able to look after themselves; also, it will promote a fuller and more rational utilization of the labour force and prevent existing tendencies towards considering certain jobs and occupations as more fit than others for the handicapped from becoming too firmly entrenched.

The programmes of rehabilitation are only in their first stages but, in contrast to earlier efforts, the problem has now been taken up on a broad front and step by step the various measures envisaged are being put into operation. A crucial point is, however, the shortage of qualified personnel – both social workers and medical staff with special insight into occupational problems being far too few in number to meet the increasing demand.

Investigations have disclosed that a considerable proportion of the handicapped may be placed directly on the open labour market if they are assisted by an effective employment service. Under the favourable conditions prevailing, impressive results have been achieved with relatively modest means in all countries. Departments solely devoted to the placement of handicapped persons have been established under the normal employment service and within a short period it

has been possible to provide work for a large number of handicapped. In the right place they have proved to be capable of filling their jobs quite as successfully as their "normal" colleagues.

It is expected that in the near future most of these departments will have at their disposal a social advisor and a specially trained medical officer; in Sweden this is already the case. The next step will be the establishment of close collaboration between the institutions which come into contact with the handicapped, i. e. the local social welfare organs, the disablement pensions' boards, hospitals, and the various specialized organs for the care of the blind, the deaf, discharged offenders, etc. Further, the placement of handicapped persons who are in need of particular consideration at the start or

require specially adapted equipment to work with will call for close co-operation between exchange services and individual enterprises. In Sweden, where about 10,000 handicapped annually have obtained employment through the employment exchanges since 1944, special arrangements for probational hiring (whereby certain grants and guarantees are offered) have been made with a number of private industrial enterprises.

Many handicapped persons are, however, unable to embark upon regular work without suitable preparation. Lack of training and skill may be due for instance to prolonged unemployment or to no trade having ever been learned; in either case training facilities are required. In many places industrial rehabilitation centres have been established

189

where disabled persons and convalescents may have their work capacity "tuned up" under medical supervision until they are considered fit for vocational training or employment. Insofar as age or other circumstances do not constitute a hindrance, existing normal educational services are, of course, drawn upon, but special institutions are needed whenever particular treatment is to be given. In Denmark so-called work schools for handicapped have been in operation for many years, but generally the training programmes have not gone beyond the simplest work performances. Recent experience shows, however, that training of handicapped persons can be successfully given also in "difficult" occupations. Blind persons are now employed as typists, telephone operators, radio mechanics, etc. The demand for handicapped persons has in some cases been more than adequate, employers having found that they are steady workers who show a positive interest in their job.

Prevention of disablement will have an important place in a comprehensive rehabilitation programme. Workers' protection, industrial hygiene, and employee counselling can do much to make working conditions more healthy and to reduce risks. On the other hand, an efficient vocational guidance and employment exchange service, together with improved vocational training facilities, will prevent many young persons from entering, or becoming disabled by, unsuitable work.

Further, it is hoped that gradually existing prejudices and resistance against employment of handicapped persons will cede to a more humane and flexible personnel policy with both private enterprises and responsible authorities. Undoubtedly a prolonged period of full employment will provide a strong stimulus toward individual experiments with employment of handicapped persons; this, in turn, may pave the way for a revision of antiquated attitudes, prevailing also among many fellow workers of the handicapped.

The employment of the handicapped has proved to be a paying proposition, not only for the persons involved, but for Society as a whole: Instead of relief cases they have become taxpayers.

CHAPTER III

THE CO-OPERATIVE MOVEMENT

Introduction

A common feature of the five Northern countries is that they have all developed co-operative organizations of considerable strength and importance within the last three generations. Indeed, it is probably true to say that the highly developed co-operative movement has long been among those aspects of Northern life which have attracted most interest in the outside world. This is due not merely to the fact that the co-operative movement has in these countries come to play an essential role in their economic and social life, a role which can hardly be fully understood without drawing into the picture both the co-operative agricultural marketing and purchasing enterprises and the well-developed consumers' co-operatives. It is also explained by a general and undoubtedly correct evaluation of the co-operative movements as significant links in the cultural and social development of these countries since the movement began almost a century ago. There is here a two-way connection. Existing conditions in these respects were unquestionably favourable to the growth of a powerful and independent co-operative movement. But at the same time the latter has itself, by virtue of its practical work and its idealist aspirations, been one of the major factors influencing the level of education and culture of the population as well as the forms and contents of public life.

The co-operative organizations of the Northern countries present a highly diversified picture and the phrase "co-operative movement in the Northern countries" should not be taken too literally since it does not denote a uniform system. This will at once be evident on noting a few characteristic differences in the organizational set-up in one country or the other. Actually, it is only with respect to the smallest country, Iceland, that it is justifiable to speak of a single national co-operative movement. In the other countries the organizations fall into two or more groups. Thus, in Norway and Sweden we find the distinction – well known from other countries – between the consumers' movement and the farmers' co-operatives. Again, in Finland the line of division goes through the consumers' co-operatives, half of which are grouped, organizationally speaking, with the farmers' co-operatives and compete vigorously with the other half. In Denmark, on the other hand, consumers' and farmers' co-operatives collaborate through a joint organization, the Central Co-operative Committee; still, this Committee does not include all Danish co-operatives, a special group of urban co-operative societies connected with the labour organizations being separately organized. In some cases the various groups have no connections or contacts, sometimes they have a certain understanding concerning division of activities, but in other cases they pursue different ideological and economic ends, or even compete with each other.

If, in spite of the marked differences, it is nevertheless justified to venture on a joint description of co-operatives in the Northern countries, this is primarily due to the fact that all of them are based more or less on the same fundamental principles of co-operation. These principles were first propounded in the classical Rochdale programme. The key points in this programme are known all over the world and have been widely accepted by co-operative enterprises, particularly consumers' co-operatives. It is probably correct to say that the Northern consumers' societies have, by and large, been modelled after these principles although, naturally enough, they have undergone numerous modifications and adjustments, the pattern of which is by no means uniform. By contrast, the producers' co-operatives in these five countries are essentially "home-grown" in origin and development. The fact that these organizations still follow very similar principles in their activities should be taken to indicate the broad validity for co-operative enterprise of the tenets first laid down by the Rochdale weavers rather than that it implies a direct line of influence. The result has been that the great majority of Northern co-operatives, on the consumers' side as well as on that of the producers, are firmly based on the main principles of open membership, democratic government, limited interest on capital, and distribution of the annual surplus to members as dividends or refunds proportional to their trade with the co-operative.

Another characteristic which the Northern co-operative organizations have in common is their independence of the State. Apart from the Finnish co-operative credit societies, the co-operatives have everywhere originated with the peoples and not with the governments. Sweden, Finland, and Iceland have introduced legislation, dating from 1895, 1901, and 1921, respectively, which lays down provisions concerning the establishment and operation of co-operatives. Recent Swedish legislation, enacted in 1951, stipulates that only associations which are co-operative in character may henceforth be registered as economic associations. In the remaining countries, where no such legislation exists, it has often presented difficulties to fit the co-operatives in among the numerous legislative provisions concerning trade, joint-stock companies, banks, etc., but on the whole the co-operative organizations have been satisfied with their position.

The sweeping expansion of State intervention in the economic field during the last two decades has obviously exercised a decisive influence also upon the activities of the co-operative movement. In some cases this has resulted in a strengthening of its position, in others it has been made more difficult.

State measures of particular importance in this connection comprise two main groups. Into the first fall those various schemes which were resorted to in the 'thirties in order to mitigate the worst effects of the depression upon the agricultural industry. They comprised a complex network of provisions aimed at the stabilization or raising of prices, in numerous cases combined with regulation of imports, domestic and foreign marketing and, not infrequently, of production itself. As a result of their central position with respect to marketing and purchases of agricultural products and necessities, the co-operatives were inevitably affected fundamentally by these measures. The second group includes those more general restrictions upon imports and production which had for their purpose to alleviate the employment situation and to protect the precarious balance of payments. Due to their rigidity and their liability to freeze trade in quotas, these restrictions often, and for long periods, impeded the continued development of consumers' co-operatives and other co-operative purchase societies, but obviously they also hampered the progress of private undertakings.

It is worth observing, however, that State intervention has not been aimed directly at the co-operatives as such. On the whole, governments have observed a policy of neutrality, trying to deal impartially with co-operatives and private enterprises.

193

Democratic government by members. The co-operative wholesale society of Iceland (SIS) at one of its yearly conferences.

Democratic government by members is one of the universal and basic features of the co-operative movement and the fact that the principle of "one member – one vote" has been applied in most of the Northern countries ever since the first co-operatives made their appearance, and is today observed practically everywhere, cannot in itself be said to constitute such a unique trait as to distinguish it from the co-operative movement in other parts of the world. Still, in the general background of the application of this principle and also in the forms in which it is implemented under varying conditions, the five countries have certain characteristics in common. In practice, this is manifest, for instance, in the special arrangements introduced to serve as links between the central organs and the rank and file to safeguard government by members.

Foreign visitors may find other features common to and characteristic of the Northern co-operatives, such as, perhaps, a preference for practical positive results and a certain hardheaded scepticism toward such radical philosophies and far-reaching goals as are sometimes put forward by co-operators in other countries. It is only a slight minority of Northern co-operators who consider themselves members of a movement aiming to revolutionize Society into a kind of co-operative

194

commonwealth. As for relations between the parallel organizations in the Northern countries, co-operators are always alert to any possibilities of extending practical business collaboration to their mutual advantage. Most of them, however, attach very little weight to vague appeals for "co-operators" to join forces and have only a non-committal smile for those romanticists who believe that the Northern co-operatives have eliminated all conflicts between producer and consumer; first and last they are practical men, each of them with the interests of his members to protect and further, and these interests also largely determine future goals.

The present chapter deals mainly with the two principal components of the co-operative movement: The consumers' co-operatives and the agricultural co-operatives; in addition, brief accounts are given of the fishermen's co-operatives and of co-operative credit institutions.

Before proceeding it may, however, be expedient to attempt a bird's-eye view of such parts of the co-operative field as are more or less by-passed in the following.

The co-operative and other non-profit housing agencies which in recent years have come to play an essential role in urban housing construction and management and which occupy a special position – also in the sense that they are favoured by the authorities – are described elsewhere in this book.

See Chapter V, Housing, pp. 288–292.

Industrial workers' production co-operatives, which are well known from such countries as France and England, play only a minor role in the Northern countries. It should be mentioned, however, that in Norway there are certain artisan societies, especially in the building trades, which collaborate with the housing co-operatives. In Denmark these co-operatives form a characteristic part of the labour movement, together with the trade unions and the Social Democratic party. They include artisan societies and several factories or other establishments, e.g. bakeries, dairies, canteens, a brewery, a shoe factory, a clothing factory, and several others. Together with some large urban consumers' co-operatives, the housing co-operatives, and the Workers' Bank they form a special Urban Co-operative Union which is independent of the main body of the Danish movement and holds separate membership in the International Co-operative Alliance. No comparable organization is found in any of the other four Northern countries.

Several insurance companies are genuine co-operatives and others work along lines which strongly resemble the co-operative principles. In Sweden, it might be added, a number of rural fire insurance societies, which are clearly co-operative in character, were established long before the other categories of existing co-operatives and even antedate the foundation of the famous Rochdale enterprise. Some of these diverse societies are closely related to other co-operative organizations, both on the consumers' and producers' side. Since they do not present special features or problems of particular interest to a description of the co-operatives in general, it is considered justifiable just to mention them and stress their importance as a link in the network of co-operative activities.

It is difficult to give a clear-cut practical definition of what is to be understood by a co-operative enterprise. Consequently, it is hardly possible to indicate the exact boundaries of the operating field of co-operatives. On innumerable occasions smaller or larger groups of people have combined their efforts and resources to undertake some project or other which might very well be considered co-operative in character. The extent to which such activities should be considered as belonging "officially" to the co-operative movement is actually a matter of rather arbitrary judgment.

There are, however, in the Northern countries a host of small local societies, institutions, and enterprises, unimpressive if taken individually but of considerable significance as a whole, which are operated strictly according to co-operative principles. Many of these societies never come within the range of any co-operative statistics or organizations. They include local water-works, societies supplying electricity, local breeding societies, animal insurance societies, drainage societies, local locker stations for refrigeration, etc. These co-operatives should not be forgotten in any total estimate of the extent to which the Northern countries have been saturated with co-operative schemes where people work together for the solution of practical tasks.

With their 8,000 shops, the Swedish consumers' co-operatives cover the entire country. An increasingly common type of co-operative shop in towns is the "super-market", while rural shops often look like the one shown here.

Consumers' Co-operatives

In spite of numerous differences, the Northern consumers' co-operatives present a relatively uniform picture. As in other countries, their basic purpose is to provide members with consumer goods, most of which are pretty much alike in all five countries. The local consumers' society remains the key unit in the system, sales being made through the retail shop or shops owned by each society and managed by salaried employees. In all countries consumers' societies are organized in nation-wide wholesale societies, the activities of which include not only imports and other wholesale purchasing, but industrial production in their own factories as well. Wholesale societies or related organizations also serve as centres furnishing advice and other assistance to local societies as well as informational and educational facilities to members. This uniformity of structure and functions also provides the background for the successful operation for more than thirty years of a joint international purchase agency for the Northern co-operative wholesale societies: The Scandinavian Co-operative Wholesale Society (Nordisk Andelsforbund).

197

DEVELOPMENT

Some of the first societies were started by the urban workers or – in Iceland – by the farmers themselves, others were sponsored by well-meaning persons outside the working class. All of them, however, aimed more or less directly at improving the economic lot of the labouring man. The first experiments in Denmark and Sweden date back as far as the early 1850's. These early ventures were in some cases built on the example from Rochdale, in other cases they were original efforts. None of them survived for long, and viable societies did not appear in Denmark until after 1866, in Sweden after 1867, and in Finland after the turn of the century. Norway experienced a vigorous development of consumers' co-operatives about the same time as Denmark, i. e. in the 'seventies, but a period of economic depression around 1880 did away with most of them and renewed progress did not start until about 1900. The oldest existing Icelandic consumers' society dates from 1882.

It is interesting to find that industrial workers were not destined to become the sole important population group within the movement. At an early stage the rural population – independent farmers as well as agricultural workers – realized that they stood to benefit materially from this innovation. As a result, new consumers' societies were soon established all over the countryside. Indeed, in Denmark this tendency was so marked that farmers came to be the dominating group in the consumers' movement already in the 1870's, a position they have maintained ever since. An important practical consequence of this development has been that Danish consumers' co-operatives have been fitted in alongside the specialized agricultural co-operatives as a natural link in one united co-operative movement. A similar development has taken place in Finland with respect to the rural consumers' societies.

In Finland, and to some extent in Iceland, the co-operatives received an additional impetus from another source, both Finns and Icelanders finding the co-operatives a valuable instrument in their endeavours to promote national economic independence, which was rightly stressed as important to their aspirations for full national sovereignty. This also explains why in Finland – alone of all five countries – we find the usual process reversed in that an important part of the initiative came from the top, especially propelled by the famous "Pellervo" society, which was established in 1899 by a group of

This is the head-quarters of consumers' co-operation in Sweden, adjoining the busiest traffic clover-leaf in Stockholm. An elevated platform leads from the building to a lift, and from the top there is a superb view of the capital.

citizens with social and national interests for the purpose of furthering co-operative enterprises in Finland. Pellervo, which in the following years came to assume a position of central importance within the Finnish co-operative movement, was and is an entirely private under-taking, the work of which includes information and propaganda as well as the development of standard statutes for co-operatives.

An important phase in the development of Northern consumers' co-operatives was entered upon when the local societies initiated joint purchases. As long as each society operated alone, the move-ment's range of action was restricted to competition with private retailers in order to improve conditions as to prices, qualities, meas-ures, and credit conditions. By combining for joint purchases they were, however, also enabled to enter the wholesale trade. The Danish wholesale society for joint purchases, the FDB (Fællesforeningen for Danmarks Brugsforeninger), was established in 1896; the corresponding Swedish organization, the KF (Kooperativa Förbundet), in 1899; the Icelandic SIS (Samband Íslenzkra Samvinnufélaga) in 1902; the Finnish SOK (Suomen Osuuskauppojen Keskuskunta) in 1904; and the Norwegian NKL (Norges Kooperative Landsforening) in 1906. Thus, in spite of the different historic development of consumers' co-operatives in the five countries, establishment of all the wholesale societies took place within a period of only ten years. In 1916 the urban branch of the Finnish consumers' co-operatives left the SOK and subsequently established its own wholesale society, OTK (Osuustuokkukauppa).

Establishment of the wholesale societies strengthened the position of the consumers' co-operatives very considerably. The wholesale societies represented a buying power far exceeding that of any single private concern and were able, in negotiations over prices and sales conditions, to hold their own against sellers, including importers and other wholesale firms as well as industrial producers. In fields where the co-operatives found themselves unable to secure what they considered satisfactory terms concerning qualities and prices the wholesale societies took up their own production of the commodities involved. Also, special laboratories were established for the continuous quality-control of merchandize. In some of the countries co-operative manufacturing has attained sizeable proportions and has unquestionably in numerous cases acted as a powerful stimulus to competition.

PRESENT STATUS

Although the basic structure of consumers' co-operatives is more or less the same in all five Northern countries, a closer view reveals significant national variations.

Denmark is characterized by the many small societies, nearly 2,000 of them, with an average of 230 members. Farmers remain the most influential group, but in recent years the towns have accounted for most of the continued growth of membership. Similarly, the Norwegian societies are rather small, averaging 240 members; the 1,100 societies are, as in Denmark, scattered all over the country, but workers and office employees dominate among the members, although farmers are also strongly represented. In Finland and Sweden, on the other hand, there are relatively few but large societies. Thus, the total number of Finnish societies is only 494 and the average membership almost 1,900, farmers dominating in the SOK group and workers in the OTK group. The corresponding Swedish figures are 682 and 1,456, with industrial workers as a clear majority of the membership. Icelandic consumers' societies occupy an inter-mediary position with an average membership of 570, the farming population constituting the largest single group among the members with urban workers in the second place.

An important practical consequence of the larger size of Finnish and Swedish societies has been that they operate through an extensive network of local branch stores, in Sweden numbering more than 8,000. In Denmark and Norway, by contrast, only the urban societies maintain branch stores, the number of which has in recent years expanded considerably.

The relative importance of the consumers' co-operatives in the five countries is indicated by their membership related to total popu-lation (1951).

	Members of consumers' co-operatives (thous.)	Members in per cent of population
Denmark . . .	455	10.8
Finland	992	24.1
Iceland	31	21.4
Norway	273	8.3
Sweden	993	14.0

Since each member generally represents a family, the percentages listed above should be multiplied by about three or four in order to arrive at the actual extent to which the population is directly or indirectly affiliated with the consumers' co-operatives. The table therefore indicates that the coverage of the societies ranges from a low of almost one-third of the population in Norway up to a high of three-fourths in Finland. On the other hand, it is important to emphasize that membership, whether personal or through a house-hold, does not mean that all goods are bought from the co-operatives; this will be evident also from what is stated in the following with respect to the co-operative share of total retail turnover.

The consumers' societies in Norway and Denmark account for a little less than 10 per cent and a little more than 10 per cent, respectively, of total retail sales while the corresponding Swedish percentage approaches 15. It should be noted, however, that there are numerous branches where the co-operatives have never been very active, either because no need for action has been felt or because co-operative enterprise has failed; Danish examples are meat, milk, vegetables, clothing, and a variety of luxury goods. On the other hand, the co-operatives handle 25–30 per cent or more of total turnover in several important commodities, viz. groceries in Denmark and foodstuffs in Sweden. The two Finnish groups of consumers' co-operatives are estimated to account for no less than a full third of total retail trade, although it should be added that rural consumers' societies in Finland sell a variety of farming necessities which in the other countries are mainly provided through the farmers' purchase societies, i.e. by agricultural co-operatives. No comparable figures are available for Iceland, but since the Icelandic wholesale society handles 30-50 per cent of imports of numerous important goods, e.g. flour, rye, oatmeal, sugar, and textiles, it may safely be estimated that the percentage in that country is high.

The particularly strong position of Finnish consumers' co-operatives is partly explained by the fact that they have been widely accepted both among farmers and among industrial workers. Actually the unique development in Finland must be viewed against the split-up of the consumers' movement into two independent and competing groups which took place in 1916, when the workers' group left the national union (YOL) and the wholesale society (SOK), and formed its own union (KK) and a new wholesale society (OTK). It should be observed, however, that even in the farmer-dominated SOK wage earners comprise no less than two-fifths of the membership. The two groups are today about equally strong, the SOK leading in number of affiliated societies and shops while the number of members and the turnover are about the same. Although evidently there might be economies to gain by collaboration between the two big wholesale societies, ideological differences have so far barred any progress in that direction. At the same time there is a general impression that the enhanced homogeneity of each organization and the very existence of a powerful "rival" have acted as strong stimuli to continuous advances in efficiency.

202

In addition to their role as great commercial enterprises, the co-operative wholesale societies have gradually developed into large-scale industrial manufacturers. Production in the co-operative factories today covers a wide range of merchandize, including such important consumer goods as margarine, soap, footwear, textiles, knitwear, leather goods, and – in Denmark, Finland, and Sweden – also flour, canned goods, chocolate, etc. Within the last twenty years, co-operative manufacturing has attained impressive proportions, particularly in Sweden. The Swedish wholesale society has established or acquired plants in almost all important industrial sectors and in 1951 the goods manufactured in these plants accounted for more than one-half of the society's total turnover. In Sweden, and to some extent also in the other countries, the larger local societies operate factories of their own. Local units are free to place their orders with private wholesalers and manufacturers, but the proportion of total purchases made with the wholesale society is considerable, in Denmark as high as 75 per cent.

Since the early days of the Rochdale pioneers it has been the general policy of consumers' co-operatives to charge current prices on their goods and to distribute the resulting surplus as an annual dividend, proportional to the purchases made by each member. On the whole, this tradition was from the beginning also followed by the Northern consumers' societies. With the increasing economic resources of the movement the societies have, however, in recent years frequently departed from this practice to pursue an active policy of price-cutting. Especially in Finland and Sweden the co-operatives have registered encouraging results of this more radical approach which – to the extent that it is successful – benefits not only members of the societies but all consumers. The most famous example of co-operative initiative in this respect is the establishment in 1931 by the Danish, Norwegian, and Swedish wholesale societies of "Luma", a co-operative federation for the joint administration of the electric bulb factory of the same name in Stockholm. This factory has successfully competed with the international cartel dominating this field. The dividends on purchases from the consumers' co-operatives are generally low, averaging two to three per cent.

It is obvious that consumers' co-operatives and private commercial enterprises have been, and still are, competitors. With this as the general background, the main controversial issue has been the existence of, or demand for, special taxation rules for co-operatives. Primarily the question is whether that part of a co-operative's surplus which is due to its trade with members should be considered income in the legal sense and thus subject to income taxes in the same way as is the case with joint-stock companies.

The co-operatives have always asserted that such surplus cannot be considered as income either for the co-operatives or for the

The co-operative
LUMA factory
in Stockholm was
established by the
Danish, Norwe-
gian, and Swedish
wholesale societies
to fight the inter-
national electric
bulb cartel.

individual members receiving a refund upon their purchases. They maintain that these are funds which members have saved out of their previously earned income by jointly taking over – through the co-operative – the trade in merchandize for their personal con- sumption. Members do so solely to obtain such merchandize as cheaply as possible and not in order to engage in trading as an occupation. If the co-operatives charge current prices instead of selling at cost prices, this is simply motivated by practical business considerations, particularly that it is an expedient method of assuring the co-operatives the necessary capital for their operation. On the other hand, co-operatives admit the justifiability of taxing that part of the surplus which arises out of sales to non-members since this must be classed with ordinary income.

Private business rejects this line of reasoning. Its representatives argue that co-operatives in their present form – with salaried employees, with considerable sales to non-members and, in general, with their widespread occurrence and large turnover – must be said to be economic ventures essentially analogous to private enterprises operated as joint-stock companies. Consequently, the net surplus of a co-operative cannot be distinguished from the net surplus of a joint-stock company and refunds to members are therefore comparable to the distribution of dividends to shareholders. They conclude that there is no justification for applying other principles in the taxation of co-operatives than those applicable to private enterprises.

The debate on this issue has gone on for decades in all the Northern countries and, whether the authorities have taken a stand favouring one or other of the two parties, it is still being continued with varying degrees of acerbity. Without attempting any evaluation of the respective arguments it may be relevant briefly to outline the actual conditions prevailing with respect to the taxation of consumers' co-operatives in the various countries.

Taxation of co-operatives, like tax legislation in general, shows considerable differences from country to country. With respect to taxes on property, private and co-operative enterprises are subject to roughly parallel provisions. It is particularly in the field of income tax that provisions differ somewhat, depending upon which point of view the authorities have taken on the issue discussed in the preceding paragraphs.

Norwegian legislation entitles the co-operatives to deduct from their taxable income that part of the surplus which is due to their trade with members. In Sweden that part of the surplus which is refunded to members according to the volume of their purchases has been tax-exempt since 1920. Danish co-operatives which traded exclusively with members were originally tax-free while co-operatives which also accepted non-members as customers were taxable on the basis of their entire surplus. However, legislation adopted in 1940 provided for taxation of all co-operatives. A reform in 1949 introduced a quite new principle whereby taxes on co-operatives are no longer based upon their surplus but solely upon their net capital (share capital plus reserves). In Finland the co-operatives were, until 1943, entitled to a tax-free deduction of fifty per cent of their surplus, but a tax reform in that year abolished this right; refunds to members are, however, still tax-exempt.

As regards the right to deduct refunds to members, it should be noted that in Finland, Norway, and Sweden private traders enjoy the same right where they pay their customers a rebate on their total purchases at the end of the year. Particularly in Sweden this practice is very widespread.

In keeping with their general line of furthering consumers' interests, the co-operatives have devoted special attention to the possibilities of rationalizing retail distribution. The co-operative societies have achieved several important practical results in this field. It has not everywhere been possible to realize the Rochdale principle of cash trading, but the emergence of consumers' societies has contributed strongly to restrict the practice of credit purchases. The societies have imposed certain limits on such purchases and in the annual dividend, or rather its retention, have an effective means of curtailing credit to members.

In several of the countries the consumers' societies have in recent years introduced a growing number of self-service stores similar to the American "supermarket". By the establishment of a special architectural unit the wholesale societies have rendered an important contribution to the improved design of stores. Also, in 1951 the leader of the Swedish consumers' co-operatives took the initiative for the establishment of an international committee to deal with the general question of rationalization of co-operative retail and wholesale trade.

As previously noted, the close relationship between the co-operative movements of consumers in the Northern countries has led to the creation – in 1918 – of the Scandinavian Co-operative Wholesale Society, which today counts all six wholesale societies as members (as already mentioned above, Finland has two wholesale societies). The Society is a joint purchasing agency, mainly for import from overseas countries. It undertakes the main part of purchases on behalf of its members of such commodities as coffee, tea, rice, spices, grain, and fruit, as well as numerous raw materials for the factories run by the wholesale societies. Restrictions and war hampered its continued development considerably, but in 1951 its turnover had reached 250 million Danish kroner. Backed by the combined strength of more than $2^1/_2$ million members, the Society today stands as one of the strongest and most influential buyers of several commodities on the world market.

Farmers' Co-operatives

Like the consumers, the agricultural producers have developed co-operative organizations to obtain by joint effort the benefits of large-scale operation otherwise inaccessible to the individual members. However, while the consumers' movement has been largely modelled on the English system, farmers' co-operatives are typically Northern, both in origin and development.

A few common features tend to give the over-all picture a rough uniformity. Thus, in all Northern countries the movement centres around co-operative dairies and slaughterhouses, which dominate the processing and the marketing of milk and of animals for slaughter; other important marketing organizations handle eggs and other farm products. Today also co-operative purchase societies for feeding-stuffs and fertilizers have come to play a considerable role.

These common features must be viewed against the background of production systems which – in spite of great differences in climatic, soil, and marketing conditions – share a number of outstanding characteristics. One is that the typical farm is nowhere very large, which means that it is not possible for farmers themselves to undertake industrial processing of milk and slaughtering of animals. Another is the key role played by animal husbandry, all five countries being normally major importers of feeding-stuffs, both grain and oil cakes. It is in this situation that Northern farmers have found the co-operative method eminently useful. The operation of dairies and slaughter-houses as well as trade in feeding-stuffs and fertilizers were in the beginning taken up by private enterprise on a commercial basis. An explanation of the rapid development and present strong position of co-operatives, therefore, must be sought for in special circumstances, some of the most important of which will be traced in the following paragraphs.

DEVELOPMENT

Farmers' co-operatives were not introduced at the same time nor for the same reasons in all of the countries. Yet it is possible to point to a number of motivating background factors which the five nations had more or less in common. Foremost among these stands the long-term trend of increasing production characteristic of Northern agri-culture in the 19th century. At the same time the distribution of the population was shifting, the number of town-dwellers growing faster than the rural population. Both of these factors rendered the farmers increasingly dependent upon the market and particularly the marketing of their products over longer distances – whether within their own country or abroad. These developments also served to accentuate the difficulties of the farmer in being dependent solely upon private merchants for the marketing of his production and for the purchase of farm necessities; with respect to the latter, the expanding demand for fertilizers and imported feeding-stuffs was of special importance. If the changes mentioned provide a general background, there can still be no doubt that the formation and growth of farmers' co-operatives received a further impelling stimulus by the reduction of ocean freight rates and the resultant flooding of the European market with cheap overseas grain during the last decades of the 19th century. Northern, and especially Danish, farmers responded to the challenge with a radical revision of traditional production patterns, shifting main emphasis to the marketing of animal products instead of grain, and – in Norway and Sweden – by the imposition of tariffs on imported grain.

Danish agriculture, traditionally an exporter, was hit particularly hard when world prices for grain collapsed in the late 1870's. Farmers had to act themselves, as nobody else at the time was prepared to enter the dairy and slaughterhouse business on the necessary scale. That they were able to introduce the new undertakings on a co-operative basis, was partly because they found a practical way of financing them – taking out loans against the joint and unlimited liability of all members – and partly because sixty years of compulsory elementary education in conjunction with the famous folk high schools had provided them with the necessary educational background. The economic advantages of joint action in the processing and marketing of milk and slaughterhouse products were so evident that in the years after 1880 the agricultural co-operatives spread with great rapidity, not only in Denmark but also in Norway and Sweden. With expanding animal production, oil cakes and other imported feeding-stuffs as well as artificial fertilizers came into increasing demand and efforts to procure these goods on a co-operative basis took their beginning in the years just before the turn of the century.

As a result of these activities all five countries found themselves with more or less well-developed networks of agricultural co-operatives in the years immediately before the First World War. These co-operatives comprised several different types of societies, but everywhere the major groups were, on one hand, dairies, slaughterhouses, and societies for egg-marketing and, on the other hand, purchase societies for a variety of articles required by farmers, particularly feeding-stuffs and fertilizers.

The preceding paragraphs have portrayed the general trend in broad strokes, emphasizing the basic similarities among the five countries. A fuller, but also a far less simple, picture emerges if the many and important differences are taken into account.

The role of agriculture varies very considerably among the Northern countries. Danish farming is primarily directed at foreign markets, almost three-fifths of Denmark's substantial export trade consisting of agricultural products. Swedish farmers are almost able to supply the home population with its basic foodstuffs, relatively small surpluses alternating with small deficits according to weather conditions and changes in production patterns. Within the past half century Finnish agriculture has made a spectacular effort to achieve a similar productive capacity and the country has now almost attained self-sufficiency. Owing to their less favourable natural conditions Norway and Iceland, on the other hand, must of necessity rely upon regular food imports, chiefly grain, to supplement their own agricultural production.

This brief statement of the varying position of agriculture in the national economy of each country provides a clue to the understanding of some of the most obvious differences found among agricultural co-operatives.

In *Denmark*, the exporting country, it was very soon recognized that the establishment of local co-operative societies could be considered only a first step toward efficient agricultural marketing and that it had to be followed up by further efforts if satisfactory results were to be achieved. The handling of butter exports obviously required resources beyond those at the command of small local dairies. Consequently, it was not long before co-operative butter export societies began to be established with a view to obtain better marketing terms through competition. But the co-operatives went further. A high and uniform quality of the product was an indispensable condition if high prices were to be obtained on export markets, and necessary standardization and export controls could be effectively introduced only by the concerted action of producers controlling a very large share of total exports. The co-operative dairies secured voluntary support from an overwhelming majority of their members for such export control safeguards and finally the government made them compulsory. Similarly, the co-operative bacon factories were successful in standardizing both pig production and processing of the pigs into bacon, the principal aim being to develop a uniform and high-class product for the British market. The co-operative egg export association was founded for the express purpose of improving quality controls and the grading of eggs in order to market a better product and obtain better prices from abroad. Likewise, the local purchase co-operatives for feeding-stuffs and fertilizers at an early stage found it expedient to combine their efforts in order to influence import trade directly and fight attempts at monopolistic practices. Central import societies were set up in the years between 1898 and 1901.

In *Norway and Sweden* the agricultural co-operatives had their first important development on the local level about the same time as in Denmark, the first Norwegian co-operative dairy even dating as far back as 1855. The second step, however, the establishment by local co-operatives of joint marketing agencies, was taken only at a later stage and then on a smaller scale. The main reason for this was that, due to the different positions of agriculture in these countries, sales of agricultural produce – cereals, milk, butter, pork, meat, and eggs – were primarily for the home market.

Due to the uneven distribution of production and population there are in these countries, and particularly in Sweden, some areas with a decided surplus and others with a deficit of agricultural produce; this fact, together with the long distances, indicated the need for collaboration to ensure a steady and properly adjusted supply to different localities. However, the co-operatives in the vicinity of the larger consumption centres had not at this time attained the size required to tackle the tasks which they would have had to assume in that case. Their activities were mainly to collect part of the local production and to sell it to private local merchants. Co-operatives in surplus areas were in this connection viewed as competitors. On occasion the societies in various regions within each country would, moreover, enter into direct business relations with each other. The conditions for collaboration on a national scale did not exist.

On the other hand, in southern Sweden – a pronounced surplus area which at the beginning of the present century regularly exported butter, eggs, and bacon – the co-operatives had a common interest in collaborating with respect to the marketing of this surplus. The years after 1900 therefore saw the foundation of export societies for butter and eggs with functions similar to those of the corresponding Danish organizations. These export societies, which competed with private firms, sold their produce not only on the foreign market but also in domestic deficit areas; on occasion they were also active as importers. In this way they functioned as organs for the adjustment of supplies to domestic demand, prices being determined, by and large, by the price level on the world market. Also, systems of standardization and export controls, similar to those found in Denmark, were introduced. Furthermore, larger associations for the marketing of milk and cream were subsequently formed around a number of consumption centres.

From their inception the local purchase societies in Sweden had a common interest in collaboration with respect to such necessities as fertilizers and feeding-stuffs, since these commodities predominantly had to be imported or purchased from larger domestic manufacturers. In 1905, therefore, these societies established the nation-wide Swedish Farmers' Selling and Purchasing Association (SLR). This organ has also been entrusted with the marketing of such agricultural products as cereals, potatoes, oilseed, etc. – and the scope of its activities in this field has in recent years almost equalled that of its purchases of farming necessities. As was the case with other co-operatives, this organization suffered a financial crisis after the First World War, a crisis which severely impeded the further development of Swedish agricultural co-operatives during the 'twenties.

The development of *Finnish* farmers' co-operatives must be viewed in connection with the general movement for national independence already mentioned above in connection with consumers' societies. Efforts to increase agricultural production and improve the backward living conditions of farmers were also stimulated by the poignant fact that real hunger years had occurred as recently as in the 1860's. In consequence, an energetic policy of expansion was embarked upon, characterized by the extensive cultivation of new areas and improvement of old farm land. The result has been that today, in spite of heavy losses of fertile lands to the Soviet Union following the Second World War, Finland is able, by and large, to cover her own needs for foodstuffs.

Although a few agricultural co-operatives for joint purchases had been established at an earlier date, it was only with the foundation in 1899 of the great Pellervo organization that large-scale development set in. Basing itself upon the experience not only from Rochdale but also from the German Raiffeisen societies, Pellervo originally favoured combined purchasing and marketing societies. Actual developments took a somewhat different course, however, with main emphasis upon societies concentrating on joint purchases. These organizations subsequently expanded to become consumers' societies, supplying members with household necessities as well as with farm requirements. Later on they became affiliated with the wholesale society SOK and many of them also with the special agricultural wholesale society Hankkija.

In several cases the societies have – in conformity with Pellervo's original plan for multi-purpose co-operatives – taken up the marketing of agricultural produce such as grain, eggs, and animals for slaughter. Slaughtering is, however, also undertaken on a co-operative basis through a separate slaughterhouse organization and there is a somewhat strained relationship between the two types of co-operatives competing in this field. Milk processing, on the other hand, is completely in the hands of specialized co-operative dairies which are organized in two central marketing societies.

An important feature of Finnish farmers' co-operatives is that in most fields activities are carried on by two distinct groups of organizations. The larger one covers the Finnish-speaking part of the population while the considerably smaller one represents the Swedish-speaking minority. This dualism is more or less evident from bottom to top of the co-operative structure and even Pellervo has its counterpart, the Swedish Co-operative Federation of Finland.

Icelandic co-operatives, as previously mentioned, resemble the Finnish in that, although primarily pursuing economic ends, they have also been instrumental in the furthering of national independence

In this part of the world, bacon is spelled D-a-n-i-s-h ! This Danish slaughterhouse turns out the staple of many an English breakfast.

– in this case from Denmark. The first important co-operative enterprises were initiated almost simultaneously with those of the other Northern countries, but due to Iceland's very different economic structure they took their own independent course. In the very thinly populated rural regions there was usually only one trader within reachable distance. The inhabitants were therefore highly dependent upon him for the marketing and prices of their produce as well as for the prices and qualities of the consumer goods and other necessities they had to buy. Both as sellers and as buyers they consequently stood to gain considerably when, by combining their resources, they were enabled to establish direct contact with the large business enterprises in the towns. The small population numbers, and consequently the restricted membership, rendered it a practical necessity in most districts that there should be only one co-operative agency, covering both marketing and purchases. Icelandic co-operatives have thus from their start been multi-purpose organizations. This applies also to the co-operative union and wholesale society, SIS, founded in 1902, which does extensive marketing of agricultural products for its members in addition to carrying on its main business, the importation and distribution of merchandize to local societies. Outside the SIS there are a few co-operative dairies and a co-operative slaughterhouse.

215

RECENT TRENDS

The disastrous impact of the world depression after 1929 also hit the Northern farmer. Not only was Denmark seriously afflicted when her vital exports of foodstuffs became all but unsaleable, but also in the other countries farm products fell precipitately in price without any corresponding decline in agricultural costs. An aggravating factor was that the majority of farmers, especially in Denmark and Finland but also to some extent in Norway and Sweden, were rather heavily in debt and thus saddled with considerable debt services. Conditions deteriorated to the point where State intervention became necessary. The co-operatives participated prominently in the implementation of the resulting programmes. In Norway and Sweden the agricultural co-operatives were to a great extent reorganized during this period in order to make them capable of accomplishing wider purposes. In those two countries the emergency situation also gave the final impulse to the establishment of closer collaboration on a nation-wide scale among existing co-operatives and for the tight centralization of co-operative marketing of farm produce.

In *Norway* a special act of 1930 concerning the trade in agricultural products became a powerful lever to this new development. Under its provisions the various central co-operative organizations were, each within its particular field, empowered to introduce marketing regulations dealing not only with control of quality and similar matters but also with the stabilization of prices. In order to finance such schemes the organizations were authorized to levy a sales tax on the commodity in question, such taxes to be imposed not only on members of the co-operatives but also on unorganized farmers. With their position thus fortified, the co-operatives were able to launch a strong organizational drive which resulted in the creation of a number of centralized bodies on the national level, the most important being the milk organization, the meat and pork organization, and the egg organization.

As for *Swedish* developments, the General Agricultural Society of Sweden submitted a comprehensive plan for the development and consolidation of the co-operative system. The plan's double aim was to strengthen the basis of the co-operatives by increasing their following among farmers and to combine the local units by branches into national organizations in charge of exports as well as of sales from surplus areas to deficit areas within the country. Large-scale organization work was subsequently carried out along these lines by the various general farmers' organizations acting in collaboration. The national organizations, finally, became affiliated with the Federation of Swedish Farmers (SL), a successor to the General Agricultural Society mentioned above. The State supported the movement by grants for the necessary informational and organizational activities; similarly, grants were made available for supervision and revision until the co-operatives were able themselves to defray the costs involved. Most important among the various organizations are the dairies, the slaughterhouses, the egg-marketing organization, the association of purchase societies, and the forest owners' organization. But even the smaller groups play a dominant role in their individual spheres.

Thanks to their general consolidation and the development of central organizations, the agricultural co-operatives of Norway and Sweden have grown into powerful instruments for the protection of farmers' interests but are also at the service of retailers and consumers. The local units have freed farmers from the bother of transportation and marketing. It may thus be mentioned that extensive transport systems have been instituted to collect the products directly from the farmers, such arrangements being a necessity for the operation of large-scale enterprises. At the same time as the co-operatives have come to handle the major part of all animal products brought on the market they have also had to undertake the task of seeing that the demand in various locations is regularly met and that prices are kept as stable as possible. This is done, in the first place, by the holding of stocks to equalize seasonal fluctuations; in the second place, the national branch organizations provide for merchandize to be transported from one location to another and also undertake exports or imports, as the situation indicates. During the Second World War and the years immediately following, the co-operatives were thus able to fulfil important tasks in connection with the implementation of the rationing system. Moreover, it was largely thanks to the distribution apparatus developed by the co-operatives that, for example, milk for consumption never had to be rationed in Sweden during all the war years. Also, in Sweden, the farmers' co-operatives, on one hand, and consumers' co-operatives and private retail trade, on the other, have concluded general agreements defining the limits of their respective fields of activity. These stipulate *inter alia* that collection and processing as well as wholesale marketing of agricultural products are referred to the farmers' organizations while retail distribution is referred to the consumers' co-operatives and private retailers.

In both countries the agricultural co-operatives have come to wield very considerable influence in the vital negotiations between farmers and State authorities concerning price and production schemes. This has been one of the means which has enabled them to secure satisfactory prices for the farmers and to stabilize production of important food items. But at the same time it has implied an obligation for the co-operatives to consider consumers' interests and to maintain stipulated prices also when world prices are higher. Another way has been the reduction of the costs of marketing. Guided and encouraged by their central organizations the individual co-operatives have consistently striven to increase efficiency in the collecting, processing, and marketing of foodstuffs. Small and obsolete dairies and slaughterhouses have been closed or disposed of, larger ones have been modernized and new ones constructed in accordance with the latest technical requirements. In the vicinity of the greater cities large co-operatives have been formed in order to ensure the regular supply and distribution of milk. Obviously, the increased financial resources of the reorganized co-operatives have greatly facilitated the undertaking of these various rationalization projects.

The extremely strong position long held by the *Finnish* agricultural co-operatives largely provides the explanation why they have been able to weather the violent changes during the last two decades without major alterations in their structure or line of activities. In the first instance the agricultural crisis about 1930 struck the co-operative village banks a serious blow when debtors began defaulting on their payments, and the government had to come to their support. Obviously, farmers' co-operatives also met with serious difficulties, but on the whole it proved possible, with the assistance of the State, to establish satisfactory arrangements for price stabilization and marketing of farm products. The most important measures adopted were a duty on imports of rye and export subsidies for dairy products, introduced in 1931 and 1932, respectively. The co-operatives were thus enabled to continue their steady development which was maintained even during the difficult war years when the co-operative organizations rendered an important contribution to the successful operation of the severe restrictions which were then necessary.

In *Iceland*, too, the world depression rendered the situation of farmers' co-operatives very difficult. The final outcome was that as from 1934 a price stabilization scheme was introduced under which the State sets the prices for meat, sheep products, and dairy goods. The central wholesale society (SIS) has retained its pre-eminent position in the marketing of agricultural produce and accounts for 86 per cent of total exports in this field.

As already mentioned, *Denmark*'s position as an agricultural exporter became extremely difficult when the agricultural crisis hit her in 1931. The long-established co-operative bodies for joint marketing, standardization of products, etc., were inevitably powerless against the rapidly declining demand for Danish products on the world market. One of the measures taken by the State was the centralization of exports or total sales of the most important agricultural products – butter, bacon, meat, horses, etc. – under the supervision of special government agencies. In some cases price differentiation was employed as a means of increasing farmers' incomes, home market prices being fixed at higher levels than the export prices obtainable. But even such measures could be only of limited effect because of the large quantities exported. Centralization was taken advantage of to obtain as high prices as possible from each separate foreign market. Due to their heavy dependence on exports, however, Danish farmers could not possibly be protected against the slump of world prices in the same way as their Norwegian and Swedish colleagues.

In these circumstances, the co-operatives carried on "as usual", with lower incomes and – especially the slaughterhouses – with lower production. An important strengthening of the movement took place in 1932 when all co-operative organizations joined their resources to increase the share capital of the new Co-operative Bank, which had been established 1925. In spite of the financially difficult situation they succeeded in making the Co-operative Bank large and strong enough to take over the main part of the extensive business in foreign exchange transacted both by export and import co-operatives. Subsequent government restrictions, however, placed all dealings in foreign exchange under the control of the National Bank, and the farmers' organizations were thus deprived of the possibility of utilizing their powerful position as chief exporters and holders of foreign currency. The agricultural co-operative organizations collaborated closely with the authorities in the implementation of export regulations and domestic marketing schemes. The co-operative leaders had seats on the national export committees and on the whole the administration of the schemes was placed with the agricultural organizations, dominated by the co-operatives. The regulations were upheld essentially unchanged during the Second World War in order to ensure satisfactory food supplies for the population, the co-operatives retaining their previous role.

As for the post-war period, the general relaxation of economic controls in the last few years has also had its effects upon the Danish regulations outlined above. The State export committees were abolished in 1950. To replace them the agricultural co-operatives and the general farmers' organizations, acting in unison with private exporters, established a number of large export organizations of their own for the purpose of maintaining the centralization of exports in the interest of all Danish farmers. Their activities do not cover sales on the home market.

In the other four countries policy has largely been determined by the overwhelming importance to agriculture of the domestic market. The general line followed in recent years has been to determine agricultural prices by agreement between the State and the farmers' organizations, taking into consideration farmers' incomes and consumer prices as well as the desirability of influencing agricultural production in one or another direction. In negotiating these agreements the agricultural co-operatives play a decisive role alongside the national farmers' organizations. The co-operatives have in this way obtained a position at the centre of influence with respect to agricultural conditions.

In all the Northern countries agricultural co-operatives are today strongly centralized as far as the marketing of the principal products is concerned. Democracy is fully preserved inasmuch as members still elect their leadership according to traditional procedure. With the development of organizations on a national scale and the growing complexity of problems encountered it is, however, inevitable that the necessary initiative and planning has increasingly come to rest with a relatively restricted group of leaders. This applies to local co-operatives, some of which have grown into large-scale enterprises with a high degree of centralization as compared with the smaller units of former years. And it applies to the national organizations, the establishment of which has been motivated primarily by the need for taking up new tasks rather than by any desire to take over the functions already performed by the local organs.

In both cases the question is involved of the growing distance between the individual producer and his organization. The importance of this problem and the resulting need to bring about closer contact between the organizations and their rank and file members and to keep the latter abreast of the work of the co-operatives has been increasingly recognized. A many-sided set of arrangements has been introduced to meet this situation. They include district meetings for the election of representatives to the co-operative assemblies, the appointment – in several of the countries – of special officials to foster contacts with members and, in general, expanded activities in the fields of education, information, and propaganda.

See also Co-operative Education, pp. 230- 231.

If centralization as a general trend is common to all five countries, there are still differences of degree. On the whole, the tightening of the organizational structure has gone further in Norway and Sweden than in the other countries, a result which must be viewed against the sweeping changes in the co-operative set-up carried out during the 'thirties in the former countries. In Denmark, with its early development of central collaboration among co-operatives, centralization has been somewhat less marked and there has been a certain disinclination on the part of farmers to delegate too much power to the central organizations. It is undeniable that this aversion to measures of centralization has in some cases hindered the prompt undertaking of desirable reforms. As an example may be mentioned the rather slow progress made in reducing the number of small dairies and concentrating production on larger and more efficient units.

PRESENT STATUS

In all five Northern countries the farmers' co-operatives today occupy a position of dominating importance to agriculture and must be considered an integral part of the economic structure. In the following paragraphs an attempt is therefore made to outline their present role.

The co-operative dairies everywhere dominate the processing and marketing of milk, accounting for no less than 90 per cent or more of all milk delivered to dairies. Nonetheless, only a rather modest percentage of Norwegian and Finnish farmers have joined the co-operative dairies, but this apparent contradiction is explained by the fact that many small farmers, especially in the northernmost areas, have no cows at all or a production which suffices only for their own consumption.

With respect to the marketing of other products the role of co-operatives is generally less outstanding than in the dairy business; only the Danish bacon factories and the Norwegian meat and pork organization command a comparable proportion of total production. The Swedish slaughterhouse organization is, however, very extensive and handles about 75 per cent of total sales of pigs, cattle, etc. The Finnish co-operative slaughterhouses account for one-third of total slaughterings and Danish co-operatives for the marketing of cattle account for a similar proportion of all cattle sold. The co-operative egg societies dominate the market in Norway and Sweden while in Finland they handle almost one-half and in Denmark one-third of total turnover, in keen competition with private enterprise. Mention may finally be made of the marketing organizations for poultry and for fruit, which are of considerable importance in Denmark, for furs, especially in Norway, and for such products as flour, seeds, potatoes, sugar beets, etc.

Feeding-stuffs and fertilizers are major items in co-operative purchases of agricultural necessities but against a background of rapid mechanization also machines and other implements have in recent years acquired increasing significance. In Sweden about 65 per cent of total turnover in fertilizers and 55 per cent of feeding-stuffs are handled through the co-operatives which also account for 65 per cent of sales of cereals. Finnish co-operatives account for 65 per cent of total trade in fertilizers and 60 per cent of feeding-stuffs. The corresponding Danish figures are about 40 per cent and 50 per cent, respectively. In Norway there are wide local variations, the co-operatives dominating in some localities, private undertakings in others.

On the whole, Northern agricultural co-operatives are rather highly specialized in comparison with similar organizations in most other countries. The farmer has to join several separate societies in order to dispose of his different products and to obtain his various requirements. Still, the extent to which specialization has been carried through varies somewhat from country to country. Denmark has gone farthest in this direction, with separate societies for the marketing of pigs (bacon factories) and of cattle, and special poultry slaughterhouse societies; purchasing societies are likewise usually split up in independent fertilizer societies, feeding-stuffs societies and – more recently – machine purchase societies and machine stations. In Norway and Sweden specialization has not been carried so far and in Finland there is no specialization at all among purchasing societies; as already mentioned the rural SOK consumers' societies supply their members also with feeding-stuffs, fertilizers, machinery, and other farming necessities for which purposes they are affiliated to specialized wholesale societies. On the whole, Icelandic conditions are very similar to those found in Finland.

Here butter is being packed for export in a Danish co-operative dairy. The churn in the background is sprinkled with cold water while in operation to maintain desired temperatures.

*Norwegian fisher-
men co-operate
on a wide scale.
The majestic
Lofoten range
furnishes the
background to this
co-operative fish-
meal factory.*

Fishermen's Co-operatives

The *Norwegian* fishermen's co-operatives deserve special mention among the Northern organizations of this category. Not because the fishing industry is unimportant in the other countries or co-operatives unknown there. But they are of modest size compared to the well-developed organization in Norway which has greatly benefited the Norwegian fishermen who comprise a large and important section of the population.

Until the end of the First World War there was hardly any co-operative marketing of fish in Norway; fishermen generally had to market their haul through the local fishmonger who was also their grocer and general merchant and, in many cases, their financier as well. With failing markets the situation deteriorated steadily during the 'twenties until, in 1926, a group of far-sighted fishermen banded together to found the Norwegian Fishermen's Association as a sort of trade union for the promotion of fishermen's interests. The principal solution advocated was the establishment of co-operatives for the marketing of fish and the purchase of nets and other tackle.

The Association soon attracted a strong following and today it includes practically all Norwegian fishermen. Co-operative marketing societies established in the following years introduced an arrangement by which the fishermen contracted to deliver their catch at a preliminary price to the society which then would market the fish and, after deducting costs, pay the fishermen the balance in their favour. But progress still proved too slow and in 1929 special legislation, enacted with the approval of the spokesmen of the Association, gave to the co-operatives the exclusive right of selling herring to wholesalers. By later enactments this privilege was extended to include other species so that today, thanks to this legislative intervention, the co-operative marketing societies dominate the Norwegian fish market. Moreover, they established herring-meal factories and factories for the salting and processing of codfish, etc., and in several fields have developed their own export organizations. Finally, special co-operatives have been formed for the purchasing of fishing tackle and other necessities.

Due to the fact that these co-operatives have, almost from their start, been based upon legislation, they clearly occupy a somewhat special position among the Northern co-operative organizations, although it may be noted that their form of operation is rather similar to that employed in the Norwegian agricultural co-operatives since their reorganization in the 'thirties. But if the system has largely been initiated "from the top", it still remains true that the organizations conduct their business according to co-operative principles. And, it may be added, under this influence fishermen have developed a far more positive attitude to the co-operative movement in general; this is reflected in the very considerable number of fishermen who have joined the consumers' societies in recent years.

On the other hand, it may be plausibly argued that what has really happened is that the State, in undertaking to support the fishing industry, has merely imitated and followed up the technique of the co-operative movement. In any case it can hardly be denied that this support has been rendered in a rational and effective way.

In the other Northern countries fishermen's co-operatives play a far more limited role.

Since the middle 'twenties, *Danish* fishermen, too, have made considerable progress in the co-operative marketing of fish, although it has proved somewhat difficult to retain a stable members' interest under changing market conditions. Although the societies have never been given any State support they have persisted and today, organized in a national association, they form a special branch within the co-operative movement. Some 20–25 per cent of the total quantity of fish caught is marketed through the co-operatives, the major part through a national co-operative agency.

Very few *Icelandic* establishments in this field are organized on a co-operative basis. However, many boat owners are organized in purchasing, marketing, insurance, and other co-operative societies. In the last ten years, moreover, a growing number of co-operatives have been established for the processing of fish products.

In *Sweden* the fishermen's co-operative movement is making rapid progress. On the east coast the greater part of the catch is marketed through the fishermen's marketing associations which in many cases have received authorization from the government to act as sole buyers of the Baltic herring landed within the territory of each association. At the same time most of these associations also function as purchasing societies for fishing tackle for their members. On the Swedish west coast co-operatives are as yet of limited importance, although several marketing associations have been established within recent years.

Co-operative credit societies are a familiar sight in the Finnish countryside, where they have played an important role in the modern development of agriculture.

Co-operative Credit Institutions

It is only in three of the Northern countries, namely Denmark, Finland, and Sweden, that co-operative credit is of major importance. By way of a brief characterization it may be said that Danish institutions in this field deal almost exclusively in long-term credit, where it is dominant, while the Finnish movement is primarily concerned with short-term personal credit, although long-term real estate credit is also important. Swedish co-operative credit institutions likewise grant both short-term and long-term credit, but are of smaller scope and wholly confined to agriculture. In Norway co-operative credit plays only an insignificant role, the banks, savings' banks and State mortgage institutions commanding the field. In Iceland, too, co-operative credit institutions are but of small importance.

In *Finland* the co-operative credit societies have been vital to the modern development of agriculture and form an integral part of the co-operative movement. The background for their creation was the lack of an adequate credit system which entailed that farmers in arrears were in many cases obliged to pay unreasonable interest charges and frequently had to give up their holdings at a heavy loss. In recognition of this state of affairs the founders of the co-operative movement from the outset incorporated co-operative credit societies as one of its central components. The societies were organized "from the top", the foundation in 1902 of a central society, the present OKO, being followed by the establishment of local societies, each of which was directly connected with the central institution. The first task falling upon the central society was to provide the local societies with funds to lend to their members – including farmers, other individual persons, co-operatives, and local authorities – in need of credit. The central society obtained these funds partly from the State, partly by the emission of bonds; it is now a joint-stock company owned and managed by the local credit societies, although the State retains a minor proportion of its capital.

The co-operative credit societies build upon the principles of the German Raiffeisen societies. Members of a society are usually jointly and severally responsible for its total obligations. The societies receive deposits from non-members as well as from members and have in this way reduced their dependence upon the central institution. Almost two-thirds of total loans are financed locally, only one-third being furnished by the central society. Loans are partly granted as short-term and medium-term credit, partly as long-term real estate credit. Accommodation bills are not used, but the cheque system is of great importance. The societies have administered the main part of the large State agricultural loans granted especially after the Second World War and these loans have in the last few years comprised 30–40 per cent of their total loans. This is a special Finnish feature. In the other Northern countries the comprehensive State loans for various purposes, notably agriculture and housing construction, have been granted directly to borrowers by the authorities.

The co-operative credit societies dominate Finnish agricultural credit which, inversely, accounts for more than one-half of their total volume of business. However, the societies also finance considerable activities outside agriculture and are the principal monetary institutions in many rural districts.

While the credit needs of Finnish agriculture were met by establishment of the credit societies as a step in the general growth of the co-operative movement, it is characteristic of developments in *Denmark* that this problem had, by and large, been solved thirty years before the emergence of other forms of co-operative enterprise. This was accomplished by the foundation, starting around 1850, of credit associations – co-operative societies of real estate holders who raise long-term loans against first mortgage security in their property and against joint responsibility. This first-class security has been one essential reason for the favourable borrowing terms obtained. Another main reason is found in the method by which the credit associations obtain their funds, i.e. the emission of fixed-interest bonds which are today the most important securities on the Danish capital market. Contrary to the Finnish credit societies the Danish credit associations have never received any funds from the public and only in special cases has the State undertaken to guarantee payments of interest.

The credit associations, together with the later second mortgage associations (similar except that bonds issued are secured by second mortgages), have contributed powerfully to assure agriculture the necessary capital. It was largely due to them that, during the last two decades of the 19th century, Danish farmers were enabled to carry out the far-reaching re-orientation of production from grains to animal husbandry which involved the partial industrialization of farming. But beyond this, these institutions have been of fundamental importance to urban housing construction, since also urban real estate holders have their own credit associations.

The co-operative character of Danish credit associations is obvious. Due to the special legislation regulating their organization and operation, however, they are viewed rather as semi-public institutions and neither administratively nor personally are they connected with the other branches of the co-operative movement. Neither do they - as is the case with the Finnish credit societies – grant loans to co-operatives except bonded loans in the real estate property of the latter. Otherwise, the commercial banks and savings' banks have been the main financiers of the Danish business community. The co-operative organizations – producers' and consumers' co-operatives – have established their own central bank, the Co-operative Bank already mentioned, which has concentrated to a great extent upon the financing of co-operative enterprises. The establishment of co-operative credit societies – along lines very similar to those followed in Finland – was begun in the years after 1914 but has never attained major proportions. There are at present about seventy societies which receive deposits and grant short-term loans to members, operations being on a rather modest local basis.

The *Swedish* co-operative credit institutions are concerned solely with agriculture and are intimately related to the other farming co-operatives. In the first place, they include ten mortgage associations which exclusively grant long-term loans against security in real estate property; the associations receive their funds from a central bank which emits bonds. In the second place, they include an organization of agricultural credit societies, for short-term and medium-term credit, which are affiliated with provincial central societies and these again center around a national institution, the Agricultural Credit Society of Sweden. Loans are primarily for current operations and the funds derive mainly from deposits, both from members and from non-members. While the mortgage associations are based upon the unlimited joint responsibility of members, the joint responsibility in the agricultural credit societies is of limited character only; moreover, it is interesting to note that the former provide a significant exception to the principle of "one member – one vote", since the larger debtors have several votes. The State has provided some support to the agricultural credit societies by making available a basic fund of State securities, both in the central and in the provincial societies.

Apart from the institutions mentioned, however, the financing of agriculture and the farmers' co-operative movements in Sweden and Denmark, and even more widely in Iceland and Norway, has in great measure been undertaken by commercial monetary institutions. Excepting Finland, it is true to say that the co-operative movements in the Northern countries have not been based upon co-operative credit enterprises as a starting point and key component, as is the case in several other countries.

Co-operative Education

One of the "minor" Rochdale principles lays down that a proportion of the annual surplus of a co-operative should be set aside for educational purposes. While the idea originally was to promote general education, elementary schools being still rather primitive a century ago, the principle today is interpreted as referring mainly to co-operative education.

There can be no doubt that the early and successful development of the co-operative movement in the Northern countries was in no small degree due to the relatively high level of education. Although particular mention is traditionally – and rightly – made of the folk high schools in Denmark and their signal contribution to the raising of the educational standard of Danish farmers, it is probably true to say that on this score all five countries have enjoyed a considerable advantage over the co-operative movements in most other parts of the world.

This fortunate state of affairs, however, also had the less desirable effect that educational work was for many years largely neglected, Finland being the outstanding exception to this general statement. It was only in the 1920's that there was a gradual recognition that something was wanting: Contacts between members and organizations were weakening and the younger generation did not view the co-operatives with the same intimate understanding and appreciation as did their fathers who had known and participated in the movement since its first frail and hopeful beginnings.

Starting with this re-orientation, the co-operatives have since developed educational programmes which aim at a strengthening of the bonds between members and co-operatives by promoting an understanding of the basic co-operative ideas and by stimulating interest in co-operative activities. Thus, at the present time most of the central organizations, of consumers' co-operatives as well as farmers' co-operatives, operate more or less comprehensive educational programmes. The means employed are manifold and include publication of periodicals, pamphlets and books, showing of films, the sponsoring of correspondence and other courses, study circles, and lectures. The interest of members in these various arrangements is highly variable and continuous efforts are made to devise new, attractive and efficient methods.

Furthermore, all the central organizations of consumers' co-operative societies have their own schools, mainly devoted to the theoretical training of their employees. In Finland, Norway, and Sweden also the agricultural co-operatives have established schools, open to young farmers as well as to. co-operative employees. The establishment of such a school was considered particularly necessary in Sweden in view of the very rapid growth of the farmers' co-operative movement during the 1930's. It should be added, however, that in all the Northern countries there would appear to be general agreement among co-operators that a broad education of the future rank and file is essential in preserving active member-interest in the work of the co-operative societies and organizations and thus also in the continued healthy growth of the movement.

Of equal importance, however, is the exchange of experience among the societies and the advice and guidance in operational and administrative matters furnished to the local co-operatives who obviously cannot master all the technical, economic, and legal problems encountered. From a relatively early date the central organizations formed by the consumers' movement have given such assistance to their local affiliates. The same applies to the agricultural co-operatives in Finland and – to a certain extent – also in Denmark. For a long time, however, such services were not thus available in Norway and Sweden, with the result that the management of local units found it difficult to undertake improvements and tackle those wider tasks which changing conditions imposed. The subsequent reorganization of the agricultural co-operatives in these two countries made it both necessary and possible to amend this situation.

In all the Northern countries there are today more or less developed programmes providing counselling and supervisory services to the societies. Numerous experts are occupied with this work which also includes the preparation of standard statutes, recommendations for operations and bookkeeping, as well as organizational and legal advice. Moreover, both central branch organizations and the top co-ordinating organs prepare statistics and furnish technical and economic information; also research is undertaken. Several organizations operate special units for the drawing up of blueprints for building construction and of plans for the equipment of premises. Separate departments, finally, undertake auditing, comparative operational analyses and investigations with a view to rationalization within the enterprises.

Evaluation of the Co-operative Movement

In general, the basic purpose of all co-operative undertaking has been to strengthen the economic position of smaller or larger groups of people who for some reason or other felt themselves at a disadvantage. It may be consumers who were dissatisfied with the quality or cost of goods offered by retailers, or it may be farmers who could not obtain satisfactory prices for their products. Assuming that such persons are right in thinking the terms available to them unfair, that they are capable of establishing and managing a co-operative enterprise and, finally, that they are able to raise the necessary funds – then obviously the co-operatives can strengthen their position and improve their incomes and standards of living.

These considerations also apply to the co-operative movement in the Northern countries. It is important to note, however, that Northern co-operators usually have not been destitute, poverty-stricken people at the very bottom of the social scale, but self-reliant men and women who either found co-operation a natural means of defence against outside influences which appeared unreasonable to them or who utilized the co-operative method to introduce economic reforms which were felt to be desirable. This general frame of mind is also reflected in the fact that co-operative enterprises have, in their wider effects, gone far beyond those relatively restricted economic tasks originally envisaged.

Co-operators and several outside observers maintain that by improving quality and lowering prices the consumers' societies have contributed significantly to the rise in living standards within the last couple of generations and that the agricultural co-operatives must be given main credit for the rapid development of agricultural production during this period as well as for the impressive increase in the standard of living of the small and middle-size farmers who dominate Northern agriculture.

While all of this may be true, it has to be admitted that it is impossible to render scientific proof of the extent to which co-operatives have contributed positively to the economic welfare of their members and, incidentally, also to that of the population as a whole. It might well be argued, and has been argued, that private enterprise under free competition could have served progress equally well in their stead. And as a matter of fact private enterprise has undeniably done so in many branches and in many places. Under these circumstances it will probably be wise not to give any narrow interpretation to the coincidence in the Northern countries of well-developed co-operative systems and relatively high standards of living.

In this connection it may be relevant to point out a basic contrast between the interests of consumers' and producers' co-operatives: Generally speaking, attempts by agricultural co-operatives to improve the conditions of farmers by obtaining higher prices implies higher prices to be paid by consumers. This issue inevitably emerges in any country where both types of co-operatives exist, although it may vary in form and importance. This holds true also with respect to the Northern countries.

In Denmark and Iceland, as well as within the rural group of Finnish co-operatives, the problem has never resulted in serious disagreement, mainly because the bulk of members are farmers affiliated to both categories of co-operatives. The Danish consumers' societies and the farmers' seed-growing society have even succeeded in establishing a unique instance of direct contractual business relations between buyers' and sellers' co-operatives, providing for annual negotiations to determine prices. The latent conflict of interests has come more to the fore in Norway and Sweden, partly as a natural consequence of the fact that here the home market is of such decisive importance to the farmers. The urban group of Finnish consumers' societies have found themselves similarly at odds with the farmers' co-operatives. It should be added that nowhere have the two groups of co-operatives been in a position to determine, independently, the prices of basic food items; outside competition and State intervention have imposed effective limitations upon the bargaining possibilities of producers' as well as of consumers' organizations.

On the positive side, mention should be made of the co-operative contribution to rationalization. By improved planning and operation, both producers' and consumers' co-operatives have continuously striven to reduce costs of processing, transportation, and distribution; through the forces of competition these advances have redounded to the benefit not only of co-operators, but of other groups as well.

It is beyond dispute that the various producers' and consumers' co-operatives today represent a very considerable concentration of economic power which gives them a strong position vis-à-vis other organizations as well as the State. Divergent points of view are found

233

with respect to the question how this strength, and the way it is utilized, fit in with the interests of the community as a whole. By way of general comment it would appear true to say that experience has shown the co-operative leaders to be sensible negotiators who are also mindful of the interests of other groups. Another matter is that the co-operative organizations will undoubtedly proceed in their development toward increasing co-ordination and concentration of power, although democratic government by members will be maintained as a matter of course.

Whatever may be the final verdict as to the extent of the special contribution of the co-operative movement toward improved standards of living, there can be no doubt whatsoever of its importance to the cause of modern democracy in the five Northern countries. Together with the trade unions, the co-operatives are the outstanding representatives of the huge network of societies, associations, and organizations created for a host of purposes and resting mainly upon popular initiative. Since their start at a time of restricted suffrage and unequal representation, the co-operatives have been managed in accordance with democratic rules. By thus serving as "schools of democracy" for broad sections of the population they have made no small contribution toward preparing the ground for the subsequent introduction of full political democracy.

CHAPTER IV

FAMILY WELFARE

Background

One of the outstanding features of social developments in Northern Europe during the last two decades has been the gradual emergence of comprehensive family welfare programmes.

So far there is nothing new in the recognition of the family as the basic unit of Society. The novel thing is the growing conviction, now shared by practically all parts of the populations concerned, that Society should take upon itself the responsibility for safeguarding and furthering the welfare of the family with respect to a number of vital needs which, save for such intervention, would be met only partially or not at all.

The reasons for this change are clear enough. The rising standards in respect of housing, nutrition, clothing, education, leisure time activities, etc., which have been characteristic particularly of urban life in recent decades, have led to a widening gap between the general living standard of families with few or no children and of families with many children. This gap alone would justify public aid to alleviate the burden of families who, simply because of a large number of children, are forced to live under conditions considered sub-standard, the granting of such aid being based on ascertained needs, regardless of any opinion harboured by authorities as to the desirability of married couples rearing few or many children. However, with the growing practice of birth control a development was started which by its far-reaching consequences was to place the matter in a totally different perspective and to bring about a radical reversal of traditional attitudes.

From the last decade of the 19th century birth rates declined continuously for four decades. By 1921–30 birth rates had fallen from more than 30 per thousand to about 20 per thousand inhabitants, the lowest birth rate being reached in Sweden in 1934 with 13.7 per thousand. The net reproduction rate – a measure for future demographic development – which, if population numbers are to remain constant; must be 1,000, fell below this level in all the Northern countries except Iceland. In Sweden the situation reached a critical point in the early 'thirties when the net reproduction rate fell to 742 (in 1934); this was even lower than in France, the country in which the demographic development had already for generations been a cause of serious concern. A spirited public discussion ensued, the keynote of which was the unanimous fear of the social, economic, and military consequences of a steadily declining population and a consequential desire to find effective remedies against these threatening prospects.

In their important study, "The Re-population Crisis", which was published in 1934, the well-known Swedish social scientists Gunnar and Alva Myrdal stated their belief that the very foundation of the social structure was at stake and that prompt action was imperative. If the alarming population trend was to be reversed, the whole attitude of the community toward individual families would have to be radically changed. The Myrdals pointed at the very core of the problem in stressing that means must be found to enable families to have children without suffering undue resultant setbacks in their standard of living.

The magnitude of the problems involved made it clear that only governmental action could be of any effect. In the following years population commissions were appointed in Denmark, Finland, and Sweden to study the matter and submit recommendations for action.

The frame of mind in which these problems were approached in the North stands out typically in the terms of reference of the Danish Population Commission. They called for the formulation of a policy in harmony with the basic views of a democratic society, a policy which would counteract depopulation while simultaneously constituting a progressive step in social development towards better, healthier, and more secure living conditions for the population as a whole; they further stressed that the efforts to arrest the decrease in birth rates should serve also as a contribution towards a better adjustment of community and family life to the changed conditions of modern times.

This formulation brings out the characteristic double ambition of family welfare policy in the Northern countries since its inception and its contrast with similar measures in some other states, where attention has been concentrated on one issue: To increase population numbers. Admittedly, in the North, too, it was the decline in births which provided the stimulus for the inauguration of a family welfare policy and it was a principal aim of this policy to arrest and in some measure to reverse this development; but its demographic ambition has been modest, limited to the prevention of a long-term decline in population. Coupled with this quantitative preoccupation is a natural concern for the improvement of the quality of the population, and with passing years increasing emphasis has been placed upon this latter aspect. In this connection it is significant that the major family welfare programmes have been introduced only during and after the last war when demographic developments – due to the considerable increase in birth rates – no longer caused the same anxiety as during the early 'thirties.

The crisis of the family was viewed mainly as a broad economic problem affecting a large number of persons in very much the same way. The solutions envisaged consequently centered on such measures as could readily be administered in the form of uniform benefits and services and which would alleviate the economic pressure on families having many children, thereby tending to equalize the standard of living of these families as compared to that of families with few or no children. This policy, tantamount to a redistribution of national wealth and income in favour of children, was also well in harmony with the general feeling of social justice in the countries concerned.

The whole body of social policy has thus been pervaded to an increasing extent by family welfare considerations, the needs of the family having come to be accepted as the central issue with priority over all others. It would hardly be feasible or serve any useful purpose to take up for separate treatment the almost innumerable instances where programmes are influenced, more or less, by such considerations. In the following pages, however, an attempt will be made to depict the more important measures specifically aiming at the furtherance of the welfare of families with children.

The main direction and content of these measures will be readily evident by a glance at the headings of the sub-sections below. Briefly, their general purpose is to improve the conditions of life under which the young generation grows up and, intimately related to this, to lighten the economic burden borne by families with children. By now the programmes extend – directly and indirectly – to all essential aspects of child life: Health, housing, nutrition, education, and leisure, although their stage of development may vary between the various aspects as well as between the various countries concerned.

Programmes are of every kind and description, having been framed to meet a wide diversity of needs. In former years it was a subject of heated debate, particularly in Sweden, whether public aid should in principle be given in kind or in cash. Advocates of the former have argued that only by providing the assistance in kind could there be any assurance of its being utilized as intended. Adherents of the cash method, on the other hand, have protested that even assistance in kind might be misused in many cases, and have further stressed the educational importance of cash grants as a means of encouraging administrative responsibility in the families themselves. However, in the course of years this divergence of principle would appear to have lost most of its original sharpness, and in its stead has come a growing recognition that the real issue is not an exclusive choice, but rather a decision in each individual case as to the comparative advantages of one method or the other.

Today the question of giving aid in cash or in kind is no longer the main issue. It has been superseded by a practical distinction between collective programmes for the benefit of families and allowances or grants to the family household. Collective programmes comprise educational institutions, health care, day nurseries and kindergartens, maternal and child welfare centres, school meals, etc.; many of these schemes simply could not be replaced by cash grants. Grants to the family household may be given in various forms according to the circumstances: In some cases they are given in cash, e.g. general children's allowances, in other cases, e.g. housing rebates, provision of children's clothing, etc., they may be given in a form that channels consumption in certain directions which are considered desirable.

The concept of family welfare characteristic of the countries under review differs somewhat from the American approach. The extensive family welfare activities undertaken by voluntary agencies in the USA have for their background a general interest in family life from a sociological point of view. This interest has concentrated on the problems arising out of the relationships between the family members, problems which were greatly accentuated during the process of absorption of large groups of newcomers from abroad into the American urban communities. The individual psychological approach characteristic of American family welfare work has as yet only been practised on a very small scale in the Northern countries of Europe, although increasing attention is being given to this important aspect of family welfare.

It would perhaps be natural to infer from the preceding observations that conditions and developments with respect to family welfare in the five countries of Northern Europe present a uniform picture. This, however, would be erroneous. Sweden, which was the pioneer in introducing family welfare measures in this region, has since maintained her leading position in this field. It is in that country that investigation into the problems of family welfare has been most thorough and systematic, and Sweden has been the first country to establish a complete family welfare scheme, of which the most important parts were passed by the Riksdag in the first years following the Second World War. Her neighbours, although following a similar line of action, have lagged somewhat behind, in part due to their more unfortunate situation during the war years. The experience gained from the Swedish programmes has, however, been of great value to the other countries and extensive reforms have been undertaken which are gradually bringing their family welfare standards up to those enjoyed by the Swedish population.

Family Establishment

Marriage Loans

Already in 1938 *Sweden* introduced a programme of marriage loans to assist young people in starting family life on a sound economic basis and, in so doing, also to encourage early establishment of families; at the same time these loans were intended to counteract unreasonable instalment purchases of furniture and other household articles. The loans, which are advanced through the Bank of Sweden, are granted under a State guarantee but on a commercial basis. The annual interest is four per cent and repayment is normally required within eight years. Loans are granted up to an amount of 3,000 kronor, but their actual size depends on the amount which the borrower is deemed able to repay. The loan is given primarily for the purchase of furniture and other household articles, and the borrowers have to submit plans for their purchases. The scheme has attained considerable proportions, marriage loans being at present

239

granted to about 20 per cent of all newly-wed Swedish couples. As from 1953 also unmarried mothers may be granted such loans on similar conditions.

In *Finland* legislation providing for marriage loans up to 50,000 Finnish marks to persons under 30 years of age was enacted after the last war. The Finnish scheme differs from that introduced in Sweden in several respects. Thus, each loan is given almost entirely in the form of coupons entitling the holder to order a certain range of furniture and other household articles, only a minor part being paid in cash. Loans are granted free of interest and are repayable within five years, but for every child born repayment is suspended by a period of twelve months. At the birth of the third child one-fifth and at the birth of the fourth child one-half of the loan is written off; if a fifth child is born, the entire loan is considered repaid.

In *Denmark* no legislation on marriage loans has as yet been enacted. The problem has, however, been taken up, by the government Youth Commission which was appointed in 1945 to undertake a broad inquiry into the problems of Danish youth and to submit such recommendations as were deemed desirable. In its report the Commission puts forward proposals for marriage loans along lines somewhat different from those followed in Sweden and Finland. It recommends loans up to 3,000 kroner, the amounts being graduated in each individual case according to the applicants' amount of savings during the preceding two years in such a way as to favour persons of smaller means. The higher the savings in proportion to income, the higher will be the loan. The proposed rate of interest is only one per cent annually, the State paying the remainder of the interest as well as guaranteeing the repayment of the loan, which is scheduled to take place over a period of (generally) six years. A bill along these lines is pending in the Danish Folketing.

In *Norway* measures have been introduced on private initiative to counteract purchases on the instalment plan, which – although regulated by identical Scandinavian laws enacted in 1916 – are still considered an uneconomical method of borrowing. Marriage loans are under consideration but, as in Denmark, no legislation has as yet been placed on the statute books.

It should be added that in Sweden experience has shown that not all marriage loans are used to their best effect. It is therefore deemed necessary to combine the granting of loans with some kind of guidance as to the most efficient use of the money. In Stockholm and a few other cities efforts in this direction have been made through the appointment of advisers to assist the borrowers, and by means of permanent exhibitions, pamphlets, etc.

Shared responsibility is the theme of modern family living. In school kitchens Swedish school boys learn how to manage a home and prepare a meal....

Home Management Education

The measures mentioned in the following aim at providing present and future housewives with an understanding of economical home management and to equip them with the theoretical and practical qualifications requisite for their household tasks.

In all the Northern countries quite extensive programmes are today in existence. They comprise, firstly, domestic training for girls, and to an increasing extent also boys, as part of the primary-school curriculum and, secondly, more advanced instruction at evening courses and secondary-school courses for girls. The public interest in assisting

241

housewives to manage their daily problems is also evidenced by sewing centres, courses in food preservation, etc., which are sponsored by local authorities and directed by professional staff. More specialized training is available at a large number of colleges, some of which – especially in rural districts – are resident institutions. A few of these institutions train future teachers for this particular kind of work.

Instruction is given in the theory as well as the practice of the subjects. Whereas formerly it concentrated mainly on cooking, it has gradually been extended to comprise related subjects such as the study of merchandize, particularly foodstuffs and their nutrition value, economical housekeeping, and other aspects of domestic work. The courses, schools, and colleges are of every description, operated by the State, by local authorities or by private persons or agencies, but even in the latter cases they usually receive considerable grants from the State.

Although the general programmes follow a practically identical pattern in the five countries under review here, their present stage of development may differ. Features common to all of the countries are, firstly, that there is a strong interest in expanding present programmes which in spite of rapid development are still considered inadequate and, secondly, that progress is being retarded by the shortage of qualified teachers. Although strong efforts are being made to overcome this difficulty, considerable time will inevitably be required to make up for this shortage.

. . . in the same way that Swedish school girls do.

Pregnancy and Childbirth

A large variety of measures share the general intention to protect the welfare of mother and child during pregnancy, childbirth, and the period immediately following. These measures may form part also of a more traditional social welfare policy aiming to assist persons most in need of help. The demographic concern of the 'thirties, however, further underscored the general importance of these measures as a means of arresting the then prevailing population trends. They aimed at easing the burden which pregnancy and childbirth inevitably places upon a family, especially the mother, and were also meant to reduce as much as possible the waste of human life caused by infant and maternal mortality. Viewed against this wider background it was quite logical – and a step forward in progressive social welfare thinking – that all services introduced were in principle designed to be rendered either free of charge or at charges so small as to cover only a fraction of the actual costs – which in many cases are quite considerable.

Roughly, these schemes may be divided into two categories. The first of these includes measures, designed within the framework of a collective programme, to provide the mother with the services and facilities required by her situation; the second covers measures assuring her the necessary means to defray some of the expenses arising out of other needs resulting from that situation. The present section outlines measures belonging to the first group which is primarily concerned with the safeguarding of the health of the mother during pregnancy and confinement, and of that of the new-born child. A subsequent section will outline the programmes included in the See pp. 251–252. second category.

PRE-NATAL SERVICES

Considerable emphasis is placed upon the provision of proper pre-natal care, although the forms under which such care is provided vary.

In Denmark all expectant mothers, regardless of their economic circumstances, are entitled to three free examinations by a medical doctor and seven free examinations by an authorized midwife.

In Sweden and Norway pregnant women receive free medical examinations as part of the services provided by the maternal and child welfare centres spread all over the country. Although, owing to the shortage of public health medical officers and midwives, the Swedish organization has not yet been completely developed, about 60 per cent of all pregnant women now attend these centres, which – starting in 1938 – are established and operated by local authorities with State support. The services rendered comprise not only regular health control but also advice and instruction, including birth control; furthermore, prophylactics and protective medicine and foodstuffs are distributed to women of small means in need of them. The Norwegian set-up, although as yet of more limited geographic coverage, especially in the more remote rural areas, is very similar, except that the large majority of centres are sponsored by local health associations and not by municipal authorities.

In Finland a comprehensive programme, completed during the years 1944–1949, has been set up, providing for an advisory centre for free maternal and child welfare in every local district and a publicly appointed midwife for every five thousand inhabitants; practically all pregnant women are now registered at these centres which today number more than 3,000, or one for every 1,300 inhabitants. Similar centres are found in most of the larger Icelandic towns and today serve about 50–60 per cent of all pregnant women.

The need for a specialized organ to help women solve their various difficulties arising out of pregnancy has been met in Denmark by the establishment in 1939 of the Mothers' Aid Institution, and in Finland by Social Consulting Bureaus which, beginning in 1947, have been established by the Finnish Population League founded in 1947. The general purpose of these semi-official agencies is to offer personal advice as well as medical and legal assistance to all pregnant women, whether married or unmarried. In case an expectant mother should wish to have her pregnancy interrupted, they investigate the possibilities of obtaining a legal abortion. Where there are no such possibilities, the agencies provide guidance and financial aid to enable the woman to proceed with her pregnancy. Thus, they will assist unmarried mothers in obtaining an affiliation order requiring the father to contribute to the costs of confinement as well as to the maintenance of the child. These institutions also help the expectant mothers to obtain accommodation before and after confinement, either in private homes or in special maternity homes, and will undertake to find a foster home for the child, or

See Chapter VII, Social Security, pp. 470–471.

make arrangements for its adoption. They also sponsor courses in cooking, care of infants, etc., to which all women are admitted free of charge.

In Norway the activities of the maternal and child welfare centres previously described are supplemented by Maternal Hygiene Offices which, although private, are subsidized by the public. Their work is mainly educational, centering on health problems of pregnancy, infant care, sexual hygiene, etc.

PROTECTION OF WOMEN WORKERS

Within the framework of the general legislation designed to protect industrial workers special attention has been given to the safeguarding of women from the consequences of arduous work immediately before and after confinement. Enactments in all five countries aim at preventing women from working in certain industries for a specified period before and after childbirth, as well as at prohibiting employers in general from employing pregnant women at work which may be harmful to them or to the expected child.

In Norway and Sweden no employer may dismiss a woman employee on account of her betrothal or marriage. Furthermore, women may not be dismissed because of pregnancy and childbirth and are entitled to a maximum leave of six months; in Sweden this provision is, however, limited to women who have been working for an employer for a year or more. The most significant aspect of these provisions is probably not the purely legal one, important though this may be, but rather the recognition by Society that it is morally wrong to subject pregnant women to fear of dismissal. In Denmark, Iceland, and Norway women are partially compensated for loss of pay during their absence from work through the health insurance societies or (in Iceland) through the national social insurance system.

Provisions very similar to these rules are under preparation also in Finland and Sweden.

CONFINEMENT FACILITIES

A very important feature common to family welfare programmes in all five countries under review is the very low cost of confinement. With respect to the conditions under which confinement takes place there are, however, considerable differences.

Sweden presents the clearest picture as regards the provision by the community of confinement facilities. Since 1938 confinement is furnished practically free of any charge for all women. More than 90 per cent of all childbirths are now institutional, as against 10 per cent in 1920. The maternity institutions are operated almost exclusively by local authorities with State subsidies. A fee of one krona per day is considered equivalent to what food would have cost the patient at home, and for the majority of women that fee is paid by the health insurance societies. Midwifery services in the home are also provided free of charge.

In the other countries institutional confinements, although steadily increasing in importance, are less widespread. In *Denmark*, two out of every three confinements still take place in the home. Maternity institutions are partly public, partly private. Every woman of small means is entitled to the free services of a midwife and, if necessary, to medical assistance, all costs being borne either by the health insurance societies or, for non-members of these societies, by the public; the same applies if the medical doctor considers hospital treatment necessary. Unmarried mothers may enter one of the maternity institutions operated by the State free of charge.

See Chapter VI, Health and Rehabilitation, pp. 338–342.

About one-half of all deliveries in *Finland* are undertaken in special hospital wards or maternity institutions. The new county central hospitals under construction will, however, increase the present capacity considerably. Midwives are in attendance at most non-institutional confinements and less than five per cent of all births take place without any trained help attending.

In *Iceland* confinement services are provided free of charge to all women, the social insurance system defraying all institutional confinement expenses or granting a sum to meet the costs of childbirth at home.

Under present *Norwegian* legislation, the health insurance system provides for free midwifery services. In the capital and in provincial towns institutional confinements are preponderant, while the opposite holds true of rural districts.

It may be noted that in all the five countries private organizations receiving State support provide special accommodation for single mothers, either in maternity homes or with private families where they may stay for some months after confinement. During their sojourn mothers are given instruction in domestic work and child care.

Up in the sparsely
populated areas
of Sweden and
Finland midwives
often have to
work without the
help of a medical
doctor. With skis
her only means
of transport, this
midwife carries
a knapsack of
supplies, which in
Sweden includes
a portable nitrous
oxide "laughing
gas" apparatus.

THE RESULTS

Inasmuch as the improved health of mother and child and the reduction of the risks of childbirth are their principal purposes, the various measures outlined above have undoubtedly been of considerable importance.

Maternal mortality rates – the number of maternal deaths per 1,000 births – which in the decades up to the middle of the 'thirties showed no pronounced downward trend, have since then declined by more than two-thirds. Present rates, which in all of the countries are below one, rank with those of the United Kingdom and the USA among the lowest in the whole world. The most striking results have been obtained with regard to the former main cause of maternal mortality: Whereas puerperal fever in 1931–40 accounted annually for 74 deaths in Denmark, the comparable average for the last few years is six to seven, or only one-tenth of the former figure. This happy development is due both to increased hygienic standards and to the new anti-biotics (e. g. penicillin). It may be noted that this decline also continued through the difficult war years.

ABORTION AND ITS PREVENTION

In recent years increasing attention has been given to induced abortions as constituting a serious problem from a social as well as a demographic point of view. In Sweden cautious estimates, made prior to the expansion of abortion legislation in 1946, fixed the annual number of illegal abortions at 10–20,000, corresponding to from 8–16 per cent of the annual number of live births.

Comprehensive investigations into this problem were undertaken during the 'thirties, particularly in Sweden, in connection with the work of the population commissions. For centuries harsh punishment under the criminal law had been the sole mainstay of Society in its efforts to dissuade women from resorting to abortion. When the question was taken up for serious re-examination in the light of modern social thinking it became clear, however, that the reasons prompting so many women to this desperate course are primarily the serious economic and social difficulties involved by their pregnancy and that, by and large, the preventive effects of traditional prejudiced attitudes and severe measures had been negligible.

The broad attention focussed upon this issue paved the way for a general re-orientation of these attitudes of long standing. Provoked abortions are still subject to criminal punishment. While increasingly severe penalties are meted out to those third persons who perform such operations illegally, the law has, however, come to deal less harshly with the unfortunate pregnant women. Increasing emphasis has gradually come to be placed upon the elimination of the motives driving women to seek abortion; it has thus been one of the important factors underlying the demand for expanded aid, economic and otherwise, to pregnant women.

In certain cases, however, abortions are legal. Thus, they may in all countries be legally induced when indicated on medical grounds (grave risk to the life or health of the mother) or, except in Norway, when justified by eugenic considerations (insanity, imbecility, etc.). The same applies in cases where the child is the result of violence or threat of violence. Similarly, abortion is legalized where indicated by mixed social and medical considerations, i.e. in cases of chronic under-nutrition, exhaustion, attempted suicide, and the like, where the risk to the life or health of the mother is deemed to be as grave as in cases of sickness proper. On the other hand, abortion for social or personal reasons only is illegal. In Norway abortion may be legally undertaken solely when indicated by medical considerations. It is, however, recognized that present statutes are too narrowly defined.

The number of legal abortions has increased very considerably within the last 10–15 years; thus in Sweden from about 500 in 1940 to 5,300 in 1952 and in Denmark from about 800 in 1942 to 5,000 in 1952. These developments have given rise to concern and to deliberations on the official level of future policies in this field.

Several measures are specially directed at the prevention of abortion. As described above, the Danish Mothers' Aid Institution is at the disposal of expectant mothers with aid and advice to enable them to proceed with their pregnancy in the many cases where it is not possible to meet the woman's request for an induced abortion. Since 1945, a number of urban communities in Sweden, including Stockholm, have on an experimental basis established counselling centres subsidized by the State to render advice and aid to pregnant women who seek to have their pregnancy broken off. The centres are directed by medical doctors assisted by women social workers; they have proved highly successful, especially in the capital where about 10 per cent of all pregnant women seek abortion. Almost 50 per cent of the women who request an abortion reconsider and complete their

Straightforward sex education is considered essential at an early age. The course given in this Swedish schoolroom is taken by young pupils all over the country.

pregnancy. Similarly, on the initiative of social and other voluntary organizations in Finland, advisory centres have been established which function as casework agencies.

Apart from the above-mentioned casework activities which are intended to ensure the necessary help to expectant mothers who wish to have their pregnancy interrupted, the campaign against criminal abortions may be said to involve two main issues:

First, it should be emphasized that insufficient economic resources constitute the foremost reason for wanting an abortion. It is the experience of the Mothers' Aid Institution in Denmark and the corresponding Finnish institution that less than one-half of the women seeking abortion are unmarried. The majority are housewives who already have children to raise and who feel that the family budget cannot bear the burden of an additional member. It follows that all measures aiming at alleviating the cost of having children also help to reduce the requests for abortions.

But, second, even with substantial economic support there may still be numerous valid reasons why expectant mothers do not wish to give birth to their child. Experience has shown that ignorance of birth control methods is still surprisingly great, and sex education programmes have accordingly been undertaken on an expanding scale in all of the Northern countries.

Apart from this, however, the increasing understanding in all quarters of the population of the situation of the unmarried mother will probably prove to be one of the best weapons against induced abortions, especially those performed by unscrupulous quacks.

Costs of Childbirth

Through the various collective programmes described above, confinement costs proper have been reduced to a minimum for the major part of the population; yet the birth of a child still places a heavy strain on most family budgets. In all five Northern countries the recognition of this fact has led to the adoption of more or less extensive programmes designed to alleviate the costs of meeting basic needs of families in cases of childbirth.

The *Swedish* programmes for this purpose are quite complicated, comprising no less than three forms of assistance. In the first place, all members of approved health insurance societies are entitled to Maternity Aid, generally amounting to 125 kronor; second, non-members having an income below a certain maximum receive a Maternity Cash Allowance of 75 kronor. More than 92 per cent of all mothers are beneficiaries under one of these schemes. Finally, supplementary Maternity Grants are given, subject to a means test in each case, such grants usually being provided in kind: Improved diet, domestic assistance, contributions to the clothing of mother and child, dental care, etc., all within a total sum not exceeding 600 kronor (800 kronor in the cases of twins or more); approximately one-third of all mothers benefit from this measure.

Similarly, Finland and Iceland have special schemes providing compensation for the extra costs necessitated by childbirth. Introduced in 1937, the *Finnish* maternity grants were given to persons of small means, as defined by their taxable income, but since 1949 these grants have been allowed without reference to income. The grant, which is conditional upon the expectant mother visiting either a medical doctor, a midwife or a maternity centre before the end of the fourth month of her pregnancy, comprises a package with baby clothing and other child-care items, distributed just before confinement, and a lump cash sum, immediately after the birth of the child.

Iceland maintains a dual system. All women are entitled to a lump sum, 950 krónur, in maternity aid at confinement. Unmarried mothers also receive childbirth allowances running for three months, provided that the woman stays away from her job during that period and meanwhile does not receive any wages; for married women the allowance is further contingent upon a means test.

As for *Denmark*, all pregnant women qualified for membership in the health insurance societies (about 90 per cent of all women) are entitled to half a litre of milk daily for six months before confinement and one litre per day for six months after the birth of the child. Through the Mothers' Aid Institution needy mothers may receive clothes, perambulators, and other necessities for the care of the child.

Norwegian legislation in this field, dating already from 1915, is more limited in scope. It authorizes assistance to destitute mothers for six weeks prior to confinement and for six months after the birth of the child. Assistance is granted by the local authorities but, within certain limits laid down by the Ministry of Social Affairs, the amount is determined in each individual case by the county governor.

The supplies in this layette form part of the assistance given to all Finnish mothers by the State.

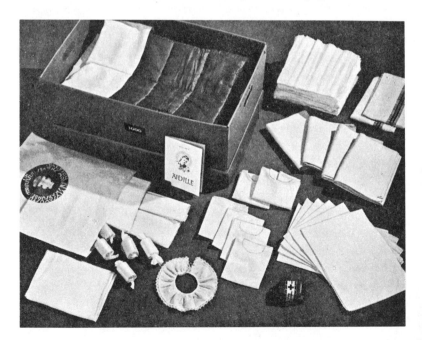

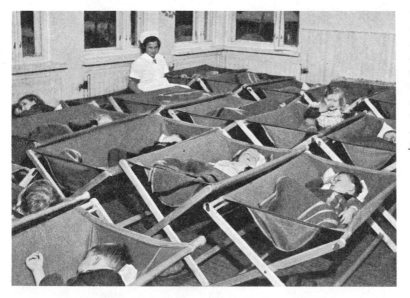

These youngsters are enjoying an afternoon nap at a Finnish day nursery, available to mothers employed at the well-known Arabia porcelain factory.

Collective Measures for Children

The measures discussed in the preceding two sections are designed to meet the needs of mother and child during pregnancy and child-birth, needs that involve considerable costs during a brief period of time. The main burden of parenthood is, however, felt during the long period, increasing in length within the last few generations, until the age is reached when the young become self-supporting. It is not primarily the initial cost of acquiring children, but the increasing cost of rearing them which in modern times has brought about the most significant and financially most far-reaching family welfare meas-ures in the Northern countries. In the present section mention is made of a number of programmes which aim to safeguard the welfare of children in various essential respects on a collective basis; in this connection special note may be taken of the increasing extent to which the schools, above and beyond their traditional functions, have been given an active part to play within the new social welfare pro-grammes. In the next section a survey is undertaken of the various *See pp. 267–272.* grants and allowances given directly to families to enable them to defray, without an unduly pinched standard of living, the cost of meeting the many needs of children, the satisfaction of which is after all, even today, still the primary responsibility of the family.

*At special centres
located all over
Sweden mothers
get free medical
examinations of
their newborn.*

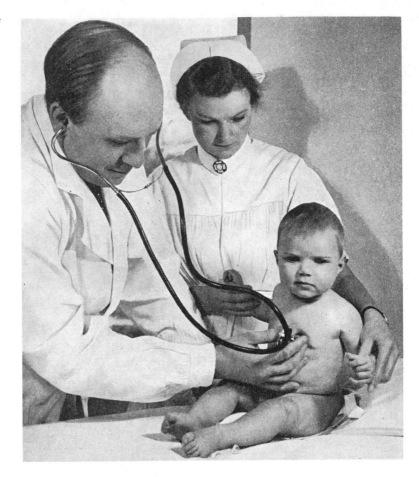

HEALTH EXAMINATIONS, ETC.

In *Denmark*, State subsidies have been given since 1937 to local
authorities appointing special public health nurses with the sole function of furthering infant health-improvement work. At regular intervals these nurses visit the home of every baby within their district
in order to examine its general condition of health, to guide the
mother as to its proper care and, where the child appears in need of
medical care, to urge the mother to see the family doctor. The programme, which is steadily expanding and now covers about 50
per cent of all infants, has been introduced in Copenhagen and in
most provincial towns, but as yet only in a small minority of rural

districts. The marked decline in infant mortality rates registered in the course of a few years in the districts where such public health nurses have been appointed is the best proof of the efficiency of this initiative. Nursing centres established by the Association of Charitable Societies in the capital and various provincial towns form a natural supplement to the work of the public health nurses. At these centres mothers may obtain free regular medical examinations and in minor emergency cases also medical treatment of their babies. Moreover, from their birth and until their seventh anniversary all children are entitled to a total of nine medical check-ups free of charge by a practising doctor. Three of these examinations shall take place during the first year. About half of all children are actual beneficiaries under this programme which, especially in the rural districts, has not as yet become sufficiently known.

Reykjavik, the capital of *Iceland*, has a similar arrangement with visiting public health nurses associated with the maternal and child welfare centre of that city.

As for *Finland*, there are about 1,000 public health nurses, the large majority of whom are active in the field, while the remainder perform

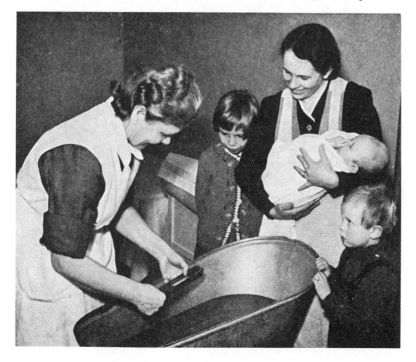

"Now this is the right bath temperature for your baby". The advice of visiting nurses is highly appreciated by anxious mothers.

255

educational and supervisory work. Their responsibilities include guidance on the health care of children, prevention of tuberculosis and other contagious diseases, as well as health care in the schools.

See above,
pp. 243-245.

The advisory maternal and child welfare centres previously mentioned likewise play a role of considerable significance in the efforts to improve the care of infants in the nursing stage.

In *Norway* and *Sweden* the duties of the advisory centres include periodical health examinations of children of pre-school age. About 90 per cent of all Swedish children under one year are examined; for the age groups between one and two years and between two and six years the percentages are 65 and 40, respectively.

The various measures outlined above have contributed greatly to the steady decline in infant mortality since the turn of the century.

INFANT MORTALITY RATES 1900–1951

(Deaths per 1,000 live born within the first year of life)

	Denmark	Finland	Iceland	Norway	Sweden
1901–10 . .	11.1	12.4	11.0	7.5	8.5
1911–20 . .	9.2	11.2	7.1	6.4	6.9
1921–30 . .	8.0	9.2	5.1	5.1	5.9
1931–40 . .	6.6	7.2	4.4	4.2	4.6
1941–50 . .	4.3	5.6	3.1	3.4	2.7
1951	2.9	3.5	2.6	2.6	2.1

It will be seen that the recent figures are only one-half or even one-third of the corresponding rates of a generation ago. They now rank among the lowest in the world. By way of comparison it may be noted that in 1951 infant mortality rates in the United Kingdom, USA, and New Zealand were 3.1, 2.9, and 2.3, respectively.

See Chapter VI,
Health and
Rehabilitation,
pp. 345-346.

In all the five countries vaccination against small-pox has for many years been compulsory and similar arrangements with respect to tuberculosis and diphtheria are under consideration.

In the schools, public as well as private, children are generally under health supervision, although this may still be lacking in rural districts of more remote regions. The school doctor's duties are preventive only: If one of the periodical examinations reveals a need for medical treatment the child is referred to the family doctor. Included in the tasks of the school medical staff is also the undertaking of annual examinations for tuberculosis, not only of the children but also of the teachers.

In Norway all school children have been entitled to free dental treatment since 1936. The Public Dental Service Act of 1949, which called for the establishment of a nation-wide public dental programme to serve the whole population, extended free dental services to all children and young persons between the ages of 6 and 18 years. At the present time schemes in operation cover more than four-fifths of all children and it is practically only in some of the northernmost rural districts that the necessary facilities have not yet been established. Similarly, Swedish legislation from 1938, as part of a national scheme, provides for free dental care to all children of school age. Although the programme is already in operation on a considerable scale, the shortage of dentists will make it some time before full coverage is attained, but approximately one-third of all school children are already under regular public dental care. As for the other countries under review, free dental services at school are maintained by the local authorities in some (mainly urban) areas.

See also Chapter VI, Health and Rehabilitation, pp. 353-354.

SCHOOL MEALS

Originally, the proposal to give children a meal at school sprang out of traditional social welfare motives and meals provided under the initiative of local authorities for quite a number of years in most of the countries under review were accordingly given only to children of impecunious families. Today, it is more or less generally accepted that the provision of a regular meal to each school child is desirable as one way of ensuring a balanced diet – by no means always assured by the adequate income of a family – and also as a way of reducing the work-load of housewives, particularly those having employment outside the home. Finally, its economic value, especially to families with many children, is obvious. The school meal is probably the most important example of that group of family welfare measures where aid is given in such a form as to guide the consumption of the beneficiaries in a direction considered desirable for the individual as well as for the community.

In this connection particular mention should be made of the so-called Oslo-lunch originating with the Norwegian doctor, Carl Schiøtz, who in 1937 urged that the traditional school meal of porridge or some other hot dish be replaced by a more balanced and vitaminous diet comprising bread with butter or margarine and cheese, liver paste, jam, etc., a glass of milk, and an apple, an orange or a carrot.

257

This proposal has been realized in many schools, not only in Norway where local authorities in many areas have introduced such meals, but also in the other countries of Northern Europe.

School meals are the subject of special legislation in Denmark, Finland, and Sweden. The Finnish scheme, dating from 1943, simply arranges for every pupil in the elementary schools to receive a hot meal free of charge during school hours, such a meal being served at a low price also to children in many secondary schools.

In Sweden, State subsidies have been granted since 1946 where school meals are provided to children regardless of their economic circumstances. Local authorities are, however, under no obligation to introduce the scheme and, although it is quickly expanding, it will take some years to be fully developed. At the present time sixty per cent of all school children in Sweden receive free school meals.

The Danish programme, enacted only in 1949, is very similar to that introduced in Sweden, although a revision undertaken in 1951 restricted its scope to the first six classes and to the six winter months. Lunches are now provided in most towns and also in a few rural areas, the total coverage being somewhat smaller than in Sweden. By and large, school meals have proved a definite success in urban communities whereas, perhaps naturally, enthusiasm has been somewhat more restrained in rural districts where the need for such a service has not been felt to the same extent.

Free lunches, consisting of a hot dish, milk, and sandwiches, are served to 600,000 school children in Sweden each day. Here we see young Lapps in a school dining-hall far up north.

"Ring around a-rosey, pocket full of posies . . ." Many different organizations, private and municipal, co-operate to give thousands of Northern children the opportunity to enjoy a healthful vacation in the country. Scene from a Finnish summer colony.

DAY-TIME CARE OF CHILDREN

Institutions in this field comprise three principal groups: Day nurseries, nursery schools or kindergartens, and leisure centres. The day nurseries are intended for babies, nursery schools and kindergartens for children of pre-school age, and leisure centres for school children in their spare-time.

The demand for such institutions is largely due to the need for providing satisfactory care of children whose parents are both gainfully occupied outside the home. Also many parents today consider it desirable for educational reasons that their children attend kindergartens or, at a later age, the leisure centres.

The programmes undertaken to meet these needs date back a considerable time; their establishment and development have until recently rested predominantly upon private initiative. Recent years have, however, brought about a considerable change in this state of affairs. In the first place, the increasing number of mothers employed outside the home and the rise in the number of births, especially noticeable after 1939, have in all of the five countries led to an acute shortage of accommodation in day-time institutions. And, in the second place, while there may have been a tendency formerly to view day nurseries, nursery schools, etc., somewhat as being on a par

259

Kindergarten supervisors deliberately keep in the background, so as to give the children free rein for their creative instinct. This view is from a kindergarten in Gävle, Sweden.

with traditional public assistance services, there has been a growing recognition of the general value, from an educational as well as from a social point of view, of these institutions as important components of a well-balanced family welfare programme.

In all of the Northern countries child welfare institutions of the categories indicated above today receive public subsidies, although to a varying extent. Also, a considerable number of local authorities have established their own institutions. In Denmark, where subsidies have been granted, although on a modest scale, ever since 1919, the State today defrays 40 per cent of operating expenses in institutions that meet certain minimum requirements, provided that the local authorities involved pay an additional 30 per cent of such expenses. Similar, although more limited, arrangements are in force in both Finland and Sweden, whereas in Iceland and Norway the local authorities not only operate numerous public institutions but provide sizeable subsidies for private institutions as well.

The result of this extended aid has been a very considerable expansion of accommodation facilities. In Denmark, for instance, a doubling has taken place since 1939 and at the present time the three groups of institutions have a total capacity of approximately 34,000, or 12 places per 100 children below 14 years of age in the urban districts. The corresponding figure for Sweden runs to about 35,000. It is interesting to note that while formerly nearly all of these institutions were situated in the towns some of the nursery schools

The quiet idyllic setting of a Swedish day nursery, also in Gävle. It is becoming more and more usual to house nurseries and kindergartens in one-storey buildings which fit naturally and harmoniously into their surroundings.

most recently established have been located in rural districts to provide for the care of children, especially during the busy agricultural seasons of the year; in Sweden there are already 110 such seasonal institutions.

In spite of the rapid increase, a very marked shortage is still evidenced by the long waiting lists found everywhere. In Denmark it is estimated that there is need for a tripling of the present capacity of day nurseries and a doubling of kindergartens; the situation in the other countries is much the same, although obviously there are differences of degree. The obstacles to an even more rapid progress are not only financial, but also due to the shortage of qualified personnel and building materials. A Swedish experiment arising out of this situation is the recent organization by local authorities of numerous "family" day nurseries, where only a couple of children are cared for at a time in private homes; such arrangements which are obviously non-institutional in character are mainly intended for children of mothers occupied away from home.

Together with the new programmes of public aid there has been a radical transformation of the type and working methods of the institutions. The kindergarten of the 19th century, which was based on private charity, often accommodated a very large number of children. Since neither the superintendents nor the assistants had any proper training for this kind of work, it goes without saying that these philanthropic depositories, while undoubtedly meeting a need, were hardly in a position to exercise any very constructive influence on the individual child. The comparable institution of our day will usually serve no more than 40–50 children, divided into groups according to age and development, and – at its best – will have an

....*pays off in the summer! This is a Danish youth club sponsored by Socialt Bolig-byggeri, a non-profit housing association in Copenhagen.*

adequate staff with a thorough knowledge of modern child psychology and pedagogics. However, in spite of the progress achieved conditions are still unsatisfactory in many kindergartens, both as to material facilities and staff qualifications.

In this connection it is worth noting that increased public aid has been accompanied by stricter supervision. In the first place, aid is only granted where, as already mentioned, the institution fulfills certain requirements as to facilities, staff, admission fees, etc. In the second place, in most of the countries under review no new institution may be established at all except with the approval of the competent authorities and such approval will only be given where certain standards are fulfilled.

The shortage of qualified staff having been noted as one of the main obstacles to further expansion, it remains to be mentioned that in almost all of the countries recent years have witnessed a rapid development of facilities for staff training. Numerous special schools have been established with public support to provide for the training of persons dedicating themselves to this work.

Children, of course, like to play in their own way. Hence the so-called junk playgrounds, started in Denmark and now popular in other Northern countries as well. These determined locomotive engineers live in Copenhagen.

HOLIDAY SCHEMES

Due to the length and severity of the Northern winter it is of special importance that the brief summer be utilized to build up the health of the children. As yet only partly developed, one of the most recent aspects of family welfare policy in the countries of Northern Europe has been the introduction on an expanding scale of holiday arrangements for children of small-income families, including particularly those who do not benefit at all, or only insufficiently, from the general holidays for wage earners decreed by law. The initiative has primarily rested with various voluntary organizations which have been active in this respect for many years. The State and local authorities have, however, to an increasing extent recognized the value of this work by granting financial support; in some of the countries special legislation has even been introduced to further such programmes. Here again Sweden has taken a leading part.

See Chapter II, Labour, pp. 94–98.

Holidays for children are promoted in various ways, either by reducing their cost or by the direct provision of vacation facilities. Most of the countries provide transportation to the vacation spot either free or at reduced rates. Since 1946 all Swedish children in families below a certain income level have been entitled to travel within the Swedish borders once a year against a nominal fee of 5–10 kronor, the mother being entitled to accompany her child, if under 10 years of age; a special feature is that it includes children in rural districts. In Denmark the railways carry all needy school children free, and in Finland the State provides transportation at a fifty per cent discount or, in case of need, entirely free.

Reduced or free transportation for children has considerably widened their possibilities of spending a holiday away from their homes and this, in turn, has greatly increased the need for low-cost summer accommodation. In all of the countries voluntary organizations and, in numerous cases, also local town authorities have for many years maintained summer colonies for children, especially those coming from families of small means. The number of such colonies is increasing at a brisk rate, in part due to the increased financial aid made available by the State. Particular mention should be made of Sweden, where a general scheme of State subsidies to children's summer colonies has been in operation since 1946; subsidies are also given to individual homes accommodating one or more children during the holiday period, such arrangements being specially favoured because of the lower cost and reduced risk of infection.

In Denmark it has been a custom for many years for farmers to extend invitations to poor children, particularly from the capital, to spend a free holiday in the country; as already indicated, transportation on the railways is in these cases provided free by the State.

"Don't forget to wash behind your ears!" Copenhagen parents bidding farewell to sons and daughters on their way to enjoy summer holidays on hospitable country farms. Transportation is provided by the State railways free of charge.

Grants and Allowances for Children

Even with the numerous services and benefits provided for under the various collective programmes described in the preceding section, children – and particularly, of course, when there are many of them – impose a heavy economic strain on most families under present-day conditions. To illustrate the order of magnitude of "child costs" mention may appropriately be made of a Swedish enquiry undertaken in 1948 according to which the annual extra cost of maintaining – on an undiminished family standard of living – a child aged one year was estimated at approximately 1,100 kronor rising to 2,900 kronor by the age of sixteen. These figures were based on the circumstances of a family with an annual income of about 7,400 kronor (exclusive of taxes). Although family welfare programmes have certainly not made it their purpose to reimburse families *in toto* for the extra costs incurred by having children, it has been their acknowledged aim to equalize to a substantial degree the living standards of large families and families with few or no children.

Among the first steps taken in this respect were those designed to raise the housing standards of families with many children. A whole series of enactments has been passed in the Northern countries for this purpose, notably in Denmark and Sweden. Since these measures are intimately tied up with general legislative programmes to further low-cost housing, this subject has been referred for a more detailed examination to Chapter V, Housing. *See pp. 299-302.*

Otherwise, the most common traditional method of contributing directly to the cost of children has been the granting of tax rebates by deductions from taxable incomes. It is by no means the aim of such rebates to provide even partial compensation for the expense of rearing children, but only to carry out the principle of equality in taxation since the rearing of children obviously affects the paying capacity of the family. In all the Northern countries, except Finland, such rebates, varying according to the number of children, the income of the taxpayer, and the locality where the family lives (capital, provincial town, or rural district), have long been the primary means of alleviating the cost of meeting current living needs of children. A slightly different system has been in operation in Finland since 1920. In recent years, however, tax rebates have in one country after the other been superseded, or at any rate outweighed in importance, by the introduction of massive schemes providing children's allowances for all or for large groups of children. It may be noted in passing that family wage systems on the classic French model have not, except for a transitory period in Finland, gained acceptance in these countries.

As for tax rebates it would not appear necessary to enter into the details of the varying schemes. Suffice it to state that while they may have functioned somewhat more equitably a generation or more ago, the steeply increasing progressivity of income taxes has brought about the obviously unintended result that the benefits obtained are today quite considerable for well-to-do families, but of practically no importance to low-income families who pay only small or no taxes at all, thus rendering the system of somewhat dubious value from a more progressive point of view.

Children's allowances proper are now taking the place of tax rebates as the principal means of achieving a more equitable spreading of the direct costs of having children over all members of Society. Since the distinction is primarily not between rich and poor, but between families with and families without children, it has been felt natural to extend, as far as possible, such allowances to all families with children. Existing tax measures and financial considerations have, however, in several countries motivated certain limitations in the present coverage of these schemes.

In addition to and independently of such general programmes, all the countries under review have more or less elaborate schemes providing for allowances to special groups: Children born out of wedlock, children of widows, etc. Unlike the general programmes, these special allowances cannot strictly be considered as family welfare measures, but rather as social security programmes since they aim to replace, not to supplement, the normal source of maintenance of the child, namely the income of the family bread-winner.

See Chapter VII, Social Security, pp. 437 and 470–471.

Among the five countries *Sweden* has been the first to take the consequence of the inadequacy and inequity of the old rebates system: In 1948 the State income tax rebates were replaced by general children's allowances financed out of current revenues. Tax rebates were retained in municipal taxation, but their discontinuance here, which took place in 1952, was of smaller significance since local taxes in Sweden are not progressive but proportional to income.

As from 1948 all Swedish children under 16 years of age, regardless of their economic circumstances, received a tax-exempt grant of 260 kronor annually; in 1952 it was raised to 290 kronor to compensate for the municipal tax deductions then abolished. The allowances are paid quarterly to the mother who is considered primarily responsible for the welfare of the child. A comparison with the figures previously mentioned will show that this allowance corresponds to almost 30 per cent of the minimum cost of meeting the living needs of an additional child. The combined effect of abolishing the previous tax rebates and replacing them by uniform allowances to all children was to favour rather substantially families in the lower income brackets and among these particularly families with many children.

In *Finland*, developments in this important field of family welfare present a more complex picture. General reforms aiming at assisting families with children were initiated in 1935 when the State income taxation system was revised. Besides the tax rebates found in the other Northern countries, Finland introduced a 20 per cent

269

surtax (increased in 1940 to 40 per cent) on those who did not support children or other relatives apart from a wife (or husband). Already in 1943 this system was replaced by another method which divides taxpayers into three different categories: Single persons are taxed according to a more severe scale than married people without children, and these in turn are taxed more heavily than families with children. The resulting tax-bill is finally reduced according to the number of children below 16 years of age.

Furthermore, the system of "family wages" has until recently played a considerable role in Finland. It was introduced in 1908 for elementary-school teachers and later extended to cover all public servants. The final step along this line was the enactment in 1947 of legislation according to which all wage earners received from their employers a wage increment in respect of every child below 17 years of age for whom they held responsibility.

However, the drawbacks of this scheme, which was mainly intended to strengthen a general policy of wage stabilization, soon became apparent. In the first place, it left out all family supporters who were not wage earners; in the second place, it proved difficult to administer. Consequently, it was replaced already in 1948 by a general system of children's allowances similar to that introduced somewhat earlier the same year in Sweden; in 1952 the allowances amounted to 14,400 Finnish marks, paid in quarterly instalments. The scheme is, however, not financed through taxation but largely by employers who now pay to the State a fixed proportion, four per cent, of total wage outlays instead of the previous wage increments. As for the effects upon the various income groups, the combination of existing tax rebates and uniform children's allowances places the higher income brackets in a more favourable position than is the case under the Swedish system.

Apart from the above-mentioned general schemes, a more limited programme of children's allowances for families of small means with many children (four or more) and for families with two children where the normal breadwinner is missing, has been in effect already from 1943. This so-called "family allowance" is not intended to contribute to the current living expenses of recipient families of modest means, but rather to ensure a lasting improvement of their standard of living by enabling them to consolidate and expand their basic economy. The allowance is therefore distributed in kind, mostly as children's clothing or bed-linen, seed or fertilizers, or even in the form of repairs of houses or sheds. At the present time approximately 80,000 families, or almost all large families in the country, are beneficiaries under this programme.

Norwegian and Danish children's allowances are less comprehensive in scope than the schemes outlined above.

In *Norway* children's allowances were introduced in 1947, but existing tax rebates were retained as in Finland and with the same effects. The annual allowance, which amounts to 240 kroner, is paid only in respect of every child after the first up to the age of sixteen, obviously a very important limitation compared to the Swedish and Finnish provisions. In 1951 the allowance was raised for large families by 100 kroner for each child, starting with the third; this increase was intended to offset the particularly severe effect upon such families of a simultaneous increase of sales taxes necessitated by the rising defence expenditures. If the supporter of the child is widowed, divorced, or single, the allowance is paid also for the first child; this applies also to orphans regardless of who the guardian may be.

In *Denmark*, too, a limited system of children's allowances and tax rebates is now in operation, although the criterion according to which the former are limited differs from the Norwegian rules. In 1949–50 a double reform was enacted by which tax rebates were increased at the same time as a graduated system of children's allowances, varying in amounts from 112 kroner to 44 kroner, was introduced. The general idea underlying this combined arrangement was that families should, as far as possible, receive the same benefit, regardless of income. In early 1953 the allowances were increased, particularly for low-income families. Hereafter, in Copenhagen the taxable income is reduced by 600 kroner for the first child, 700 kroner for the second and 800 for each following child under 16 years of age. Children's allowances are paid to all families having a taxable income below 16,000 kroner, the allowances being granted in full with 182 kroner for each child in respect of incomes not exceeding 5,000 kroner and reduced according to a sliding scale for higher incomes. The same arrangement, although with somewhat lower rates, applies to families living in provincial towns and in rural districts.

Icelandic programmes of this character comprise a general reduction of taxable incomes by 2,750 krónur for each child under 16 years of age combined with a system of family allowances paid to families for each child beyond the first. In the towns the allowances amount to 628 krónur for the second child, 942 krónur for the third, and 1,884 krónur for the fourth and every subsequent child; rural rates are 25 per cent lower.

The general programmes of children's allowances reviewed in the preceding paragraphs are indisputably the most important component of family welfare policy in Northern Europe today. Even against the wider background of social welfare provisions as a whole, they carry remarkable weight. This applies particularly to Finland and Sweden, where these allowances today account for about 25 and 18 per cent, respectively, of the total social welfare budget. The less comprehensive provisions in force in the other three countries naturally result in correspondingly smaller costs, but even here children's allowances today figure among the largest social welfare items.

The Welfare of Housewives

There is probably general agreement as to the vitally important role of the housewife, individually as the central figure of the family and collectively as the largest professional group. Yet it is remarkable that for a long time housewives were considered outside the scope of the increasing number of legislative provisions which aimed at safeguarding the welfare of the working population. It is only in very recent years that a spreading recognition of the unmitigated strain to which many housewives are subject – especially in large families of small means – has resulted in the gradual emergence of more comprehensive measures for the benefit of this group. Such measures are primarily designed to promote the rationalization of housework; second, to assure housewives of an annual leave from their daily duties and, third, to provide for the replacement of housewives temporarily incapacitated.

RATIONALIZATION OF HOUSEWORK

In the five countries under review housework is still carried out by rather old-fashioned methods in the majority of homes, at any rate when compared with the standards prevailing in the United States. This particularly holds true in rural districts which have long lagged behind in the development of such essential utilities as water supply, sewerage, and electricity. Thus in Sweden 62 per cent

of all rural homes still have neither running water nor adequate sewerage, while 17 per cent are without electricity. In recent years, however, rapid strides have been made to amend this situation. One main reason for this has been the increasing awareness of housewives as to the possibilities of easing their work-load by rationalization. Another reason arises out of the fact that ever more housewives are employed outside the home in full- or part-time jobs and that domestic assistance has become increasingly expensive and scarce.

The authorities are taking an active part in such efforts, but this is obviously a field well suited for the display of private initiative and, indeed, in all the countries we find numerous organizations actively engaged in this work by research, education, and propaganda.

To a large extent progress is clearly dependent upon the raising of housing standards in general, e.g. sewerage, central heating, hot water, etc. In this connection it is interesting to note that in Reykjavik the last two problems have been solved once and for all by the utilization of the hot springs situated outside that city.

A very important point is that of laundry. Until recently it has been an almost universal custom in Northern Europe for each family to wash its laundry without mechanical aid. A growing part of this hard and time-consuming work is now being undertaken outside the home by modern laundries operated either commercially or as a

273

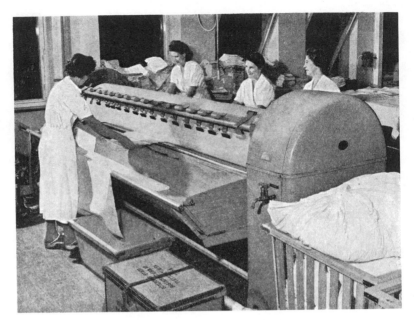

Many Northern housewives still sweat over wooden washboards and tubs, but laundry "automats" are being installed in increasing numbers under municipal and co-operative auspices. Here is the interior of a modern laundry in Stockholm.

community service. As for the latter it may be mentioned that since 1939 the Swedish State grants subsidies for the establishment of laundries all over the country where housewives may either deliver their laundry for washing or wash it themselves in modern machines under the supervision of trained attendants.

Specialized organizations have developed to meet the need for further scientific investigation into the problems of what may be termed "domestic science". Thus, in Denmark the National Council of Domestic Science and Household Economics (Statens Husholdningsråd) and in Sweden the semi-official research institution (Hemmens Forskningsinstitut) together with Active Housekeeping (an organ operating under the Price Control Board) have already for some years been working actively with household rationalization. Investigations into the economic aspects of domestic work and the quality of standard consumer goods have formed the basis for proposals to rationalize housework, which afterwards have been publicized by means of pamphlets, lectures, and radio broadcasts. This programme has been realized on an extended scale, especially in Sweden, and has further been followed up by a considerable improvement in kitchen standards: During the 'forties more than 450,000 well planned and well equipped modern kitchens were installed in Sweden, primarily in new houses.

There is also a growing movement, sponsored by co-operative and progressive business organizations, for a fuller and franker guidance of consumers on the quality of goods marketed. Especially in textiles, a field where consumers cannot undertake such an evaluation themselves, this movement has made considerable headway.

Besides rationalization, the above and similar institutions have also taken up investigations in the field of food hygiene and provide practical advice on this subject, followed up in some instances by measures of food control.

A more recent initiative has been the appointment of home management consultants who give lectures all over the country and organize exhibitions and competitions, thus promoting a general interest in the subjects.

Also, in 1946 a chair in home economics and in 1947 one in nutritive chemistry were established at the University of Helsingfors.

HOLIDAYS

Annual holidays with pay for wage earners have been on the statute books of the Northern countries since before the war. An annual leave of two or three weeks is today no longer a privilege for the few. The chief beneficiaries of such legislative provisions were, however, the male workers or single female workers, while housewives, even when gainfully occupied outside the home, very often benefited insufficiently or not at all from these schemes.

See Chapter II, Labour, pp. 94–96.

As in so many other fields voluntary organizations have also been pioneers here, for many years maintaining special holiday homes for weary housewives of small means. In recent years the public has, however, lent increasing support to such efforts.

In 1946 Sweden thus introduced a number of measures assuring a large number of housewives of an annual holiday. State subsidies are now given to holiday centres operated by voluntary associations; housewives who fulfill certain conditions as to income and number of children are also granted transportation once a year to holiday centres as well as to other holiday locations of their own choice against a nominal fee of 10 kr. In 1951 about 35,000 mothers received free transportation, the large majority going on holidays privately arranged. It might be added that many more were entitled to this grant. Since the lack of someone to take care of the children is often the main obstacle to a much needed holiday for the mother, the State and local authorities also grant subsidies to needy families to enable them to pay for domestic assistance or to have the children cared for outside the home during the mother's absence.

In the other countries such holiday arrangements have not yet reached the legislative stage although the State in some cases provides financial support to non-governmental organizations active in this field. Also, some large enterprises operate holiday programmes of their own. In Norway a private organization, "Norsk Folkehjelp", which receives subsidies from local authorities, maintains arrangements for providing housewives of small means with summer holidays, but the number of beneficiaries is still relatively unimportant. In Denmark, Finland, and Iceland the situation is very much the same, though it might be mentioned that a Danish scheme providing for greatly expanded State aid to voluntary organizations active in this field is at present under consideration.

HOME HELP SERVICES

It is a common saying that a housewife cannot afford to fall ill. Certainly, when she becomes incapable of discharging her tasks because of confinement or illness, it is realized how indispensable she is to the daily smooth operation of the household. In our urbanized industrial society only a small minority can afford a domestic servant. A striking picture of the declining use of domestic assistance is furnished by Swedish statistics showing that the number of domestic servants in full-time employment fell from 220,000 in 1930 to 96,000 in 1950. The moment the housewife becomes incapacitated, the large majority of families are faced with the question of her replacement, a problem which obviously becomes particularly acute where there are small children.

Some local authorities in large towns and some voluntary organizations have already for many years operated schemes, usually of rather modest scope, providing for assistance in such cases. *Sweden*, in 1943, was the first of the Northern countries to enact special legislation placing such schemes on a national basis. The Social Home Help Act contains provisions for subsidies to local authorities or voluntary organizations who recruit home helps, provided that certain conditions, particularly relating to the training of these persons, are complied with. Home help is specifically limited to temporary domestic assistance in critical situations such as illness,

When mother is ill, it is a reassuring feeling to know that a friendly home help will come to tidy up, cook the meals, and manage the household. Such help is available through local authorities or voluntary organizations which receive State subsidies.

childbirth, etc. The service is free for persons of small means, while others pay according to a sliding scale.

The scheme has proved highly successful and the supply of trained home helps has fallen short of the demand. In consequence, it has become necessary to take steps to provide for the effective training of a larger corps of home helps. Today, State subsidies are paid with respect to approximately 3,000 full-time home helps employed by the local authorities, including 122 towns, and the programme is steadily expanding.

Comparable *Danish* and *Norwegian* provisions date from 1949 and as in Sweden they have proved a success. Here, too, special training courses have been instituted to accelerate the expansion of the number of home helps to be able to satisfy the acute demand for their services. Finnish provisions in this field date from 1950 and likewise provide for considerable State subsidies to local authorities who establish home help programmes. Special training courses for such home helps have been in existence already since 1939.

Equal Access to Higher Education

Among the costs of bringing up children are the expenses involved in their schooling and higher education. To many families of small means, particularly those with many children, these expenses are a heavy burden; with respect to higher education it is, in fact, often of such magnitude as to constitute an effective barrier against the equal access to educational facilities for every youngster, contingent only upon his intellectual qualifications.

At the present time numerous measures designed to reduce such expenses have already been taken. In several of the Northern countries, however, much still remains to be done, especially in the field of higher education which, for economic reasons, is also today beyond the means of many young people in modest circumstances.

In all the Northern countries the free instruction provided in the public elementary school is still, as it has been for generations, the basis of the educational system. Nowadays pupils are also provided with the necessary textbooks and other materials required at public expense. In Finland the local authorities furthermore supply children of small means with clothing and other articles necessary for them to attend school; in rural areas where distances from the home are often considerable the public also contributes to transportation costs and, in remote Northern regions, even maintains free pensions for pupils who would otherwise be unable to attend school regularly.

As for secondary and high schools (grammar schools), the situation in Iceland is analogous to that of the elementary schools. In the other four countries parents pay a modest tuition fee (usually graduated according to income and not exacted from families of small means) and have to supply their children with books and materials; in Sweden, however, it is proposed to abolish the remainder of such fees in the near future.

Unlike conditions in most other countries, the universities and most of the other institutes for advanced education in the five countries offer their services either at a nominal charge or without any charge at all. This is obviously of great value as a means of opening up higher education to all qualified students, regardless of their economic resources. On the other hand, this is clearly not sufficient by itself, since students have to subsist during their long years of study and by no means all homes are able to mobilize the necessary funds.

A considerable number of scholarships are available for distribution to deserving students. The old universities, in particular, have for centuries disposed of considerable resources for this purpose. Also, in recent decades, there has been an expanding interest in the establishment of students' hostels where out-of-town students are given board and lodging at very low rates or, in some cases, even free. One of the oldest of these hostels is "Regensen" which was established in Copenhagen by King Christian the Fourth more than three hundred years ago and which houses more than a hundred students who have successfully passed their first two or three years at the University of Copenhagen.

Nevertheless, the rapid increase in the number of students at universities and other scientific colleges together with the steadily advancing rise in prices have rendered existing resources for aiding qualified but impecunious students clearly inadequate. To a certain extent students take outside jobs to carry them through, but at many faculties it is difficult to combine regular attendance with outside employment; such studies thus become more or less inaccessible to students lacking the necessary economic support.

Even less desirable, not least from the family welfare point of view, has been the widespread practice of students, particularly in Finland and Sweden, of taking up often quite considerable private loans to enable them to carry on their studies. Thus, in 1946 more than 50 per cent of all Finnish students financed their studies wholly or in part by this method. In many cases the obligations resulting from such loans (often contracted at high rates of interest) have obliged the borrower to postpone for years the setting-up of a family.

It is only within rather recent years that the question of establishing comprehensive unified scholarship programmes for academic students has been taken up for thorough examination and action. In 1939 the Swedish Riksdag passed legislation providing for such a scheme. Since then the scholarship programme has been extended step by step for academic students as well as for the pupils of schools for higher education. Some 30 million kronor a year are allocated to this purpose, and around 60,000 students benefit from the scheme. High-school pupils from rural districts who cannot live at home during their studies are granted substantial scholarships irrespective of their economic circumstances. Already since 1919 the State has granted study-loans free of interest to gifted students of small means.

In 1946 a system of State guarantee for private loans contracted by students was further added. In Finland, scholarship legislation to better the lot of deserving students of small means was enacted in 1948. Several programmes for the granting of low-cost loans to students have also been developed under State auspices in recent years. In Norway, a State Loan Institution to serve students of small means was established in 1947 and now grants loans at an annual rate of five million kroner, including one million kroner to students abroad; these loans are free of interest, repayment being scheduled to take place over a period of up to 15 years after graduation. The Danish Study Foundation, active for more than a generation, carries on similar operations although on a more limited scale. Icelandic programmes of this character centre on scholarships for studies abroad.

Conclusion

In the preceding paragraphs an attempt has been made to present the multifarious measures undertaken with the furthering of family welfare as their specific purpose.

When reviewing the large number of schemes now in operation these might appear to constitute a far-flung "system" of family welfare with programmes of general children's allowances as their basic component. And, indeed, it is probably true to say that almost every essential aspect of family welfare has been made the subject of more or less comprehensive action. Closer examination, however, leads to the sobering reflection that the "system", if such it may be called, is still far from complete. In the first place, there are considerable differences in the stages of development in the five countries, with Sweden still in the lead. Secondly, even where best developed not all the various programmes are as yet in full operation.

Having granted this it would, however, appear fair to conclude that in their entirety the measures undertaken in these five countries remain an impressive manifestation of the present-day will of the Northern peoples to protect by common action the basic unit of our Society: The family.

CHAPTER V

HOUSING

The Community and Housing

The historical background for the housing problem today, in the Northern countries as elsewhere, is the rapid growth of towns and urban districts which followed in the wake of advancing industrialism. To be sure, the issue is a live one also in rural districts but here it is primarily a question of quality rather than quantity of dwellings. In urban centres, on the other hand, although quality is certainly a vital consideration, the particular acuteness of the problem has arisen out of the inexorable demand for a greatly increased quantity of dwellings to accommodate growing populations.

The assumption by the community of major responsibility for the provision of adequate housing accommodation for the broad masses of the population is of recent date in the Northern countries – as in other parts of the world. Prior to 1914 the intervention of the public authorities was, by and large, confined to the establishment and gradual expansion of what might be called "passive" legislation – that is, bye-laws and regulations aiming at better construction, reduced fire risks, improved hygiene, etc. Provisions of this character date back centuries, although it was not until the 19th century that more comprehensive statutes were adopted, the first Norwegian Building Act being passed in 1827 and comparable Finnish and Danish legislation in 1856–58.

By contrast, it was the general view that house-building proper was the exclusive responsibility of private enterprise and no concern of the community. It was only slowly that this traditional attitude gave way to a more active housing policy based upon social welfare considerations. Up to 1914 government initiative was limited to a few modest schemes in Denmark, Norway, and Sweden under which government support was provided for the building of dwellings for certain low-income groups. The housing shortage which developed during the First World War led to a considerable expansion of public intervention in all five countries, not only in the form of rent controls but also through a variety of government loans and subsidies for new housing projects and through the construction of new dwellings – in part of an emergency character – by local authorities. These activities were largely allowed to lapse in the 1920's. That decade, however, also witnessed the strong development of the housing co-operatives which have come to play an important role in the provision of dwellings for better-paid workers and the lower middle classes.

The early 1930's may be said to mark the beginning of modern government housing policies, particularly in Denmark, Iceland, and Sweden. Social and statistical surveys made during this period showed that large numbers of people inhabited obsolete dwellings lacking all modern conveniences; this was the case not only in the towns but also, and especially, in the rural districts. Moreover, although the findings indicated a general decline in the habitation density of former years there was still widespread overcrowding of urban and rural dwellings. In Sweden, for example, no less than 2.5 million persons lived in overcrowded dwellings, i.e. with more than two persons per room. The main sufferers were, of course, the low-income groups, notably families with many children and aged persons.

The programmes adopted subsequently in the three countries mentioned entailed broad State support for the building of dwellings for low-income groups; at the same time government controls over State-supported housing were tightened. New features were the special provisions enacted in Denmark and Sweden in favour of large families, old age pensioners, and agricultural labourers. All these measures fitted in naturally with the family welfare and social insurance reforms introduced during this period and were also linked up with the employment programmes to mitigate the effect of the depression.

Throughout the interval between the two World Wars the situation in Norway was characterized by a persistent housing shortage. It is interesting to find that in the 1930's public support of housing construction was left mainly to the local authorities, the contribution of the central government being of secondary importance only. The housing co-operatives figured prominently among the builders of subsidized housing in Oslo but were of no significance elsewhere.

Storgarden, Copenhagen, showing a profile typical of Danish urban housing construction in the 1930's. The screens of the balconies ensure privacy as well as shelter against the wind.

The collapse of housing construction following the outbreak of the Second World War and the ensuing critical housing shortage gave the final impetus to the full-scale development of the massive housing programmes now in effect. Obviously, national developments show many differences but their basic features have been essentially the same. State financing and subsidies have been expanded on a grand scale, co-operative and other non-profit housing being particularly favoured. The result has been that a high proportion of new construction (in Denmark and Sweden no less than 80 per cent) has come to be undertaken with government support. At the same time the central governments have assumed a greatly increased measure of direction over housing activities. In this connection a

283

fundamental consideration has been the integration of the construction of new dwellings within a general investment programme compatible with economic conditions and the overall economic policies pursued. These measures have been supplemented by strict rent controls and regulations concerning the allocation of housing accommodation.

The assumption by the community of primary responsibility for the improvement of housing conditions may be viewed as the result of a twin line of development. In the first place, experience gained in the past has led to a widespread conviction that government support and planning on a national scale is essential if the general population is to be assured of suitable dwellings at a cost within their means. Viewed in this light, the new housing programmes in the Northern countries emerge as an integral part of present-day welfare policies, on a par with programmes in such fields as employment, family welfare, and health. In the second place, economic developments since the 1930's have shown that the building industry occupies a position of vital importance to the national economies of these countries – not only as regards employment, but also government finance and the balance-of-payment situation. Housing policy has thus become a key factor in the general economic policies pursued by governments.

The vast increase within recent years of the housing responsibilities assumed by the central governments has led to radical administrative changes, particularly the centralization of housing administration in new autonomous State agencies.

In 1946 a special Housing Directorate was created in Norway and the National Housing Bank was organized. In Denmark a separate Ministry of Housing was established in 1947. The following year the Swedish housing administration and loan agency, established already in 1933, was reorganized as a new independent organ, the National Housing Board, with 24 regional committees. The corresponding Finnish agency is the Housing Production Committee (ARAVA) which was created in 1949 for the purpose of developing and administering a new long-term housing policy.

The tasks entrusted to these agencies are largely the same in all the countries. They include the planning of housing policies, the rationalization of housing construction, the administration of government loans and subsidies, and – as a rule – the regulation of building activities, including industrial and other construction, on the basis of the available supply of building materials and manpower.

Basic Features of Housing Policy

Many housing problems may be essentially the same in all developed countries situated in the same region or having the same climate. Still, the measures undertaken by the various nations for their solution are widely divergent. Below an attempt is made to bring out the basic features which the Northern countries have in common and which distinguish their housing programmes from those of most other nations. These features include the important position attained by co-operative and non-profit housing as well as the forms which such housing activities have assumed. They further include the methods devised by the central and local governments for the support of housing construction and, finally, the measures used to provide accommodation for particularly vulnerable population groups.

285

Although the public authorities have, within the last 10–15 years, become a decisive factor in the construction of housing in the Northern countries, it is important to note that this has not changed the basic structure of the building industry. In the large majority of cases the actual building of new housing, whether for the account of central or local governments, co-operative or other non-profit associations, or private persons, has remained in the hands of private architects and construction firms. Only in Denmark and Sweden are co-operative construction firms of a certain importance.

On the other hand, important changes have taken place with respect to the type of builder. In all the Northern countries it has been government policy to give preference to non-profit housing agencies and to persons wishing to build for themselves rather than to commercial building enterprises. It is worth noting that this policy, and its successful implementation, has had for its corollary that in none of the five countries does the State or local authority normally appear as a builder or administrator of housing, as is the case, for instance, in the United Kingdom. Direct building by local authorities has been limited to dwellings for old age pensioners, for homeless families and, to a certain extent, for low-income families in general. The overwhelming share of all new construction – whether for own use or for letting – is undertaken by private builders or by co-operative and other non-profit housing agencies.

During the inter-war period commercial builders dominated the housing market in all five countries. The decisive expansion of non-profit housing organizations dates from the emergence of the "new" housing policy, in Denmark and Sweden in the late 'thirties, and in Finland, Iceland, and Norway only after 1945. Everywhere the resulting legislation has given preference to such organizations. This gives at least a partial explanation of their subsequent rapid expansion, which has continued up to the present time. In the last few years almost half the dwelling units completed in Denmark, Finland, and Sweden, and about one-third in Iceland and one-fifth in Norway have been erected by co-operative and other non-profit housing organizations.

Multi-family rental housing plays a far greater role in the towns of the Northern countries – notably in Denmark and Sweden – than in many other countries. Recent years have, however, seen a growing movement, supported by the public authorities, in favour of owner-occupied dwellings which today account for an increasing share of new construction. Thus, in Norway, where this type has always been of great importance, approximately 75 per cent of all new dwellings erected in recent years are small single-family houses built by the prospective occupant, or two-family houses built by the future occupant of one of the dwelling units.

Company housing is practically unknown in Denmark and Iceland. In the other three countries, however, and especially in Finland and Sweden, the localization of many large industrial undertakings in small and isolated communities has resulted in the development of a considerable number of employer-sponsored housing programmes, often with public support. In some cases the firms have provided financial and other assistance to help employees build a house of their own, in others they have built large housing projects to let.

Modern company housing is often characterized by new architectural approaches, as witness these row houses built for employees of the Nuojua power station in Finland.

287

NON-PROFIT HOUSING AGENCIES

Non-profit housing in the Northern countries dates back to the latter half of the 19th century when the first housing co-operatives were established in Denmark, Norway, and Sweden. In its subsequent development the movement has followed no uniform pattern and the present-day organizations in this field differ considerably in type, not only among the five countries but also within each of them.

Viewing the Northern countries as a whole, three main types of non-profit housing agencies may be distinguished:

First, the *housing co-operatives* which, especially in their early phases, were strongly influenced by the Rochdale principles of consumers' co-operatives and which are governed by the tenant-owners as shareholders in the organizations.

Second, *the non-profit building societies* founded mainly on the initiative of trade unions or consumers' co-operatives and frequently organized as joint stock companies. Formerly, such societies were often organized by unions in the building trades during periods of declining construction and employment.

Third, the *community housing associations*, which represent a rather new type. They are organized in close co-operation with the local authority which is usually strongly represented on the governing board. Residents in dwellings constructed by these organizations are tenants only, and are not shareholders in the association.

The organization of non-profit housing has been approached in a highly pragmatic manner. Consequently, no hard and fast distinction can be drawn between the various types. A few general observations may, however, illustrate the general line of development.

In their early stages the housing co-operatives usually confined their activities to the building and administration of dwellings for the members who founded the organization for this purpose. In a sense these agencies might be viewed as attempts to introduce consumers' co-operation into the field of housing. However, while consumers' co-operatives are based on the recurrent everyday needs of their members, and thus automatically continuous in character, the situation is different with respect to housing. Once a housing society had completed the contemplated number of dwelling units for its members, no further construction was generally undertaken since the members had no longer any personal interest in continued building operations.

Housing co-operatives of this kind are still common in several of the Northern countries, notably in Denmark and Norway, but with the passing of time the inadequacy of this approach has been increasingly recognized. In all five countries growing emphasis has therefore been placed on those types of co-operative housing organizations which ensure the continuous construction of dwellings for a steady flow of new members. Except in Iceland, this development has been accompanied by the emergence of large-scale organizations which function as planning and financing centres for subsidiary building societies located throughout the countries.

The contribution by the prospective tenants of a share of construction costs is an inherent feature of the co-operative housing movement. Although this contribution has usually been rather modest, the result has been that co-operative housing is generally confined to better-paid workers and salaried employees. This provides the background for the more recent development – notably in Sweden but to some extent also in Denmark and Finland – of the so-called public utility or community housing associations which build dwellings to let without down payments or share capital requirements.

Danish non-profit building associations comprise three main groups. The first of these includes the co-operatives which are joined by individual persons for the purpose of obtaining a dwelling. Members contribute a share of the construction costs, usually three per cent. The second group comprises joint stock companies, which have frequently been founded by trade unions or co-operative construction firms. The third type, the community housing associations or social housing societies, have usually been established by interested persons and are operated in close connection with the local authorities.

The common purpose of all of these agencies is the building and administration of dwellings on a non-profit basis. While the housing constructed by the partnership societies are intended for members only, the projects of the other two types of organization are available to the general public. Since 1933 it has been a fundamental requirement for all these government-supported organizations that any surplus funds accumulated, especially through amortization, cannot be passed on to the tenants but must be set aside for the construction of new dwellings.

Apart from Copenhagen, housing associations in Denmark are usually locally organized and have no strong central organization.

However, a national agency has been established for the purpose of furnishing advice on the technical, economic, legal, and administrative problems arising in connection with the undertaking of construction and management of housing by the various organizations.

Non-profit housing in *Sweden* before the Second World War was undertaken mainly by co-operative organizations. However, as a result of new legislation enacted in 1946, public utility or community housing associations have developed rapidly in the last few years and today account for almost 40 per cent of all new construction as against about 20 per cent built by the co-operatives.

The most important co-operative organization is the strongly centralized Tenants' Savings and Building Society (HSB), which today is alone responsible for about 15 per cent of all new housing construction. The HSB is organized on three levels: The "national office" performs architectural, engineering, and financing functions and is in general charge of relations with authorities and outside enterprises. "Parent societies" are found in about 160 towns throughout the country. They take the initiative in building dwellings for their members and represent the continuity of the movement in each locality. When a new project is completed, it is turned over to a "daughter society" composed of the occupants who own and operate the unit with the assistance of the parent society. Members pay an initial deposit, usually amounting to about five per cent of the prorated cost of their dwelling. Contrary to the Danish housing co-operatives, any savings achieved redound to the benefit of the tenant-owners in the form of lowered annual costs.

Among the other Swedish housing co-operatives one of the more important is the Swedish National Builders (SR), which is sponsored by the labour unions of the building trades.

Under the new legislative provisions introduced in 1946 municipally chartered community housing associations were assured 100 per cent government financing and the following years witnessed the rapid increase in the number and scope of activities of such organizations. These new associations today dominate Swedish non-profit housing.

In *Norway* the bulk of non-profit housing associations are organized as joint stock companies or building associations; each member contributes his share of necessary capital beyond the loans obtainable through commercial and government credit institutions and subsequently becomes the owner of his house or flat. As distinct from

these more traditional types, there are, however, a growing number of co-operative societies which aim at continuous building and are organized along the lines of the Swedish HSB. The largest "parent society" within this category is the OBOS which has built about half of all post-war dwellings in Oslo. Altogether there are today about 60 such societies which constitute the Norwegian Building Societies' Association.

The *Finnish* housing co-operatives are usually joint stock companies. They fall into two main groups, the HAKA and the SATO. The HAKA organization is directed by the central organ of the urban consumers'

See Chapter III,
The Co-operative
Movement, p. 202.

movement (KK) and its affiliated building societies usually include among their members the local consumers' or farmers' co-operative as well as the local authority. Similarly the SATO organization comprises a number of local societies – the members of which are generally firms engaged in the building industry – and the local authority. Activities of these organizations include the planning and financing of housing projects. Members contribute 10–25 per cent of the costs.

Community housing associations, also, have gained increasing importance in Finland. These agencies, established by urban local authorities and essentially under their direction, may in large part be viewed as special organs entrusted with municipal housing construction. Dwellings constructed are sold to subscribers, payment being usually spread over a period of ten years.

In *Iceland* non-profit housing is mainly in the hands of two groups of organizations, the workers' housing associations and the co-operative housing societies. Their activities are supported and regulated by special legislation which was most recently amended in 1946. The associations, which are today found in all Icelandic towns and most urban settlements, are limited to workers of small means. They erect dwellings to let for their members, who contribute 15 per cent of building costs. The societies, which have in recent years spread to an increasing number of towns, build houses for sale to their members, who contribute one-quarter of the building costs.

In Iceland, one-family houses are predominant even in the towns. Still, there are also numerous modern co-operative multi-dwelling projects, although each unit rarely houses more than 4–6 families, as shown in this picture from Reykjavik.

GOVERNMENT AID FOR CONSTRUCTION

It is characteristic of the Northern countries that government aid has been extended to the various categories of builders primarily by means of State loans on easy interest and repayment terms. To a varying extent also direct subsidies have, however, been utilized. The preference for loans as the main form of aid is due to the experience gained after the First World War when it was found that large-scale direct subsidies tended to raise building costs. The advantages of the present method are that it entails a smaller immediate burden on the Exchequer and is more easily adjusted to changing circumstances.

The extent to which State financing of housing construction supplements or takes the place of traditional credit sources varies greatly among the five countries. A rough distinction may be drawn between Denmark, Sweden, and Finland, on one hand, and Norway and Iceland, on the other. In the three former countries government financing centres on junior liens, while in the other two countries it extends also to first mortgage loans. To a large extent this difference reflects the varying degree to which the traditional credit institutions have been able to provide adequate financing for house-building.

In *Denmark, Sweden*, and *Finland* the loan arrangement generally assumes that the builder has taken a first mortgage loan (and in Denmark and Sweden also a second mortgage loan) from a bank, savings bank, insurance company or co-operative credit association.

See Chapter III, The Co-operative Movement, pp. 226–229.

Up to the outbreak of the Second World War government loans for urban housing construction in general – as distinct from building on behalf of certain special groups – were of limited importance. The breakdown of housing construction and the housing shortage which developed during the war years led to a decisive change in this respect. The State has everywhere taken over the risky "top" financing by granting third (in Finland also second) mortgage loans at low interest and on easy repayment terms, thus covering nearly all construction costs that could not be financed by loans through the real estate credit institutions. As already mentioned, the result has been that today only a minor proportion of new housing – in Denmark and Sweden as low as 20 per cent – is financed without public support.

State loans are granted to all types of builders, although the terms vary with their character, community or public utility housing associations being the most favoured category, with housing co-operatives, home-ownership building, and commercial building following, in the order named. There is also a certain differentiation according to the type of dwelling – single-family or multi-family housing. Loans are in all cases contingent upon approval by the authorities of plans and construction costs, the general rule being that projects should satisfy certain minimum requirements but must not be of a luxury character.

Though similar in approach, the provisions relating to State housing loans show significant differences from country to country. In this connection it may be noted, moreover, that these provisions have been subject to frequent amendments with respect to loan limits, rates of interest, repayment conditions, etc., and that they will undoubtedly be modified again in adjustment to changes in the costs of building and financing.

Under the provisions of the *Danish* Building Aid Act of 1951 the size of the State loan varies automatically with the amount obtained through first and second mortgage loans in the open market, usually 30–35 per cent of building costs. The upper loan limit depends on the extent to which the local authority will guarantee the loan as well as on the type of builder and the character of the project. For non-profit housing associations the maximum limit is 97 per cent of total building costs, while in the case of commercial builders of tenement housing the limit is 90 per cent. This means that the maximum State loans range from 55 to 67 per cent of the costs of building. All groups of builders are exempted from building taxes for 22 years.

Non-profit organizations and low-income owner-occupants are also favoured in so far as the rate of interest is concerned. For example, the interest and repayment charges on loans granted to non-profit associations erecting detached or terrace houses are at the present time only 2.2 per cent, while the corresponding rate for a third mortgage loan in the open market is 7–8 per cent. The lowest capital charges are paid by an owner-occupant with two or more children. In this case the charges are reduced to 1.2 per cent; administrative costs account for 0.2 per cent of this amount, the remainder being earmarked for repayment. These rates compare with charges of 5–6 per cent for first and second mortgage loans in the open market.

The amortization period is usually about 60 years. This corresponds to the duration of first mortgage loans granted by the co-operative credit associations; the fact that these have provided such long-term credit is at least a partial explanation of the rather low rent level in Denmark as compared with most other European countries.

In *Sweden* the first and second mortgage loans obtainable through the various credit institutions usually add up to as much as 50–70 per cent of the capitalized value of the property (production costs minus subsidies); this is higher than in most other countries. The balance is in large part covered by State financing in the form of third mortgage loans and so-called supplementary loans granted under provisions most recently amended in early 1953.

For multi-dwelling construction third mortgage loans may thus be granted up to 100 per cent of the property's capitalized value when the builder is a local authority or a community housing association; for co-operative housing societies the loan limit is 95 per cent and for private builders 85–90 per cent. The interest rate is three per cent and the loans are redeemable over 30–40 years, depending upon the building material (timber or brick and concrete). The borrowers are further guaranteed an interest rate of three per cent on their first mortgage loans and a slightly higher rate on their second mortgage loans, thus largely eliminating the risk of future upward changes in credit costs.

It was originally a basic principle of Swedish post-war housing policies that rents, also in new housing, should be kept at the pre-war level. However, the capitalized value of these rents, which provided the basis for the size of the State loans, has been smaller than actual building costs. The difference was covered by a conditional capital subsidy in the form of a supplementary loan. As from 1946 this loan has been granted with a fixed sum per square meter floor area, which is graduated according to locality. Due to the steep rise of building costs since 1950 the size of the loans has been materially increased and now corresponds to the capitalized value of an annual contribution of 3.30–5.00 kronor per square meter. Under certain conditions these loans are subject to interest and repayment charges.

Builders of one- and two-family houses intended for their personal use are entitled to a so-called homestead loan. This is a three per cent loan of 25 years' duration which is granted up to 90 per cent of the approved costs of production. It includes a fixed capital subsidy of 8,000 kronor (about twenty per cent of average construction costs) very much on the same lines as the above-mentioned supplementary loans. Both forms of capital subsidies are viewed as provisional expedients only and are not part of the long-term housing programme.

In *Finland* the first mortgage loans, supplied through savings banks, insurance companies, etc., usually cover about 50 per cent of building costs. The strains to which the Finnish economy has been put since 1939 are reflected not only in the disproportionate increase in these costs as compared to the other Northern countries but also in very severe credit terms. Thus, first mortgage loans are typically of relatively short duration – 25 years – and usually carry $7^1/_2$–8 per cent interest.

Government loans are granted through the Housing Production Committee (ARAVA) under regulations most recently amended in 1949. Loans may be granted up to 90 per cent of the building costs for co-operative housing projects and one- and two-family houses built by persons in the low-income brackets; for multiple-dwelling construction by community housing associations the loan limit is 95 per cent. The loans, which for the time being bear interest of one per cent, are redeemable over 25 years in the case of wooden houses and 45 years in the case of brick houses. In practice, the very low rate of interest on these loans works out in the same way as a subsidy of 35–40 per cent of total building costs.

While prior to 1939 the *Norwegian* State left it mainly to local authorities to grant financial aid for housing, post-war policies have entailed a radical expansion of central government financing which, today, in some respects goes further than in any of the other Northern countries. The programme is implemented mainly through two State banks, the National Housing Bank of Norway, established in 1946 with urban housing as its primary field of activity, and the fifty-year old Norwegian Smallholders' Bank, which mainly serves the rural areas. The statutes of the latter were reformed in 1948 to conform with the basic principles of the Housing Bank. In the last few years 80–90 per cent of all Norwegian construction have been financed by these two institutions, the volume of transactions handled by the Housing Bank being more than double that of the Smallholders' Bank.

The Housing Bank represents a new departure in two main respects. In the first place, the loans granted cover not only junior liens but first and second mortgages as well. In the second place, the calculation

Blocks of more than four or five storeys are fairly unusual in the Northern countries, but they do dot the urban landscape here and there. This tower building was erected outside Oslo in 1950-51 by a co-operative housing society with support from the National Housing Bank of Norway.

of loans and subsidies is based upon the principle that, in order to be equitable from the social point of view, the rent of a "normal" dwelling – identified as three rooms plus kitchen – should not exceed 20 per cent of the average income in each locality. The capitalized value of this rent provides the yardstick for determining the size of the loans which are granted up to a maximum of 90–95 per cent of this amount for co-operative building societies, 85–95 per cent for home-ownership building, and 75 per cent in other cases. The rate of interest is $2^1/_2$ per cent and the loans are of very long duration – generally 100 years for brick and concrete houses and 75 years for timber houses. However, the capitalized value arrived at according to the above-mentioned method falls considerably short of actual construction costs and in practice the loans granted do not – on an average – go higher than 55–60 per cent of these costs. The remainder is in part contributed by the builder (usually 10–15 per cent in the case of co-operative building societies, otherwise 20–25 per cent) and in part by a subsidy granted by the Bank and normally free of any interest or repayment charges. The subsidy is determined according to the size of the dwelling and reaches its maximum at a floor area of 80 square meters (corresponding, roughly, to three rooms plus kitchen). This whole procedure, it will be seen, is similar to that found in Sweden, the main difference being the Norwegian insistence upon a constant rent in terms of income as contrasted with the Swedish idea of a constant rent in terms of money.

The Smallholders' Bank operates according to similar principles although loan limits and subsidies are lower; moreover, its facilities are available only to persons of limited economic resources.

Although less comprehensive in scope, the *Icelandic* system of government aid to housing construction is largely similar to that of Norway. Since 1929 the Building Fund, a government-sponsored institution, has been entrusted with the granting of aid for the construction of workers' dwellings in towns and urban settlements.

The Fund, which obtains its capital in part by the issue of State-guaranteed bonds, and in part by annual contributions from the central and local governments, grants loans up to 85 per cent of building costs for the erection of dwellings by workers' housing associations. The loans, which are secured by first mortgages on the building erected, carry an interest of two per cent and are repayable within 42–90 years, depending upon the wishes of the individual association. In addition, the State guarantees the loans contracted by the co-operative housing societies up to 75 per cent of building costs, each loan being the joint responsibility of those persons who occupy the dwellings thus financed. This method, it may be added, is essentially the same as that practised in the United States during the 1930's.

HOUSING FOR SPECIAL GROUPS

It was early realized that a number of low-income groups, notably large families, aged persons, and farm workers, encountered particular difficulties in obtaining their share in the general improvement of housing standards. It was found, moreover, that they could not even afford the rents charged in projects erected with government support. Consequently, most of the Northern countries have adopted special measures to ameliorate the housing conditions of these groups.

Families with Children

With respect to families with children, these measures may be considered an integral part of the broad family welfare programmes which grew out of the discussion of the population problem during the 'thirties and which have for their common purpose the improvement of the living standards of families with children.

See Chapter IV, Family Welfare, pp. 235–280.

Beginning about 1935, Sweden, Denmark, and Finland introduced legislation (since repeatedly amended and extended) which authorized cheap government loans for the building of approved *housing projects for large families*, as well as rent subsidies to the individual families. Extensive construction of blocks of flats and of one- and two-family dwellings (detached, semi-detached, and terrace houses) has been undertaken in subsequent years under these provisions which, particularly in Sweden, have been an important instrument in the long-term policy of combating overcrowding and improving the general housing standard.

Due to the acute shortage of suitable accommodation, the multi-family projects were originally leased exclusively to large families. However, the resulting congestion soon proved to entail serious drawbacks, economic (high maintenance expenses) as well as psychological and educational. In recent years it has therefore become the practice in Denmark and Sweden to lease a major proportion of such dwellings to "small" families, thus also preventing the stigma which easily attaches to projects inhabited solely by families with many children. In Sweden, moreover, the building of these special projects was definitely discontinued in 1948 and the large families who receive rent subsidies (see below) are now able to take up residence as ordinary families in any category of housing projects.

Rent subsidies have become an increasingly important feature of housing measures designed for families with children. The provisions under which such subsidies are granted share the characteristic that they cover only families with incomes below a certain limit. The term "low-income family" is, however, given a far wider interpretation than, for instance, in the USA. While in the latter country the maximum income recognized for low-income families includes only about 25 per cent of all families, the corresponding limits in the Northern countries are so high as to include the large majority of the population (in Denmark and Finland about 90 per cent, in Sweden about 70 per cent). The practical result is that not only low-income but also middle-income families are eligible for subsidies.

The Danish and Swedish rules are rather similar in scope and character. Subsidies are given both to families living in multi-family projects and to families inhabiting one- or two-family houses, whether as tenants or as owners. Formerly restricted to housing built with government support, they have in recent years been extended to all new dwellings that satisfy certain minimum standards. Moreover, while early regulations were limited to families with three or more children, post-war legislation has also authorized subsidies for families with two children.

Rent subsidies vary according to the number of children. Thus, as from 1950, the *Danish* rent subsidies applicable to new multi-family dwellings rise from 20 per cent for families with two children to 75 per cent for families with seven or more children. Large families living in a house of their own are entitled to a reduction of the capital charge on the State loans from two per cent to one per cent. About 17,000 families are beneficiaries under these provisions.

In *Sweden*, under legislation enacted in 1953, tax-exempt rent rebates of 150 kronor are granted annually for each child. A supplementary allowance, ranging from 150 to 300 kronor per dwelling, is granted to compensate for the rise in fuel prices since 1939. Families with very low incomes or many children receive an additional 210 kronor. In 1952 the number of families receiving rent subsidies was about 78,000, of whom 38,000 lived in their own houses.

In *Finland*, low-income families who reside in housing built to let for large families are granted a government subsidy ranging from 20 to 70 per cent according to the number of children. The number of actual beneficiaries under this scheme is, however, rather limited.

Although special housing projects for large families are not found in *Norway*, present legislation authorizes rent subsidies for families

Second floor.

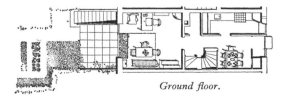

Ground floor.

Row or terrace houses have become increasingly common within recent years. The above houses, built in 1942 by the city of Copenhagen, are intended for families with many children. The date of construction explains the lack of a bathroom proper.

301

with at least two children who live in government-financed housing. The local authorities decide on the introduction of these subsidies which may vary between 30 and 120 kroner annually per child; two-thirds of the costs are met by the State. Up to the present time the scheme has been adopted by about 60, mainly urban, municipalities.

Pensioners' Dwellings

As already mentioned, aged persons of small means were among the categories of persons found to be frequently confined to substandard dwellings. The provision of low-rent housing for this group forms a special part of housing programmes and at the same time it may be considered a supplement to other measures adopted on behalf of aged persons, particularly in the field of social security.

In 1937 and 1939, respectively, *Denmark* and *Sweden* introduced special legislation authorizing government subsidies to local authorities for the construction of pensioners' dwellings. Thus, the Danish act provides for the State to cover half the annual operating deficit of old age pensioners' dwellings erected by local authorities. The corresponding Swedish measure, by contrast, provides for a capital subsidy ranging from 25 to 80 per cent of building costs according to the economic circumstances of the individual municipality.

The dwellings provided under this legislation are intended for aged persons in good health as well as for disablement pensioners who are desirous and capable of maintaining an independent existence in their own homes. The projects are consequently quite independent of the old people's homes which care for pensioners who are so old or infirm that they cannot live alone or be placed in private care.

See Chapter VII, Social Security, pp. 461–468.

It has therefore been considered important that the accommodation should be normal dwellings without institutional character. The projects, which must be provided with modern installations, consist of one-room flats with an alcove and kitchen for single pensioners while married couples have either a somewhat larger one-room flat or two rooms. In most of the projects there are recreation rooms, laundries, and other community facilities. The rents are very moderate. In Copenhagen, for example, they amount to about one-third of the normal rent for a similar flat in the open market, corresponding to 12–15 per cent of the old age pension.

The construction by local authorities of these dwellings has assumed sizable proportions. The number of aged persons thus accommodated

in Sweden has reached a total of 33,000 and in Denmark 14,000
(about 6 per cent of all old age pensioners). Most projects have been
undertaken by urban local authorities.

In *Norway* greater emphasis has been placed upon the institutional
care of aged persons, but the city of Oslo has on its own initiative
established a number of special housing projects for the accommodation of old age pensioners. Plans for similar projects are at an
advanced stage of preparation in other towns.

The pensioners' dwellings have everywhere proved a great success
and there are generally long waiting lists for admittance. At the
same time there has been a growing recognition of their inadequacy
as the sole answer to the housing problems of aged persons, many
of whom prefer to live among younger families in ordinary housing,
provided the rental is kept within their means. The result has been
that in 1950 and 1951, respectively, Sweden and Denmark have made
subsidies available also for pensioners who take up residence in new
government-supported dwellings intended for "normal" families.

A variety of measures have been undertaken during the last decades to improve the formerly very meagre living conditions of agricultural workers, in part as a means of checking the continued migration of rural youth to the towns.

Beginning in the middle 1930's, Denmark and Sweden introduced legislation (since amended) calling for government subsidies for the building of approved houses for this group. Under the present *Danish* provisions, which date from 1947, married agricultural workers may receive cheap loans up to 100 per cent of the cost of purchasing or building their own dwellings. Three-fifths of the loan are free of interest, while the remainder bears interest at four per cent; the annual repayment charge is one per cent.

The comparable *Swedish* programme, enacted in 1939, aims primarily at assisting farmers in establishing good dwellings for their employees. Farm workers wishing to build their own houses are eligible for the benefits available under the general housing legislation.

Moreover, far-reaching measures have been adopted to improve rural housing standards in general. The government loans for construction or renovation of one- or two-family houses, first granted in 1904, have since 1946 acquired an ever-increasing importance. Furthermore, since the early 1930's the State has granted loans and subsidies for improvement of old one- and two-family houses, particularly in rural districts. It is recognized that the raising of rural housing standards to the level of new urban construction will require considerable time and that it therefore is desirable that the government assist in the less costly improvement of existing sub-standard rural houses. Improvement loans, generally free of capital charges, are at the present time granted up to 8,000 kronor for both one- and two-family houses. In many cases these loans have been used to finance sewerage, water, and electrical installations, etc. Particular attention has in recent years been given to the modernization of old dwellings with a view to accommodating aged persons who wish to remain in their accustomed environment.

In *Finland* a special housing problem arises in connection with the seasonal employment of about 50,000 forestry workers and raftsmen who have to live away from their homes for considerable periods. In former times the accommodation offered was frequently extremely poor, but since 1928 special regulations have placed the

Here is a typical State-financed farm worker's house in Sweden, where improvement of rural dwellings in general forms an important part of housing policies.

employer under obligation to provide temporary dwellings that satisfy certain minimum requirements for workers thus employed in isolated areas. The houses are usually built of timber, but frequently movable camps are also used.

RENTS

The regulations pertaining to rent controls and security of tenure are a key feature of modern Northern housing legislation.

Rent controls were originally introduced during World War I and remained in force after the close of the war. In Finland, Iceland, and Sweden they were abolished as early as 1922–23, and in Denmark and Norway some ten years later. After 1939, however, stringent controls were re-imposed, the general rule being the pegging of rents in existing dwellings at their pre-war level. These regulations have been retained essentially unchanged during post-war years in order to prevent a rise in rents above that motivated by increased maintenance costs.

In *Denmark* the rent freeze was applied to all dwellings under lease prior to September 1939. It was not until 1951 that an increase of about six per cent was permitted to cover increased maintenance costs. Moreover, all rents in government-supported housing, whether erected by private builders or non-profit housing agencies, have been subject to approval by the central government throughout the period, rents here being determined on a cost basis; finally, non-supported housing is subject to local rent-controls. Similarly, *Finnish* and *Icelandic* war-time regulations pegged the rents of pre-war housing at the 1939 level though they permitted increases to cover higher costs of maintenance; moreover, rents in new dwellings were fixed on the basis of costs. As from 1949, however, no rent controls are imposed on new construction in Finland. Further, Icelandic legislation, enacted in 1951, introduced a novel principle of rent control by dividing all dwellings into three categories according to their date of construction (before 1942, 1942–45, and after 1945) and establishing a uniform maximum rent per square meter for each of these categories. In *Norway* interest charges on mortgage loans were reduced by 20 per cent in 1940 at the same time as rents in existing housing were reduced by 10 per cent. Rents have since remained at this level in such housing although house owners may apply individually for a raise in case the property is operated at a deficit. In post-war houses rents are determined by costs. *Swedish* regulations, introduced in 1942, stabilized rents in existing dwellings at their 1941-level. Since 1951 limited increases in rents to cover rising maintenance costs have, however, been permitted.

Rent controls in all five countries are supplemented by provisions for the protection of tenants with respect to their *tenure*. In several of the countries comprehensive regulations to this effect had already been enacted before the outbreak of the Second World War and were subsequently further strengthened. Their main characteristic is that they void the right of the landlord to terminate the lease. As long as the tenant fulfils his obligations he is thus assured of automatic prolongation of his contract on the existing terms.

The various regulations outlined above have been highly effective and large population groups have benefited from the stability of rents thus ensured. Since money incomes have increased very considerably since 1939 (in Denmark, Norway, and Sweden by 150–200 per cent), the result has obviously been a marked improvement in the *rent-income ratio*. Due to the extensive support rendered under the government housing programmes, the same holds true of newly constructed dwellings, although to a much smaller extent. Thus, the proportion of income used for rent and heating by a worker living in a new two-room flat built by a non-profit housing association has since 1939 declined from about 25 per cent to 20 per cent in Denmark, from about 30 to 17 per cent in Norway, and from about 30 to 20 per cent in Sweden. The rents in such dwellings are everywhere, except in Sweden, considerably higher than in pre-war housing, since they are determined on the basis of construction costs. The renewed rise in building costs since 1949 has not only accentuated this discrepancy but has also entailed much higher rents for new construction than those charged in early post-war building. The result has been an irrational use of available housing to the particular detriment of those, mainly younger, families who find it all but impossible to obtain accommodation except in the new and expensive projects. In Sweden the situation is not the same since the rise in construction costs has largely been offset by increased subsidies.

Town and Country Planning

In all the Northern countries the rapid growth of towns and urban settlements within the past two or three generations has generally proceeded in a rather haphazard manner – as has also been the case in most other countries. In some instances the result has been an unfortunate mixing-up of residential and industrial building as well as scattered developments combining a marked lack of amenities with highly uneconomical features such as long transportation distances, excessively costly sewerage and water installations, etc. This provides the background for the introduction of increasingly comprehensive town planning and building legislation. In spite of many differences in national statutory provisions, the methods applied and the extent of regulation in the five countries show considerable uniformity.

Private ownership rights to land and buildings are safeguarded by the national constitutions and in principle have not been changed by increased government intervention. These rights have, however, become subject to increasing regulation by public authorities.

In regulating new development the main line of approach is to establish a preventive framework which will forestall undesirable

307

subdivision, roadbuilding, and housing. The actual work of development, on the other hand, is undertaken mainly by private land owners or non-profit organizations, although in practice the community may exert considerable positive influence by means of loans and subsidies for the construction of housing.

The active land policies pursued by many of the large towns – and especially the capitals – in all the Northern countries have served as important auxiliary instruments in guiding urban development along the lines staked out by town planning and building legislation. By acquiring large tracts of land in the suburban areas the public authorities have obtained considerable – in Sweden even dominating – influence over land prices as well as a large measure of actual control, beyond and above that implied by statutory provisions, over the general layout and type of housing of new urban districts.

GENERAL LEGISLATIVE PROVISIONS

The *Swedish* Building Act and Building Code of 1947 in many respects represent the most advanced town planning and building legislation in the Northern countries. Particularly, it includes far-reaching provisions to avert premature or inexpedient urban development. Such development is permitted only where a town plan or building plan has been approved for the area in question and – as stated in the Act – such plans may not be approved if, from a community point of view, the area is unsuitable for extensive building.

Town planning is undertaken on two levels. General planning (master plans and regional plans) and detailed planning (town plans and building plans).

Master plans are prepared by the local authorities and since 1947 such plans have been established for about 110 Swedish towns and urban settlements. The plans may be submitted for approval by the State authorities but there is no obligation to do so. On the other hand, the plans are usually forwarded to an advisory State organ, the Building Board, for expert review; in undertaking this task the Board consults railway, road, defence, and other authorities concerned.

Detailed planning usually takes the form of town plans, the preparation of which is in reality compulsory. They are prepared by the local authorities subject to approval by the government. A town plan normally includes detailed provisions on the siting, height, width, and utilization of buildings, on the siting and width of thoroughfares,

Suburban idyl in Copenhagen, or what happens when laissez-faire is left to do the planning. The catty propaganda on behalf of milk is eye-catching...

...but the harmonious whole of this large-scale urban development in Kärrtorp, Stockholm, is an indubitable improvement.

on sites for public purposes, etc. Each town plan usually covers only a limited section of the town involved, but added up the plans will cover most of the town area. Building plans, with somewhat more detailed provisions than town plans, apply to urban centres in the rural districts.

While hitherto Swedish town plans have usually gone into great detail, in the last few years there has been a certain trend toward allowing the local authority and the builder a somewhat greater freedom of choice.

To a considerable extent the Swedish system, with its distinction between general and detailed planning, is typical of Northern town planning. General planning is emphasized particularly in Denmark and Iceland, somewhat less in Finland and Norway. Another common feature is the important and independent role which the statutory provisions assign to the local governments in charge of the preparation and the administration of all town planning. At the same time, the procedure of submitting town plans for approval to the competent State authorities ensures that development is based on uniform considerations, except where otherwise warranted by special local conditions.

The *Danish* Town Planning Act of 1938, as amended in 1949, provides that town plans shall be prepared for all towns and built-up areas with a population exceeding 1,000 inhabitants (about 235 localities). Plans have been adopted for most of these towns. It may be added that plans also may be introduced in areas that are not as yet built-up. Special Building Acts apply to the capital and the provincial towns, respectively. In addition, special building bye-laws apply to most towns and a large number of rural districts; these bye-laws frequently include provisions relating to town planning.

The *Norwegian* Building Act of 1924, as amended most recently in 1949, applies to all towns and a large number of urban centres in the rural districts. The local authority is generally under obligation to establish town plans covering all the various built-up areas. On the other hand, the Building Act does not require the towns to prepare a master plan as a primary step, but in many cases such plans are nevertheless introduced.

The *Finnish* Town Planning Act of 1931 assumes development in towns to be regulated by town plans. A number of such plans have been adopted but, generally speaking, their coverage is as yet limited.

This panorama of modern housing is the 1952 achievement of a Danish co-operative housing society in Hvidovre, a suburb of Copenhagen. This and similar projects in the Northern countries are the result of careful, overall planning: Dwelling types are differentiated and open spaces landscaped, varying traffic functions are assigned to the lanes and streets, and emphasis is placed on community facilities.

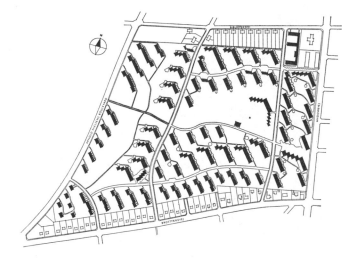

311

In *Iceland* the Town Planning Act of 1921, as amended most recently in 1938, requires the establishment of town plans for all towns and urban centres with more than 200 inhabitants. Contrary to the other countries, these plans are worked out by the competent central government agencies, although in close collaboration with the local authorities involved.

In certain emergency situations the normal division of responsibility between central and local governments has been departed from also in the other countries. Thus, in Norway a separate State agency was established in 1940 with the task of framing draft plans for war-damaged towns and areas. Operating through a number of regional offices, this agency has served as an effective instrument in promoting the reconstruction work which is today practically completed. Similar measures were undertaken in Finland where the problems involved in the repairing of war damages were further complicated by the simultaneous need for resettling evacuees from the eastern areas ceded to the Soviet Union.

COMPENSATION AND EXPROPRIATION

The problem of how to deal with the two interrelated questions of compensation and expropriation (compulsory purchase) occupies a position of key importance in all town planning work.

It has always been the legal interpretation of the constitutional provisions relating to the protection of private ownership rights that general restrictions on the use and enjoyment of property (as imposed *inter alia* by town planning and building legislation) do not entitle the owner to compensation. On the other hand, full compensation must be paid in case of expropriation. Certain general restrictions under town planning regulations are considered such extensive encroachments on ownership rights that compensation must be given. Rules pertaining to this issue vary somewhat from country to country. Thus the Swedish Building Act usually does not provide for any compensation to owners of land for which the authorities refuse to establish a town plan or building plan. In Denmark, on the other hand, compensation is granted to a certain extent in cases where the owner is deprived of the possibility of utilizing his land for urban development. With regard to compensation it may be relevant to stress that the former British system of levying development charges is not known in the Northern countries.

In addition to the expropriation rules contained in town planning and building regulations, several of the Northern countries have introduced separate and more trenchant expropriation legislation. In Norway, provisions enacted in 1946 allow for compulsory purchase of land on behalf of State or local authorities, certain co-operatives, and other non-profit housing agencies for the purpose of housing or other (including industrial) development. In certain cases the same procedure applies to the purchase of land for the building of houses for occupancy by the owner. Under the corresponding Swedish legislation, which in its present form dates from 1949, the local authorities may expropriate property – whether it is built upon or not – when this is deemed necessary to ensure the availability of land for urban development. Moreover, new Swedish legislation of 1953 has introduced potentially far-reaching provisions concerning expropriation of land in connection with comprehensive redevelopment of central urban areas.

NATIONAL AND REGIONAL PLANNING

Although the activity of the responsible State authorities ensures a certain degree of uniformity of town planning in the various localities, there is no *national planning* proper in the Northern countries. Another matter is that planning along national lines takes place in a number of other fields – railways, harbours, airports, power stations, etc. – which inevitably influence town plans to a greater or lesser degree.

Interest in *regional planning* has grown out of a recognition of the need for co-ordinating the master plans and town plans of neighbouring communities, mainly by the establishment of a framework for the general and detailed planning of each locality involved.

As yet, regional planning is in its infancy. Mention may be made of the 1949-amendment to the Danish Town Planning Act which empowers the Ministry of Housing to set up co-ordination committees to assist local authorities in preparing town plans for an area covering several municipal districts; a considerable number of such committees have since been established, notably for towns and adjacent districts of a more or less pronounced suburban character. In general, though, regional planning has been confined to the large towns, particularly the capitals, where comprehensive plans for the metropolitan areas have been prepared during recent years in all the Northern countries, except Iceland.

BUILDING REGULATIONS

Town planning and building legislation, as well as the local bye-laws, include numerous provisions relating to the construction of buildings. In the first place, these provisions lay down requirements aiming at solid construction and fire prevention. Second, they establish certain standards for roads, water supply, and sewerage. To a greater or lesser extent they also contain rules governing ceiling heights, minimum floor space, etc., as well as stipulations concerning maximum heights of building, site exploitation, etc. It may be added that the gradual raising by the administrative authorities of the requirements stipulated under these various regulations has proved an effective instrument for the promotion of improved housing standards.

EFFECTS OF TOWN PLANNING

In evaluating town planning efforts in the Northern countries it should be recalled that most buildings predate the legislation introduced in this sphere. In already developed sections the influence of town planning measures therefore will not be evident for many years. In order to see the effects of more recent town planning concepts it is necessary to investigate the suburban sections developed within the last two decades. The character of these sections has in large measure been determined by the large-scale projects made possible by government housing programmes. In the large towns it is not infrequent to encounter projects comprising 5–10,000 inhabitants, large figures by Northern standards.

The individual buildings in these projects have not always been erected by the same builder (generally a non-profit housing association), but they have all been built within a few years, thus retaining the integrated character foreseen in the plans.

The large-scale projects, moreover, provide the necessary economic basis for the establishment and operation of community facilities, including schools, recreation centres, laundries, day nurseries, etc. It must be admitted, however, that even in recent years such facilities have not always been introduced to the desired extent. This is due in part to the housing shortage which has necessitated that available resources be first and foremost concentrated on the production of dwellings; furthermore, the comparatively high cost of establishing and running such facilities has made it necessary to carry out these programmes by stages.

Housing Production and Housing Shortage

In all the Northern countries the volume of *housing production* has in recent decades been subject to marked fluctuations, reflecting the alternate periods of prosperity and depression, the influence of two world wars and, in the years immediately after 1945, the shortage of manpower and building materials.

In the early 1930's building activities were on a rather low level in all five countries. However, the subsequent expansion brought housing production in the following years up to capacity volume, i. e. in Denmark and Finland about 20,000 dwelling units annually, in Norway about 15,000, and in Sweden about 50,000 units.

315

In Denmark, Finland, and Sweden production during the war years amounted to only 25–50 per cent of normal and was lower in Norway where only about 1,000 dwellings were constructed annually in 1942–45. With the single exception of 1940, Icelandic construction was, on the other hand, maintained at a higher level than in 1939 throughout the war years. After the conclusion of hostilities the volume of new construction remained modest for several years in Denmark and Norway due to shortages of labour and materials. In Finland and Sweden, on the other hand, it was possible to attain the pre-war level by 1946–47. By 1948–49 new construction had reached or surpassed pre-war figures in all the Northern countries.

			Dwelling Units Completed *(Thousands)*					Annual number of units per 100,000 population constructed
	1936–40	*1947*	*1948*	*1949*	*1950*	*1951*	*1952*	*1948–52*
Denmark .	20	13	19	25	20	21	19	490
Finland . .	22	31	23	29	26	29	30	680
Iceland . .	0.5	1.1	1.0	0.9	0.9	0.7	0.8	600
Norway . .	13	15	17	18	22	21	32	670
Sweden . .	47	58	48	42	44	40	45	630

As the above figures show, the number of new dwellings completed in the last few years have, except in Norway, shown relatively modest variations, construction remaining at a fairly high level. The steeply rising prices and the balance-of-payments difficulties which followed after the devaluation of the Northern currencies in 1949 and the outbreak of the Korean conflict in 1950 entailed considerable difficulties for the building industry. However, thanks to the intensified public efforts and the improved economic conditions prevailing as from 1952, these difficulties have now been overcome, Norwegian construction showing, indeed, a marked expansion over former years.

In spite of the extensive residential building which has taken place during the post-war period, the marked *shortage of housing* originating in the war years persists in all five countries. This has been roughly estimated at 30–40,000 dwellings in Denmark, 60–70,000 in Sweden, 65–75,000 in Finland, and no less than 100,000 in Norway (which has the smallest population). In Iceland the shortage is particularly acute in the capital, Reykjavik, which has grown at an astonishing rate and today accounts for 40 per cent of the entire population.

Among the main factors responsible for this unfortunate situation have been the steep decline in housing production during the Second World War, the continued large-scale migration from rural districts to the towns, and the marked increase during the 'forties in the number of marriages and births. The higher employment level and the improvement in the rent-income ratio of large population groups have obviously had a similar effect. Moreover, in Finland and Norway the war resulted in extensive destruction, notably in the Northern regions; as mentioned above, Finnish conditions were further aggravated by the influx of evacuees from the ceded eastern areas.

The housing shortage has given rise to more or less severe regulations authorizing the allocation of available dwelling accommodation. Most radical have been the measures adopted in Finland and Norway which until 1950 authorized the requisitioning of "surplus" dwelling-space from tenants or owners. Introduced during the Second World War, these regulations have been retained, although with modifications, in post-war years. In administering the allocation system priority has everywhere been given to families with children, families without children coming next, and single persons last.

317

Housing Standards

GENERAL CHARACTERISTICS

Any comparison of Northern housing standards with those of other countries will have to take into consideration various fundamental factors of a technical and organizational character.

Due to the relatively severe winters, especially in the northernmost regions, insulation is of decisive importance in the choice of building methods and materials; similarly, expenses for fuel carry considerable weight in family budgets. As for construction materials, there are significant differences among the five countries. Practically all Danish construction is in brick while light concrete dominates in Iceland. Swedish construction uses both materials. In Finland and Norway, on the other hand, brick and light concrete are used extensively only in the large towns, timber being otherwise the traditional building material.

Naturally enough, the countryside is dominated by one- and two-family houses, which generally account for more than 90 per cent of all dwellings in the rural districts. On the other hand, it is characteristic of the Northern countries that most urban housing takes the form of multi-family dwellings. As shown in the table below, urban one-family houses in the USA comprise almost three-fifths of the total number of dwellings while the comparable Danish and Swedish figures are only one-seventh. In Norway the two-family house is the most common type and even multi-family houses are usually rather small, comprising only 3–9 units.

URBAN DWELLING UNITS BY TYPE

	Denmark (1945)	Norway (1946)	Sweden (1945)	USA (1940)
One-family houses . .	15	27	15	59
Two-family houses . .	7	39	16	17
Multi-family houses .	78	34	69	24
	100	100	100	100

In all five countries, but especially in Norway, there has been in recent years a movement in favour of home-ownership. As yet, however, tenement housing remains the most widespread form of accommodation, especially in Denmark where it accounts for four-fifths of all urban dwellings. Even in the latter country, however, one-family houses have gradually gained increasing importance, accounting for about 45 per cent of all new dwelling units completed in the last few years.

SIZE OF DWELLINGS

Space standards, as measured by the number of rooms, are illustrated by the following table. In explanation of the figures given it should be emphasized that in the Northern countries kitchens and bathrooms are never counted as separate rooms; a two-room modern flat, for example, will therefore comprise two rooms proper, a kitchen or kitchenette, and (in practically all cases) a bathroom.

URBAN DWELLINGS BY NUMBER OF ROOMS

	Denmark (1945)	Finland (1945)	Iceland (1940)	Norway (1946)	Sweden (1945)
One room	7	60	9	23	38
Two rooms	38	19	31	37	36
Three rooms	29	10	30	24	14
Four rooms	15	5	15	9	6
Five rooms or more .	11	6	15	7	6
	100	100	100	100	100

As the table shows, there are marked differences among the four countries. While in Finland and Sweden three-fifths and (almost) two-fifths, respectively, of all dwellings were one-room units, the corresponding figures for Denmark, Iceland, and Norway, where two-room dwellings are most common, were only 7, 9, and 23 per cent, respectively. However, it should be mentioned that, in Sweden especially, kitchens are usually of such size and equipment that they also may serve as dining rooms. Still, with these figures for a background it is easy to see why the building of larger dwelling units has become a major goal for the post-war housing programmes of the Northern countries.

As a result, construction in the last few years has shown a decided trend away from the very small types of dwellings.

CONSTRUCTION OF URBAN DWELLINGS BY
NUMBER OF ROOMS (1950)

	Denmark	Finland	Iceland	Norway	Sweden
One room.	4	26	1	3	16
Two rooms	18	47	19	13	41
Three rooms	42	18	36	45	30
Four rooms	28	8	24	29	9
Five roms or more . .	8	1	20	10	4
	100	100	100	100	100

A comparison of the above figures with the previous table shows a decided change. In Denmark, Iceland, and Norway the three-room dwelling has come to be the dominant type while in Finland and Sweden the emphasis has shifted to two-room dwellings.

TECHNICAL EQUIPMENT

Simultaneously, there has been a considerable improvement in technical equipment. Practically all urban dwellings in the Northern countries today have electricity and water closets; in Denmark, Iceland, Norway, and Sweden one-third or more have a bathroom; central heating has been widely introduced, particularly in Sweden. Almost all new construction in the towns has these installations as a matter of course. Rural housing, however, still lags considerably behind with respect to modern conveniences although the last 10–15 years have brought very considerable improvement also here.

Many Northern cities are faced with the problem of how to relieve the congestion of time-worn houses at their cores. The maze of buildings shown here is a condemned quarter in the heart of Copenhagen.

SLUM CLEARANCE

It is frequently stated that there are no slums in the Northern countries. This may be true in the sense that one does not encounter the extensive sections of substandard dwellings characteristic of some cities in other parts of the world. Nevertheless, a great number of families are still living in housing unfit for habitation.

In Denmark it has recently been estimated that approximately 100,000 dwelling units, or about seven per cent of total housing, are ripe for clearance. A rough Swedish estimate some years ago indicated that about 200,000 urban dwellings should be cleared in order to eliminate various technical and town planning deficiencies. No figures are available for the other countries, but even here there is a great need for clearance. The dwellings which are considered ready for clearance fall into two distinct categories. The first of these includes houses which due to age, or faulty construction or maintenance, are beyond repair; they are found mainly in the central districts of the large towns. The other comprises houses which were erected shortly after the industrial revolution and which, in the absence of adequate building and town planning legislation, were constructed

321

with such intensive exploitation of the site that the resulting excessive density of housing renders them obsolete regardless of other technical qualities. Special slum-clearance programmes have been introduced in several of the Northern countries and a considerable amount of such housing has been razed within the past 15–20 years. Nevertheless, the continued housing shortage has presented a serious obstacle to rapid progress in this field since the Second World War.

RESEARCH

Today it is generally recognized that the reduction of the costs of building depends – both in the short and the long run – upon research in the widest sense of this term and upon the dissemination of the results of such research. Research into various aspects of building and housing has long been carried out by numerous institutions and agencies, governmental and non-governmental alike. The assumption by the State of major responsibility in the housing field has in recent years been accompanied by a trend toward the co-ordination and integration of such activities and by the establishment under government auspices of new central research organs.

Thus, the Danish Building Research Institute was established by the State in 1947 with the main object of following, promoting, and co-ordinating technical, economic, sociological, and other inquiries likely to contribute to the improvement of building and the lowering of construction costs. The Institute, which co-operates with laboratories, organizations, and specialists in various fields, carries out most of the development work and economic research and also takes an active part in the publication and implementation of its findings. The Norwegian Building Research Institute, with very similar functions, was founded in 1953. In Sweden, where a number of agencies have long undertaken extensive research activities, the government established in 1953 a co-ordinating agency for research into and rationalization of housing construction methods, to be financed in part by the building industry itself. A similar organ was established by the Finnish State in 1951, but since 1953 its responsibilities have been transferred to the Housing Production Committee (ARAVA). No comparable agency exists in Iceland although the Technical Institute of the University of Reykjavik has in the last few years conducted investigations into the question of building materials (Iceland has no local resources and is obliged to import cement).

322

Although the form of organization varies somewhat from country to country, the approach has followed a similar pattern.

Among the main fields of activity is research into production techniques, aimed at further mechanization of the building industry (covering such problems as the relative merits of working methods, prefabrication, means of transportation, and the organization of the industry as a whole). As heating equipment and fuel consume a large share of the costs of construction and maintenance, respectively, of Northern dwellings, the research programme also includes all aspects of insulation and heating. Ever since the Danish institute was created, winter construction problems have been one of its most important topics of study. Research into construction materials has for its special aim the production of new and improved materials and the standardization of materials and parts. Module investigations, which are very important to the future of standardization, are not yet completed. In both Denmark and Sweden modules have been recommended which correspond to the 10 cm module gradually being adopted in other countries.

New techniques overcome the climatic obstacles to winter construction. Steam is used to thaw frozen building materials.

In view of the broad aims pursued by present-day housing policies, and the large sums expended in their implementation, it is quite natural that the building research programme is not limited to construction research. In Sweden, especially, thorough studies have been made of the functions of the home with a view to establishing dwelling plans suitable for different types of families. The proper layout of the kitchen – the home's principal place of work – is given special attention. Moreover, Danish and Swedish government commissions are at present inquiring into methods of providing community facilities such as laundry centres, day nurseries and kindergartens, hobby rooms, and playgrounds.

CHAPTER VI

HEALTH AND REHABILITATION

Introduction

Among the most conspicuous features of welfare policy in the Northern countries has been the early and sustained interest in the development of health and medical services. The safeguarding of the health of the population has long been considered a natural responsibility of the community on a par with other public functions. How the necessary facilities should be established has thus mainly come to be a question of organization.

Present programmes are predominantly organized and financed by the central and local governments but are operated both by public authorities and by private persons and organizations. Public health authorities are responsible for the general promotion of health and hygiene throughout the countries. Medical care is furnished by general practitioners and specialists working either under public auspices or in a private capacity, the costs being covered wholly or in part by the State-subsidized health insurance schemes in respect of all insured persons. The vast majority of hospitals are public and available to the whole population either entirely free or at very low charges. The mentally and physically handicapped are dealt with under special government schemes. The result is that the community covers considerably more than one-half of total health costs.

The direct responsibility for health programmes is shared by local authorities, the counties, and the State which is in central control. Although conditions vary somewhat from country to country, the situation may perhaps very roughly be summarized by saying that local authorities are primarily entrusted with the supervision and promotion of general conditions of health and hygiene; county and city boroughs are in charge of most of the major general hospitals and the larger part of preventive health programmes; and the State operates the national health service as well as certain categories of

325

hospitals and related institutions. From a financial point of view the role of the State is, however, considerably more important than this would seem to indicate since considerable subsidies are given both to the health insurance schemes (except in Finland) and to county and local district authorities.

See Chapter VII, Social Security, pp. 409–410.

Traditionally, curative medical care has been the main object of attention, the basic principle being that everyone, regardless of economic circumstances, should be assured of the necessary care and treatment when afflicted by sickness or disablement. In harmony with the general re-orientation of social thinking and action, the preventive aspects of health work have, however, increasingly come into the foreground in recent decades. A rounded programme has thus gradually been developed and although the Northern countries have by no means reached the point where the manifold problems involved in providing the population with adequate health and medical care can be said to have found a final solution, the following pages will show that they have at least gone a considerable distance towards this goal.

Public Health Administration

The basic features of public health administration are practically identical in all the Northern countries. A national organ (in Denmark and Iceland termed the National Health Service, in Finland and Sweden the Medical Board, and in Norway the Health Directorate) has been entrusted with central responsibility for health and medical services, although the actual administration may to a varying extent be in the hands of other agencies. Through a nation-wide network of public health medical officers the central authority is in touch with both county and borough councils as well as with the public health committees found in practically every local district.

The functions of the National Health Services (or comparable bodies), which are largely staffed by medical experts, are threefold: Advisory, supervisory, and administrative. They are chief advisers to the central administration and to county and local authorities in all matters requiring medical knowledge. They must keep a close watch on the development of health conditions and ensure that health regulations and bye-laws are complied with. They supervise all hospitals, public or private, as well as other institutions and premises subject to special health rules. Physicians, dentists, mid-

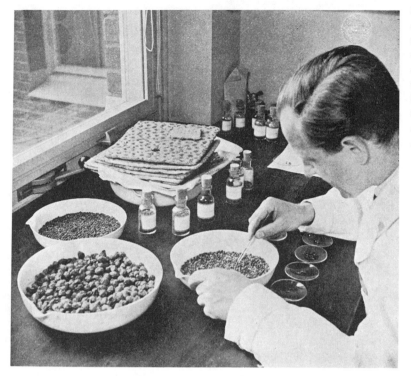

The community is strongly concerned with the problems of food handling and hygiene. Here we see foodstuffs being analyzed at the Swedish State Institute of Public Health.

wives, etc., receive their authorization from the Services and are, in their professional capacity, subject to their jurisdiction. To these varied tasks should finally be added a general obligation to inform and guide the population on health matters and to submit such proposals for the improvement of public health as are deemed necessary.

The National Health Services are assisted by several specialist organs, e.g. on nutrition, forensic medicine, psychiatry, etc. Particular mention might here be made of the Swedish State Institute of Public Health which was established in 1938 with the support of the Rockefeller Foundation to deal with specific practical problems taken up by health authorities, to undertake independent research in public hygiene, food hygiene, and industrial hygiene, and to serve as a school for public health nurses. Similarly, a semi-official Institute for Industrial Hygiene has been in operation in Helsinki since 1951.

Work in the field rests mainly with the specially trained public health medical officers employed directly under the central authority.

In principle, if not in practice, the system (which in Sweden dates back more than 250 years, while it is of more recent origin in the other countries) is very much alike in all five countries, every county having a county medical officer assisted by district medical officers. Iceland, with its limited population, may in this connection be considered equal to a county, there being no intermediary organs between the central government and the local districts. These officials in the first place serve as statutory advisers to local health committees and ensure compliance with national and local regulations pertaining to health and hygiene. They are, moreover, responsible for a growing variety of preventive health programmes, including those relating to tuberculosis, epidemic diseases, and venereal diseases. But while in Denmark public health medical officers are quite few, leaving the overwhelming part of direct medical care to private practising physicians, the situation is the opposite in Iceland, Norway, and Sweden where public health medical officers are spread in considerable numbers all over the country and are primarily practising doctors for the major part of the rural population. The Finnish set-up resembles the Danish system with respect to the role played by the State-employed public health medical officers, but as in the other three

See Medical Care, pp. 331-336.

countries rural medical care is also here predominantly in the hands of public doctors, only these are appointed by the local authorities.

County and borough councils are the principal organs in charge of hospital care in rural districts and towns, respectively, their responsibility in this field having been laid down by the State long ago.

The basic unit of the system is the special public health committee found in all towns as well as in the large majority of rural districts and entrusted with the main responsibility for preventive health work. In Finland and Norway all local authorities are under legal obligation to establish such a body, while in Iceland and Sweden small rural districts may let the local council cover its functions. Although corresponding Danish provisions are mandatory only upon the towns, practically all local authorities have in fact set up health committees. Committees are selected among the elected district or town councillors. The number of members varies somewhat, being usually 3-5 in rural districts and 5-11 in the towns, the public health medical officer being an *ex-officio* member (often chairman) or entitled to attend meetings; in Iceland the constable is always chairman of the committee.

General Health and Hygiene

Starting with the Danish Act of 1858 on the Establishment of Health Bye-laws, and followed up in 1860, 1874, and 1879 by similar Norwegian, Swedish, and Finnish measures, all the Northern countries today have on their statute books legislation providing for control over and regulation of health and hygiene by local authorities. In several of the countries it is only within the last generation that these controls have been extended to rural districts where sanitary conditions are still generally far behind those prevailing in the towns.

The key organ is the local health committee, the terms of reference of which are very wide. In the typical words of the Norwegian Health Act of 1860 "the health committee ..... shall strive to promote health and to eliminate circumstances which further illness and the spreading of disease". It is thus their task to enforce existing health regulations, to eliminate hygienic defects, to prevent epidemic diseases, and to promote health conditions in general.

But if there is a broad similarity as to the intended role of local authorities in this field, the basic legislative provisions still differ considerably. In Sweden the main regulations to be observed all over the country are directly spelled out in the Health Code, adopted in 1919, which contains one set of rules for rural districts and another stricter set for towns. Finland has a similar Health Act and Code from 1927. The Norwegian Health Act comprises very similar provisions, but these are supplemented by local health bye-laws which the towns are under obligation to adopt and rural districts may adopt; there is, however, a growing tendency towards greater uniformity also of bye-laws. In Denmark and Iceland, on the other hand, main emphasis rests upon these provisions which, as in Norway, are mandatory upon the towns, but in principle optional for rural districts. The difference is, however, more formal than real, since also in these countries the central authorities exercise considerable influence upon the contents of local bye-laws which are subject to their approbation. Thus in Denmark the individual bye-laws are largely patterned upon "Standard Health Bye-laws", one for rural districts and one for towns, recommended by the National Health Service. Similarly, in Iceland special regulations set out the minimum provisions which all bye-laws must contain, at the same time as they define the powers of the committees.

As a consequence, the general regulations governing the health activities of local authorities in practice are largely identical, comprising rules pertaining to drinking-water, sewerage, refuse disposal, and cleanliness on public and private property.

In the course of time these general regulations have been supplemented by a lengthening series of national enactments covering special problems of hygienic importance. They include legislation concerning prevention of epidemic and venereal diseases, and of tuberculosis; control of the manufacturing and distribution of foodstuffs, particularly bread, meat, milk, and margarine; and supervision of hotels and restaurants, barber-shops, etc. A special category comprises those measures relating to the promotion of maternal and child health which have been introduced mainly during the last two decades within the general framework of family welfare policy; the same applies to the general inspection of industrial premises.

See pp. 344-353.

See pp. 243-257.

See pp. 79-81.

The health committees have contributed greatly to the attainment of a high general level of hygiene and sanitation throughout the five countries. Continuous participation by elected members has ensured close contact with the population and has helped to prevent health activities from stiffening in bureaucratic routine. One of the difficulties of the system is that modern society requires a highly complex technical and organizational machinery in order to assure satisfactory conditions of hygiene. As a result increased demands are made upon the expert services of public health medical officers, veterinarians, engineers, etc., and it has been necessary to provide health committees with larger staffs, including public health nurses who, especially in Finland and Sweden, play a very considerable role. Obviously these difficulties are particularly manifest in the smaller, mainly rural districts, while the towns have largely solved the problem by the appointment of special health inspectors to assist the public health medical officer in his work.

An interesting feature of post-war developments has been the increased interest in industrial hygiene, including the organization of specialized medical services in industrial undertakings. As an example may be mentioned the conclusion in Norway of an agreement between the Medical Association and the central organizations of employers and workers, calling upon larger enterprises and public utilities to appoint special medical doctors to keep a continuous check upon the health conditions of all employees as well as to supervise work-hygiene in general; these doctors do not directly treat patients but refer them to other physicians in case of sickness. The scheme is administered by a central committee, which collaborates with the Health Directorate, and today covers about 100,000 wage earners, mainly in large undertakings.

Industrial hygiene is an important and rapidly expanding concept in the Northern countries. Here a company doctor is vaccinating workers in a Norwegian plant.

Medical Care

All the five Northern countries are fortunate in commanding the services of a first-rate medical profession. In each country medical instruction has always been provided only at one or a few government-operated medical schools, usually attached to the universities. This concentration of educational facilities has obviously greatly facilitated the establishment and maintenance of high and uniform standards. Training of a doctor usually requires 7–8 years, including hospital service as an intern. But also after acquiring their licence as physicians only a minority go immediately into general practice while the rest continue their training for years, an increasing number in order to qualify as specialists.

There are considerable differences in the set-up under which *medical care outside hospitals* is provided for the population. The following figures show medical doctors distributed according to their main practice. It should be noted that a considerable number of hospital doctors are also active in private practice and that, inversely, many private practitioners perform official duties to a varying extent.

PERCENTAGE DISTRIBUTION OF MEDICAL DOCTORS (1949)

	Denmark	Finland	Iceland	Norway	Sweden
Private practice. . .	58.1	39.8	46.7	50.7	38.1
Public health. . . .	1.5	33.0	31.1	14.1	15.5
Hospitals	40.4	27.2	22.2	35.2	46.4
Total	100.0	100.0	100.0	100.0	100.0

It will be seen that the Danish figures stand apart from those of all the other countries, the proportion of doctors employed in private practice being higher and that in public health lower than anywhere else. The explanation is found in the basically different systems of medical care. In *Denmark*, the voluntary health insurance societies, which today comprise four-fifths of the adult population, are under statutory obligation to assure their members of free medical care. The societies have consequently contracted with the general practitioners and specialists all over the country to provide such care to members. The doctors thus employed are, however, at the same time free to serve non-member patients. As a result of these arrangements practically all medical care outside hospitals is in the hands of private doctors, while the relatively very limited number of public health medical officers concern themselves predominantly with their public health functions.

See Chapter VII, Social Security, pp. 405–409.

The other four countries present a rather different picture. Mainly due to the difficulties of providing regular medical attendance for inhabitants of the vast, sparsely populated areas characteristic of these countries, it was early realized that the public had to step in with appropriate measures. The result has been a combined system under which, in addition to their supervisory and preventive tasks with respect to general health conditions and hygiene, a large number of public health officers spread all over the country are also in charge of almost all general medical care of out-patients in rural districts. In the towns, on the other hand, arrangements are more similar to those found in Denmark, public health officers leaving the main part of general medical care in the hands of private practitioners.

Sweden has been the pioneer in the establishment of this highly important public health scheme, which here dates back to the end of the 17th century. The country is divided into 570 districts, each with a "provincial physician", as the public health medical officer is called. Receiving a basic salary from the government, they treat patients for fixed low fees, make sick calls, issue certificates, etc. They are furthermore responsible for maternity and child health services, often serve as school doctors and carry out preventive investigations concerning tuberculosis, as well as contagious and venereal diseases. In the remote and sparsely populated regions of North Sweden they also operate "cottage hospitals" for cases which do not require transfer to the larger hospitals. An important feature is that each provincial physician is assisted by one or more trained public health nurses of whom there are now about 1,200. Their duties include the dissemination of information and guidance

See Chapter IV, Family Welfare, pp. 243–244 and 256.

concerning domestic hygiene, maternal and child care, and general hygiene, including prevention of disease as well as bedside care in the home.

The system is generally acknowledged to have been of fundamental importance in raising general health standards, particularly in the rural areas where the provincial physician will usually be a prominent community figure. A major difficulty arises out of the shortage of doctors, the individual districts being considered too large to be handled satisfactorily by one officer. There are, of course, private practitioners but they are very unevenly distributed, most of them being located in the towns and thus leaving the provincial physicians pretty much to themselves in the rural areas. In the towns the major part of out-patient medical care is provided by the private practitioners, but large numbers of patients are also treated at low fees in out-patient departments of the public hospitals.

Norwegian programmes follow practically the same lines although districts are usually smaller (measured by the number of inhabitants). The same applies to *Iceland*, although due to the acute shortage of trained nurses only few rural districts include such persons on their medical staff.

As already indicated in the preceding section, the *Finnish* set-up is somewhat different, general medical care in the rural districts being mainly in the hands of medical doctors employed by local authorities. This system of "municipal doctors" is found throughout the country and legislation enacted in 1951 authorizes special State grants so as to encourage their appointment also in the smaller districts. The towns, where the majority of the private practitioners are located, similarly employ one or more public physicians. A special feature, which has gained increasing prominence in recent years, is for private enterprises to appoint special company doctors who furnish general medical care to employees, the costs being defrayed by the employer, the employee, and the health insurance according to varying criteria.

In contrast with several other countries, such as the United Kingdom and the United States, *hospital medical services* in the Northern countries are in principle quite independent of other medical care and are provided by special hospital doctors. They everywhere make up a large proportion of the medical profession, although figures vary considerably (from 22 per cent in Iceland to 46 in Sweden).

See table, p. 332.

334

Vital health functions are furthermore carried out by the large cadres of trained nurses and midwives. The great majority of the former group are employed in hospitals and similar institutions. A considerable number who have received special supplementary training are also employed as public health nurses; of particular importance in this connection are the many nurses who take part in the work of the public health medical officers, especially in the rural areas.

MEDICAL DOCTORS AND NURSES PER 100,000 POPULATION (1949)

	Doctors	Nurses
Denmark	102	215
Finland	47	151
Iceland	115	100
Norway	88	219
Sweden	69	177

While Denmark, Iceland, and Norway are considered to be about adequately covered with doctors, except in certain categories, Finland and Sweden, where enrollment for medical training is subject to the *numerus clausus*, suffer from a marked shortage. By comparison, the corresponding figure for the United States is 130–140 per 100,000 population, or higher than in any of the Northern countries.

In all five countries there would appear to be a more or less pronounced shortage of trained nurses; this is largely explained by their rather exacting working-hours schedule as compared with the more attractive conditions offered in other occupations of recent years. The situation became particularly acute in Finland during the last war when the Red Cross instituted the training of "relief sisters" to alleviate this shortage. In post-war years the Finnish Medical Board has for the same purpose introduced courses of eight months for the training of "assistant nurses". The basic shortage, however, still persists in all five countries, although numerous improvements in the working conditions of nursing staffs have been introduced in the last few years.

The activities of midwives are subject to special regulations. Starting with a Danish decree dating as far back as 1672, all five countries today have introduced legislation providing for the training of midwives and laying down rules governing their working conditions and duties. The general set-up is very much the same everywhere,

335

the countries being divided into a large number of districts, each with a publicly appointed midwife who is remunerated by a basic salary, supplemented in some of the countries by fees (which are usually paid by the health insurance). In Denmark and Norway there are, however, also numerous midwives who practise privately. The total number of midwives has increased only slightly or not at all within recent decades; this is partly a result of the improved means of transportation in rural areas but mainly it is due to the fact that an increasing proportion of births takes place in hospitals or other institutions where all modern medical facilities are at hand and staffs may be more economically utilized.

See Chapter IV, Family Welfare, pp. 245–246.

Engraving of the first Danish public hospital, built in 1757 and now the Danish Museum of Decorative Arts.

Hospitals

There is a long tradition in the Northern countries for the community to carry the main responsibility for assuring the whole population of hospital care. The first Swedish public hospital, the Serafimer Lazaret, was founded in 1752 to serve as a national hospital for both Sweden and Finland (at that time under the Swedish Crown); its capacity was eight beds! In 1757 King Frederik the V. erected the first public hospital in Denmark, named after himself. Somewhat later public hospitals also made their appearance in Norway.

As far back as 150 years ago government decrees in Denmark and Sweden placed upon county and borough councils the duty of pro-

336

viding general hospitals and operating them in such a way that all citizens received the necessary treatment, irrespective of economic circumstances. In all five countries the great majority of hospitals have always been publicly owned and operated, and available to the whole population at low fees. The problem of how to ensure the common man of hospital care – a controversial issue in several other countries – was thus decisively solved long ago. A number of private hospitals are maintained in the larger cities by religious and other non-governmental organizations, frequently with more or less extensive public support, but they are of secondary importance only, varying from less than 3 per cent of the aggregate number of hospital beds in Sweden to 15–20 per cent in Iceland and Norway.

Total capacity of the hospital systems is illustrated by the following figures which cover general, epidemic, tuberculosis, and mental hospitals. A number of special institutions, excluded because of the difficulties of compiling data on a uniform basis, play only a minor role in the general picture.

BEDS PER 100,000 POPULATION (1949)

Denmark	940
Finland	680
Iceland	840
Norway	850
Sweden	1050

As will be seen, there are quite considerable differences among the countries. In none of them, however, is present capacity considered fully adequate. In Finland, Iceland, and Norway the present situation is one of acute shortage. But also in Denmark and Sweden there is need for further expansion. This is due partly to the increasing number of aged patients who occupy the wards for longer periods, partly to the demand for further enlargement in a number of special categories.

General hospitals account for about one-half of total accommodation in Finland, Norway, and Sweden, and a somewhat higher proportion in Denmark and Iceland. Between 25 and 30 per cent fall upon the mental hospitals in all countries except Iceland, where the percentage is only 10. Finally, the tuberculosis hospitals have 10–15 per cent of all beds in Denmark and Sweden, but more than 20 per cent in the other three countries.

337

GENERAL HOSPITALS

General hospitals are primarily the responsibility of district, county, and borough authorities. In Denmark and Sweden practically all these hospitals are administered by the county and borough authorities while in the other three countries the rural population is predominantly served by hospitals operated under the direct auspices of local district councils. It should be added that, as a rule, the State operates one or more larger general hospitals, connected with the universities, as training centres for medical students; in Finland, alone, there are also numerous other general State hospitals throughout the country, largely taking the place of the county and borough hospitals found in the other countries.

In former days when communications were poor it was only natural to concentrate upon the building of many small hospitals in order that they might be within easy reach of the patients. This applied to all five countries but obviously less to Denmark than to the other countries with their extensive and sparsely populated rural areas, particularly in the northern regions. This difference is still clearly discernible today: While there are only 155 hospitals in Denmark, the corresponding Finnish and Norwegian figures run to no less than about 450 and 300, respectively, most of them being rather small. The consequence was a system of hospitals primarily intended for the treatment of the more common diseases. Since surgical cases required quicker treatment and surgery made revolutionary advance in the 19th century, this discipline became predominant, with the result that the typical hospital had a trained surgeon as its only chief medical officer, his duties also including, however, the treatment of medical and other diseases.

Within the present century this situation has been fundamentally changed. Due to the improved means of transportation the sick may now be quickly and safely conveyed over relatively long distances. Moreover, the sweeping progress of medical science has rendered it impossible for any single medical doctor to master, even approximately, all the specialties required for up-to-date treatment; at the same time medical apparatus has multiplied and today involves such heavy expenditure that hospitals on a large scale are required for its economical use.

As a consequence, the last decades have witnessed a thorough reorganization of the traditional hospital set-up, particularly in Denmark

and Sweden. Briefly, the new policy, which has been strongly advocated and promoted by the national health authorities, has aimed at the establishment of a network of specialized central county hospitals in addition to the many smaller and older local hospitals.

The pattern has been for each county to establish a central hospital equipped not only with a medical, a surgical, and an X-ray department, but wherever possible also with departments for diseases of the ear, nose, throat, and eyes, as well as pediatrics and gynaecology. These general hospital facilities are supplemented by out-patient departments and by laboratories which not only serve the hospital, but are also at the disposal of general practitioners for the undertaking of analyses, X-ray examinations, etc. Another new feature, as yet only partly developed, is the employment of social workers to assist patients in solving their personal problems. Practically all Danish and Swedish counties have erected such hospitals, although here and there some of the specialist departments are still lacking.

These large institutions are supported by the numerous smaller hospitals which deal with the less complicated cases. In Sweden two types are distinguishable within this group. There is the "three-way" hospital with separate medical, surgical, and X-ray departments, each with its own specialist in charge. And there is the "mixed" hospital

339

where one chief physician, usually a trained surgeon, is in general command, assisted by one or more junior medical doctors. The latter type is the prevalent category in Denmark. Finally, at the bottom of the scale, there are in the remote regions a considerable number of "cottage-hospitals" or sick-wards attended to by the provincial physician; these small units, it may be added, are found in all of the countries except Denmark.

The large cities, primarily the capitals, maintain their own hospital systems which have developed along lines very similar to those of the central county hospitals. In fact, the latter may be considered the solution to the problem of how to provide the more scattered population in rural areas and smaller towns with hospital services of the same high standard as that prevailing in the large cities.

In the other Northern countries, too, reorganization of the hospital system along the lines described above has long been under consideration, although it is still in the initial stages of implementation.

In Norway, where it has long been a complaint that the hospital set-up was suffering from a lack of planning, a national programme for the construction of hospitals has been under preparation since 1932. Numerous projects were about to be initiated when the war and the German occupation brought activities to an abrupt, if temporary, halt. It is therefore only in post-war years that it has been possible to resume this work. The plan, which aims not only at reorganization but also at large-scale expansion of existing hospital facilities, corresponds very closely to Swedish developments. Central hospitals, one in each county, are to be supplemented by "three-way" hospitals in towns and by "mixed" hospitals in smaller urban settlements; in the northern regions local sick-wards are retained under the management of public health medical officers. – Considerable progress has already been made during the last few years in implementing this ambitious programme, although the scarcity of building materials has put a limit to the speed of construction.

Finnish legislation dating from 1943 likewise calls for the construction of central hospitals all over the country, but due to the financial difficulties and shortages of materials resulting from Finland's troubled post-war situation the implementation of this programme has been considerably delayed. The first central hospital is, however, already in operation while four more are under construction. Present plans envisage the completion of the whole building programme by 1966.

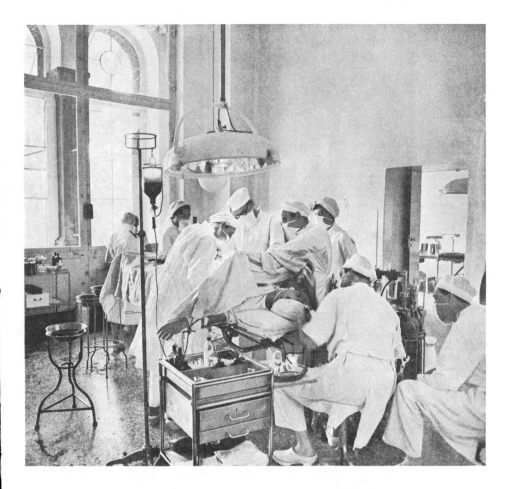

The smaller picture shows the operation room in Copenhagen's Municipal Hospital as it looked 90 years ago; the larger as it is today. The fact that only interior changes have been necessary to transform the old premises into a fully modern operation room is a high tribute to the vision of the original architect.

341

The hospital system in Iceland must be viewed against the basic structure of the country, with a very slender population scattered over a considerable territory. Apart from a State hospital situated in the capital and a few private hospitals, the large majority of general hospitals are owned and operated by local urban and rural districts. Most of them are very similar to the "cottage hospitals" of the northern regions of Finland, Norway, and Sweden, being quite small – with a capacity of less than 10 beds – and attended to by the local provincial physicians.

As already mentioned, it is a characteristic feature of hospitals in all the Northern countries that they are exclusively manned by regular medical staff employed on a whole-time basis. Some of these medical doctors make hospital work their life career, ending up as chief physicians in charge of one of the smaller hospitals or of a department in one of the larger hospitals; others leave after some years of service in junior positions to become public health medical officers or take up a private practice, often as specialists. The practising physicians take the initiative in having patients admitted to the hospitals, but once hospitalized, patients are dealt with solely by the hospital staff. It may be added that Swedish hospital doctors are usually also entitled to treat out-patients in premises made available by the hospital. This staff system, which is considered highly practical, must obviously be viewed against the fact that most hospitals are public and thus in a position to afford secure tenure of posts; today it also applies, however, to private hospitals. It provides the principal explanation of how hospital work, as previously indicated, has come to account for such a considerable proportion of the total number of medical doctors.

In keeping with the basic policy of providing hospital care irrespective of economic circumstances, fees have traditionally been low, not only for the poor but for the population as a whole, and today cover only a fraction of actual costs. The Danish county hospitals charge 6–9 kr. a day, the corresponding Swedish fees being 3–5 kr.; in Finland the fees are approximately the same as in Sweden. Actual costs average 35–50 kr. per day. In Iceland and Norway, on the other hand, fees have been adjusted to some extent to the rising costs. However, since in all five countries the health insurance pays these fees in respect of all insured members, the final result is that the large majority of the population receive hospitalization free of charge.

SPECIAL HOSPITALS

Among the diseases singled out for treatment in special hospitals
and related institutions are mental ailments, epidemic diseases, tuberculosis, cancer, etc.

There are considerable variations between the countries as to the
auspices under which these hospitals are operated, although the public
everywhere carries the main responsibility. Some of them are maintained directly by the State – this applies to practically all mental
hospitals in Denmark and Sweden; others are primarily in the hands
of county, borough or district authorities; and, finally, a considerable number of institutions, notably for the treatment and care of
patients suffering from tuberculosis and cancer, are private, although
the central and local governments contribute heavily towards their
costs of operation.

More details concerning the measures undertaken on behalf of these
groups will be found in the following two sections where an attempt
is made to give a general outline of the principal methods employed
in the prevention and treatment of the so-called major diseases, and
in the care and rehabilitation of the physically and mentally handicapped, respectively.

343

The Struggle Against Major Diseases

A number of diseases have occupied, and partly still occupy, such a prominent place in the general picture of health developments that they would appear to merit special mention. Epidemic diseases, tuberculosis, cancer, and venereal diseases are the chief among these maladies, and the struggle against them constitutes a weighty chapter in the history of modern health and medicine. Some of them have been almost eliminated or sharply reduced, others still loom as largely unsolved problems. It has previously been stated that a major characteristic of more recent health programmes has been their growing emphasis upon preventive work. This is nowhere better illustrated than in the activities undertaken to combat the major diseases. Well into the present century curative efforts commanded the centre of the stage but in recent decades the weight has been definitely shifted to measures of prevention and control, although facilities and methods of treatment have clearly also been very considerably developed.

Victims of alcoholism constitute a group somewhat apart. As against the purely condemnatory attitude of former times, measures undertaken in recent years reflect the increased understanding that alcoholics are essentially sick persons and, consequently, that the problem of their treatment and rehabilitation is a legitimate object for the combined efforts of medicine and social welfare.

Similarly, the feeble-minded and the mentally ill are increasingly viewed on a par with victims of other diseases. For practical reasons these groups are, however, dealt with in the following section on the care and rehabilitation of the mentally and physically handicapped.

See pp. 359–377.

Northern scientists have made important contributions to the advancement of medicine. A few of the results obtained in the present century may be cited. Danes prominent in this field include four Nobel-prize winners: Finsen, who developed methods of light treatment for a number of serious diseases, including lupus; Fibiger, a pioneer in cancer research; Dam, the discoverer of vitamine K; and Krogh, known for his epochal inquiries into the capillary system. The Finnish scientist Savonen is internationally known as a pioneer in the fight against tuberculosis; Ylppö is famous for his work with premature infants. As for Norway, special mention should be made of Holst and Frölich, who found the cause of scurvy in the lack of vitamine C, and of Owren's renowned investigations into blood coagulation. Famous Swedish contributions include the inquiries of Fahraeus into the sedimentation of red blood corpuscles, the production by Lehmann of PAS (paraaminosalicylic acid) for the treatment of tuberculosis, and by Ingelman and Grönwall of dextran, a blood-substitute; in the fields of brain and heart surgery the names of Olivecrona and Crafoord are known all over the world.

EPIDEMIC DISEASES

Undoubtedly our ancestors considered epidemics and diseases as largely synonymous terms for the good reason that the ferocity of epidemic diseases heavily restricted the range of operation for the other, slower working ailments. To illustrate this we need go no further back than the beginning of the 18th century when a small-pox epidemic is estimated to have torn away a full third of the whole Icelandic population. In the Northern countries, as in other parts of the world, one of the key aspects of health developments during the past century has therefore quite naturally been the sustained campaign waged against epidemic diseases, primarily cholera, small-pox, and plague, and, secondly, typhoid, paratyphoid, diphtheria, and the like.

The first organized measures to combat epidemics date back to the closing decades of the 18th century when notification of cases of such diseases was made compulsory in several of the Northern countries and all persons infected were obliged to submit to treatment; also quarantine regulations for foreign traffic were early introduced. The decisive period of progress, however, did not set in until the later part of the following century when, against the background of the great development of bacteriological research, the Northern countries, one after another, passed special legislation covering this field. Provisions which originally aimed only at the most critical of these diseases have gradually been broadened in scope and today apply generally to all epidemic diseases.

In the Northern countries it has long been a rule that all children must be vaccinated at least once against small-pox before entering school (usually at six or seven). The local authorities are in charge of this service which is rendered free of charge. Within recent years inoculation against diphtheria, while not yet compulsory, has also been undertaken on a large scale. In this connection mention should be made of one of the existing national institutions, the Danish State Serum Institute in Copenhagen, which for several decades has been

345

one of the leading institutions in the world as regards production of sera and research into epidemic diseases.

The basic legislative provisions, almost identical in all five countries, call for free medical treatment and hospitalization of patients suffering from any of the more serious epidemic diseases at special hospitals or sick-wards, usually operated by county or local authorities. While there are a large number of independent epidemic hospitals in Sweden and Finland, these cases are in the other three countries largely cared for in sick-wards attached to the general hospitals. While hospitalization is compulsory in Finland and Sweden, in Denmark the patient is generally free to decide for himself whether he wants to be treated in hospital or at home.

Results have been highly gratifying. The most deadly epidemic diseases, e.g. cholera, small-pox, and the plague, ceased to be of any importance long ago and are by now virtually extinct. Others, such as typhoid, paratyphoid, diphtheria, scarlatina, etc., have been sharply curtailed and today hardly exist as a serious problem. The following figures relating to diphtheria may serve as an illustration of the spectacular advances made in reducing mortality due to these causes.

Deaths Due to Diphtheria per 100,000 Population

	1911–20	1950
Denmark	8.7	0.1
Finland	...	0.9
Iceland	9.1	0.6
Norway	19.0	0.9
Sweden	18.3	0.1

Epidemics still occur, poliomyelitis being today the most frequent among the serious diseases, dreaded not only because of its rather high mortality but also because of the lasting disablement which is so often its result. But on the whole epidemics center on such "milder" diseases as influenza, angina and tonsillitis, whooping cough, etc., which, although for climatic reasons widespread, are of relatively brief duration and involve few fatal cases. The only major exception in the last 10–20 years was a serious diphtheria epidemic in Finland 1942–46 which caused considerable loss of life. But generally epidemic diseases today figure only modestly in mortality statistics. Thus, while in Denmark they still accounted for 10 per cent of all deaths in 1927, the percentage has now declined to less than 2.

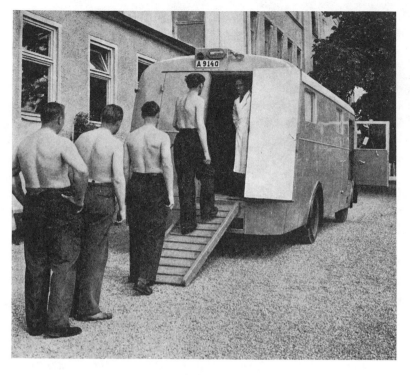

Among the devices resorted to in the unremitting fight against t.b. are mobile X-ray units, such as the Swedish Roentgen-bus shown here.

TUBERCULOSIS

In former times a veritable scourge to many European countries, tuberculosis has for generations been the focus of intensive efforts in the Northern countries, closely associated with those directed against epidemic diseases. The first steps were everywhere primarily due to voluntary initiative. In all five countries the various interested organizations long ago joined to form National Societies for the Combating of Tuberculosis. Today, these societies remain in active charge of important anti-tuberculosis activities, though the central and local governments have by now everywhere taken over main responsibility in this field.

As in the case of epidemic diseases, two main lines of approach have been pursued: Cure and prevention. Naturally enough, work in most of the countries concentrated from the start upon the establishment of hospitals and sanatoria to provide treatment and care for those afflicted, at the same time isolating them and thus preventing the disease from being spread.

347

The first sanatoria were founded in Denmark and Sweden in the 1870's and 1890's, respectively, on a purely private basis. Shortly after the turn of the century both countries introduced State subsidies for the construction and operation of tuberculosis hospitals and sanatoria, the general policy being that the government would leave the direct management of such institutions to local authorities and interested voluntary organizations.

At the present time a comprehensive network of these establishments has been developed, Sweden having a large number of rather small institutions, Denmark a somewhat smaller number of larger institutions. Most of the hospitals are under the auspices of county and borough authorities, while numerous sanatoria are maintained by the National Societies. For practical reasons the institutions, usually situated on scenic spots, have largely been specialized, some of them receiving adults, others children; special seaside hospitals and sanatoria have also been established for patients suffering from surgical and glandular tuberculosis. Denmark and Sweden are today amply covered with hospital and sanatorium accommodation, and with the continuous decline in the number of patients it has actually been possible to release several sanatoria for other uses.

Developments in Finland and Norway have followed a rather similar pattern. A Finnish act of 1930 authorized government subsidies for tuberculosis sanatoria and in the following years many large sanatoria were built by municipalities, associating for this purpose. Under the present Tuberculosis Act of 1948 the country is divided into 18 districts, each with its central sanatorium. All tuberculosis institutions are operated by the local authorities, although under State direction and supervision. The Norwegian situation is characterized by a shortage of hospital accommodation for the surgical treatment of tubercular patients while sanatoria intended for chronic patients show surplus capacity. Iceland has three sanatoria, two of them State-operated while the third is maintained by the Society of Former Tuberculosis Patients (though with State subsidies) and concentrates upon the vocational rehabilitation of patients.

As previously indicated, tuberculosis institutions today are an important part of the hospital systems of the Northern countries. Total capacity of tuberculosis hospitals and sanatoria varies from 104 beds per 100,000 inhabitants in Denmark to 178 per 100,000 inhabitants in Iceland, the other countries occupying intermediary positions.

348

*First-class archi-
tecture need not be
a monopoly of
cultural centres or
office buildings.
This fine Finnish
sanatorium is
located in Pemar.*

Treatment and care are everywhere given at very low fees and since
in most cases these are paid by the health insurance or by the public
the practical result is that the large majority of the population receives
services free of charge. It may be added that examination of persons
considered liable to spread the disease is everywhere compulsory;
in Norway also hospitalization of such cases is compulsory.

With the rapid progress made in hospital treatment of tuberculosis,
increasing emphasis has come to be placed upon preventive measures.
In all countries developments have followed very much the same line,
the National Societies or – in Denmark – the National Health Service taking the initiative in establishing dispensaries, mainly in the
larger towns, and the public subsequently taking over and expand-

349

ing the programme. Practically all county and city boroughs are today provided with one or more of these dispensaries operated by local authorities with State support, usually in connection with a tuberculosis hospital; in Sweden the central dispensaries are supplemented by a large number of smaller district units.

The central dispensaries, which are equipped with X-ray apparatus and staffed with medical specialists, occupy a key position in the campaign for the prevention of tuberculosis. They serve primarily as diagnosing centres to which general practitioners refer persons suspected of the disease for detailed examination. Also, they are in charge of check-ups in the private homes of patients hospitalized for tuberculosis, their effectiveness in this respect being based upon the duty to notify all new cases of the disease. They further undertake mass investigations, covering whole population groups, either all inhabitants in selected regions or all members of certain occupations, e.g. students, employees of certain categories of enterprises, etc.; and, finally, they are generally active in promoting the hygienic and social conditions of those suffering from tuberculosis. X-ray testing has assumed very large proportions in all countries. In Iceland a scheme calling for the testing of the whole population has been in process of implementation since 1940; thus, in 1945 all citizens over one year of age in Reykjavik were examined. Similar programmes have been initiated in the other four countries in the years 1946–1950. Mobile units are utilized in order to reach the most remote areas. Also vaccination against tuberculosis has been introduced on an ever-growing scale and in most of the countries it is becoming the general practice to vaccinate newborn infants, before their discharge from maternity hospitals, and school children. Generally, participation in the programmes is voluntary, but in Norway the central health authorities may, since 1947, decree compulsory vaccination for any group of the population or for the population as a whole, and in Finland, Iceland, and Sweden any person may be forced to undergo examination if this is deemed necessary. It remains to be added that all the various preventive services are generally rendered free or at a nominal charge.

It has not yet been possible to eliminate tuberculosis entirely. It remains a serious disease afflicting large numbers of people. But its incidence, and especially tuberculosis mortality, has been greatly reduced, as will be apparent from a glance at the following figures.

350

DEATHS DUE TO TUBERCULOSIS PER 100,000 POPULATION

	1911–1920	1950
Denmark	144	14
Finland	254	91
Iceland	177	20
Norway	231	29
Sweden	188	22

As a death cause tuberculosis has today been reduced to modest proportions in all countries except Finland where it is still considered public-health enemy number one, accounting for one out of every twelve deaths. The other four countries, on the other hand, today rank among those having the lowest mortality rate from this cause. For the last ten years Denmark has had the lowest tuberculosis mortality in the world (closely followed by New Zealand and Holland).

CANCER

The prevention of cancer is still beyond the reach of medical science, but considerable progress in methods of treatment has been made within the last 20–30 years. As with tuberculosis, private initiative has also here played a pioneer role. In all the Northern countries special societies have been founded for the combating of cancer.

Focal points in this campaign are in all five countries a number of radiological clinics operated in the large cities and equipped with the most up-to-date apparatus. Special mention may here be made of the Danish Finsen Institute in Copenhagen and the Swedish Radiumhemmet, both world-famous centres for X-ray and radium treatment of diseases. Thanks to public subsidies, fees are everywhere very low and are usually paid by the health insurance. Considerable appropriations are also made for cancer research. The voluntary societies conduct extensive propaganda among the population, particularly with a view to inducing people to present themselves for examination and treatment immediately on observing suspicious symptoms; it may be added that it is often quite difficult to persuade people to do so.

In recent decades cancer has shown a slow but consistent upward trend and figures today as one of the most dreaded diseases, accounting for 10–15 per cent of all deaths. Denmark has the highest and Finland the lowest rate among the five countries.

351

In evaluating this trend it should, however, be observed that cancer mainly afflicts persons in middle and later life. Thus in Denmark almost three-fifths of all deaths due to this cause occur after the 65th year, while there are practically no fatal cases in the age groups under 30 years. The real explanation of the increasing frequency of cancer is consequently found in the general aging of the population since the turn of the century, and mortality rates calculated on the basis of an unchanged distribution of the population according to age actually show a decline. Moreover, the improved methods of diagnosis have raised statistical figures without any corresponding real increase occurring in the incidence of the disease.

VENEREAL DISEASES

Already in 1790 Denmark, as the first country in the world, introduced legislation providing for free and compulsory treatment of venereal diseases. Within the present century all the other Northern countries have followed suit. Basic statutory provisions are practically identical. Any person who has contracted a venereal disease is entitled to free public treatment, ambulant or in hospital. He may also be treated privately but in all cases he is under legal obligation to undergo treatment. Any patient who evades this obligation or refuses to follow instructions received may be placed in hospital by force. The physician shall endeavour to elicit information as to the source of infection and criminal punishment is inflicted upon those who knowingly transmit the disease.

Serious cases are hospitalized, but the general rule is for patients to receive ambulant treatment from the public health medical officers or from other specially appointed physicians. In the large cities treatment is usually given at out-patient departments attached to general hospitals. Great emphasis is placed on the informational aspect of the problem and at their first visit to the doctor patients in most of the countries are furnished with a pamphlet outlining the nature of venereal diseases and their contagiousness, as well as the main legislative provisions. A recent development has been the employment in some of the urban out-patient departments of social workers to assist in tracing sources of infection, to guide patients, and to assure them of social assistance if required.

Statistics concerning the incidence of venereal diseases clearly reflect the effectiveness of these measures. There have been marked variations, especially during each of the two World Wars, but the general trend has been strongly downward. This especially applies to syphilis. Thus, in the years before 1914 the number of registered cases of syphilis in Denmark – which then had the highest incidence – corresponded to about 100 per 100,000 inhabitants, while by 1940 the rate had fallen to only 10; Swedish and Norwegian figures were still lower. Real progress was even more marked than these figures indicate since, due to the early treatment of patients, the worst forms of syphilis, particularly in its final stages, had been all but eliminated. The frequency of gonorrhea also fell off considerably during the inter-war period, but in 1940 it still ranged between 150 and 200 cases per 100,000 inhabitants.

The unsettled conditions prevailing during the years of the Second World War brought about a violent reversal of this downward trend in all countries. The effects were most pronounced for syphilis which increased many times over pre-war levels within a few years. But also the incidence of gonorrhea multiplied, doubling in Norway and Sweden and tripling in Denmark and Finland.

Following a culmination in the years 1944–1946 the figures declined, however, and at the present time the number of registered cases of both syphilis and gonorrhea is approaching or has already reached the low figures of 1940.

CARIES

Although hardly comparable in seriousness to the diseases dealt with above, caries·has, due to its widespread occurrence, come to attract increasing attention as an important health problem. For several decades school dental services have been in operation to a varying extent in all the five countries and more recently comprehensive measures for the further improvement of existing facilities have been undertaken.

Sweden has been a pioneer in this field, special legislation from 1938 calling for the establishment, under the auspices of county and borough authorities, of a nation-wide programme of public dental care. The country is divided into a large number of districts, each of which is to be provided with a dental clinic, every county having a central clinic for the treatment of more complicated cases. Clinics are open to the whole population, children being treated free of charge while adults pay a modest fee or – in the case of less well-to-do persons – also receive treatment free of charge. A serious bottleneck, which has hampered quick realization of this scheme, is the shortage of dentists; new training institutions have been decided upon in an effort to relieve this shortage. At the present time the service employs about 800 dentists, but when completed their number will have increased to more than 2,000.

In 1949 Norway introduced a similar system. In the initial years the emphasis was placed upon the quick development of dental services in the northern regions, where the lack of facilities was particularly pronounced. Urban school-children have for many years received free dental care and this is now being introduced also in the rural districts.

No comparable programmes exist in the other countries under review. Numerous local authorities, mainly towns, provide free dental services for school-children, while the adult population is to a varying extent entitled to more or less comprehensive dental care by dentists attached to the health insurance systems.

ALCOHOLICS

A special problem with important repercussions on health is that of alcoholism. At the beginning of the 19th century the Northern peoples maintained a dubious eminence as large-scale consumers of alcoholic beverages. Indeed, according to an official report from 1882, Denmark then still carried the world record in this respect.

Within the past 75 years this traditional state of affairs has undergone considerable change. Under the triple onslaught of temperance movements, public restrictions and prohibitive taxes, consumption of alcohol has everywhere declined materially; in Denmark where this development set in later than in the other countries the decline has been particularly pronounced, consumption of alcohol having been throttled to a meagre fraction of its former volume.

ANNUAL PER CAPITA CONSUMPTION OF PURE ALCOHOL (LITRES)

	Denmark	Finland	Iceland	Norway	Sweden
1881–1890	10.2	2.5	...	2.6	4.8
1931–1940	2.1	1.2	0.9	2.0	3.2
1941–1945	2.4	1.3	1.1	1.3	2.8
1946–1950	2.9	1.7	1.8	2.3	3.5
1951	2.7	1.8	1.4	2.1	3.5

As shown in the table tne years since 1940 have, in spite of renewed heavy tax increases, been accompanied by a limited rise, but
consumption is still lower than for instance in the United States (to
say nothing of wine-producing nations such as France and Italy).
It should be added that there is a significant difference in consumption habits between Denmark, where beer accounts for about
two-thirds of total consumption, and the other four countries, where
strong liquor is dominant.

Although dating back for more than a hundred years, it was only
around 1880–1890 that the temperance movement really gathered
momentum. Today the Northern temperance organizations command
a following which runs into hundreds of thousands in several of the
countries. The movement has undoubtedly contributed importantly
to the voluntary reduction of liquor consumption. At the same
time it has acted as a powerful and highly vocal pressure group
upon legislative authorities and has thus exercised considerable
influence also beyond its own ranks. It is a notable fact that teetotallers
in every one of the countries comprise a disproportionately great
percentage of parliamentary members. The activities of temperance
societies have in recent years been supplemented by cultural and
athletic organizations which have taken up the promotion of temperate
drinking habits without going so far as to advocate total abstinence.

Although the beneficial effects of voluntary efforts should not be
underrated, it is probably a realistic appraisal that the main explanation of declining alcohol consumption must be found in public
taxation and regulation.

In all five countries ever-increasing taxes upon spirits have been
imposed, particularly during the two World Wars. A sudden, and
drastic, tax increase in 1917 within a short time changed the position
of Denmark from that of the most "alcoholic" country in the world
with respect to strong liquor to that of one of the most "temperate".
In the other Northern countries taxation has increased at a slower
rate and with less dramatic effects. The desire to promote temperance
may have played a certain role, but hard fiscal considerations have
without any doubt been the main motivating factor. The result has
been that the Northern countries, especially Iceland and Norway,
today boast liquor prices that are among the highest in the world.

With respect to regulations and restrictions concerning production,
distribution, and consumption of alcoholic beverages there are, on

355

the other hand, decisive differences. Danish legislation provides for control, through a licencing system, of public houses dispensing liquor but no general restrictions have ever been introduced. Differently in the other countries. Already during the 19th century consumption of alcohol was here materially reduced thanks to legislative provisions and the activity of the temperance movement. In Finland, Iceland, and Norway total prohibition was in force for considerable periods in the present century but its manifest fiasco led to final repeal. Today the liquor trade is subject to a government monopoly in these countries as well as in Sweden. In Iceland and Norway the question of whether alcoholic beverages may be placed for sale is decided by local referendum. Sale of liquor is permitted only in a number of the towns and prohibited all over the countryside. In Finland and Sweden the situation, although not so extreme, is similar. No referenda are held, but special permits are required for the purchase of liquor and such permits are cancelled for alcoholics. The Swedish situation is, moreover, characterized by a unique rationing system which has existed for more than a generation but which has not prevented consumption from being higher than in any of the other countries. One striking illustration of the differences prevailing in this field among the Northern countries is found in the fact that while Iceland has none, Norway less than a hundred, and

Finland and Sweden only a few hundred public houses offering strong liquor, the number of such establishments in Denmark is no less than about 4,000.

In spite of the general trend outlined above, alcoholism remains quite an important problem, especially in Finland, Iceland, and Sweden. As an example may be mentioned that in the latter country the number of alcoholics is estimated at no less than 50,000 or almost two per cent of the male population. Alcoholism in women is extremely rare in all five countries. Sweden has taken the lead in developing measures for the care of alcoholics, its Act on Alcoholism from 1913 having been emulated in both Finland and Norway. Main responsibility for combating alcoholism rests upon local authorities, usually operating through special Temperance Committees. If advice and warnings prove of no avail, a person who abuses alcohol to such an extent that he is a danger or serious nuisance to his surroundings or neglects his duties toward dependents or others may be placed under supervision or in one of the special institutions established for the treatment of such persons, if necessary compulsorily.

Until not very long ago provisions governing institutional care of alcoholics were very harsh in all five countries and remnants of this traditional attitude are still found in existing statutes. In recent years, however, modern medical treatment and economic assistance issued

The rehabilitation of alcoholics has been markedly facilitated by modern medical treatment. This includes the Disulfiram cure, one phase of which is shown here.

357

by the social assistance authorities have increasingly been co-ordinated in order to restore alcoholics to normal life. Efforts are made to have alcoholics apply voluntarily for medical assistance and the Danish invention of the medical preparation Disulfiram (Antabuse) – now known all over the world – has proved of great value in their treatment. Intensive research is being carried out in order to ascertain the causes of alcoholism and the best methods of treatment.

Particularly in Sweden scientific investigations have been undertaken to measure the effects of alcohol, even in minor quantities, upon the human organism. The blood test, initiated by the Swede Widmark, is today applied in a large number of countries for the examination of motorists. All the Northern countries, particularly Iceland and Norway, maintain severe regulations against driving while under the influence of alcohol. The blood test is obligatory where the driver is suspected of intoxication and, if a certain alcohol percentage in the blood is exceeded, fines and other sanctions are imposed regardless of whether any accident has occurred or not.

Also sociological studies into the question have been undertaken, especially in Finland and Sweden. Thus, a Swedish government commission has, during the 'forties, carried out comprehensive enquiries into the alcohol customs of various population groups, particularly young persons; one conclusion, it may be added, has been that the rationing system has not furthered temperance.

"Sober at the wheel...". Campaigns against drunken driving employ a rich arsenal of propaganda weapons. The poster attached to the milk truck urges motorists to stick to milk.

Care and Rehabilitation of the Mentally and Physically Handicapped

BACKGROUND AND DEVELOPMENT

The Second World War confronted the warring nations with strong demands for the best possible rehabilitation service for disabled persons, including not only medical treatment but also social rehabilitation by way of training or retraining and placing in employment. One important result of the urgent war-time need for manpower to replace the large numbers enrolled in the armed forces was that handicapped persons who had not previously been gainfully occupied were now drawn into production and thus given the opportunity to prove that they were actually capable of doing useful work. Both in the United States and in England the rehabilitation of handicapped persons – civilians as well as war-disabled – was taken up on a broad basis and already during the war years legislation was enacted which provided for a series of measures covering the rehabilitation and resettlement of all groups of handicapped persons.

As for the Northern countries, it will be found that, with the exception of Finland, they do not possess any comparable general legislation, the main reason being that the number of disabled ex-servicemen and other war-victims has been relatively limited and, consequently, also the weight with which the problem has pressed upon the communities. Present-day provisions concerning rehabilitation are frequently found scattered in various legislative statutes enacted on behalf of special groups. Naturally enough, legislators have taken a primary interest in those most severely affected, such as the mentally ill, the feeble-minded, the blind, the deaf, and cripples.

Measures taken on behalf of some of these categories were among the very first manifestations of organized welfare in the Northern countries. Already in the late Middle Ages St. John's Asylums were found in numerous towns, intended primarily for the mentally ill, the feeble-minded, and other cases of abnormity. Under conditions then prevailing serious treatment was obviously out of the question and the institutions served mainly as depositories with the double function of providing subsistence for the mixed clientele of unfortunates and ridding Society of a nuisance.

359

This general state of affairs remained essentially unchanged far up into the 19th century; it is only within the last two or three generations that the care and rehabilitation of the mentally and physically handicapped have been developed into important branches of health and medical services, comprising nation-wide networks of specialized institutions. Denmark and Sweden have led the way in these reforms, but in more recent years the other countries have caught up to a considerable extent. Private initiative has played a pioneer role during the initial stages of this transformation but today the public, and particularly the State, has in all five countries assumed the main responsibility for the maintenance, care, training, and placing in employment of these groups.

A corollary to this whole development has been that assistance to the handicapped, which was formerly considered as poor relief with all of its accompanying disabilities, has gradually been relieved of this stigma and today nowhere entails any legal effects to the recipient. Assistance is available to the large majority of the population without any charge, costs being defrayed directly by the public or by the health insurance. In none of the countries has it been felt advisable to regulate the placing in employment of handicapped persons by "quota legislation" on the British model.

See Chapter VII, Social Security, p. 384.

There are differences among the five countries as to the stage of development attained in the various fields. Nevertheless, it is correct to say that existing programmes for the handicapped nowhere as yet measure up fully to the standard considered desirable. Although all five countries have made considerable progress in providing handicapped persons with an adequate measure of economic security and with appropriate care and treatment, the resettlement of these persons in gainful employment represents an aspect which has long been somewhat neglected. This particularly holds true with respect to post-hospital rehabilitation work in retraining handicapped persons. Furthermore, the fact that legislative provisions in most of the countries are scattered and administered by a number of different organs has been somewhat of a hindrance to the establishment of an integrated rehabilitation and resettlement programme.

There would, however, appear to be a general recognition that this is a field which offers a wide margin for constructive efforts. Substantial advances have been made in post-war years and further reforms are in varying stages of preparation. The experience of the

Finland's many war invalids are determined to rejoin the ranks of the gainfully employed. Picture from a rehabilitation centre, surrounded by some of the 10,000 lakes.

former warfaring nations has here provided many fruitful impulses. This, combined with the favourable employment conditions in recent years, has greatly stimulated activities within this field in the Northern countries with the result that the problems of the handicapped have come to occupy a prominent place in present-day social policy.

It should be added that while earlier measures were developed separately for each group, such as the blind, the deaf, cripples, etc., the new programmes are more integrated in character. There is no longer the same concentration upon the specific problems of each category, but rather an emphasis upon the co-ordination of measures taken, not only as between the various groups but also between the handicapped as a whole and able-bodied persons.

As already mentioned, *Finland* is the only of the Northern countries to have established a general legislative framework for its rehabilitation work. The Disabled Persons Act of 1946 (amended in 1952) covers disablement whether civilian or military in origin. It comprises provisions concerning not only medical treatment, elementary and

361

advanced schooling, and vocational training, but also specialized employment services and financial aid for working implements and materials as well as for the setting-up of an independent business. In large measure this comprehensive statute has for its background the heavy losses suffered by Finland during the Second World War. The number of disabled ex-servicemen totalled 45,000 out of a population of 4 million. The country was consequently faced with a large-scale problem of training or retraining a considerable proportion of these invalids. In the past years many thousands of them have been given training, including vocational training, and more recently the proportion of civilian disabled persons among those in need of such services has been steadily increasing.

Danish legislation concerning handicapped persons contains, first, a number of general provisions: Under the National Insurance Act of 1933 the Disablement Insurance Court may require insured persons to submit to curative and training measures at the cost of the insurance whenever the Court considers that a substantial and not merely temporary reduction in earning ability is likely to take effect in the near future if such measures are not undertaken. Moreover, grants-in-aid may be given for the acquisition of implements and machinery and – in special cases – for the setting-up of an independent business. Aid may finally be given for the purchase of surgical appliances, artificial limbs, invalid chairs, and hearing aids. The Public Assistance Act, moreover, places upon the State the general responsibility for the education, maintenance, curative treatment, and care of a number of special groups of severely handicapped: The feeble-minded, epileptics, the crippled, persons suffering from defective speech, the blind, the deaf, and the extremely hard of hearing, provided that the persons concerned submit to institutional treatment or placement under supervised family care.

See Chapter VII, Social Security, pp. 432–435.

Already from 1914, under the provisions of the National Pensions Act, the *Swedish* Pensions Board has been responsible – in the same way as the Danish Disablement Insurance Court – for the initiation of curative and training measures for the disabled as well as for the granting of financial assistance for the establishment of such persons in small independent businesses. During the last war, when the conscription in the military forces attained considerable dimensions even in Sweden and a large number of military accidents occurred, the Labour Board was entrusted with the rehabilitation and resettlement of the military disabled. With this for a start, the programme has subsequently been expanded to cover also civilian cases and today includes all groups of disabled persons as regards vocational guidance, work tests, work training, vocational training, and placing in employment. The local authorities are under obligation to make grants available for preventive purposes, *inter alia* for the setting-up of an independent business. Most county councils and large towns operate special workshops where disabled persons may be given work tests, work training, and sheltered employment. As is the case in Denmark, the general measures outlined above are supplemented by special programmes of older origin, providing for the care, treatment, schooling, vocational training, and employment of groups with severe handicaps, such as the blind, the deaf, cripples, etc.

The only *Norwegian* provisions bearing upon handicapped persons in general are found in the Unemployment Insurance Act of 1938 and stipulate special allowances to such persons while undergoing theoretical or practical vocational training, including advanced education. Moreover, the Norwegian Act on War Pensions of 1946 provides for vocational training or aid to setting-up in business of war-disabled persons. Assistance to certain special categories of handicapped persons is provided under the Tuberculosis Act of 1900 and the legislation concerning cripples enacted in 1936. Here it may be noted that there is as yet no comprehensive disablement insurance in Norway.

GENERAL PROVISIONS

The following paragraphs briefly outline the main features of social rehabilitation services in the five countries, excepting those aspects which relate to the placement in the open labour market of handicapped persons. A number of particularly severely handicapped groups will be dealt with in a subsequent section.

See Chapter II, Labour, pp. 186–190.

Registration

Since it is essential for ultimate success that action be undertaken at an early stage, cases of mentally and physically handicapped persons are everywhere subject to compulsory registration, mainly through the local social welfare organs, private practitioners, and the school authorities. The main object of this rule is obviously to secure the prompt treatment and training of children and young persons. A special Finnish feature is the arrangement by the non-governmental Invalid Foundation, acting in collaboration with local authorities, of disablement surveys in various parts of the country. Carried out by specialist medical and social welfare personnel these surveys result in the annual detection of several hundred "new invalids" in need of treatment.

Educational Measures

A variety of special residential schools serve children of pre-school age who are so severely handicapped that they cannot remain in their own homes. This applies to feeble-minded, deaf, blind, and crippled children, and – most recently – also to children suffering from cerebral palsy. However, gradually the opinion has been gaining ground that, in the interest of the child, restraint should be shown in removing it from its mother and natural environment and that the child should, whenever its condition and family circumstances permit, remain in its own home. This, on the other hand, presupposes that parents are given expert guidance with respect to correct methods of education and appropriate treatment in general. Organized parent counselling has only been established on a very modest scale as yet but there is increasing recognition of the need for such services. It may thus be mentioned that the new Danish and Swedish legislation concerning deaf and hard-of-hearing persons, which dates from 1950 and 1952, respectively, includes provision of parent counselling. In Copenhagen, for example, a special clinic for examination of and guidance with respect to children in this category has now been established, its functions including visits in the family home. Special nursery schools are operated for such children. Experiments are, however, being made in Denmark at present with the placement of children who are hard of hearing or suffer from defective speech in ordinary nursery schools, with specially trained staff, in order that the special education may be started as early as possible.

As for children of school age whose defect is not so serious as to necessitate their placement in boarding-schools or day-time schools for the severely handicapped, special educational facilities have been established to a varying extent within the framework of the normal school system in the form of separate classes or schools. Special education is provided in the elementary schools for children who are mentally retarded, hard of hearing, partially sighted, or word-blind or who suffer from speech defects.

364

Deaf children require special measures and methods of instruction. The scene is from a Danish day-time school. All children are equipped with hearing-aids.

In most of the Northern countries educable children with mental defects, children who are blind or whose sight is severely reduced, and deaf, hard-of-hearing, crippled, and epileptic children are accommodated in special boarding-schools where the pupils are, as far as possible, given elementary education corresponding to that of the normal schools. Day-schools are found in some of the larger towns where it is possible to gather the necessary number of pupils. Moreover, secondary school facilities are available for crippled and blind children, sizable numbers of whom attend such instruction; gifted children are given the opportunity of qualifying for a university degree.

There is increasing recognition of the danger of isolation which is inherent in life in a boarding-school and which may impede the future transfer to regular employment. Consequently, during recent years, there has been evidence of a trend away from such institutions and in favour of day-schools permitting the children to remain in their own homes. This applies not only to feeble-minded educable children but also to children who are deaf or hard of hearing; for the two latter groups, the new Danish legislation of 1950 authorizes State subsidies for the operation of such day-schools established by private initiative or by local authorities.

Occupational Therapy

Programmes for handicapped persons have placed increasing emphasis on measures to promote their earliest possible return to working life. Already while still in hospital the disabled and sick person starts training with this purpose in view. Also, experience has shown recovery to be more rapid if medical treatment is combined with suitably adjusted occupation. In the Northern countries there is so far nothing new in the occupational employment of patients while in hospital but it is only in recent years that modern occupational therapy has found wide application. As in England and the USA, occupational therapy has been introduced as part of the treatment in many hospitals at the same time as the training of therapeutists has been organized.

In 1934 Denmark established special training of $2\,^{1}/_{2}$ years for occupational therapeutists. Sweden followed suit in 1949 with a two-year training programme. In Norway courses of 5–6 months' duration for previously trained artisans were introduced in 1952.

Occupational therapy is prescribed by the medical doctor in co-operation with the therapeutist. The most usual occupations include sewing and knitting, weaving, cardboard-work, simple carpentry, and metal work as well as study-groups in various subjects. Therapy is used rather extensively in hospitals with long-term patients, such as cripples, tuberculosis cases, mentally-ill persons, alcoholics, etc.

Working Tests and Work Training

Except for occupational therapy as a part of hospital treatment, measures aiming at the re-training and adjustment to work of persons who have suffered from working incapacity of long duration have up to now been applied to a limited extent only. Experience has shown, however, that thorough working tests and work training are of great value for the vocational guidance and re-adjustment to working life. These measures make it possible to give a more exact assessment of the individual person's aptitude for certain occupations. This is particularly important in cases where, due to sickness or disablement, a change of occupation is necessary; but a period of work training is necessary also in cases where, due to disablement, there are difficulties to overcome in returning to a former occupation.

The Working School in *Copenhagen*, which was established in 1932 by private initiative to serve such handicapped persons, origi-

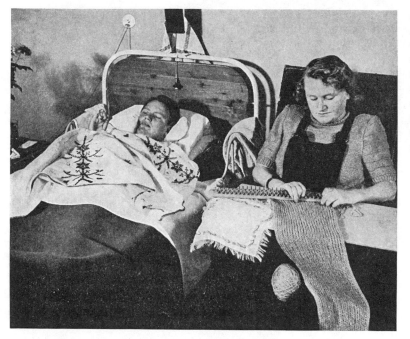

Mental depression always looms where sickness imposes prolonged idleness. So as to prevent this, modern hospitals make increasing use of occupational therapy.

nally had a double purpose: In the first place, to observe the working capacity of clients referred to it and to examine their employment opportunities and, in the second place, to re-train them. In recent years the School, which includes a number of workshops, has almost exclusively concentrated upon the former purpose and has functioned notably as a vocational diagnosis centre for the Disablement Insurance Court. A reorganization of this School is at present under consideration. Furthermore, under the public emergency relief programmes a number of training projects, covering mainly out-of-door work on a piece-work basis, have been initiated all over the country with State subsidies for the benefit of such handicapped persons.

Although it was only with the Disabled Persons Act of 1946 that comprehensive legislative provision was made for the schooling and re-training of disabled persons in *Finland*, non-governmental organizations were active already before that time. Thus, starting in 1942, the Finnish Association of Disabled Civilians and Servicemen has established four training institutions accommodating 530 trainees. Similarly, the Invalid Foundation operates two such schools with a total of 415 trainees. Other institutions include a vocational school

367

in Liperi for war-consumptives, a rehabilitation centre for cases of brain-injuries, and an institution for work training, all of them maintained by the Disabled Ex-Servicemen's Association.

The *Norwegian* State Rehabilitation Centre, established in Oslo in 1946 by the Norwegian State for the benefit of war-victims, primarily seamen, has continued its activities even after this task had been completed. Staffed with medical officers, industrial psychologists, labour market specialists, and social workers, the Centre now has three departments: One where the disabled persons are received for thorough examination (medical and psychological) in order to assess their working capacity; another comprising mechanical and other workshops where patients are trained while gradually improving their working capacity; and a third instituted for the specific care of former tuberculosis patients and special cases in need of rest in sheltered surroundings. As the employment service is not as yet developed with special reference to disabled persons, the institution has also temporarily taken up the task of providing its patients with suitable employment, in which connection follow-up work aimed both at control of results obtained and continued help and guidance is undertaken.

On the initiative of the *Swedish* Labour Board a number of local authorities throughout the country have in recent years established training workshops which are subsidized by the State. The programme is designed to bring about a gradual adjustment of the trainees to different machine-types and to normal working rhythm and working conditions as a prelude to their placement in regular vocational training or employment, (in some cases "sheltered employment"). The year 1952 witnessed the establishment of two Swedish work clinics – one in Stockholm under State auspices and one in Gothenburg operated by the city authorities – for the purpose of investigating the working ability of severely handicapped convalescents. The patients are tested at various working assignments and examined by medical doctors and other specialists in order to reach the most complete work diagnosis. The clinics are also equipped to undertake research, and to train staff for the local public workshops.

The special problems posed by the rehabilitation of tuberculosis patients have, in Finland and Norway, led to the establishment of separate vocational schools which combine reconditioning and work training under medical control. Mention should also be made of the Icelandic institution, Reykjalundur, which since 1946 has operated a rehabilitation centre for former tuberculosis patients. This centre was founded by the Association of Former Tuberculosis Patients with liberal support from the public. The patients, who are under close medical control, are given training and employment in a variety of manual professions until they are considered capable of resuming their former work or entering a new occupation.

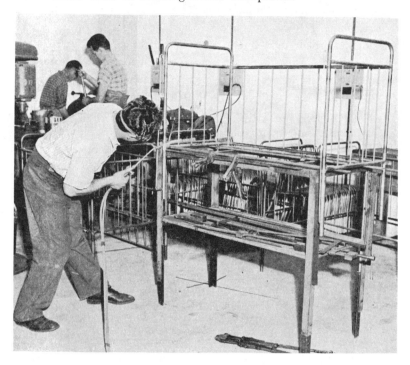

Vocational rehabilitation of t.b. patients at Reykjalundur, Iceland. All hospital beds in that country are supplied by this workshop.

Vocational Training

Vocational training of handicapped persons has been practised for many years with favourable results.

Wherever possible such training is given in a skilled occupation since skilled workers, and persons with higher education as a whole, stand the best chance of retaining employment during depression periods. The standards laid down with respect to vocational training are identical with those normally applied and the handicapped person who wishes to become a skilled worker thus has to undergo the customary period of apprenticeship. The arrangement arrived at in England, where disabled persons may obtain special training in a

369

number of occupations with a training period shorter than that normally required, is not so common in the Northern countries. Still, the system has been practised with good results in Finland, Norway, and Sweden for older disabled persons, civilians as well as ex-servicemen, such training being given not only in the normal trade schools but also in special schools for disabled persons.

It is the general opinion that in order to avoid the isolation resulting from vocational training of handicapped persons in special institutions – particularly residential schools – and in order to facilitate the transfer to normal employment, training should as far as possible be given at the same places as are normally used for that purpose, e.g. industrial establishments, independent craftsmen, and ordinary technical schools. Conversely, it is felt that special workshops for the handicapped should be relied upon only where absolutely necessary; such workshops are mainly of importance for cripples, for the blind, for cases of contagious tuberculosis, and for nervous cases.

SPECIAL GROUPS
The Feeble-minded

Starting about the middle of the 19th century special institutions for the feeble-minded were established in the various countries, all based on private initiative. During subsequent decades these establishments formed a foundation for the development of the present system of care for this large group of handicapped persons. Main responsibility has now everywhere been assumed by the community.

Measures for the feeble-minded are directed partly at the educable (imbeciles, deficient), partly at the ineducable (idiots) and include placement in institutions as well as supervised extra-mural care.

Institutions are generally operated, directly or indirectly, by the State or by local authorities with government subsidies. Apart from their educational function they are mainly devoted to the care af the ineducable and of the antisocial or asocial individuals who would otherwise end up in prisons and workhouses. On the other hand, a large number of the feeble-minded under public care – in Denmark close to one-half – are accommodated outside the institutions; they may be placed under supervision with families who can offer suitable employment (normally small farmers, gardeners, and the like) or with their own relatives. The obvious advantages of this arrangement are that many feeble-minded persons are thus enabled to lead an

370

existence approaching the normal and to perform useful tasks within their competence.

The community having by now assumed main responsibility for the care of the feeble-minded, and in recognition of the great importance of heredity in this field, it is only natural that efforts should be made to prevent an increase in their number. In Finland, Iceland, Norway, and Sweden special legislation, adopted during the 'thirties, authorizes sterilization where indicated by social, medical or eugenic consideration; the corresponding Danish provisions authorize sterilization only for social reasons, although the question of heredity is an important factor in arriving at a decision. Similarly, castration may be undertaken in certain cases, when motivated by criminological or humane considerations. While sterilization is performed rather frequently, often as a prelude to the placement of the individual under extramural care, the provisions concerning castration are only rarely applied. Under certain conditions, it should be added, sterilization may also be performed upon mentally-ill persons.

Although conditions vary considerably from country to country, the number of feeble-minded persons under public care has everywhere shown a steeply rising tendency during the last two or three decades; as a particularly striking example may be cited that Danish figures show an increase in this group from less than 6,000 in 1933 to more than 14,000 in 1950. This trend is due partly to improved contacts between institutions and local bodies, resulting in the more complete registration of observed cases, partly to improved medical methods for ascertaining mental defects. Neither accommodation nor medical staff is adequate at present and institutions are often badly overcrowded with the result that individual care cannot be provided to the extent desirable. It may be added that in Denmark, Norway, and Sweden plans for further development are under consideration.

The Mentally Ill

With the realization that mental diseases like all other diseases are amenable to treatment, the primitive asylums of former days have been supplanted by proper hospitals staffed with medical specialists and trained nurses. In the Northern countries measures for this important group of handicapped persons are today primarily in the hands of the State which generally operates the large majority of hospitals and heavily subsidizes all other hospitals for the mentally

371

ill; only in Finland are most of these hospitals maintained by the local authorities. A few among the largest cities maintain their own institutions and furthermore include special psychiatric departments in their general hospitals; in Sweden there are also a number of county mental nursery homes for the treatment of milder cases. Moreover, numerous county and borough hospitals have special psychiatric wards providing preliminary accommodation for persons in need of treatment.

Institutional facilities are supplemented by extra-mural care. Two forms are distinguished: In the first place, considerable numbers of patients who are but mildly affected are placed in free surroundings with private families, although under supervision; in the second place, recent years have seen the gradual expansion of ambulant services for the mentally ill. With the establishment of out-patient departments at some mental hospitals in the large cities, especially in Denmark and Sweden, a beginning has been made in the development of psychiatric counselling. At the same time supervision by the hospital doctors of patients living at home has assumed increasing proportions. These undertakings, apart from their general desirability, are also of great importance from a practical point of view since they serve to alleviate the persistent heavy pressure upon hospital capacity.

Rules governing the admission of patients to institutional care are rather similar. If a mentally-ill person does not himself request to be placed under care, it is incumbent upon his relatives to have him examined by a physician. If the latter considers hospital treatment necessary, and if the competent authorities concur, the family is entitled, in serious cases even under obligation, to take the necessary steps to have the patient admitted to a mental hospital. Existing regulations, however, also provide for social welfare, health, and police authorities to take the initiative for such removal, following a medical recommendation to that effect.

As an illustration of the general statement made above concerning the overwhelming extent to which the public today carries financial responsibility for the care of the handicapped, it may be mentioned that in Denmark about 70 per cent of all mentally-ill patients are treated at the expense of the State while most of the remainder are paid for by the State-subsidized health insurance.

The general intensification of programmes has obviously led to a radical increase in the demands made upon facilities. Hospitals for

the mentally ill have expanded enormously within the last fifty years and today occupy an important place in the hospital systems of the Northern countries; as previously mentioned, their proportion of total bed-accommodation now amounts to about 25–30 per cent, except in Iceland where the percentage is considerably smaller. Even so, capacity has not been able to match the rapid growth in demand for institutional care with the result that overcrowding and long waiting lists are everywhere familiar phenomena. One regrettable consequence is that in all the countries, except Denmark, numerous patients who are only mildly affected have to be cared for in non-specialized establishments such as old people's homes; although separate wards are provided wherever possible, this mixture of clientele obviously does not enhance the sense of well-being of normal residents.

Generally speaking, the care of the mentally ill has not yet reached the high level attained in other branches of the hospital system. Large-scale reforms, calling for the establishment of special homes for milder cases as well as for the expansion of existing capacity in mental hospitals, are, however, at an advanced stage of preparation. This particularly holds true with respect to Denmark and Sweden where considerable new construction is under way.

Cripples

The crippled and deformed include persons whose actual or expected working ability is permanently and seriously impaired due to congenital or acquired infirmity or defect of bones, joints or muscles.

It is characteristic of the measures undertaken in behalf of these groups in the Northern countries that the rehabilitation of cripples as useful members of society was early placed at the centre of efforts. From the outset the pioneers in this field directed their efforts towards the development of an integrated programme of care and treatment based upon a series of specialized institutions: Orthopedical treatment – including provision of prostheses and braces – in clinics and out-patient departments; vocational guidance and training; social services; special schooling facilities for crippled children; and homes with "sheltered workshops" for severely crippled adults.

The idea of such an integrated programme was taken over from Germany during the closing decades of the 19th century. The first Northern institution within this field was that founded by a voluntary organization "The Society and Home for Cripples" in Copenhagen in 1872. During the next 10–15 years the other countries followed suit with the establishment of similar institutions of which there are now four in Sweden, three in Finland and one in Norway, usually situated in the capitals and large towns. They are all operated by voluntary organizations although with generous support from the public. The below figures give an indication of their capacity:

CAPACITY OF INSTITUTIONS FOR CRIPPLES (1952)

	Denmark	Finland	Norway	Sweden
Orthopedical beds	365	235	90	500
Places for vocational training .	150	890	125	540
Places for school children . . .	75	140	75	280
Places for severely crippled children	60	30	–	80

Orthopedical care is not confined to these institutions. Especially in Sweden an increasing number of orthopedical clinics have been established in connection with general hospitals. In Denmark "The Society and Home for Cripples" maintains clinics in several of the large provincial towns in addition to the main institution in Copenhagen. The Society has recently also taken the initiative in establishing

two homes for the medical treatment and education of spastic children below and of school age.

Nowadays there are several other possibilities open for obtaining vocational training than at the special institutions for cripples. Public grants are given to cripples undergoing training in the open labour market and at the "normal" training institutions. It should be added that because of the large government subsidies, the State authorities on the whole exercise a very considerable influence upon the various programmes for the crippled.

At the same time the crippled persons' own organizations also play an important role. In Finland these organizations maintain several large institutions for vocational training and direct employment of cripples, and also operate 20 holiday-homes for such persons. Their Norwegian counterparts maintain a number of homes for severely crippled persons while the corresponding Swedish organization has taken the initiative to solve the recreational problems of cripples by the establishment of holiday-homes. Finally, the Danish organization operates a rehabilitation centre of its own in Copenhagen.

No specialized facilities for cripples are found in Iceland; in that country cripples are given treatment in the general hospitals and are assisted in their social and vocational problems by the agencies providing such services in general.

In all five countries blind children are legally required to attend instruction – given free of charge – at special residential schools, most of them State-operated. The oldest among these is the Royal Institute for the Blind in Copenhagen, founded already in 1808, while the most recent is the School for the Blind established in Reykjavik 1933 as the first of its kind in Iceland.

Instruction includes elementary education for 9–10 years, followed by more advanced schooling, including vocational training. Young men and women, who are found to be eligible, frequently receive a musical education, which qualifies them to enter for examination as organists or piano-tuners. Otherwise, training is most frequently still in the traditional occupations for the blind such as – for men – brush-making, basket-making, and weaving and – for women – weaving, machine-knitting, and embroidery. Others may be placed in sheltered employment, thus in Denmark with the Blind People's Work Company Ltd., a State-subsidized institution which not only employs a considerable number of blind persons, but also purchases and markets the products of blind people working at home.

In recent years increased efforts have, however, been made in all five countries to improve the situation by introducing the blind in regular employment. For years blind persons have been trained as telephone operators, clerical workers, and physiotherapists and a growing number have been given training as industrial workers. The organizations of blind persons have been very active in this respect. Thus, in 1938 the Danish National Association of the Blind founded an enterprise for the manufacture of locks, where blind persons are trained during a nine-month period under normal working conditions with a view to their future employment in the open market. Similarly, following a proposal by the Swedish organization for the blind, a basic course in metal work was started in 1952 at the Handicraft School for Blind Men at Kristinehamn. Training lasts 48 weeks with an average of 48 hours of instruction per week, the curriculum including occupational practice, materials, machinery, accounting, hygiene, and civics. This basic training is followed by advanced training at one of the occupational courses arranged by the Labour Board and the Vocational Training Board. The Norwegian organization has given particular emphasis to the placement of blind persons in industry through personal contacting of individual employers.

As the possibilities of creating new training outlets for the blind are limited, *inter alia* by the relatively small number of blind persons in each country, attempts are being made to extend the opportunities by co-operation among the Northern countries. Thus, at a conference in Stockholm in 1952 among representatives of organizations for the blind in all five countries a working committee was appointed, its assignments including, first, the continuous collection and exchange of information concerning, among other things, new opportunities for choosing an occupation in the various countries and, second, the planning of an exchange of trainees among Northern training centres for the blind.

The Deaf and Hard of Hearing

Programmes for deaf children and young persons follow very much the same lines as for the blind, general education and – to a lesser extent – vocational training being given in a number of special institutions, most of them public.

The most recent legislations in this field are the Danish and Swedish acts of 1950 and 1952, respectively, on the care of the deaf and hard of hearing. Apart from their emphasis upon the treatment of children of pre-school age, they call for intensified State efforts with respect to the vocational training of deaf persons who are not able to obtain suitable work in the open labour market. Finally, the Danish act provides the first legal basis for the establishment of public services in behalf of the hard of hearing, such services to include hearing centres where these persons may be examined with a view to determining the proper hearing aids, training courses, counselling and placement in employment.

Conclusion

Even if due account is taken of the favourable effect of rising standards of living and medical progress in general, there can be no reasonable doubt that the high level of health services has contributed substantially to the spectacular improvements in the health of the Northern peoples within the last generation or two.

Since the turn of the century average life expectancy has increased by 10 to 15 years in all five countries and now ranks among the highest in the world. Present figures vary between 55 and 68 years for men,

377

and 61 and 72 years for women, Norway showing the highest and Finland the lowest averages. Mortality rates have declined sharply, from 1.5–2.0 per cent fifty years ago to 0.9–1.1 per cent in 1950. Epidemic diseases have been largely eliminated or brought under control; the same applies to venereal diseases. And considerable results have been obtained with respect to chronic diseases, especially tuberculosis.

Even so, there are still considerable health problems to solve. In several fields, notably the care of certain special groups, existing facilities are as yet manifestly inadequate. Several of the major diseases present a wide margin for further improvement. Employment injuries and diseases today demand an alarmingly high toll. Preventive work and rehabilitation measures need to be further developed and offer a promising field for the collaboration of social workers and medical science.

Sickness and disability remain a source of grave losses to the national economy. Only little documentation is available but mention may be made of an enquiry which revealed that Swedish public and private costs in 1952 arising out of sickness (excluding accidents) totalled 1,800 million kronor. Another Swedish investigation, covering the year 1945, showed that sickness accounted for a loss of about 300,000 working years equivalent to a reduction in the total labour force by 7 per cent; it is estimated that three-fifths of the working time lost may be set down to the more chronic and disabling major diseases.

Against this background it is understandable that, notwithstanding the successes scored in the struggle for improved health and the high standard of hospital and medical services, health problems still hold a place among the central issues of present-day social policy.

CHAPTER VII

SOCIAL SECURITY

Role and Character

Prevention is better than cure. This axiom lies at the root of Northern welfare policies today. Labour Welfare, Full Employment, Family Welfare, Housing, and General Health Policies are the captions sweeping the expanse of those broad programmes whose common denomination is that they go beyond the symptoms of social ills in an effort to eliminate their causes. However, it is only within comparatively recent years that this ambitious objective has come to occupy the centre of the stage. Historically, a firmly established rock-bottom of social security proved a prerequisite for the launching of an offensive against those maladjustments of which distress was only the symptom. And, this offensive once launched, the protection afforded by social security schemes remains a basic component of the whole structure of present-day social policies.

For centuries poor relief administered by local authorities was Society's principal instrument used in assisting its members in misfortune. Starting in the last decades of the 19th century, the Northern countries were confronted with the greatly increased risks to the individual which the industrial revolution entailed. Under the circumstances it was natural that attention should focus upon the relief of those already in need. Subsequent efforts therefore centered upon the establishment of a minimum of security against the consequences of the most widespread causes of destitution, i. e. sickness, unemployment, employment injuries, old age, and disablement.

The social security programmes which have developed during the past 60–70 years are the result of a multitude of reforms, each of which may be viewed as a step toward a better adjustment of social organization to the changing economic and political environment. This development has been accompanied and sometimes propelled by a slow but decisive shift in the prevailing attitude toward community life: From individualism to an increased sense of mutual responsibility and common welfare. The establishment of the various social security schemes has itself contributed strongly to this change in attitude; thus, from the psychological point of view also, these schemes may be regarded as a necessary preliminary to the general acceptance of the more active spirit underlying the modern approach to social welfare problems.

Since their establishment, social security programmes have held a key position in the social welfare structure of the Northern countries, and though the emphasis during the last decade or two has moved decisively from protection to prevention, this does not mean that the chapter on social security is a closed one. The rock-bottom defence against poverty needs to be strengthened in many spots and even at the present date some glaring holes show that the mason has not yet completed his work.

Social security is traditionally conceived as comprising two main parts: Insurance and assistance, and this conception is used also in the following presentation. A few remarks may serve to illustrate the way in which these two components of present-day social security systems have developed and the real contents of these terms as applied in the Northern countries.

Less than one hundred years ago the poor-law authorities, supplemented to some extent by charitable societies, were the sole recourse of distressed persons who had no relatives capable of coming to their aid. This system had withstood the strain of centuries, the main change being the gradual assumption by the community of primary responsibility, as climaxed by the enactment – in Denmark at the beginning of the 19th century, somewhat later in the other countries – of comprehensive poor laws.

The industrial revolution and the social upheavals following in its wake were to result in decisive changes in this traditional set-up. With the gradual emergence of the new class of wage earners the number of relief cases rose rapidly and need was found increasingly attributable to a few uniform causes. These developments burst the existing organizational framework of relief.

The dole and the poorhouse were "emergency exits" – anything but attractive to the destitute, nor meant to be. Early Liberalism with its emphasis upon the right and responsibility of the individual to fend for himself without public interference, whether restrictive or protective, found it quite consistent with the belief in free enter-

*This alms box in
the carved head of
a wooden figure
stands outside a
church at Karls-
krona, Sweden, as
a reminder of past
days when Society
relied mainly on
charity to care
for the poor.*

prise that poor relief should be so administered as to encourage actual or potential recipients to seek gainful employment if at all possible. An expression of this attitude is found in the general tightening of poor-relief statutes in several of the Northern countries shortly after the middle of the 19th century.

However, the same general attitude also inspired the establishment of voluntary mutual benefit organizations through which the common people strove by their own efforts to secure protection against the increased risks arising out of the changing economic environment. As the movement gathered momentum, savings banks, health insurance societies and, somewhat later, unemployment insurance societies were established in ever increasing numbers throughout the five countries. These activities were by no means limited to the growing towns; in

381

many cases the farmers played a prominent role as pioneers. The fact that these new institutions found their origin not with the State but in a spontaneous "grass roots" initiative, was perhaps the most significant aspect of this development which was destined to exercise an enduring influence upon subsequent social welfare programmes.

With the passing of time the pressure for positive community action grew steadily in force. The continued extension of the franchise to lower-income groups and the incipient organization of what later were to become the powerful Labour parties were important factors in this connection. Simultaneously, the idea of State intervention in these matters received strong impulses from the series of great social insurance reforms enacted in Germany during the 'eighties. Following many years of continued and often heated debate, inside and outside the parliaments, the first decisive steps towards the establishment of comprehensive social security programmes were finally taken during the closing decade of the 19th century.

The basic conception was simple and all-inclusive: Effective and non-humiliating help should be given to those who were in need due to circumstances over which the individual had little or no control. Applied in practice it led to a dual approach.

In the first place, a number of nation-wide insurance schemes were set up to deal with certain broad and well-defined causes of need, liable to be encountered by large groups of the population. In the second place, the former indiscriminating attitude of condemnation towards persons receiving poor aid gave way to a growing understanding of the need for differentiated and more liberal treatment of those in distress. As a consequence, certain kinds of assistance were freed of the retaliatory elements attaching to poor relief.

Viewing the Northern countries as a whole, the period of basic constructional reforms in the field of social security took its beginning in the 1890's. In the course of the following generation the main foundations of present-day social security systems were established. The general re-orientation of social policy along more expansive lines, which gained ground in the 1930's, gave the impulse for a second wave of reform which resulted in decisive improvements in the scope and effectivity of social security programmes. It has been characteristic of these developments – especially in their earlier phases – that the various programmes were not conceived as parts of any master plan, each scheme being dealt with essentially upon its own merits. Hence the various reforms were introduced in rather hapha-zard order, varying from country to country. It is only in later years, when most components of social security were already established, that the co-ordination of the various programmes within an integrated system has become an issue of practical politics.

The past 60 years have been dominated by the gradual development of *social insurance*. In some cases, e. g. health insurance and un-employment insurance, the schemes have built upon the mutual benefit societies voluntarily developed to provide a measure of pro-tection against these short-term risks. What happened here was essentially that each of these groups of institutions was organized within a solid framework and given an official status, which entailed government supervision as well as government subsidies and greatly facilitated their consolidation and subsequent expansion. In other cases, e. g. employment injuries insurance, disablement and old age insurance, where the issue was predominantly one of securing pro-tection against certain long-term risks, the schemes were the direct result of legislative initiative.

On the whole, Denmark took the lead. By 1922 that country had created schemes covering old age, disablement, health, unemployment, and employment injuries under varying forms of social insurance. The other Northern countries reached this stage only at a later date, meanwhile relying to a greater extent upon public assistance granted under the gradually liberalized poor-law provisions. Thus, all the contingencies enumerated were not covered by social insurance schemes until 1934 in Sweden, 1936 in Iceland, and 1939 in Finland. With the planned introduction of general disablement insurance also Norway will have completed this series of schemes.

However, these dates tell only part of the story. Even at the present time the scope and effectivity of the various schemes vary sharply among the countries. Thus, the Finnish health insurance and un-employment insurance are of extremely limited significance as com-pared with the corresponding schemes in Denmark, Norway, and Sweden; and the Icelandic unemployment insurance, although for-mally established in 1936, has never become operative.

The order in which the various programmes were placed on the statute books has followed no uniform pattern. On the whole, the first schemes to be organized under national legislation were health insurance and employment injuries insurance which by 1911 and

1917, respectively, were found in all the Northern countries. The dates on which the other branches of social insurance have attained similar status are scattered throughout the period right up to the present day. Thus, State subsidies to and State supervision of unemployment insurance were introduced in Norway and Denmark already in 1906–1907, in Finland in 1917, and in Sweden not until the middle of the 1930's. Likewise, the first – though very limited – old age pensions scheme was introduced in Iceland in 1890 while the last such scheme to take effect was in Finland as late as 1939.

The development of social insurance has been parallelled by a progressive diminution of the scope of poor-law provisions. Simultaneously the character of these provisions has undergone a gradual transformation, which may be briefly characterized by saying that poor relief has been replaced by *social assistance*.

There was no abrupt break with the past. Local authorities retained their traditional position as main carriers of responsibility for the care of those in need. What happened was essentially that the discretionary powers of municipal organs were increasingly circumscribed by national legislation. A lengthening series of enactments have stipulated the duty of local authorities to render assistance in specified cases of need and have also to some extent prescribed the kind and amount of benefits to be given. This line of differentiation according to uniform rules, moreover, has had for its corollary a differentiation also in the conditions and legal effects attaching to the receipt of benefits.

Thus, there has been a steady trend toward liberalization of relief granted in cases where the contingency is not as yet covered by social insurance or where an insurance scheme is still restricted in coverage; the same applies where the insurance benefits are insufficient to meet individual need. Public care and rehabilitation of mentally *See pp. 359–363.* and physically handicapped persons has been relieved of the stigma of poor relief. A similar development is found with respect to the *See pp. 461–468.* care of old people, their former maintenance in poorhouses having been replaced by accommodation in old people's homes where they pay for themselves with their old age pensions. The care of children *See pp. 469–484.* has been disassociated from ordinary relief and entrusted to special child welfare organs.

These have been the main categories of poor relief to be transformed into social assistance. It should be stressed that this development was
a natural corollary to the effectivization of assistance rendered.

The above represents a highly simplified picture of actual developments in the field of social assistance. Thus, there are marked variations among the five countries regarding the dates on which and the extent to which such reforms have been carried out. In Denmark the first important step forward along these lines was taken already in 1891 with the adoption of a new poor law and the simultaneous enactment of legislation providing old age assistance outside the scope of poor relief. During the following decades, new poor laws were passed also by the other countries: Norway in 1900, Iceland in 1907, Sweden in 1918, and Finland in 1922; it should be added, though, that this chronology of events, however important in itself, cannot be accepted as an adequate yardstick of developments in the field of social assistance.

At the present time poor relief plays a very modest role in all the Northern countries. It should be noted, moreover, that poor relief itself has undergone improvements toward a more humane treatment and – perhaps most important – toward greater efficiency. Poor-relief cases are increasingly considered and treated as social illnesses.

The insurance schemes have provided more effective help and gradually freed large groups of persons from the odium of seeking aid under the provisions of the poor law. In their initial phases, moreover, they cost the taxpayers relatively little. This was an important consideration with the political parties then in power. The principle of providing "Help for Self-Help" which had occupied a key position in the formation and struggle for recognition of mutual benefit societies, offered a practical working formula which modified Liberalism could accept. As compared to these schemes social assistance may – in the light of present-day social thinking – be viewed as a "shortcut" solution to the problem of social security. However, it lays the financial burden directly and fully upon the taxpayers. This may largely explain why the traditional vestiges of poor relief have been only gradually removed from assistance programmes.

Whether initiated on a voluntary basis or by parliamentary action, the social insurance schemes originally took over many of their guiding principles from commercial insurance. However, most of the features typical of commercial insurance have been eliminated or so drastically altered in the Northern countries as to be hardly recognizable, the most important development being the assumption by

Society of a greatly increased measure of financial responsibility in regard to most of the schemes. Apart from the term itself, the use of which today is in many respects rather misleading, the main feature uniting the various branches of social insurance is essentially this: The social insurance programmes furnish exactly specified benefits in certain standard situations of need, involving the vital interests of large numbers of people, provided a number of precise and easily ascertainable conditions are met; the most striking development being the progressive abolition of the actuarial interdependence of contributions and benefits. This leaves only little of insurance in the classical sense.

Roughly speaking, the existence or absence of these features also provides the main dividing line between social insurance and the remaining social security programmes which, for the sake of convenience, have been classed under the term "social assistance". In principle this distinction may be said to reflect a real difference in the character of the needs covered. Social insurance, embodying an indisputable right of the insured to certain specified benefits, appears the natural solution where a great many cases of need present themselves as essentially similar to each other with respect to cause and effect, the principal examples being sickness, unemployment, employment injuries, disablement and old age, and death of breadwinner. The more heterogeneous categories of relief cases cannot be adequately dealt with according to a uniform schedule but must be treated on a more individual basis. In consequence, it is primarily within the field of social assistance that discretionary decisions on the kind and amount of benefits have been more or less retained together with their traditional corollary, the individual means test.

This may be a generally valid statement of principle. Actual developments show, however, a picture considerably more diversified.

In large part, social assistance may be considered a residuary form of help under the social security systems. The establishment of one comprehensive insurance scheme after the other has reduced its scope decisively. A similar effect has followed from the formation in more recent years of schemes of family welfare and public health where benefits – some of them formerly granted within the framework of poor relief – have increasingly taken the form of public services.

To the extent that social assistance covers cases which are predestined for inclusion in a separate social insurance scheme, or where the cause of need is such as to affect large numbers in a similar way, there is a strong tendency for provisions to approach those of the so-called insurance schemes: Benefits are granted at standard rates and subject only to the fulfilment of certain precise and objective conditions. Important examples are the Danish and Swedish children's maintenance advances granted to single breadwinners – primarily unmarried or divorced mothers – and the Norwegian disablement benefits granted by some of the large towns.

The discretionary decision as to kind and amount of benefits – and its companion, the means test – are thus primarily applied with respect to the remaining groups where the need for individual treatment is particularly pronounced. They include not only those cases which fall through the cracks of the "rock-bottom" furnished by social insurance, but also those categories which may be termed the "hard core" of poor relief. Today assistance is generally given without any accompanying legal disabilities, although the beneficiary is in principle under obligation to repay the amount received. It is only with respect to certain, numerically very limited groups, such as – in Denmark – negligent family supporters, alcoholics and vagrants, that the strict terms attaching to poor relief are still retained.

One of the important factors underlying the transformation of social security programmes during the past two generations has been a general preference of insurance to assistance. Nevertheless, in most of the Northern countries – Denmark being the exception – it is only within the last twenty years that the scope and effectivity of social insurance has become such as to reduce assistance to second place. In several fields where the experience of other countries indicates insurance as the natural solution, but where it has not yet been introduced, it will undoubtedly be established. The progressive dilution of the terms "insurance" and "assistance" and the ensuing levelling-out of the former sharp differences with respect to conditions attaching to the receipt of benefits have, however, in recent years led to a certain rehabilitation in the public mind of social assistance as a form of help. This is particularly evident with respect to those services, still in their beginning, which are based upon the modern concept of concentrated treatment of the individual in order to reach the roots of social maladjustment. Here social assistance with its greater flexibility quite obviously provides the most practical framework of organization.

Social Insurance

Social insurance, as understood in the Northern countries, today comprises the following six branches: Health insurance, unemployment insurance, old age pensions, disablement pensions, survivors' benefits, and employment injuries insurance. There are important differences, both as regards form and contents, among the schemes established by the five countries but on a number of points they are quite similar. The following presentation emphasizes the similarities but also attempts to bring out the significant differences.

BASIC FEATURES
Organization

Recalling the piecemeal development of Northern social security programmes, it is quite natural that each contingency normally has been dealt with under a separate scheme. Limited steps to combine different social insurance branches have been taken, the main examples being old age and disablement pensions which in Denmark, Finland, and Sweden are organized within a single programme. As yet, however, the British post-war example has been emulated only in Iceland where a scheme combining almost all social insurances under one system was adopted in 1946.

All five countries, on the other hand, share the characteristic that the schemes are national, not local, in character. For historical or other reasons some programmes may be organized in a multitude of local units but such organization is according to standardized patterns which apply to the country as a whole. The extent to which local differences in the actual implementation of programmes are possible varies with both scheme and country. It is of importance chiefly with respect to health and unemployment insurance, particularly in Finland but also, though to a lesser extent, in Denmark and Sweden.

The problem of co-ordination has been on the agenda with each expansion or revision of social insurance. In Iceland the comprehensive reform of 1946 represented an attempt at a final solution of this issue. As for the other four countries, special mention may be made of the Social Reform enacted in Denmark in 1933, whereby the previous multitude of scattered and often conflicting provisions in the field of social security were rationalized and merged into a body of only four separate laws. In Norway, moreover, a full-fledged social security plan has recently been placed before Parliament. This plan *inter alia* calls for the introduction of a general scheme of disablement pensions. As with the Danish Social Reform, however, the focal point is effective co-ordination of existing programmes rather than real innovations. In Sweden, the general overhauling of social security schemes in post-war years has brought the need for improved co-ordination to the foreground once again. An important recent step was the co-ordination of employment injuries insurance and health insurance decided upon by the Swedish Riksdag in May 1953 as part of a bill on the general reform of health insurance.

The administrative set-up largely reflects the situation outlined above. It is only in Iceland that the administration of the whole system of social insurance has been concentrated in the hands of a single organ, the National Insurance Institution in Reykjavik. In the other four countries it is possible to point to schemes, e. g. the Swedish and Finnish old age and disablement pensions, where a unified administration is today in existence, but on the whole the various branches of social insurance are still administered as essentially separate entities, although under central government control.

While the Icelandic system represents a high degree of centralization, there are in the other countries important fields which are characterized by a considerable measure of decentralization. This applies particularly to the health insurance schemes in Denmark, Sweden, and Finland, which are based on local self-government within the general framework of national legislation.

In Denmark, Finland, and Norway the ministries of social affairs are usually the top organs to which all matters of principle are referred. In Sweden, on the other hand, the situation is similar to that found in Iceland in so far as final administrative authority has been delegated to independent organs, but here there are three: The National Pensions Board, which administers the various pensions schemes, the Labour Board, which supervises the unemployment insurance, and the National Insurance Office for the administration of employment injuries insurance and health insurance. Institutions with similar names and tasks are found also in the other three countries, but most frequently they are subordinate to the ministries of social affairs to which their decisions may usually be appealed; moreover, the ministries carry direct administrative responsibility in some spheres, e. g. with respect to old age pensions in Denmark and Norway and health and unemployment insurance in Finland.

Uniformity of administration is secured in part by the detailed provisions on this subject contained in national legislation concerning the various insurance schemes, and in part by directives issued from the competent central authorities. Moreover, the voluntary insurance institutions must submit their bye-laws for approbation in order to obtain State approval and subsidies. Thus, standardization has been carried quite far even where self-government is in principle retained. This has resulted in a high degree of equality of treatment throughout each of the countries, an advantage which has been bought, however, at the price of a considerable decline in individual influence over and interest in the affairs of local authorities and voluntary insurance institutions.

Coverage

The early German conception of social insurance as largely synonymous with industrial workers' insurance has never gained general acceptance in the Northern countries. From their inception it has been a basic principle with most Northern programmes that they should not be limited to certain special categories but should wherever possible be available to the whole population or the large majority; with the passing of time this feature has become ever more pronounced.

There is a twofold explanation of this phenomenon. First, in spite of a considerable degree of industrialization the class of industrial workers never became dominant to the same extent as in some other countries. Large groups of the population remained attached to agriculture, the crafts, and retail trade in an independent capacity and also these groups evinced an interest in the idea of social insurance, notably in so far as sickness and old age were concerned. Second, the development of social insurance legislation was in these countries initiated and furthered by parliaments where the middle and lower classes of the population were represented in growing strength. Hence there was not the same political background as in some European countries for a social insurance legislation in favour only of workers to the exclusion of other large groups.

From the beginning the scope of social insurance has generally aimed at covering either the whole population or at least all of the more "humble" classes, the latter including not only the urban industrial workers but – to the extent technically possible – also fishermen, agricultural labourers, medium farmers and smallholders, independent craftsmen, and shop proprietors. Where limitations were initially stipulated, subsequent reforms have almost invariably entailed a widening of coverage. The re-orientation in social thinking which took place in the 1930's has been of particular importance in this connection. With the development of extensive programmes of family welfare, public health, and housing, the traditional view of social legislation as being essentially confined to citizens of small means has given way to broader welfare considerations. One important practical consequence of this trend toward total coverage has been that married women occupied at home are generally separately insured; this contrasts with those countries where social insurance is linked to the employment of the insured person and where the wife is therefore covered only through her husband.

However, the general trend toward the inclusion of the entire population under the various schemes is not completed as yet.

In the first place, present legislation still embodies various technical hindrances to universal coverage, usually remnants of the principles of commercial insurance which guided the establishment of the various schemes. Thus, employment injuries insurance has developed out of the concept of employers' liability toward employees and as a result does not usually cover self-employed persons. To the extent that health and disablement insurance have attained more or less universal coverage, this limitation is, however, only of restricted significance. Similarly, unemployment insurance has been limited to wage earners employed in some specific trade and a certain length of employment is generally a condition for admission. A third example is furnished by health insurance, which in Denmark and Finland is open only to persons in good health when applying for membership.

In the second place, a main modification of the principle of universal coverage stems from the principle of voluntary membership, which has played an important role in the Northern countries, notably with respect to health insurance and unemployment insurance. To accept the admittance of the entire population to social insurance is one thing, to secure that everybody avails himself of this opportunity is quite another.

The fact that compulsory membership has been introduced in schemes which originated as voluntary institutions does not necessarily imply that a general trend in that direction governs present developments. To a large extent it is a question of the relative success of voluntary organization. Danish and Swedish experience with voluntary insurance has been distinctly more favourable than in Finland, Iceland, and Norway. In Iceland the 1946 reform rests entirely on automatic compulsory membership in the National Insurance System. In Norway an increasing measure of compulsion has been applied to health and unemployment insurance which in Denmark and Sweden have remained voluntary. In Sweden a compulsory health insurance has now been decided upon, to come into existence in 1955, but the unemployment insurance will retain its voluntary character. In Finland the slow development of voluntary programmes in these spheres has not as yet led to the introduction of compulsory measures.

No similar problems exist with respect to old age pensions, disablement pensions, and employment injuries insurance, where the inadequacy of voluntary support was early recognized. In consequence all these schemes are either compulsory for or apply automatically to all persons covered by the legislation involved.

To sum up: Social insurance schemes in the Northern countries are generally and increasingly based on the total coverage of all persons who are exposed to the contingencies dealt with. Thus, the old age pension schemes of all five countries in principle cover the whole population. The same applies to disablement pensions, except in Norway where only limited provisions for disabled persons are in force. Employment injuries insurance everywhere ensures automatic coverage to all employees while others are usually not included. Health insurance covers the whole population in Iceland and more than four-fifths in Denmark and Norway; the comparable Swedish figure is three-fifths at the present time but the recently enacted reform will cover the entire population as from 1955; in Finland only 10 per cent of the population are covered. Unemployment insurance is confined to manual and office workers. The Danish, Norwegian, and Swedish schemes include approximately the same proportion, about one-third, of the actively employed population. In Finland the coverage is much smaller, about two-thirds of those workers who are organized in trade unions, or approximately 170,000 persons, being insured against unemployment; this corresponds to less than 10 per cent of the actively employed population.

Benefits

Actuarial considerations have long since ceased to be of importance in the determination of social insurance benefits in the Northern countries, the only exception being the Finnish old age and disablement pensions scheme. To the extent that it is at all possible to formulate any principle of general validity at the present time, it would rather be simply: That help should be effective. This establishes the need of the insured as the central issue and, although by no means implying any aversion to a basic uniformity, permits a differentiation of benefits according to the actual conditions prevailing in various categories of cases.

Insurance benefits may be granted in kind or in cash. Since it is a main object with all six branches of social insurance to provide a measure of security against loss of the normal income, it is only natural that cash benefits should be of paramount importance when viewing the system as a whole. Although there are scattered instances where benefits in kind are used as an alternative method of promoting income security, their primary importance lies in the field of medical care. This applies notably to the free, or almost free, medical treatment and hospitalization offered under the health insurance schemes. Equivalent services, including rehabilitation facilities, are available also to the numerically more limited groups who become beneficiaries under employment injuries insurance or disablement insurance.

Some cash benefits are intended to cover specific expenditures, examples being funeral allowances and grants for transportation. On the whole they are, however, of limited importance. Main interest attaches to those cash benefits which aim at assisting the beneficiary who has been cut off from his normal source of income.

With respect to these benefits it has been a fundamental consideration in all the Northern countries that rates should be such as to assure, in themselves, at least a minimum living income. The compensation principle – in the form known from the classical Central European worker's insurance – has influenced the Northern schemes only to a limited extent. Apart from the employment injuries insurance which has always been modelled on the compensation principle – although with considerable practical modifications – the large majority of insurance schemes have traditionally had for their primary aim to ensure a certain minimum standard. This line of thought still dominates many programmes in all the Northern countries, notably in

393

Denmark and Iceland where the compensation principle has never gained wide acceptance. In the other countries, however, modern reforms are increasingly based upon this principle. In contrast to the classical insurance systems, however, the application of the compensation principle in recent Northern reforms has for its background the previous establishment of certain minimum standards based upon the maintenance principle. It may thus largely be viewed as a method of obtaining a further improvement of social standards by diminishing the discrepancy between benefits and the incomes of ensured persons in the medium income brackets. Main examples are the Norwegian and Swedish health insurance and unemployment insurance and the Finnish old age and disablement pensions, where benefits are to a considerable extent graduated in accordance with the earnings of the insured persons.

In practice the benefit rates have in most cases emerged as compromises between the needs of prospective beneficiaries, on the one hand, and the financial possibilities, on the other. Still, the absence of an "objective standard" – such as formed a basis for the benefits in the British Beveridge Plan – has not necessarily involved any serious disadvantage since benefits have been adjusted repeatedly, generally upward, to changing conditions and conceptions.

The principle that benefits should cover at least actual costs of maintenance has led to a growing differentiation according to the living conditions of the beneficiaries. Thus, in all five countries it is a recurring feature that family circumstances are taken into account by the granting of special supplements for spouse and children. In this connection it may be noted that men and women receive benefits at the same rates. Moreover, some benefits are differentiated according to locality to correspond with geographical differences in the costs of living. This applies notably to old age and disablement pensions which are thus graduated in all the countries.

Another characteristic feature has been the automatic adjustment of benefits to changes in the costs of living, an effective and practical means of upholding their real value without repeated debate and legislative action. Starting in Denmark as far back as 1922, this method has been introduced in a growing number of schemes. Today practically all Danish and Icelandic social insurance benefits have thus been safeguarded against changes in the price level as measured by the cost-of-living index. Since 1950 the same applies to the Swedish old age and disablement pensions. In Finland the supplementary old age and disablement pensions have been similarly adjusted since 1944. Norway has not adopted the arrangement, though repeated revisions of rates and income limits in post-war years have more than compensated the rise in prices. The same applies to most of those Swedish benefits and income limits which are not automatically adjusted to changes in the costs of living.

In certain social insurance schemes benefits are contingent upon an income test. However, it bears only slight resemblance to the traditional means test, since it simply involves the establishment by legislation of a precise sliding scale which graduates benefits according to the income and property of the beneficiary without any discretionary element entering the picture. It is found in those branches of social insurance, notably old age and disablement pensions, which are farthest removed from ordinary insurance. Thus, the income test applies to the Danish, Icelandic, and Norwegian old age pensions and, in part, also to the Danish disablement pensions. In Finland and Sweden pensions are issued with their basic amounts to all persons who meet the general conditions; however, the supplementary pension benefits – of importance in both countries but especially in Finland – are granted only after an income test.

In other schemes the benefits are granted to the insured without any restriction arising from their incomes. This is the case in health and unemployment insurance where contributions by the insured cover a considerable proportion of total expenditures; and it applies also to the employer-financed employment injuries insurance.

Financing

Individual contributions were originally the sole or dominant source of financing in most branches of social insurance in the Northern countries. They were long the only source of revenue of the voluntary insurance schemes against sickness and unemployment. Likewise, the small basic old age and disablement pensions provided under the first State-sponsored programmes were determined by strict actuarial computation of contributions paid by the insured; a remarkable exception is the Danish old age pension scheme, which from its early start in 1891 has been financed exclusively out of public funds. In all five countries employment injuries insurance was from its inception financed entirely by employers' contributions.

With the gradual development of social insurance, however, government financing out of general taxation has come to cover an increasing proportion of total insurance expenditures. But also employers' contributions have, in some of the countries, constituted an important method of financing social insurance. Considering that the various schemes have generally been established singly without much regard to the creation of a uniform system, it is hardly surprising that also their financing should show significant differences, not only among the five countries, but also among the various schemes within the same country.

The starting point for government intervention in the field of social insurance was the realization that the low-income groups of the population would never be able to make contributions on the scale necessary to ensure adequate protection.

Viewed against the general preference for universal coverage of social insurance in the Northern countries, it is only natural that a main answer to this problem has been found in government financing. This applies to all countries, but especially to Sweden and Denmark where two-thirds or more of total social insurance expenditures are today defrayed out of current public revenues, main emphasis being upon those programmes which in principle cover the whole population, e. g. old age and disablement pensions. Contributions by the insured have been retained but cover a major proportion of costs only in those schemes, e. g. health and unemployment insurance, which were developed upon a voluntary basis and which have in Finland and (for all practical purposes) also in Denmark retained this character. In Sweden, it is interesting to note, the introduction of compulsory health insurance will be accompanied by higher contributions, in part because of the increased differentiation of benefits according to income, in part for purely financial reasons.

In Finland and Norway, government financing has not 'attained the same proportions and covers only about 30 per cent of insurance expenditures. On the other hand, employers' contributions are here more important than in Denmark and Sweden. Norwegian employers carry a sizable proportion of the costs of unemployment insurance and also contribute to the compulsory part of health insurance, the historical explanation being that these schemes are confined to wage earners. At the same time contributions by the insured have remained of great importance, not only in the two schemes just mentioned but also with respect to old age pensions. In Finland employers' contributions are found in the voluntary health insurance but their main importance is in the contributory old age and disablement pension schemes. Also in the new compulsory Swedish health insurance employers pay a considerable share of total expenditures.

In Iceland, finally, the National Insurance Act of 1946 introduced a uniform system of financing for all branches of social insurance, except employment injuries insurance which remains the sole responsibility of employers. A general insurance contribution is levied upon the whole adult population between 16 and 66 years of age. It is determined as a flat-rate amount, independent of income but graduated according to two "price zones" and according to sex and marital status. For the year 1953 it ranges from 384 krónur for an unmarried woman in the rural zone to 714 krónur for a married man in the towns. Employers pay a similar although somewhat smaller contribution for each employee. Also the local and central governments contribute fixed amounts, the central government assuming responsibility, moreover, for any deficit that may occur. In practice this means that the total costs of social insurance are paid as follows: Approximately one-half by the public, two-fifths by the insured, and the rest by the employers.

Apart from Iceland, the financing of social insurance in the Northern countries thus generally presents a rather caleidoscopic picture, characterized by varying combinations of State and local taxes and contributions by insured persons and employers.

A consistent pattern is found only for employment injuries where employers pay practically the whole cost in all four countries.

Old age pensions are in Denmark financed exclusively out of public revenues, while in Sweden about one-quarter and in Norway about one-half of the pensions are covered by a separate percentage-tax on individual incomes. The Finnish contributory old age pensions are unique in the Northern countries today by being based on the accumulation of a pension fund; supplementary pensions are, however, financed by public means. Contributions, which are determined as a percentage of income, are levied upon all adults, employers paying half the premium in respect of employees.

Disablement pensions are in Sweden and Finland financed jointly with the old age pensions. The Danish scheme features small contributions from insured persons and from employers, but three-quarters of total expenditures are publicly financed. As previously noted, Norway has no general disablement pensions.

Member contributions everywhere cover a major share of unemployment insurance expenditures, thus at present in Finland 50 per cent, in Sweden 40–50 per cent, and in Denmark and Norway approximately 40 per cent. State grants play an important part in all four countries, particularly in Denmark. Employers' contributions are in Norway equal to member contributions but are of minor significance in Denmark and entirely lacking in Sweden and Finland.

The Danish and Norwegian health insurance schemes rely for about two-thirds of their revenue upon member contributions. Under the new Swedish scheme the corresponding proportion will be about 45 per cent. In Norway and Sweden these contributions vary to a certain extent with the income of the member while no such differentiation is found in the other countries. The remaining costs are shared by the State and the employers, except in Denmark where no employers' contributions are collected. In Finland the overwhelming part of expenditures is covered by members, the remainder being contributed by employers; no public subsidies are given, however. The high proportion of expenditures contributed by members in all four countries conveys a misleading impression of the real situation in so far as public health services and hospitals are available to the whole population at low rates or free of charge. The public thus actually defrays a much larger share of "health costs" than is indicated by the distribution of expenditures under the insurance proper.

Without going into details regarding the varying ways in which contributions and public subsidies are determined, it may still be pertinent to touch briefly upon a few features arising out of the general principle of adjusting benefits to the actual living conditions of the beneficiary.

The existing graduation of cash benefits according to locality is to a certain extent balanced by a corresponding graduation in contributions, but the same result is obtained where contributions are a percentage of incomes, which may be expected to vary more or less with the local level of living costs, or where costs are covered out of taxes. On the other hand, the contributions levied, for instance, under the Danish disablement pension scheme are fixed amounts which apply to the whole country, in spite of the fact that benefits are graduated according to locality.

The growing tendency to adjust benefits for changes in the costs of living would appear to motivate a similar adjustment of contributions. In Iceland such adjustment is, indeed, prescribed by the 1946 reform and wherever contributions are fixed in proportion to incomes roughly the same result is bound to obtain. In other cases, e. g. the health and unemployment programmes of Denmark and Finland, there is no comparable mechanism, contributions being regulated essentially on the basis of financial needs. Again, the contributions under the Danish disablement pension scheme have been left untouched for 20 years although benefits have meanwhile more than tripled, in large part due to the adjustment for price increases.

The regular payment of contributions by the insured, wherever prescribed, is mostly an absolute condition for the granting of benefits under the insurance. Apparently self-evident, this rule has nevertheless been criticized on the ground that those who stand in the greatest need will frequently be incapable of fulfilling their obligation of payment. In Sweden this point of view has entailed practical consequences, in that the old age and disablement pensions and the benefits under the new health insurance scheme are granted regardless of the extent to which contributions have been paid up. The same applies to the Norwegian old age pensions.

The preceding paragraphs have shown social insurance in the Northern countries to be financed in varying proportions by funds subscribed by governments, by the insured, and by employers. As ever more programmes approach or attain national coverage, the distinction between the various sources of revenue takes on a changed meaning. To the extent that the insured become identical with the whole population, they obviously have to pay the full costs themselves, whatever method of financing is resorted to, be it in the form of increased taxes, higher prices, or enlarged individual contributions. However, the choice of procedure decisively influences the ultimate distribution of costs among the individual members of Society, which explains the intermittent political struggles over this issue.

Most of the early insurance schemes were exclusively financed by contributions from the insured members. The non-insured part of the population thus not only did not share in the costs but even benefited to the extent that the establishment of the schemes resulted in the reduction – or slower growth – of expenditures for poor relief. With the gradual expansion of government financing of social insurance this situation has been radically changed. Increased taxation along the lines most poignantly exemplified by the progressive income tax has enabled the public to carry an increased share of the cost of expanded social insurance programmes as part of a general, though limited policy of income redistribution. Moreover, this development has been hastened by the continuous rise in prices during the past half century. Benefits have been raised to a corresponding extent, and even higher, but individual contributions have in many cases followed the upward trend only slowly and partially.

The conception that burdens should be distributed according to paying ability has signified also an expansion in the financial responsibility of central governments as opposed to local authorities. While earlier the latter were in sole charge of social welfare within their respective boundaries, it is a general feature of social insurance schemes today that a large share of public expenditures falls upon the central government.

If financing by general taxation through the central government is accepted in principle as representing the most equitable – as well as the most practical – method of sharing the costs of social security, it might be asked why mixed financial systems have nevertheless been retained in almost all branches of social insurance in the Northern countries, including even the most recent schemes.

In explanation, reference should first be made to the strong influence of tradition. Historically, the idea of social insurance is inextricably tied to the payment of contributions and it is only slowly that this tie is being loosened.

Second, the administration of social insurance in many cases rests either with local authorities or self-governing insurance institutions, and it is considered natural that this should entail also a certain measure of economic responsibility. The partial financing out of local rates or contributions thus appears as a corollary to a certain amount of independence.

Third, it is a psychological fact that the payment of contributions "dignifies" the benefits and conveys to many people a feeling of self-respect, which will be missed where they receive benefits without "having contributed". This attitude is also interpreted as implying a greater willingness on the part of the population to accept expanded programmes as long as the increased costs are assessed as special contributions instead of general taxes which are already considered high enough. Whatever the intrinsic value of this reasoning, it carries heavy weight in all discussions on these issues and there is today a certain tendency discernible to favour the increase, rather than the reduction, of individual contributions toward social insurance schemes. In large part, however, this must be ascribed to the mounting resistance to any increase in ordinary taxation which is encountered in all Western European countries, rather than to any change on the part of the authorities in their basic views on methods of finance.

Finally, there is the question of employers' contributions. These are principally connected with employment injuries insurance, the general idea being to charge the costs of such injuries to the goods produced in proportion to the occupational dangers involved. But they are also found in other schemes, notably the Icelandic National Insurance System, the Norwegian health and unemployment insurance, and the Finnish pension schemes. Generally, such contributions will have effects similar to the introduction of sales taxes. Largely, they must be evaluated as an expedient means of obtaining the funds required for the financing of social insurance and which it would be politically difficult to raise by ordinary taxation.

HEALTH INSURANCE

Health insurance was the first branch of social insurance to be developed in the Northern countries. Starting just after the middle of the 19th century in Denmark and Sweden and somewhat later in the other countries, local groups of citizens in modest circumstances joined to form health insurance societies for the purpose of ensuring each other help in case of sickness. Coming at a time when the foundations were laid for the modern popular movements – folk high schools, co-operatives, trade unions, etc. – the attempt to secure help in case of sickness by the establishment of health insurance societies fitted in naturally with the general spirit of the period. These voluntary societies have furnished the basis upon which the present systems have been built.

The health insurance societies may in part be traced back to the old gilds, the social functions of which included assistance to sick members and help for funeral expenses. The early trade unions – in many crafts the direct successors to the former journeymen's gilds – frequently provided such benefits to members and gradually these activities were separated from the unions and organized in special

401

The success of health insurance societies in Denmark has set the pattern for the other Northern countries. This health insurance office is located on the outskirts of Copenhagen.

societies. Other societies emanated in a similar way from the temperance organizations (especially in Sweden) or were established by individual factory owners on behalf of their employees. In the small urban settlements and in the rural districts, where the idea of health insurance gained ground at about the same time, societies were established on the initiative of medical doctors, teachers or farmers. Within a few decades a large number of such societies, aiming solely at providing help in time of sickness, came into being.

Already in 1891 and 1892, respectively, the parliaments of *Sweden* and *Denmark* placed the stamp of approval upon the movement by enacting legislation which authorized State support to recognized health insurance societies. These voluntary societies remain the backbone of the nation-wide systems of the present day. In Denmark their activities are now regulated by the provisions of the National Insurance Act of 1933 and in Sweden primarily by a decree of 1931 concerning approved health insurance societies (both instruments repeatedly amended). The Swedish scheme is, however, at present being reformed. Legislation passed in 1946 called for a scheme of compulsory health insurance for the entire population to enter into force in 1950. For reasons primarily financial, however, the reform was repeatedly postponed. In May 1953 the Riksdag passed a revised

402

proposal which retains many of the basic provisions of the 1946 act. The new scheme will begin operating in January 1955.

In the other Northern countries developments have pursued somewhat different lines. Thus, in *Norway* voluntary health insurance was largely superseded already in 1909 by a compulsory system based upon the establishment of local societies operating under centralized State supervision. This legislation remains basically unaltered today although its originally rather limited scope has been widened gradually to include ever larger groups of the population.

In *Iceland* a similar development is found, although with a considerable time-lag. Voluntary health insurance was still of modest significance when, in 1936, a compulsory scheme was introduced for the towns; in 1946 it was extended in principle to the entire population as part of the comprehensive social security reform then enacted.

Finland, finally, is the only Northern country where an integrated national health insurance scheme is still lacking. Contrary to developments elsewhere, the establishment and operation of health insurance societies has generally taken place on the plant level by the initiative of employers, or employers and trade unions in collaboration. The movement has not taken root among the population at large and particularly has not spread to the rural districts. The societies, although regulated by special legislation since 1897 (now by an act of 1942), have never received any public subsidies.

Here is an interior view of the same office building.

403

Scope

In contrast to the "classical" State-sponsored insurance schemes known from Central Europe it is a common characteristic of the Northern health insurance schemes, except in Finland, that they have never been limited to certain occupational classes but have from the start been open either to all low-income groups or to the whole population. Still, their organization and coverage vary considerably from country to country.

The *Danish* system includes two main branches. The one – by far the more important – comprises about 1,600 State-subsidized health insurance societies, distributed all over the country. Membership is restricted to persons whose incomes do not exceed the annual earnings of a fully employed skilled worker; in practice this means that about nine-tenths of the population are eligible. Within this qualification any person between 14 and 40 years of age may be admitted as a member. The other branch consists of 79 insurance associations for the more well-to-do groups of the population. They are supervised by the State but receive no public subsidies.

Everyone who has attained the age of 21 years is under legal obligation to register as a contributing or "passive" member of one or the other of these two categories of institutions. Full or "active" membership in one of the two branches of health insurance is optional. Compulsory membership involves only the payment of a nominal annual premium and confers no right to benefits.

At the present time health insurance covers 96 per cent of the population over 14 years of age. The success of the voluntary principle is illustrated by the fact that no less than 87 per cent are full or "active" members, 77 per cent being affiliated with the subsidized health insurance societies and 10 per cent with the non-subsidized health insurance associations.

In *Sweden* the voluntary health insurance in existence up to now comprises about 1,000 local societies – rather similar to the Danish – and 37 central societies, some of which cover the large towns while others are organized on a county basis and entrusted with certain major tasks on behalf of the local societies. Membership in the societies has been entirely voluntary, all persons between 15 and 55 years of age being eligible regardless of their economic circumstances. The membership in 1953 corresponded to 60 per cent of the population above 15 years. The new compulsory scheme is built upon the existing societies. Membership will be compulsory for practically all citizens 16 years old or more.

The *Norwegian* scheme builds upon local insurance offices – usually one in each town or rural district. It is open to everybody, irrespective of financial status; since 1951, moreover, members are admitted regardless of their age. At the same time the insurance is, however, compulsory for all wage earners. Today the system counts more than 1,400,000 compulsory members and about 400,000 voluntary members, corresponding to a coverage of 85 per cent of the population. The extension of compulsory insurance to the entire population is under active consideration.

In all three countries children are automatically covered by the insurance of their parents; in Norway also the wife and other dependents are covered by the insurance of the husband. Under the Danish and the voluntary Norwegian scheme admission to the insurance is contingent upon the applicant being in reasonably good health; on the other hand, no such limitations are found in the compulsory Norwegian programme or the new Swedish scheme.

In *Iceland* the 1946 reform called for a compulsory health insurance embracing the whole population. However, only the new provisions concerning daily sickness allowances have entered into force. Otherwise, the older health insurance act of 1936, which in 1951 was made compulsory for the whole country, has remained in force pending the complete implementation of the 1946 reform. Thus, today all persons aged 16 are members of a local health insurance society.

The *Finnish* health insurance societies are generally confined to industrial workers. Although their establishment is quite voluntary, membership may be made compulsory for all employees with the approval of the employer if the society is exclusively intended for employees of a specific firm; actually, most societies are compulsory. In most cases the insurance does not cover dependents.

Benefits

There are numerous formal and real differences with respect to the scope of the benefits provided under the Northern health insurance schemes. Also, in several of the countries, there are frequent minor differences between the local societies. As regards Denmark there is, moreover, a decisive difference between the dominant State-subsidized health insurance societies and the non-subsidized health insurance associations, the benefits granted by the latter being more restricted; only the subsidized societies are dealt with below.

With these qualifications in mind it is still true to say that the benefits provided in the five countries are basically much alike. Roughly, they may be divided into two main categories:

1) Medical care, including principally hospitalization and medical attention; and

2) Sickness allowances, maternity benefits (see pp. 251–252), and funeral benefits (see p. 436).

In all five countries the insurance provides its members with *free hospitalization*, treatment and maintenance being paid according to the rates prevailing in the public wards of the local hospital. Only in Finland the insured will in some cases be charged a minor fee. When evaluating the role of the health insurance as regards this important benefit it should be recalled, however, that in Denmark, Finland, and Sweden the large majority of hospitals are available to the whole population at very low fees, the central and (especially) the local governments paying the deficit. Thus in these countries the insurance actually pays only a fraction of the total costs; in Denmark, moreover, the health insurance societies enjoy the privilege of paying only half the normal charge.

See also Chapter VI, Health and Rehabilitation, pp. 338–342.

The form in which, and the extent to which, *out-patient care* is furnished varies somewhat. The Danish and Icelandic health insurance societies provide their insured members with free medical attention. This has been implemented by contractual arrangements under which general practitioners undertake to provide such care to insured members. The doctors are remunerated either by a fixed annual sum per member – this being the rule in the towns – or by a fee for each service rendered. These contracts, which today have been concluded with almost all general practitioners as well as many specialists, are subject to approval by the competent central authorities.

In the other three countries medical attention is provided according to the refund principle. The insured person selects his own doctor in each case of sickness and pays the bill himself whereupon the health insurance refunds the major part of his outlay – thus in principle two-thirds in Norway, between one-half and three-quarters in Finland, and three-quarters in the new Swedish scheme (as compared with two-thirds under the present system). It should be noted, however, that these fractions refer to standard fees which are not binding for the doctors. In major Norwegian towns, it should be added, there is direct settlement between the insurance and the doctor, the patient paying the difference between the fee charged and the amount refunded. The non-subsidized health insurance associations in Denmark are also operated according to the refund principle.

Except in Norway, the health insurance societies pay for *medicine*, although to a varying extent. Thus, in Denmark the insurance pays three-quarters of the cost of more than 200 specially listed vital medicines as well as other essential drugs prescribed by a doctor. Under the Icelandic scheme the insurance pays the whole cost of a few vital and expensive medicines and from one-half to three-quarters for other essential drugs. In Finland the situation varies between the different societies but many of them refund half the cost of medicine prescribed by a doctor. Up to now the same has been the case in Sweden, but under the new compulsory scheme vital medicine will be distributed free of charge by the pharmacies, while other drugs prescribed by a doctor will be rebated by one-third.

Also, except in Iceland, *transportation expenses* incurred by the patient are defrayed by the insurance.

The benefits enumerated thus far cover the basic services furnished by the health insurance. Subject to the approval of the supervisory authorities, additional benefits may be granted. Such benefits are today provided to a very considerable extent and include physiotherapy, medical baths, home-nursing, convalescent homes, etc.

Thanks to the health insurance schemes and the hospital systems, the direct costs of adequate treatment in cases of sickness have been reduced to a minimum. The other main problem is that of establishing economic security where sickness is accompanied by loss of the ordinary income.

Daily sickness allowances are known in all five countries but, in many cases, they are still rather inadequate. This applies particularly to Denmark and has also been true up to the present time of Sweden. Apart from a compulsory minimum (in Denmark 0.40 kroner), the insured are free to insure themselves for a daily allowance up to a certain maximum (in Denmark 6.00 kroner). However, experience shows that comparatively few members have been willing to pay the extra contributions required for allowances above the stipulated minimum. The result has been that the daily allowances actually paid are on a very low average, thus in Denmark only about 1.65 kroner – or less than half an hour's wages – for members sick at home. In Sweden the corresponding amount during the last few years has been 2.25 kronor, excluding children's supplements. To some extent this unsatisfactory situation has been alleviated by voluntary sick aid societies which in Denmark count about 100,000 members, mostly workers, and which provide daily allowances of 3–5 kroner during periods of sickness.

In Norway the insured members are grouped in six classes, the corresponding allowances ranging from 0 to 6 kroner, the latter amount being reached already at annual earnings of 4,500 kroner. These basic allowances are supplemented by 2 kroner per day for married persons and a further 1 krone per day for each child under 16. However, no member may receive total allowances in excess of 12 kroner per day or 90 per cent of his normal earnings. The average allowance paid is 5.50 kroner. This is less than the daily allowances paid by the unemployment insurance, but there are plans to raise sickness allowances to the level of that scheme.

See p. 417.

Comparable allowances are provided in Iceland under the National Insurance Scheme. At the present time they amount in the towns to 28 krónur for married men and 24 krónur for others and in rural districts to 21 and 18 krónur, respectively. This corresponds to about 30 per cent of the earnings of an industrial worker. In respect of each child under 16 a supplementary benefit is granted of 5 krónur in the towns and 4 krónur in the rural districts.

In Finland such allowances form perhaps the most important benefit granted by the health insurance societies. In large part this is probably due to the fact that almost all members are industrial workers, who normally lose their income in case of sickness. Ordinarily, the daily allowances amount to 60 per cent of average wages.

Under the new Swedish compulsory scheme all members with an earned income of 1,200 kronor or more will be under obligation to insure themselves for a basic allowance of 3 kronor a day; the same applies to married women working at home. Further, there will be children's supplements of 1–3 kronor a day. All employed persons with an earned income exceeding 1,800 kronor (approximately 2.4 million persons) shall secure supplementary daily allowances varying according to the size of their earnings from 1 to 17 kronor. The maximum daily allowance will thus amount to 20 kronor. For a single person this will usually imply that he is compensated for about 75 per cent of the income lost. The daily allowance, which is tax-exempt, will be payable from the third day of sickness up to a maximum of 730 days. Independent workers, farmers, etc., will be entitled to secure, on a State-subsidized voluntary basis, the same allowances as if they were employed.

Financing

The health insurance is financed primarily by member contributions and by public subsidies. In Denmark, member contributions cover roughly 70 per cent of costs, the rest being financed by the State. The Icelandic health insurance societies are financed to a slightly lesser extent by members, almost 40 per cent of costs being borne by the central and local governments. In Norway, members cover about 60 per cent, the remainder being shared by employers and central and local governments. Finnish conditions are characterized by the absence of public subsidies. Members cover most of the costs, with employers contributing to a certain extent on a voluntary basis. The Swedish voluntary scheme has been financed very much in the same way as its Danish counterpart. However, under the new compulsory system member contributions, which will be levied by the tax authorities, cover only about 45 per cent of the costs while the remainder is shared by the State and the employers. The introduction of employers' contributions coincides with the coordination of health insurance with employment injuries insurance, the former taking over a considerable part of the latter programme, which heretofore has been financed exclusively by employers.

In Denmark, member contributions vary considerably, primarily on account of variations in the optional benefits granted by the individual health insurance societies. They average about 80 kroner, or 160 kroner for a married couple. This corresponds rather closely to the Norwegian contributions which, although graduated according to income, nowhere exceed 165 kroner for compulsory members and 220 kroner for voluntary members, respectively; these contributions, it should be remembered, cover also the wife of the insured and entitle automatically to daily sickness allowances. Under the new Swedish scheme contributions are estimated at about 160 kronor for a married member with the income of an industrial worker. In all three countries these contributions amount to somewhat less than a week's wages for an unskilled labourer.

409

The Icelandic contributions to the health insurance societies range between 120 and 324 krónur per annum, the difference being particularly pronounced between rural and urban health insurance societies. To these premiums should be added a part of the compulsory national insurance premiums.

Administration

The health insurance societies remain the basic administrative unit of health insurance schemes in all the Northern countries, except Norway. In spite of an increasing measure of State regulation they have retained their character of independent institutions. They elect their governing boards from among the insured members and – with Sweden as another exception from 1955 – themselves determine the contributions to be levied. Although their administration is largely regulated by legislation, they have also retained a degree of independence with respect to provision of benefits beyond the requirements of law. In Finland, it should be added, also the employers are entitled to participate in the management of the individual society.

In Denmark, Iceland, and Sweden the area covered by a society is generally identical with that of the local district. This distribution along geographical lines obviously implies considerable administrative advantages. Particularly, there has been no need for several institutions to operate in the same locality, as would have been the case were the societies distributed along professional lines. The Finnish societies on the plant level offer the same advantages.

With the passing of time there has been a growing tendency toward co-ordination of the activities of the many local societies. One expression of this may be found in the Swedish central societies which have taken over from the local organs a number of major tasks, particularly with respect to cases of protracted illness. As for Denmark mention may be made of the increasingly close organization of local societies into regional associations which are again affiliated with a national body. Although local self-government has in principle been fully preserved there can be no doubt that the increasing growth and consolidation of the schemes along these lines have entailed that individual interest in and influence upon the management of the societies have waned. This does not apply so much to Finland where the health insurance has never acquired the same status as in the other countries.

Supervision of health insurance is vested in central State organs, in Denmark the Health Insurance Directorate, in Iceland the National Insurance Institution, in Sweden the National Insurance Office, and in Finland the Ministry of Social Affairs. These bodies audit the accounts of the local societies, settle disputes between them and members, approve bye-laws, and in general see to it that legislative provisions are complied with in the daily administration.

The Norwegian set-up may be considered a first step toward the unified administration of social insurance on both the local and the national level. The National Insurance Institution in Oslo, which is also in charge of employment injuries insurance, is the central agency. It supervises the activities of the local offices and the application in general of the Health Insurance Act. It also serves as a binding court of appeal. On the local level the municipal health insurance office is in charge of day-to-day administration. Its chief officer is appointed by the Institution upon nomination by the local authority which also appoints the board of directors. This is a five-member board with at least three insured persons and one contributing employer. Although administration is in the hands of a locally appointed board, self-government is more limited than in the other countries. The Norwegian scheme knows of no individual bye-laws for each society and the supervision exercised by the central agency is closer than in the other countries.

UNEMPLOYMENT INSURANCE

In Denmark, Norway, and Sweden the history of unemployment insurance has followed a course rather similar to that of health insurance. In all three countries the schemes originated with voluntary societies established on the initiative of trade unions during the closing decades of the 19th century. The intimate relations between unions and societies, which are still characteristic of Danish and Swedish conditions, were an important factor underlying the development of unemployment insurance.

Already in 1906 and 1907, respectively, *Norway* and *Denmark* introduced State subsidies to approved unemployment insurance societies which were simultaneously subjected to government supervision. The subsequent period witnessed a rapid growth of the number of societies and of their membership. A setback occurred, however, during the depression following the First World War when widespread unemployment emptied the coffers of the societies.

The effects were particularly severe in Norway. The number of insured declined by two-thirds and the societies recovered only slowly and partially from the blow. Following many years of debate and preparation, the voluntary system was finally abandoned in 1945 and replaced by a compulsory scheme. In Denmark, on the other hand, the voluntary societies have remained the basis of unemployment insurance. Following the crisis in the early 'twenties they have expanded almost uninterruptedly up to the present day. The earlier legislative provisions on unemployment insurance were finally incorporated in the Social Reform of 1933. By repeated amendments, most recently in 1952, the scheme has been continuously improved. Still, its basic features have remained unchanged since 1907.

Swedish developments have essentially pursued the same course as in Denmark, but with a considerable time-lag. The late introduction of State grants to approved societies bears a part of the responsibility for the slower growth of this branch of social insurance in Sweden. At the same time it should be noted that trade unions long opposed such subsidies on the ground that they represented an attempt on the part of the authorities to escape full responsibility for the consequences of incompetent economic policies. As a result, it is only in the last twenty years, and particularly since 1940, that the Swedish unemployment insurance has become of primary importance.

In contrast to the countries mentioned above, the trade unions in *Finland* have not shown a similar interest in this line of activity. This, together with the late emergence of industrialism, may explain why government initiative, which already in 1917 resulted in State grants to voluntary unemployment societies, has not met with much response among the workers. Moreover, the full-employment situation characteristic of recent years has not been favourable to the establishment of new societies nor to the expansion of existing ones.

Iceland has never known any unemployment insurance in practice. During the 'thirties the country witnessed a period of widespread unemployment. In 1936 legislation was passed which authorized State grants to approved workers' relief funds but the act never became operative. Since the outbreak of the Second World War and up to the present day ample employment possibilities have in fact rendered unemployment insurance provisions superfluous. In consequence, the otherwise comprehensive social reform of 1946 did not feature any provisions for unemployment insurance.

Scope

As a natural consequence of the different lines of development the actual coverage obtained varies rather much from country to country. Keeping in mind the relative size of the countries, the table below indicates that while membership is roughly of the same order in Denmark, Norway, and Sweden, it is much lower in Finland.

	Membership of unemployment insurance (1952)
Denmark	655,000
Finland	170,000
Norway	720,000
Sweden	1,140,000

In Norway, unemployment insurance is organized as one national system with 750 funds including all insured workers in each of the local districts. In the other three countries the insured are members of nation-wide societies grouped along occupational lines. The strong craft traditions in Denmark are reflected in the fact that there are no less than 64 such societies, while in Sweden and Finland, where trade unions are today largely grouped along industrial lines, the number of societies is only 41 and 9, respectively.

413

In Denmark the overwhelming majority of the insured are urban workers in crafts and industries where the coverage approaches 90 per cent of all workers. In the rural districts and among salaried employees, on the other hand, coverage does not exceed 20 per cent. In Sweden the situation is much the same, although the relative number of insured among urban industrial workers probably is slightly lower. In both countries the societies have remained closely connected with the trade unions although they are legally entirely independent institutions. Membership is in principle voluntary and open to all persons employed as wage earners within the trades or industries covered by the particular society. However, with few exceptions the bye-laws of the unions require their members to join the unemployment insurance societies. In consequence, the societies have attained their largest coverage in those sectors where trade union organization is strongest. Membership is contingent upon the attainment of a certain age, 16 years in Sweden and 18 years in Denmark; in the latter country a further condition is that the applicant is not above 60 years of age.

The compulsory Norwegian scheme covers in principle all wage earners who are under obligation to take out health insurance. However, certain groups, such as civil servants, fishermen, domestic workers and home workers, are still excepted. Consequently, the number of persons covered by unemployment insurance is still approximately 25 per cent smaller than that of persons insured against sickness. Overall-coverage is today slightly larger than under the voluntary Danish and Swedish schemes.

As already noted, Finnish unemployment insurance has remained modest in scope. The societies are almost exclusively confined to industrial workers in the large cities and count most of their members in the pulp, metals, and building industries.

Benefits

The granting of benefits is contingent upon a number of *conditions* being met.

In the first place, it is a matter of course that benefits are payable only to members who are involuntarily out of a job and willing and able to work. Consequently, an unemployed person will not be entitled to benefits if he refuses to accept employment offered when it is suited to his skill and physical ability. Thus, there is no question of an occupational insurance inasmuch as the unemployed person may frequently have to accept work in another trade. The rules governing this subject are practically identical in the four countries but are on the whole administered along stricter lines in Sweden and Finland than in the other countries. The proffered work must, however, in all cases be remunerated according to the rates normally applying to the occupation and locality involved.

Second, it follows naturally from the granting of subsidies by the government or (in Denmark and Norway) by employers, that benefits may not be paid to members who are out of employment because of participation in a labour conflict. On the other hand, refusal to accept employment at places of work closed by such a conflict does not deprive a member of his right to benefits.

Third, the member must be fit to work. Thus, sickness will generally rule out any granting of benefits, this situation being in principle taken care of by the health insurance. The same applies in the case of old age or disablement.

Unemployment of a quite transitory character is not covered. The schemes of all four countries operate with a waiting period of 6 days (some Swedish and Finnish societies even going as high as 12 and 18 days, respectively). In Denmark this condition is considered fulfilled for a whole year as soon as the member has accumulated six unemployed days. The Norwegian and Swedish provisions are considerably more strict, generally requiring the waiting period to fall within the last ten days and three weeks, respectively; in Finland the situation is in practice almost the same as in Norway.

A further condition, arising out of the insurance character of the schemes, is that the member qualifies for benefits only upon having paid his contributions for a specified period. In Finland this period is ordinarily 6 months, in Denmark one year. In Norway the member must have paid a minimum of 45 weekly contributions during a period of four years while the Swedish provisions require a minimum of 52 weekly contributions, 20 of them during the last 12 months.

The unemployment insurance schemes provide a variety of *cash benefits* among which the daily allowances plus family supplements are by far the most important. It is characteristic of all four schemes under review that the allowances and supplements may not add up to more than a certain proportion of normal earnings in the various occupations covered, this limitation being considered necessary in order to avoid abuse. Thus, in Norway total benefits may not exceed nine-tenths of the normal earnings of the beneficiary. In Denmark the limit is four-fifths for breadwinners and two-thirds for others while the corresponding ratios are in Sweden four-fifths and three-fifths, respectively, in Finland two-thirds and one-half, respectively. However, these limits are seldom applied as benefits actually granted are as a rule lower. Another natural limitation is that benefits are payable only six days a week.

In *Denmark* the Unemployment Insurance Act prescribes maximum amounts for the daily allowances as well as for the various supplements. Within these limits the individual societies are free to decide but in practice almost all of them grant the maximum. As from April 1953 the maximum daily allowance is 11.80 kroner for breadwinners and for single members of 15 years' standing; for other members the amount is 10.50 or 8.70, depending upon length of membership. The allowance is supplemented by up to 1.30 kroner a day for each child. Breadwinners and long-time members who have accumulated at least 25 unemployed days within a one-year period, may further obtain a rental allowance determined according to the actual housing costs of the beneficiary, subject to a ceiling amount. Other special benefits include allowances for fuel (during the winter season), for transportation, and for moving. Practically all benefits are adjusted annually to changes in the official cost-of-living index.

In Norway and Sweden the daily allowances are more differentiated in character, being graduated more or less according to the previous income of the recipient.

In *Sweden* the size of the daily allowance was formerly optional with the insured, the result being that most members secured inadequate benefits. Members are now grouped in benefit-classes depending upon their earnings, place of residence, age, etc. Until recently the maximum allowance was 8 kronor which was also the amount most frequently paid in 1952. However, in early 1953 the allowances were raised considerably, the maximum being now 20 kronor per day and the highest amount actually paid 16.50 kronor. Supplements granted include 1.25 kronor in respect of wife and 1 krona for each child. Rental allowances are not furnished by the insurance but in cases of prolonged unemployment the member is entitled to a grant for this purpose out of social assistance funds (which are normally not available to the beneficiaries of unemployment insurance).

The compulsory *Norwegian* scheme operates with daily allowances up to 10 kroner. Except for the highest benefits, these amounts are identical with the allowances granted under health insurance. The same holds true of family supplements. The close connection between the two schemes is further illustrated by the fact that the unemployment insurance pays the health insurance contributions of its members during periods of unemployment.

Finnish benefits are on the whole considerably lower. They include daily allowances up to 160 finmarks as well as allowances to cover expenditures for rent, clothing, and transportation.

Finally, in Denmark and Norway the unemployment insurance is authorized to grant assistance to enable unemployed members to attend courses of vocational training or retraining. In Sweden such activities are financed directly by the government.

It is a matter of principle with all four unemployment insurance schemes under review that they are intended to cope only with temporary unemployment. Benefits are therefore limited in *duration*, although provisions in this respect vary considerably among the countries, being most liberal in Denmark and least so in Norway. Under Danish legislation it is possible to grant benefits for a whole year; actually, the maximum period of help stipulated in the bye-laws of the various societies averages 250 weekdays a year. In Sweden the ordinary maximum is 138–156 days during the course of 12 months while in Finland and Norway the corresponding maxima are 120 and 90 days, respectively.

Financing

In all four countries the unemployment insurance is financed in varying proportion out of member contributions and public funds; Denmark and (especially) Norway also make use of contributions from employers.

The contributions levied upon members vary with the size of benefits provided and, except in Norway, also with the unemployment risk prevailing in the different trades. The Norwegian system is thus today the only one not open to the criticism that the workers who run the greatest risk of unemployment pay the largest contributions. Public grants-in-aid are everywhere organized in such a way as to follow the level of unemployment. In this connection it is important to note that while in Denmark, Finland, and Sweden the voluntary societies carry final responsibility for the financing of the insurance, the compulsory Norwegian scheme assigns this role to the State. Employer contributions are of importance only in Norway. In Denmark such contributions were introduced in 1921, the motivation being that employers should contribute to the maintenance during bad times of the manpower which they draw upon under normal conditions; however, they have always remained of minor importance only. The absence of employer contributions in Finland and Sweden (as well as their rudimentary status in Denmark) is explained in part by a general reluctance to have employers participate in the administration of the often rather delicate questions concerning claims for benefits, in part by a preference for public subsidies as the more equitable method of distributing the burden involved in supporting unemployment insurance.

Under the *Danish* Unemployment Act member contributions are flat-rate amounts and must be so determined by each society that, when supplemented by the public grants, they are sufficient to cover estimated expenditures. In 1951–52 they averaged 145 kroner per member or about two per cent of average annual earnings of all insured persons. However, since unemployment varies considerably among the trades, there were societies where the percentage ran as high as 4.0 and others where it was as low as 0.2. While the individual societies charge a flat-rate amount of all members, there is thus a high degree of differentiation between the societies. Public grants are provided in proportion to member contributions and vary inversely with average annual earnings within the particular trade. They range from a minimum of 15 per cent of contributions to a maximum of 110 per cent. In addition to these general subsidies the State reimburses the societies – wholly or in part – for expenditures for family, rental and fuel allowances. The overall result is that members contribute 35–40 per cent of total costs, employers almost 5 per cent, and the public the remainder.

As in Denmark, the *Finnish* contributions shall be determined so as to cover the expected outlays when the public grants are added. The societies may classify members according to occupation, seniority, earnings, and family circumstances, with a corresponding graduation of contributions (as well as benefits). The public contributes one-half or two-thirds of the benefits paid, the proportion depending upon the size of benefits and the family circumstances of beneficiaries.

418

In *Sweden* the member contributions vary according to the class of benefits and the unemployment risk in different occupations. The weekly contribution today normally ranges from 1 krona to 1.50 kronor. State grants are graduated according to a sliding scale and range from a minimum of 40 per cent of the daily allowance to a maximum of 75 per cent, the percentage being progressive with the incidence of unemployment. On an average, State grants cover roughly half the total benefits paid. The Government further refunds the societies 75 per cent of their expenditures for family allowances. Finally, the State provides a grant-in-aid for costs of administration, graduated according to the number of members.

The *Norwegian* financing of unemployment insurance is rather different from that of the other three countries. Contributions, which are paid one-half by employees and one-half by employers, are stipulated in the law. They are graduated according to seven income classes but are otherwise the same for all insured persons. The local authorities contribute one-quarter of the total contributions paid. A highly interesting feature is that the local insurance offices are required to pass on 10 per cent of the contributions levied to a national reserve fund established to assist offices that have exhausted their funds due to high unemployment. By this method it has been possible to ensure equal contributions all over the country, regardless of regional differences in the level of unemployment. Moreover, if the national reserve fund should become insolvent, the State guarantees the expenses. The insured members are thus in all circumstances sure of receiving the stipulated benefits.

Due to a state of almost full employment, the expenditures of the Norwegian and Swedish unemployment insurance schemes have in recent years been quite modest. Thus, in 1952 they aggregated only 14 million kroner and 23 million kronor, respectively. In Denmark, where unemployment figures have been considerably higher and where benefits are also on the whole granted along more liberal lines, the costs have been on an entirely different scale, in 1952 totalling almost 300 million kroner. In all three countries the unemployment insurance has, however, pursued a conservative policy, aiming at financial consolidation. As a consequence, the Norwegian scheme today boasts reserves amounting to almost 400 million kroner, while the corresponding Danish figure is 330 million kroner and the Swedish 200 million kronor.

Administration

In *Denmark*, *Finland*, and *Sweden* the individual societies are today, as they have been since their establishment, governed by the members themselves. Supreme authority rests with a delegates' assembly elected by the members while the daily management is entrusted to a governing board elected by the assembly. The local branches are mostly operated by the accountants of the trade unions under the general control of the national society.

The societies are in all the three countries supervised by central government organs: In Denmark the Labour Directorate, in Sweden the Labour Board, and in Finland the Ministry of Social Affairs itself. These organs are at the same time responsible for the operation of public employment services and thus in close contact with general developments in the labour market. Although self-government has remained a reality to a rather higher degree than is the case with the voluntary health insurance societies in the same countries, there has been a steady growth in the influence of the supervisory institutions upon the conduct of affairs by the unemployment insurance societies. An illustration of the degree of control is furnished by the Swedish Labour Board which appoints a member to the governing board of every society. Moreover, in Denmark the supervisory authority is assisted in its task by an advisory Labour Committee, including representatives of the societies as well as parliamentary representatives of the political parties. The Committee also serves as appeal tribunal in certain disputes between insured members and the societies as well as among the societies themselves. In Sweden disputes between members and societies are dealt with by the ordinary civil courts.

The *Norwegian* set-up is somewhat different from that of the other countries, the compulsory unemployment insurance being administered by the district health insurance offices under the general direction of the local Employment Boards. Since the scope of unemployment insurance is in principle identical with that of health insurance, this arrangement obviously involves very considerable practical advantages with respect to the handling of files, collection of contributions, payment of benefits, etc. Indeed, the possibility of obtaining these advantages was one of the reasons why the unemployment scheme was largely modelled upon the health insurance scheme in so far as scope and size of benefits were concerned. Central control with the insurance is vested in the Labour Directorate in Oslo.

See Chapter II, Labour, p. 155.

OLD AGE PENSIONS

In contrast to health and unemployment insurance, the pension schemes, including old age pensions, disablement pensions, and survivors' benefits, have been established exclusively to ensure beneficiaries a measure of permanent income security, the basic assumption being the lasting decline or disappearance of earning ability. Existing schemes within these fields are today in each of the Northern countries intimately co-ordinated within a single legislative system: In Denmark and Iceland the National Insurance Acts, in Finland and Sweden the respective National Pensions Acts, and in Norway – where a general disablement insurance is still lacking – the Old Age Pension Act. However, for reasons of expediency, they are dealt with separately in this presentation.

The old age pension schemes of the present day provide the most important illustration of the transformation of former poor relief into social insurance in the five countries under review. Many differences may be found with respect to development and present set-up, but in all the Northern countries the old age pension has today in the public mind acquired the status of a right – although subject to conditions of varying importance – at the same time as the pension has everywhere been raised to a level where, by and large, it satisfies at least the elementary necessities of decent living.

Denmark is probably the only country in the world which has consistently attempted to solve the problem of income security in old age by non-contributory methods alone, i.e. exclusively by financing out of ordinary taxation. As far back as 1891 the Danish Parliament enacted legislation by which assistance to "worthy" old people was separated from poor relief with all its humiliating effects. Assistance was granted at the discretion of local governments and authorized even where the claimant was not entirely without means. It was usually given for as long as the circumstances of the beneficiary remained unchanged. Denmark thus became the first of the five countries to provide for its aged citizens without recourse to poor relief (apart from exceptional cases). A new phase was entered upon in 1922 when old age assistance was replaced by non-contributory pensions specified in the law and granted subject only to an income test. Numerous amendments have been made since then – notably in 1933 and 1946 – but, although greatly improved, the scheme has remained basically unchanged.

In *Sweden* compulsory old age insurance of the whole population, based upon the payment of contributions into an accumulating insurance fund, was introduced in 1913. However, as the indemnity was small – and necessarily would remain insignificant for many years to come – supplementary pensions, financed out of ordinary taxation, were issued, subject to an income test. The supplements were substantially increased in 1937 but even so a major proportion of pensioners had to rely upon poor relief to eke out an existence. The decisive change came only with the entry into force in 1948 of the National Pensions Scheme (since repeatedly amended), the main purpose of which was to provide all aged and disabled persons with pensions that were sufficient for adequate maintenance. The accumulation of funds has been abandoned and although individual contributions are retained the scheme is now predominantly financed over the Exchequer.

In *Norway* the first proposal for nation-wide measures on behalf of aged persons was made as early as in 1844 but almost a century lapsed before such legislation was passed. It was not until 1936 that the entirely locally sponsored schemes established by a growing number of towns were superseded by the Old Age Pension Act which

The realization of schemes ensuring a reasonable measure of economic security in old age figures as one of the most important social advances obtained by the Northern countries in recent decades.

introduced a national system of fixed minimum pensions. These were financed – very much as in Sweden – out of public funds and individual contributions and granted subject to an income test; local authorities were, however, free to grant higher pensions at their own expense. The Act is still in force although its provisions have been greatly improved in recent years.

The first *Icelandic* measures in this field date from 1890 when municipal funds were established for the relief of "old and weak commoners". In 1909 legislation providing for old age assistance – along lines very similar to those previously adopted in Denmark – was enacted but its practical effects were small. A compulsory old age insurance scheme introduced in 1936 had not yet reached maturity when it was replaced by the comprehensive 1946 reform. The latter provides, *inter alia*, for general old age pensions to all aged Icelanders, financing being undertaken jointly with the other insurances by means of contributions and public subsidies.

Following decades of preparation, *Finland* in 1937 enacted a scheme of compulsory old age pensions which is remarkable by featuring largely the same principles of "pure" insurance as were adopted by Sweden in 1913 but abandoned by that country in 1946. Payment of

There are national differences of method, but in all the five countries the present programmes have for their common purpose to provide the aged population with pensions sufficient to live on as a right.

pensions was begun in 1949 but since the actuarial amounts are as yet insignificant main reliance is placed in supplementary pensions granted out of public funds and subject to an income test. Thus, for the time being, and indeed for decades to come, Finland will have both contributory and non-contributory old age pensions.

The programmes outlined above represent the main answer of the five countries to the question of how to provide income security for the aged population under present-day conditions. However, these principal instruments are everywhere supplemented by numerous other schemes.

Thus, in all the countries under discussion public servants employed by the central and local governments are entitled to retirement pensions, graduated according to salary and length of service. Contributions are paid, but the larger part of costs is covered out of public funds. In Norway and Sweden a similar arrangement applies with respect to manual workers who have been in public employment over a period of many years. Somewhat different in character are the special pensions introduced for certain arduous occupations. In Sweden a State-aided pension scheme for seamen has been in operation since 1864. Provisional benefits are granted to seamen who retire at the age of 55, the benefits being payable until the beneficiaries become eligible for a regular national old age pension. Officers in the merchant marine receive a retirement pension at the age of 60. A similar Norwegian scheme was introduced in 1948, the main differences being that the pensionable age is here 60 years for all persons covered and that the pensions are in all cases granted for life; also survivors' benefits are provided. In 1951 Norway introduced a comparable scheme covering all forestry workers and providing a pension from their 65th year as well as survivors' benefits. All three schemes are financed by contributions from employees and employers supplemented by State grants.

In addition to the community-sponsored programmes there is a rapidly growing number of schemes, as a rule financed by contributions from both employer and employee, which provide retirement and survivors' pensions to salaried employees and executives in industry and business. Many large undertakings, usually joint stock companies, have established special pension funds for this purpose. Other firms have contracted with life insurance companies or special pension societies to administer their pension arrangements.

Scope

The Northern old age pension schemes in principle cover the whole population in the sense that they are not – as in some other countries – limited to certain social or occupational groups. However, this does not mean that all old age pension benefits are granted to aged persons regardless of their economic circumstances. To be sure, in Finland and Sweden this is the case with the basic pensions, but supplementary benefits – of particular importance in Finland – are subject to an income test. And the Danish and Norwegian old age pensions are entirely conditional upon such a test, the result being that only 55 and 75 per cent, respectively, of all persons above pensionable age actually receive a pension; however, a large proportion of non-pensioners would appear eligible for a reduced pension but do not claim it. Also the Icelandic pensions are granted subject to an income test – which is, however, so lenient as to exclude less than 10 per cent of all aged persons. Moreover, the test is scheduled for abolition in 1955.

Pensionable age varies somewhat from country to country. In Denmark and Finland pensions are payable from the age of 65 – the same as in the United Kingdom and the USA; single women in Denmark, however, are entitled to a pension already at 60 years. The corresponding age limits are 67 years in Iceland and Sweden while Norway has the highest pensionable age, 70 years. Especially in Denmark there has been some discussion of the possibility of raising the present age limit. Although such a proposal may appear justified by the presumed improvement over the last generations in the working ability of elderly people, its realization would require further development of measures to improve also the employment opportunities of aged persons – as yet a rather neglected problem in the Northern countries, as elsewhere.

See Widows' Pensions, pp. 436–437.

Contrary to the British and American systems, retirement from regular employment is not a specific requirement to obtain a pension. However, where the income test is applied, full-time employment will in practice rule out the granting of benefits.

Other provisions which circumscribe the actual scope of the schemes pertain to nationality and residence, eligibility being usually confined, except in Norway, to nationals who have been residents for a certain number of years. Moreover, Danish old age pensions are contingent upon membership in the health insurance.

425

Benefits

The main purpose pursued by the Northern programmes of the present day is that aged people should receive a pension sufficient to live on as a right. This implies that the pensioner without private means should be freed of the need to apply for additional help from the public assistance authorities. Although benefits vary considerably from scheme to scheme, it would appear correct to state that, by and large, this purpose has been attained today in all five countries.

The principle of fixing pension rates at a level which covers at least the subsistence minimum has entailed a certain differentiation of benefits according to the actual maintenance conditions of pensioners. Of particular importance in this respect is the graduation of benefits according to regional differences in the costs of living (in Sweden especially differences in the individual housing costs), on the one hand, and the special supplements granted to pensioners who support a child or spouse, on the other. As a result, the schemes present a more or less complicated picture of benefit-graduations and supplements. For the sake of clarity the following table is therefore limited to an illustration of the aggregate benefits – including pensions proper and certain standard supplements issued in several of the countries – which are payable to pensioners with no children and no (or only small) private means in each of the five capitals.

AGGREGATE ANNUAL OLD AGE PENSIONS PAYABLE
IN THE FIVE NORTHERN CAPITALS (1953)

	Copenhagen (kroner)	Helsinki (finmarks)	Reykjavik (krónur)	Oslo (kroner)	Stockholm (kronor)
Married couples (both spouses pensioners) . .	3,988	91,880	10,250	3,840	4,692
Single persons	2,611	45,940	6,406	2,364	3,074

The aggregate pensions of married couples are in Denmark, Iceland, Norway, and Sweden about 50 per cent higher than those of single persons, while in Finland the dominant supplementary pensions are paid to married couples as two single persons.

The above figures indicate the highest pensions normally granted today in each of the countries concerned. Under all five schemes the benefits are lower for recipients living in other parts of the country, such *regional graduation* being in principle undertaken according to the costs of living, methods varying. Except in Norway and Sweden,

A welcome visitor! In most Danish towns the monthly old age pensions are paid directly to pensioners in their own homes.

this graduation is specified directly in the relevant legislation. Thus, all Danish pension benefits are 12 per cent lower in provincial towns than in the capital, and 26 per cent lower in rural districts, while in Iceland – where there are only two "cost-of-living zones" – the reduction is 25 per cent. The Finnish contributory pension is the same all over the country, being determined by the size of contributions paid as well as by the number of years for which these contributions have been made. When the scheme reaches full maturity in 1994, the pensions will be payable with amounts that vary between 6,900 and 53,000 finmarks. As yet they are, however, insignificant, amounting, for a person having earned the income of a skilled worker, to only 3,700 finmarks. At the present time non-contributory supplementary pensions are therefore by far the most important, the figures for Finland given in the above table comprising a contributory pension of 3,700 finmarks and a supplementary pension of 42,240 finmarks, thus showing a typical workers' pension in Helsinki. The supplementary pensions are graduated according to three "cost-of-living-zones" in the proportion 100:83:67. The Swedish basic

427

pensions, 2,800 kronor for married couples, where man and wife both draw a pension, and 1,750 kronor for single pensioners, are the same all over the country. Graduation here takes place by means of differentiated housing allowances which are granted to pensioners of small means by decision of the local authorities, the State contributing towards the costs. In Stockholm these allowances account for more than 35 per cent of the aggregate pension benefits, while in low-rent rural districts they are lower and in a few districts fall to zero.

The Norwegian scheme assumes pensions to be determined by the local authorities according to the local costs of living and confines itself to the stipulation of minimum pensions, namely 1,800 kroner for married couples and 1,200 kroner for single pensioners, which apply to the whole country. Most rural districts pay only the minimum rates while the towns usually pay higher pensions; as shown in the table above, the aggregate Oslo pensions are thus 100 per cent above the statutory minimum.

The above-mentioned standard benefits are supplemented by a number of *special allowances*. Thus, all five schemes provide for an allowance for each child under 16 years (in Denmark 15), which the pensioner maintains. In Iceland it amounts to more than 35 per cent of the pension of married couples where both spouses are pensioners; in the other countries it is, relatively speaking, much smaller, varying between 8 and 15 per cent of the pension of married couples. Except in Iceland, these allowances are granted in addition to the general children's allowances provided under family welfare programmes. The real difference between Iceland and the other countries is therefore smaller than the above figures indicate.

Moreover, in all the countries except Finland, a married pensioner whose spouse is not entitled to a pension will receive a special supplement. In Norway the aggregate pension granted in these cases will actually be the same as that of a couple where both spouses are eligible. Almost the same holds true of Sweden where this supplement, however, is payable as a rule only in respect of a wife and only provided she has attained the age of 60. In the other countries the supplement is considerably smaller.

The Danish and Icelandic schemes further provide for so-called "waiting allowances". A Danish eligible person who postpones his application for a pension to his 67th or 70th year will receive an increment of 5 or 10 per cent, respectively, of the basic pension;

the Icelandic claimant similarly obtains an increment increasing with the length of postponement from five per cent up to 40 per cent, the latter figure applying where the pension is claimed only at the age of 75.

The *income test* is applied in all five countries, although there are wide variations with respect to its scope of application.

In Denmark, Iceland, and Norway all pension benefits are conditional upon the economic circumstances of the claimant. Thus, under the principal Danish rule pensions are reduced by 60 per cent of any income exceeding half the amount of the basic pension (in case of earned income: The full basic pension). The reduction rate is 50 in Iceland and 60 in Norway and applies to income in excess of the full pension (in Norway the statutory minimum pension). In Finland the contributory pensions are payable regardless of the economic circumstances of recipients, but the dominant non-contributory pensions are subject to reduction by 50 per cent of income above a certain maximum. The Swedish basic pensions, which account for more than three-quarters of total costs, are paid without any income test, but the housing and children's allowances as well as the wife's supplement are only granted subject to such a test, very similar to that of the other countries mentioned.

A highly important feature of benefit provisions is that in all of the countries except Norway *pensions are automatically adjusted to changes in the general cost-of-living index* to ensure their unchanged buying power. In Finland, it should be added, only the supplementary pensions are thus safeguarded. These adjustments are carried out quarterly in Finland, Iceland, and Sweden, twice a year in Denmark, and once a year in Norway.

It is difficult to give any accurate comparative appraisal of pension benefits in the five countries. Still, there can hardly be any doubt that, on the whole, the Swedish and Danish pensions are the highest, followed by those of Norway, Iceland, and Finland in the order named. However, the schemes may also be evaluated according to the size of pensions offered as compared to the incomes which they are in principle supposed to replace. Thus, the aggregate benefits of a married couple with no private income in Copenhagen, Oslo, and Stockholm are equal to about two-fifths of the annual earnings of a fully employed unskilled labourer. The corresponding proportion is one-third in Reykjavik and slightly less in Helsinki.

Financing

Under the double impact of legislative improvements and the progressive aging of the population, the costs of old age pensions have in recent years attained very considerable proportions. In all five countries today they take first or second place on the social welfare "budget", in Denmark, Iceland, and Sweden accounting for about one-third of total expenditures. It is therefore hardly surprising that their financing is a subject of intense interest and perennial debate.

As previously indicated, *Denmark* is alone among the Northern countries in adhering to a strictly non-contributory system, old age pensions being financed exclusively by the central and local governments out of general taxation in the same way as most other public expenditures. Proposals to introduce contributions have, indeed, been put forward time and again but the more than 60-year old tradition of tax-financing has by now struck such firm roots that any innovations on this point may be expected to encounter strong resistance.

By contrast, all the other countries feature varying combinations of individual contributions and public financing. Three of them – Finland, Norway, and Sweden – share the characteristic that contributions are in principle determined as a percentage of income, the same method employed today in the USA. The Icelandic contributions, on the other hand, are flat-rate amounts, as in the United Kingdom, but unlike the latter country the Icelandic contributions are adjusted automatically to changes in the cost-of-living index.

The most elaborate of these contributory systems is undoubtedly that of *Finland*. Contributions are two per cent of annual income, with a minimum of 500 and a maximum of 5,000 finmarks; employers pay one-half of the premium in respect of their employees. The scheme calls for the accumulation of contributions in a special fund which – when the insurance has reached maturity – is intended to provide the main financial basis for the old age pensions scheme. A novel feature of this otherwise traditional structure is that the growing resources of the fund are invested, not in government securities, but in projects destined to develop the national resources, such as power plants, factories, etc. The scheme has only been in operation for 14 years and the pensions paid under its provisions are necessarily insignificant as yet. Consequently, the overwhelming part of old age pensions granted at the present time are supplementary pensions paid out of the public purse.

The Norwegian and Swedish methods of financing are in principle rather similar. In both countries the costs of old age pensions are covered in part by special contributions determined as a percentage of income, in part by public funds. In *Norway* the contribution takes the form of a 1.2 per cent tax on all incomes exceeding a certain low minimum. The proceeds are administered by the Old Age Fund which defrays about three-fifths of the costs of the minimum pensions, the remainder being apportioned between the central and local governments; moreover, the latter carry the entire cost of supplementary pensions. The final result is that total costs are covered by contributions and public funds approximately in the proportion 50:50. The *Swedish* National Pensions Scheme provides for the joint financing of old age pensions, disablement pensions, and survivors' benefits. As from 1954 the contributions will be 1.8 per cent of the assessed income, with a minimum contribution of 11 kronor and a maximum of 180 kronor per year. The remainder, about 75 per cent of total costs, is paid directly by the central and local governments.

As for *Iceland*, the old age pensions are financed within the framework of the general social security programme.

See above, p. 397.

Administration

The administrative set-up varies somewhat, in part reflecting the different methods of financing. The Danish non-contributory system is administered together with Social assistance programmes by the assistance committees which are elected by each of the local authorities with the Ministry of Social Affairs as supreme supervisory and appeal organ. The situation in Norway is similar but the local organs are here special pension committees.

In the other countries centralization is more marked. Although special local committees are in charge of daily administration, the principal decisions, e. g. on applications, size of pensions, etc., are entrusted to autonomous national bodies – in Finland the National Pensions Institute, in Iceland the National Insurance Institution, and in Sweden the National Pensions Board.

DISABLEMENT PENSIONS

See pp. 437-445.

While old age pensions aim to provide security against the economic consequences of that inability to earn a normal living which usually accompanies advanced age, the disablement pension schemes fulfill a similar function with respect to premature disablement arising from other causes than employment injuries. The basic identity of issues involved finds natural expression in the narrow connection existing between the two categories of schemes, the main provisions of which generally apply equally to both groups of pensioners.

Thus, since their inception in 1913, the Swedish old age and disablement pensions have been dealt with jointly within a single legislative framework, at present the National Pensions Act passed in 1946. The same applies to the corresponding Finnish legislation of 1937. In Denmark disablement insurance was introduced in 1921, the direct impulse being the return from German rule of the South Jutland provinces, where such a scheme had existed for decades. It was not until 1933, however, that old age and disablement pensions were combined into a single programme, the National Insurance Act. The first general Icelandic provisions concerning disablement insurance date from 1936 but – as in the case of the old age pensions – before they entered into operation they were superseded by the enactment in 1946 of the National Insurance Reform, of which the disablement insurance forms part.

Norway does not yet have a general disablement insurance scheme, although detailed plans for the gradual introduction of such a programme are at present in an advanced stage of preparation. Meanwhile a number of local authorities, including about half the towns, have on their own initiative established special pension programmes for disabled persons, usually limited to the age group 60–70 years. Moreover, under an act of 1936 blind and totally crippled persons are entitled to a State pension grant equivalent to the minimum old age pension.

The disablement pension schemes, it should be noted, form only part of existing community programmes on behalf of invalids, being *See pp. 186–190* supplemented by the various employment and rehabilitation measures *and pp. 359–377.* for handicapped persons.

Scope

In all the four countries, where national disablement insurance has been established, the scheme covers all or practically all citizens from the age of 16 in Iceland and Sweden, 18 in Finland, and 21 in Denmark up to the pensionable age stipulated by the old age pension schemes. Disablement pensioners who pass the latter age limit automatically become old age pensioners although provision continues to be made for their special needs.

Benefits

The granting of a disablement pension is preceded by an evaluation of the degree of disablement suffered by the individual claimant. Although the national provisions are somewhat differently worded, the basic qualification in all four countries is that the claimant, due to physical or mental disablement, is incapable of providing for his maintenance by gainful employment. In Denmark, Finland, and Sweden this is generally interpreted to mean that a reduction by two-thirds of earning ability qualifies for a pension; the Icelandic scheme requires a reduction by three-quarters.

Pensions plus supplements are in principle paid according to the same rules and at the same rates as apply to old age pensions. In Denmark they are, however, further supplemented by certain grants motivated by the special needs of disabled persons.

Thus, the Danish disablement pensioner receives a disablement supplement which amounts to 15–20 per cent (varying somewhat according to locality) of his regular pension. Moreover, if the invalid is blind or his condition requires the personal assistance of others, an

433

additional "assistance supplement", equivalent to 25–30 per cent of the pension, is issued; in cases of virtual helplessness a "care supplement", equivalent to 65–75 per cent of the pension, is granted instead. The income test characteristic of the Danish old age pension provisions applies also to disablement pensions, although with important modifications. Thus, the pension cannot be reduced below one-third of the basic rate whatever the economic circumstances of the pensioner. Moreover, earned income is entirely disregarded up to an amount equal to the full pension, implying that a disablement pensioner may have an income of approximately half the earnings of an unskilled worker without any reduction of his pension. Finally, supplements for "assistance" and "care" are granted entirely without any income test.

By contrast, the Swedish scheme stipulates stricter income deduction rules for disablement pensioners than for old age pensioners. For claimants of small means the pensions are, indeed, the same in both cases. But only 200 kronor of the pension are payable regardless of the pensioner's economic circumstances, the remainder being subject to an income test. Still, blind persons receive a supplementary grant equivalent to the Danish "assistance" supplement. Moreover, the Swedish scheme features sickness benefits, equal to the disablement pensions, in cases where incapacity for work extends well beyond six months but where ultimate recovery may be expected.

Financing

See above,
pp. 430-431.

In Finland, Iceland, and Sweden the financing of disablement pensions is identical with that of old age pensions. The Danish scheme, on the other hand, has always been financed under separate rules which still show some remnants of the influence of the old German disablement insurance. Thus, unlike the entirely non-contributory old age pensions, disablement pensions are in part paid for by a small poll-tax levied on all insured persons and by even smaller employer contributions assessed according to the number of employees, the deficit being defrayed by the State and local authorities. Since neither poll-tax nor contributions have followed rising expenditures, but have remained unchanged for several decades, the result has been that a steadily increasing proportion of total costs – at the present time about 80 per cent – is covered out of public funds.

It is a matter of course that, numerically and financially, the disablement pension schemes are on a quite different and more modest

434

scale than that of the old age pension programmes. Thus, in Denmark and Sweden the disablement pensioners number only one per cent and almost two per cent, respectively, of the total population while old age pensioners are about five times as many. Roughly speaking, the relative costs are in the same proportion.

Administration

The disablement insurance in Finland and Sweden is administered jointly with the old age pensions and in Iceland within the general framework of the National Insurance Institution. In Denmark, on the other hand, final administrative responsibility has been vested in a separate collegiate body, the Disablement Insurance Court.

Claims for a pension, which must be accompanied by the necessary documentation concerning the state of health and other personal circumstances of the applicant, are in all four countries submitted for decision or review to a central organ (the staff of which includes medical experts), thus ensuring that all cases are uniformly treated. The direct administration of the individual pensions is in Denmark entrusted to the local authorities which in most cases determine the rate at which the pension, including supplements, is to be paid in each individual case, according to the relevant legislative provisions. In Finland, Iceland, and Sweden, on the other hand, the central institution is also in direct charge of pension payments.

Other activities of the central organs include continuous control and inspection, particularly with a view to ascertaining whether disablement pensioners continue to qualify for a pension. Moreover, they carry general responsibility for programmes concerning the rehabilitation of such pensioners.

See Chapter VI, Health and Rehabilitation, pp. 359–370.

SURVIVORS' BENEFITS

The death of a breadwinner will very often leave the surviving dependants in a difficult economic situation. Measures designed to meet the presumed need of support mainly include certain immediate grants, plus widows' pensions and special children's allowances. The extent to which such measures have been introduced, as well as the legislative framework within which they are provided, varies considerably among the Northern countries. Benefits payable to survivors of persons fatally injured in the course of their work are dealt with in the following section, Employment Injuries Insurance.

435

Immediate Grants

As for the immediate needs arising out of the death of a family member, a funeral allowance is granted under the Danish and Finnish health insurance schemes as well as under a double set of provisions in the Norwegian health and old age pension schemes. The Danish allowance has recently been raised to 450 kroner, which should be sufficient to cover the costs of a modest funeral; in the other countries the amount is somewhat smaller.

Under the Icelandic National Insurance Act of 1946 any woman widowed before the age of 67 is entitled to compensation for three months, payable at almost the double rate of old age pensions to tide her over the most critical period; if she supports children under 16 years, the compensation is extended, at a somewhat lower rate, for a further nine months. A similar, although more modest compensation is granted under the Finnish contributory old age pensions scheme. It ranges between 500 and 30,000 finmarks, depending upon the amount of contributions paid up; in 1952 the average compensation was about 8,000 finmarks.

Widows' Pensions

General provisions for the granting of widows' pensions are found only in Iceland and Sweden where they form parts of the National Insurance Scheme and National Pensions Scheme, respectively.

Thus, the *Icelandic* legislation authorizes the payment of such a pension to women widowed at the age of 50 or later. The amount is determined according to the age and economic circumstances of each applicant but cannot exceed the pension issued in fatal cases under the employment injuries provisions.

See below, page 444.

The *Swedish* National Pensions Act similarly stipulates that any woman who is widowed at the age of 55 or more is entitled to a pension provided the marriage has lasted at least five years. For widows of small means the pension, which is subject to an income test, amounts to about two-thirds of the old age pension. The same amount is paid, irrespective of age, to widows with children under 10 years of age.

No comparable schemes are in operation in the other countries. However, in Denmark the absence of such provisions is in part compensated for by the exceptionally low age limit for old age pensions, which for single women – including widows – is only 60 years as

436

against 65–70 years in the other countries. In Norway, moreover, the widow of an old age pensioner is entitled to an old age pension if, at the time of death of her husband, she has passed her 60th year. As for Finland, special mention should be made of the large number of war-widows who receive a pension which – as in Iceland – is determined on the basis of the employment injuries scheme.

Children's Allowances

Special allowances for children who have lost one of their parents are granted in all five countries, although under divergent provisions.

Thus, in Denmark, Iceland, and Sweden a widow will receive, for each child that she maintains, an allowance equal to that paid for children of old age and disablement pensioners. Widowers either receive a smaller amount (as in Denmark and Iceland) or none at all (in Sweden). In all three countries the allowances are subject to an income test which, however, excludes only a small minority from benefits. It should be added that these allowances, which are financed by the central and local governments, are independent of the general children's allowances provided as part of family welfare programmes.

See Chapter IV, Family Welfare, pp. 267–272.

In Norway, where the general children's allowance is paid normally only for the second and each following child, widows and widowers are entitled to receive this allowance, without any income test, also in respect of the first child. The planned introduction of special child maintenance pensions – payable at the same rate as the minimum old age pensions – for single mothers with children under 16 years of age will render unnecessary this arrangement. As for Finland, a widow of small means with at least two children is entitled to a "family allowance" in kind, such allowances being normally paid only to families with four or more children; general children's allowances are payable in addition.

EMPLOYMENT INJURIES INSURANCE

Norwegian miners were the first group in the Northern countries to benefit from a regular social security scheme in case of injury during their dangerous work. This was already in 1812, long before the industrial revolution broke through in this part of Europe. Developments in the second half of the 19th century resulted in growing pressure for community action with efforts directed along two main lines: Prevention and compensation. This double approach to the problem of employment injuries has been maintained ever since, the emphasis shifting from one front to the other. As previously described, industrial safety regulations were among the very earliest social welfare enactments in these countries. And although subsequent decades have witnessed the establishment and continued improvement of compensation schemes, preventive action has for many years been in the foreground.

See Chapter II, Labour, pp.72-90.

Except in Norway, compensation for employment injuries in the Northern countries was initially based on legislation similar to that found in the United Kingdom in that it simply stipulated the liability of employers to compensate workers for injuries sustained in the course of their work. Norway, on the other hand, already in 1894 adopted the Austro-German pattern by combining such liability with the obligation for employers to insure against the ensuing claims.

This latter principle has since gained acceptance in all the Northern countries. Finland followed the Norwegian example already in 1898 and in 1903 Iceland introduced a limited compulsory scheme for seamen, supplemented in 1925 by an act covering industrial workers. The year 1916 saw the simultaneous introduction in both Denmark and Sweden of similar legislation.

Although repeatedly revised, the Danish and Swedish acts of 1916 have remained basically unchanged to the present day. In Iceland the scheme was incorporated in the 1946 National Insurance Act along with the other branches of social insurance, while Finland put a new revised and enlarged scheme on the statute books in 1948. Norway has ended up with three separate schemes: A revised edition of the 1894 Act, mainly covering industrial workers, a Fishermen's Employment Injuries Insurance Act introduced in 1909, and a Seamen's Employment Injuries Insurance Act which came into force in 1911. Through subsequent revisions these three schemes have been brought into line so that today only minor differences remain.

Scope

The *categories of persons* covered by the compulsory schemes of employment injuries insurance are essentially the same in all the Northern countries, encompassing practically all workers as well as salaried employees – with Norway forming only a partial exception to this principle. The non-covered groups are mainly made up of self-employed persons, including employers; persons who work for

438

Timber floating in Finland – – a dangerous job! An adequate scheme of compensation for employment injuries forms a vital part of social security programmes for persons in risky occupations.

others but do so on their own premises; and (usually) family members employed by the head of the family. However, those who are not compulsorily insured are to a certain extent free to join the national insurance schemes. This applies particularly to Denmark where the scheme is open to all farmers, craftsmen, tradesmen, etc., provided their income does not exceed a certain limit. Fishermen occupy a special status in several of the countries: In Denmark they are under obligation to insure themselves under the general scheme and in Sweden they are covered by a special voluntary programme. Also many private insurance companies provide employment injuries insurance, often on a group basis.

Norway, in contrast to the other countries, specifies each kind of enterprise or work which is covered, exempting all less dangerous occupations. The result is that the Norwegian scheme does not apply to non-manual workers nor to such activities as non-mechanical agricultural work, forest cultivation, etc.

The provisions relating to casual labour also show certain national differences. While the employment of casual domestic servants generally does not entail any liability to pay insurance contributions – or the liability to do so is often not complied with – the

439

employed persons are nevertheless insured to the same extent as workers regularly covered. This, however, does not apply for Iceland, where only "dangerous" casual work brings the worker within the scope of the Act. Moreover, while employment injuries insurance generally aims at the actively employed groups, it is characteristic of Finland, Iceland, and Sweden that persons training for an occupation at specified vocational schools are also included.

The *range of injuries* which qualify for benefits is practically the same in all five countries. In the first place, the insurance covers all accidents suffered by the insured in the course of his work, unless they are brought about wilfully or by gross negligence on the part of the injured person himself. Second, it comprises all occupational diseases specially listed, including, as a minimum, the diseases enumerated in the ILO Conventions on this subject. While the disablement pensions scheme applies only to serious cases of invalidation, the employment injuries insurance issues disablement indemnities for degrees of invalidity as low as 15 per cent in Iceland, 10 per cent in Finland and Sweden, and even 5 per cent in Denmark.

National differences are found, however, when comparing the stipulations applying to accidents occurring on the way to and from work. In Denmark and Finland such accidents are normally not covered by the insurance and the same applies to the Norwegian industrial insurance; in Iceland and Sweden, on the other hand, they are covered. Curiously enough, however, it is the Norwegian Seamen's Insurance which is the most liberal in this respect: An employed Norwegian seaman is insured 24 hours a day, irrespective of what he is doing or whether he is on board his ship or not.

Benefits

The fact that employment injuries insurance covers both sickness, disablement, and death of breadwinner logically entails a corresponding diversity of benefits. This, again, raises the problem of relations between the employment injuries programme and the other branches of social insurance. While overlapping has generally been prevented by stipulations regulating the simultaneous reception of benefits from two or more sources, it must be admitted that the co-ordination of the various benefits is far from complete as yet. This lack of co-ordination, which manifests itself primarily in discrepancies in the size of benefits, may largely be traced to the fact that employment injuries insurance, as contrasted with the other branches of social insurance, has since its inception been based upon the principle of compensation for loss of income. It is quite another thing that this principle is applied today only in modified form. As previously stated, however, Sweden in 1953 enacted a new compulsory health insurance scheme, effective from 1955, which takes over all cases of employment injuries of less than 90 days' duration; benefits hereafter will be the same for most cases of sickness whatever their cause, and for cash allowances the compensation principle will be applied.

Cash benefits are in principle very similar in the five countries. They include daily allowances, disablement indemnities, survivors' pensions, and funeral grants, and are generally graduated to a certain extent according to the previous earnings of the injured person. Benefits in kind include medical treatment, bandages, artificial limbs, etc. In Finland – and at present also in Sweden – such benefits are granted in full under the employment injuries scheme, while under the other schemes medical treatment is primarily provided by the health insurance. It is characteristic of benefits issued under the various programmes that – except for certain grants to surviving parents – they are granted without any income test as known from the old age and disablement pensions schemes.

In *Denmark* the graduation of cash benefits is subject to the important modification that, for the purpose of fixing benefits, the annual income is not reckoned above a certain maximum, at present 6,250 kroner, which is considerably less than the actual income of the majority of fully employed workers.

The daily allowances, which are issued from the seventh day of incapacity for work, amount to three-quarters of the previous earnings (figured on a weekly basis), subject, however, to the modification resulting from the maximum mentioned above. The disablement indemnity is in principle issued as an annuity pension. However, this is of small practical significance since the pension may be capitalized to a lump sum, this procedure being indeed compulsory in all cases – about 97 per cent of the total – where the degree of invalidity is assessed at less than one-half. At total permanent disability the annuity is two-thirds of the annual income of the injured person, proportional reduction being undertaken for lesser degrees of invalidity. Survivors' benefits are similarly computed, but, contrary to the above benefit, the actual amount is differentiated according to the number of dependants. A widow is thus entitled to four times the annual income of her husband plus an indemnity for each child under 18. However, total survivors' benefits may not exceed seven times the annual income of the deceased. A funeral grant supplements the above indemnity and the funeral benefit granted under the health insurance. It is worth noting that all continuing payments are adjusted annually for changes in the cost-of-living index.

Medical treatment, it should be added, is ordinarily not provided by the Danish employment injuries scheme since it is presumed that the beneficiary is insured with the health insurance societies. However, to the extent that the latter do not furnish the special services required by the injured person, it is incumbent upon the employment injuries insurance to provide them.

The *Swedish* set-up is now in a state of transition. Besides the above-mentioned co-ordination of health insurance and employment injuries insurance, the latter is scheduled for general revison in 1954 so as to fit in with the new health insurance. The principal provisions, however, will remain essentially unchanged with respect to those injuries that cause sickness of more than 90 days' duration, disablement, or death. The provisions of the present scheme are in several respects somewhat more liberal than in Denmark, as may be seen from the fact that in 1953 the maximum income reckoned with when computing the benefits was 7,200 kronor as against 6,250 kroner in Denmark. As from 1955 the maximum limit will be considerably higher. The daily allowances have up to now been paid from the day following the accident and include a family supplement. Under the new co-ordinated arrangement there will be a waiting period of three days. While total disablement entitles the victim to an annual pension equal to eleven-twelfths of his annual income, a supplement of up to 1,800 kronor may be added to this amount in cases where special care is needed. In case of death the widow receives a survivors' pension of one-third the annual income. Each child under 16 years receives a pension equal to one-sixth of that amount. The parents of the victim may be granted a pension corresponding to the amount of assistance they received from him, subject, however, to a maximum of 25 per cent of the annual income of the deceased. Aggregate survivors' pensions, however, may not exceed five-sixths of the earnings of the deceased. Finally, a funeral benefit of 500 kronor is granted.

The three *Norwegian* schemes of employment injuries insurance present a fairly uniform picture with respect to benefits granted.

In the first place, they provide free medical treatment as long as such is needed. However, this rule is decisively modified in practice since the health insurance is under obligation to care for injured members during the first 52 weeks. This obligation also extends to the granting of daily allowances.

The maximum and minimum incomes upon which disablement and survivors' indemnities for industrial workers are computed amount to 5,000 and 2,400 kroner, respectively. Seamen are, however, classed according to their position while in employment, with income limits varying from a maximum of 7,000 kroner for ship's-officers to a minimum of 4,500 kroner for plain sailors. For fishermen the maximum income is only 3,000 kroner but individual voluntary insurance may bring the maximum up to 4,000. Complete disablement entitles to a pension of 60 per cent of the annual income and, contrary to Denmark and Sweden, substantial supplements are granted for dependants. Thus, the married pensioner is entitled to a further 600 kroner and also 300 kroner for each child under 16, subject to a maximum of 90 per cent of annual income. As in Sweden, an additional grant is made in cases where special care is required by the disabled person. Where disablement is less than 20 per cent, a lump sum is paid, equal to three times the annuity due in each case.

Survivors' pensions amount to 40 per cent of the annual income of the deceased plus 600 kroner for the first and 300 kroner for each subsequent child. Subject to very strict rules and a means test in each case, the parents may also in Norway receive a compensation if the deceased contributed in a major degree to their maintenance. The funeral benefit amounts to 200 kroner, or 300 kroner for seamen in foreign trade when buried in Norway; in other cases the allowance usually covers the actual costs.

The *Finnish* benefits comprise, as in Sweden, medical and other care, as well as the four cash benefits enumerated above. The daily allowances, which include a breadwinner's supplement, amount to about 75 per cent of the daily wages of the lowest paid workers and correspondingly less for the more skilled professions. For permanent disablement ranging from 10 to 30 per cent a lump sum indemnity is granted in proportion to the annual wages. For higher degrees of

443

disablement annual pensions are issued which consist partly of a basic sum graduated according to the degree of disablement, partly of a supplementary pension computed on the basis of the loss of earnings involved and differentiated according to the number of dependent children. In case the victim is reduced to a state of helplessness a special supplement is granted. In fatal cases a survivors' pension is issued to the widow, to dependent children under 16, and under certain conditions to other relatives. A maximum of 80 per cent of the full disablement pension sets the limit of the survivors' pension. Unlike conditions in the other countries, the funeral allowance varies according to the income of the deceased.

The *Icelandic* scheme is peculiar in that the income of the beneficiary affects only the maximum daily allowance to which he is entitled. Otherwise the benefits are fixed amounts, regulated according to the cost-of-living index.

Daily allowances are issued from the eighth day of incapacity and run for 26 weeks; if the injured person supports one or more children the allowance is supplemented by the ordinary children's allowance otherwise issued only to families with two or more children. The total allowance may not exceed three-quarters of the daily wages of the recipient. Permanent disablement of 75 per cent or more entitles to an annual pension of 6,406 krónur (1953) or for lesser degrees of invalidation a corresponding percentage of this amount. As in Denmark, invalidity below 50 per cent is indemnified by payment of a lump sum. In all cases where disablement exceeds 50 per cent the pension is supplemented by grants in respect of spouse and children and to possible other dependents, especially parents. In principle these grants are determined in the same way as survivors' benefits. A survivors' indemnity is issued to the spouse and amounts to a lump sum of 14,100 krónur. If the widow (or widower) is more than 50 years old, or has lost more than half her (or his) earning capacity, the indemnity is followed up by a pension equalling the disablement pension, and computed according to rules similar to those governing the personal disablement pension. Each child under 16 receives an annual pension of 3,768 krónur, or one and a half time this amount in the case of orphans. Other relatives, notably parents, may be granted a lump sum indemnity ranging from 4,700–14,100 krónur according to the degree of dependence on economic assistance from the deceased.

Financing and Administration

In principle the employment injuries programmes are *financed* exclusively by the employers. Contributions are in Norway as a rule determined as a percentage of the earnings of insured employees but elsewhere are levied on the basis of the number of man-days worked in the enterprise concerned during a year. Moreover, they are in all five countries differentiated according to actuarial estimates of the hazards prevailing in the different industries, which, for this purpose, have been divided into a number of "danger categories".

The *administration* is in all five countries highly centralized, but there are differences with respect to the way in which the "insurance business" proper is handled. Moreover, in Sweden the co-ordination with health insurance will occasion a decentralization with respect to more than 90 per cent of all cases of employment injuries handled under the present scheme.

In Denmark, Finland, and Sweden employers contract insurance with one of a number of approved insurance companies, while final control rests with a central office or directorate supplemented by an appeals body. In Denmark and Finland the companies are sole underwriters of the insurance. The Swedish employers, on the other hand, may also take out their insurance with the National Insurance Office directly and if not insured with any company the employer is automatically insured with the Office. Decisions on claims, and administration of the schemes as a whole, are in Denmark entrusted to the State organ mentioned, while in Finland and Sweden the primary decisions on compensation are taken by the insurance companies. Whether made by the State administration or by the companies, these decisions may be appealed to an Employment Injuries Insurance Court for final award.

The administrative set-up in Iceland and Norway is somewhat different, insurance companies playing no part in the employment injuries insurance. In Iceland the administration has been vested in a division of the National Insurance Institution which decides upon claims put forward under the act and collects contributions from the employers. The three Norwegian schemes are jointly administered by a government-appointed organ, the National Insurance Institution in Oslo. For the collection of contributions and other routine administration the Institution relies upon the local health insurance office. Its decisions are subject to appeal to a special board.

Social Assistance

Assistance from the community as a legal right of the citizen in need is barely a century old. However, evidence of more or less organized aid to the destitute is found far back in history.

Iceland stands out among the Northern countries by virtue of the early and sustained part played in this field by the public authorities. Thus, already in the 12th century that country boasted a written law rendering the local councils (samkomur) responsible for the care of distressed people with no relatives able to come to their rescue. This early form of social assistance was maintained up through the centuries with a single lapse of 100 years, during which the county governors were in charge of local administration. It was re-introduced in modernized shape in 1872, when the handling of local affairs reverted once more to the local authorities. A new poor law took effect in 1907 and remained in force – although with repeated amendments – until 1946 when a thorough revision took place simultaneously with the introduction of the National Insurance Scheme.

Although a similar responsibility of local authorities has existed in principle also in the other four countries, the Catholic Church, including the various monastic orders, here remained the centre of practically all organized charity throughout medieval times. The Protestant Reformation in the 16th century brought these activities to a sudden stop. The State took over the property of the Church but the accompanying social welfare responsibilities were only to a limited degree shouldered by the secular power. The charitable hospitals founded by the Church were in some instances continued by the Crown and functioned right up to modern times as combined sickwards, poorhouses, and lunatic asylums. Otherwise, organized poor relief largely disappeared. Begging and vagrancy were widespread phenomena and in troubled times attained the proportions of veritable menaces to peace and order. Counter-measures resorted to by central and local governments were essentially repressive. Vagrancy was made a criminal offense and begging was subjected to general prohibition. Later still, special begging licenses were locally granted as a privilege to certain inhabitants of each locality.

Slowly, and in part under pressure from the Crown, the care of those who, because of poverty or infirmity, were unable to fend for

This former poor-house in Sweden still looks almost as it did when built about 250 years ago. In those days, however, its single room had no windows and housed poor persons of both sexes. They would receive some food from a nearby estate, but otherwise eked out a meagre existence by begging.

themselves became more firmly established as a primary concern of local authorities. Still, the relief granted retained the character of charity. A decisive forward step was not taken until the first genuine national poor laws were enacted in the 19th century under the influence of the liberal-humanistic ideas emanating from the French Revolution.

The first *Danish* legislation which firmly established the duty of local authorities to care for their poor dates back to 1799 and 1803 (applying to the capital and to the rest of the country, respectively). Subsequently, the right to public assistance in case of distress was written into the constitution of 1849 which terminated almost two hundred years of absolute monarchy. However, this pledge did not become effective until almost twenty years later when local self-government was reorganized on a democratic basis and entrusted with the implementation of the poor relief "programme" laid down in the constitution. Subsequent legislation, particularly the Poor Law of 1891, brought about an increasing differentiation of assistance provisions and progressively curtailed the discretionary powers of local authorities. Finally, the older provisions were streamlined and *See above, p. 388.* incorporated in the comprehensive Social Reform of 1933 under the title of the Public Assistance Act.

In 1845 *Norway* made public relief a legal right of the aged, the sick, the crippled, lunatics, and orphans; the decisive responsibility in this field was entrusted to the municipal poor commissions simultaneously established. Within the next decade *Finland* and *Sweden* enacted poor laws affirming the obligation of local authorities to care for their poor; moreover, both statutes established the right of the poor to appeal local decisions to higher authority. However, these reforms were only shortlived. Less than a generation passed before revisions of the poor laws again made aid to the poor an act of charity to which no legal right could be established, exception being made only for certain categories (thus, in Norway, sick persons, lunatics, and orphans). It was not until 1900 and 1922, respectively, that new Norwegian and Finnish poor laws re-established mandatory assistance to all those unable to provide for themselves. The Swedish Poor Law of 1918 was essentially similar although the right to assistance was confined to persons incapable of work; the local authorities were, however, free to aid also able-bodied, unemployed persons in need. Although frequently amended and from many points of view overruled or rendered obsolete by modern social security measures, all three statutes are still in force at the present time. In Norway and Sweden, however, a general revision is imminent.

The dates enumerated above stand out as milestones on the road to improved public relief for those in need of help not otherwise available. However, development has been continuous and must be viewed primarily against the gradual change in the general attitude of the peoples toward their less fortunate fellow citizens. The former condemnatory attitude toward the poor and the narrow scope and harsh character of older relief provisions which were its reflection hardly permitted any positive approach to the social rehabilitation of the individuals involved. Gradually the assistance rendered has improved at the same time as the local assistance organs, under the leadership of interested, locally elected citizens, have developed into institutions where the problems of clients are dealt with in a spirit of understanding and constructive effort, including a growing emphasis upon the preventive aspects of social welfare work. The effects of this development within the framework of social security reform in general have already been outlined at an earlier juncture. It should be added that the process described is by no means completed as yet and that there is still ample room for further improvements.

See above, pp. 385–387.

448

The transformation of poor relief into modern social assistance as a supplement to ever-widening social insurance schemes has also involved the independent branching out of two lines of community action. Within the last 50–60 years the care of the aged and the care of children deprived of a normal home life have increasingly acquired identities of their own, as distinct from general assistance.

Present-day institutional measures on behalf of old people have for their main background the poor laws of former times with their general provisions for maintenance in poorhouses or workhouses of those who, whether young or old, because of poverty or infirmity were unable to fend for themselves. The traditional procedure, even if originally unintended, of lumping together persons with only one thing in common – that they were destitute and/or in need of care not otherwise available – has gradually been replaced by classification and separate treatment according to the specific needs of each group. The chronically sick, the mentally ill, vagrants, and others have to an increasing extent been transferred to special institutions, in large part operated by State or provincial authorities. Old people in need of institutional care have, on the other hand, remained the responsibility of local authorities who have either modernized the old poorhouses or erected new old people's homes. In recent years the gradual aging of the population has brought about a renewal of public interest in the problems of old age and a series of special welfare services on behalf of old people are at the present time in process of development.

At the same time there has been a radical expansion of measures in favour of children, notably those deprived of a normal home life or otherwise socially handicapped. Practically all present-day child welfare provisions have emerged within the past half century and have for their common background a marked change in the general attitude towards children. Humanitarian considerations, coupled with an improved understanding of childhood as the formative prelude to adult life, have been among the decisive motives behind this development in which voluntary initiative, frequently organized in charitable associations, has taken a leading part.

The child welfare programmes developed during these decades have all emphasized normal family life as the ideal environment for the child. The first and most urgently needed reforms were designed to alter radically the conditions under which the community provided for children committed to its care. The early child welfare institutions

449

with their impersonal character and harsh discipline have progressively been supplanted by smaller and more differentiated children's homes permitting an increased measure of individualized care. At the same time efforts have been made to expand and improve the system of placement in foster homes of children who are in social or moral danger. Second, while this process is still in full implementation, there has in recent years been a growing recognition of the importance of preventive measures as a means of restoring to a normal home life such children as would otherwise have to be placed under permanent public care.

THE ROLE OF LOCAL GOVERNMENT

Although the general trend toward centralization has also influenced this field of community activity, local authorities have on the whole retained primary responsibility – financially and otherwise – for assistance to destitute persons in general as well as for measures on behalf of children and old people in particular.

The relative independence preserved by local authorities in these matters places an important limitation upon the following presentation. In contrast to the nation-wide social insurance programmes, the social assistance schemes established by national legislation are essentially frameworks, the contents of which may exhibit considerable local variations. True, an increasing degree of standardization has been achieved in various ways. However, the individual administrative bodies are still entrusted with discretionary powers, or stand in an optional position with respect to the establishment of numerous social assistance activities, the result being that practice varies from district to district. This is not altogether as undesirable as it may at first appear, since it is generally acknowledged that social assistance should conform to local customs and living conditions. Moreover, the local administration of social assistance has profited by collaboration with voluntary relief organizations and socially interested individuals who have found here a field of activity which allows a certain amount of freedom of action as well as personal contact with the assisted.

Still, there is no denying that the wide differences among the various municipalities with respect to size and economic and social conditions inevitably cause disparities in the ability of local authorities to meet the standards established by the increasingly complex provisions of national legislation.

Thus, in Denmark, Iceland, and Norway a large number of rural districts count only a few hundred inhabitants or less. Obviously these small communities frequently find it difficult to maintain social assistance services that measure up to those operated by the more populous, particularly urban, municipalities. In Sweden the situation was similar until a radical reform in 1952 merged a host of small, mostly rural, municipalities into larger units with (as a rule) more than 2,000 inhabitants. Most rural municipalities in Finland have a population even larger than that and the whole problem is, consequently, of practically no importance in that country.

Perhaps an even greater obstacle to the proper implementation of social assistance programmes has arisen out of the financial weakness of local authorities. Contributions to the relief funds established by the early poor laws were strictly voluntary. The introduction of a local poor tax was the first decisive improvement in this crucial matter. The reorganization of local self-government in the later half of the 19th century brought about the unified financing of all local government expenditures out of general taxation. However, these financial reforms could not change the fact that in all the countries there were marked local differences in social assistance needs, on the one hand, and in available resources, on the other. When, after the First World War, social assistance programmes were amended, systems of inter-municipal equalization and State refunds of all or part of certain expenditures were introduced in order to enable even the financially weakest localities to carry out the programmes. Obviously, the progressive establishment of nation-wide social insurance schemes has had a similar effect by reducing the number of persons in need of social assistance.

The overall result is, first, that assistance institutions of various kinds are rather unevenly distributed throughout each country and, second, that the small municipalities encounter difficulties in establishing those social services which require expert personnel. Co-operation between neighbouring localities or the establishment of central institutions at the county level present themselves as natural solutions to this problem and have in fact attained increasing importance. In the long run, however, municipal reforms on the Swedish model may prove necessary also in the other Northern countries to ensure the satisfactory adaptation of local self-government to present-day requirements.

Even with the gradual elimination of the main impediments to the achievement of national uniformity in social assistance standards it is not to be expected that all diversities will vanish as long as local self-government is retained in the field of social assistance. Minimum standards are laid down and enforced by the central governments, but in many instances the introduction of new programmes is made optional with the local authorities, thus preserving their traditional right to set their own pace of development. Likewise, the existing legislation allows a certain latitude in the practical administration of numerous provisions, thus enabling interested local authorities to experiment with improvements of social services – frequently as a prelude to the adoption of similar measures also in other districts.

ADMINISTRATION

The present administrative set-up in the field of social assistance in the Northern countries reflects the working of the above-mentioned two currents of influence, efforts to preserve local self-government being balanced to a certain extent by strivings for greater national uniformity of programmes. At the same time the increased differentiation of these programmes according to categories served has resulted in important administrative changes, notably the drawing of a more or less pronounced line of division between the administration of child care programmes, on the one hand, and that of other assistance activities, on the other.

It follows from the dominant role of local authorities that *local organization* occupies a place of key importance to the whole system. In all five countries the municipal councils are under legal obligation to establish special organs for the administration of assistance programmes. Except in Finland, two separate bodies are provided for: The *assistance committee* and the *child welfare committee*.

In *Denmark* the members of the two committees are selected by the local district or borough councils out of their own midst; interested non-members with special insight may, however, be called upon to join the child welfare committees. Moreover, all towns and all rural districts exceeding a certain minimum population must maintain a social welfare office with daily hours.

The Norwegian and Swedish provisions concerning the composition of these organs are more detailed but, in contrast to Denmark, the local councils are free to appoint members outside their own ranks.

In *Norway* the statutory members of the assistance committees include the vicar and – in the towns – a public servant appointed by the central government. Otherwise, the local authorities decide upon the number of members, one of whom shall be a woman. While the administration of child welfare has hitherto been scattered among several organs, the new Care of Children Act of 1953 introduced child welfare committees which – as in Denmark – are in charge of all activities on behalf of children deprived of a normal home life. The committees comprise members – men and women – appointed among persons with special insight into care of children.

The *Swedish* assistance committee must comprise at least five members in towns and three in rural districts. The child welfare committee must include one member of the assistance committee, a vicar, a public school teacher, and the public health medical officer, provided he is a resident of the municipality; in addition, the committee must have at least two other members known for their active interest in child welfare work. In the assistance committee as well as in the child welfare committee at least one member shall be a woman.

As for *Iceland*, the assistance committees are appointed by the local councils and comprise three to five members. The child welfare committees are appointed in the same way and have five to seven members.

In contrast to the countries mentioned *Finland* has pursued a policy of centralizing local social welfare administration. Thus, each local council appoints a single social welfare committee with at least six members. However, a certain division of labour is undertaken in so far as the committee is in principle grouped into two divisions, one of which is in charge of family welfare, child and youth welfare, and programmes for disabled persons, while the other administers general assistance, including measures pertaining to alcoholics. As in Norway and Sweden, both sexes must be represented. Moreover, one member should be familiar with public health and another have experience in the teaching and upbringing of children.

Within the general framework laid down by national legislation the local bodies described above enjoy full powers of decision. This applies particularly to the Norwegian assistance committees whose competence is absolute in that their awards cannot be overruled by higher authority. In all other cases, however, *supervision and control* are exercised in varying measure by State authorities at the county level and by the ministries of social affairs (in Sweden the Social Welfare Board) in conjunction with certain autonomous child welfare agencies.

Local decisions on general assistance may be appealed, first, to the county authorities and, second, for final award to the ministries of social affairs (in Denmark and Iceland) or to special administrative courts (in Finland and Sweden). With respect to decisions taken by the child welfare committees the appeal-procedure is different in each of the five countries. Finland and Sweden apply roughly the same methods prevailing in general assistance cases. In Denmark and Iceland the most important decisions – pertaining to the removal of children from their homes – may be appealed to the national child welfare boards, whose verdicts are final; appeals on other decisions are dealt with, first, by the county authorities and, second, by the ministries of social affairs. The latter procedure also applies to all child welfare cases under the new Norwegian Care of Children Act. It should be added that the adoption of a new Danish constitution in June 1953 has made necessary certain changes in the previous structure of child welfare administration in that country. Thus, the National Child Welfare Board will be transformed in the near future to conform with the stricter formulation given by the new constitutional provisions to the traditional and basic principle that only the courts should be competent to deprive anyone of his liberty.

Generally speaking, the primary role of the higher administrative organs is to ensure that local authorities adhere to the minimum rules of uniformity stipulated by national legislation. However, an important part of their activities consists in the rendering of guidance and advice to local organs. This is done, in the first place, by circulars and directives concerning the proper interpretation and implementation of legislative provisions. Second, by the furnishing of advisory services by expert staff. In this connection mention should be made of the State-appointed Finnish, Icelandic, and Swedish public assistance and child welfare officers who operate at the county level and during tours of inspection render advice and information to the municipal organs; a similar arrangement has now been concluded in Norway. It might be noted that in Denmark the absence of such services is to a certain extent balanced by the fact that Danish legislation is on the whole considerably more detailed than that of the other Northern countries with respect to the forms and conditions prerequisite to the granting of assistance.

Social assistance remains a primary responsibility of local authorities, operating through popularly elected organs. This is a typical Danish assistance committee at work.

GENERAL ASSISTANCE

Although in slightly different terms, the laws of all the Northern countries establish the *right to assistance* from the public of any citizen who lacks the necessary means to provide for himself and his dependants and who is unable to earn his living. This applies whatever the cause of need. Moreover, the role of the public authorities is not confined to relief of persons in distress; to a varying extent mandatory assistance is supplemented by optional assistance when warranted by the circumstances, notably in such cases where it may serve to forestall future need. In all cases the overriding consideration is the establishment of conditions necessary to enable the individual to support himself; obviously, in promoting this end the assistance authorities will co-operate with other competent agencies, notably the employment services.

The duty of the public authorities to rescue persons in distress is secondary in character. It is thus a *condition* for the granting of assistance that the situation of the person involved cannot be alleviated

455

by other means. The primary obligation of every citizen to provide for himself and his family is age-old in all the Northern countries. However, the extent of this obligation vis-à-vis the public shows considerable variation among the five countries, being least comprehensive in Denmark and Iceland and most in Finland and Norway, with Sweden in an intermediary position. Its significance lies in the fact that assistance rendered to one for whose maintenance and care another person is responsible may be considered as having been received by the latter, who is thus involved in any legal effects – notably the question of repayment – resulting from the granting of such assistance.

Accordingly, in all the Northern countries married couples must provide for each other as long as the marriage remains in force. Similarly, both spouses are severally responsible for their common children, including adopted ones. This obligation runs for the entire lifetime of the child in Norway but only to the age of 18 in Denmark and 16 in the three other countries. As for children born out of wedlock the mother carries the same responsibility as for a child born in marriage, while the father normally only has to contribute towards its maintenance under an affiliation order. Except in Denmark, parental responsibility is to a certain extent matched by a maintenance obligation of children towards their parents, in Finland also their grandparents.

In general it is from the *assistance committee* in the locality where he resides at any given time that the citizen in need may claim help. The duration of residence is irrelevant as regards his right to assistance and is of importance only in respect to the question of the final incidence of expenditures. According to circumstances, another local authority or – in exceptional cases, e. g. as regards aliens – the State is ultimately responsible for the cost of maintenance. The former practice of sending applicants for assistance from one district to the other in search of some authority willing to accept final responsibility has today been virtually eliminated. In this connection it is worth noting that, as a result of the mutual agreements concluded among the Northern nations, the right to assistance is enjoyed by their citizens irrespective of their immediate place of residence within the territories of the five countries.

See Chapter VIII, Co-operation in Social Affairs, p. 490.

The basic statutory requirement governing the *level of assistance* is that it should be adequate and continue for as long as the situation of need persists. Danish legislation adds the qualifying clause, however, that as a rule assistance in the home may not exceed an amount equal to the old age pension. Within this general framework it is the

456

assistance committee alone which – with due regard to all relevant circumstances – decides how much should be granted in each case.

Likewise, the committee decides what *form* the assistance is to take, the guiding legislative directive being simply that the welfare of the needy person should be the paramount consideration. Traditionally, a basic distinction is drawn between assistance in the home and institutional care (outdoor *versus* indoor relief).

While indoor relief of various descriptions – poorhouses, workhouses, asylums, etc. – predominated in former times, present-day legislation is in all five countries based on the principle that whenever possible help should be given in such a way as to enable the recipient to continue living in his own home. As a result, *assistance in the home* today accounts for the large majority of cases – thus in Sweden almost 75 per cent, in Denmark even more. Such "domiciliary" aid involves allowances in cash or in kind, e. g. housing, fuel, food, clothes, medical care, etc. The general trend has been decisively towards a preference for cash grants, in part for pedagogical reasons, in part because it is considered the less humiliating form of help. In Denmark, indeed, it is specifically prescribed that assistance must normally be rendered in cash and that it should be given in kind only when indicated by special circumstances (e. g. extravagance, risk of abuse, etc.).

Since each case is in principle dealt with individually, it is natural that the assistance rendered varies considerably. Still, in several of the countries many large municipalities have found it expedient to draw up standard rates for the guidance of the administration in applying the law; this is of particular importance in Denmark where the legislative provisions concerning assistance to be rendered in the different categories of cases are more detailed and specific than elsewhere. However, these standard rates are always subordinate to the circumstances in each case. The large majority of recipients draw assistance only for brief periods, rarely exceeding two or three months. It is thus but a small minority – in Finland and Sweden about one-fourth of all cases and in Denmark an insignificant proportion – that receive permanent assistance.

Institutional care is provided in two main categories of cases: As a solution to the care and maintenance problems of persons unable to manage for themselves, on the one hand, and as a measure directed at the maintenance and rehabilitation of certain destitute or anti-social persons, on the other.

457

The first, and by far most important, group includes certain categories who are either non-members of the health and disablement insurance schemes or have exhausted their right to benefits under these schemes and who are maintained and treated in general hospitals, tuberculosis hospitals, mental hospitals, etc., at public expense. Aged persons who, because of sickness or infirmity, are no longer able to continue an independent existence are to an increasing extent – varying from country to country – taken care of under special programmes which are separately reviewed below.

See Care of the Aged, pp. 461–468.

The second group comprises not only middle-aged and young persons unable to maintain themselves because of their slight capacity for work but also vagrants, including prostitutes, negligent family supporters, etc. It is with respect to these categories that indoor relief is still a principal form of assistance. There are considerable differences among the five countries concerning the exact forms in which these categories are dealt with. Still, even here differentiation has made headway, at the same time as growing emphasis has been placed upon the rehabilitation of such persons. Voluntary initiative has rendered important contributions to this development by the establishment of numerous specialized institutions in addition to those maintained by the public authorities. It may be added that in recent years increased interest has been paid to the need for further improvement of existing facilities in this field, which is generally acknowledged to have lagged behind assistance programmes in general.

Vagrants who, despite repeated warnings and admonitions, do not conform to a socially acceptable conduct of life may be subjected to public care and – ultimately – to placement in workhouses or corrective institutions operated especially for such elements in all the countries except Iceland. Roughly the same procedure applies throughout the five countries to negligent family supporters. Moreover, in exceptional cases they may be required to perform forced labour. This clientele is today numerically extremely small and at no given time does it exceed a few hundred persons in any of the countries. In Denmark, however, the workhouses are also relied upon, usually on a temporary basis, to provide shelter and care for destitute people, mostly men, whom the local authorities have not been able to accommodate otherwise. Though unsatisfactory, this situation should be viewed against the uncompromising firmness with which the authorities have carried out the transformation of the former poorhouses with their mixed clientele into old people's homes intended for and exclusively inhabited by normal aged persons. By contrast, such destitute persons in the other countries will usually be placed in special wards still attached to the old people's homes.

Alcoholics, who traditionally form an important group among the inmates of workhouses, have increasingly been placed in special institutions, maintained by public authorities or private organizations. This applies particularly to Finland, Norway, and Sweden where this category is today dealt with under separate legislation. In Denmark and Iceland, on the other hand, alcoholics are still the primary responsibility of general assistance authorities although here as well specialized services for such persons are gradually being developed.

See Chapter VI, Health and Rehabilitation, pp. 354–358.

It remains to mention that the boarding-out of needy persons with private families at public expense is only rarely resorted to in the case of normal adults, while it is very common for children deprived of a normal home life and for certain categories of the mentally handicapped. The ancient rural practice of auctioning off destitute and handicapped persons for placement with the lowest bidder as well as that of letting the poor rotate among the local farms is today extinct in all the Northern countries.

See pp. 476–479 and pp. 364–365.

To a varying degree the granting of assistance entails certain *legal effects* for the assisted as well as for any third person responsible for his maintenance.

Thus, assistance rendered is in principle considered not as a gift but as a loan which must be repaid. However, there are important exceptions to this general rule. In the first place, no one is under obligation to repay assistance received as a child. In Denmark the same applies to the so-called Special Relief which is ordinarily granted in cases of transitory and unforeseeable distress or to meet situations which – although equally beyond individual control – are not covered by the ordinary social insurance programmes. Such relief, it may be added, entails no legal effects whatsoever. Moreover, also in other cases repayment may be remitted by the assistance committees, the principal consideration being the estimated paying ability of the person or persons against whom the claim may be raised. Recent decades have seen an increasingly liberal attitude on the part of the committees with respect to the question of repayment and as a matter of fact it is only a minor proportion of general assistance expenditures – in none of the countries more than 5–6 per cent – which is actually recovered.

Other provisions stipulate, *inter alia*, certain restrictions of the civic rights of persons assisted. Thus, in Norway assisted persons are excluded from serving on an assistance committee for a certain period while in Sweden persons under permanent public care are ineligible for membership on local councils and committees. Danish and Finnish rules are stricter, both franchise and eligibility for local and national elections being forfeited in certain cases. In Finland this applies solely in cases where the recipient is under permanent care which is expected to last for his lifetime. Danish legislation maintains a distinction between assistance rendered as Special Relief, Municipal Relief, and Poor Relief. These terms do not denote different kinds of assistance but rather may be said to indicate degrees of desirability or worthiness. As previously indicated, Special Relief entails no legal disabilities at all. At the other end of the scale, assistance to vagrants, negligent family supporters, alcoholics, etc., is granted as Poor Relief which always entails the temporary loss of the right to vote and of eligibility; moreover, Poor Relief recipients will be excluded from obtaining old age pensions for a certain period thereafter. In most cases, however, assistance is given as Municipal Relief, which entails such effects only in certain cases, notably if indigence must be ascribed to laziness, extravagance, or disorderly living, or if assistance has to be granted for a protracted period or in the form of institutional care (workhouses, etc.). A bill calling for a decisive modification of these strict Danish rules was submitted in 1953 and is pending in the Folketing.

The numerical *scope* of assistance programmes has shown a steady downward trend, especially within the last 10–15 years. This may be ascribed in part to the greatly improved employment situation prevailing throughout the five countries, in part to the marked expansion and improvement of social insurance schemes during this period. These developments are nowhere more strikingly illustrated than in Norwegian statistical returns which show that from 1939 to 1950 the number of assistance recipients declined by more than two-thirds, from 4.6 per cent of the population to 1.1 per cent. Corresponding figures for the other countries show a simultaneous decrease by almost one-half. This trend is reflected in the steadily declining importance of general assistance expenditures which today in none of the Northern countries account for more than a very small percentage of the total social welfare budget.

The care of the
aged requires
proper training –
and sympathetic
understanding
as well.

CARE OF THE AGED

The vast majority of old people lead essentially normal lives either in their own homes or as lodgers with their children or others. The old age pension schemes have largely solved the problems of income security with which most old people are sooner or later confronted. With advancing years, however, an increasing proportion of aged persons inevitably reach the stage where they find it difficult to

461

continue an independent existence and, consequently, where more comprehensive care becomes necessary. Thus a recent Swedish investigation showed almost one-fifth of those aged 65 or more to be in greater or smaller need of permanent care. Half of them are ill and require hospitalization or placement in special wards for the chronically sick, mentally ill, etc. The other half, i. e. one out of every ten old people, most of them single, are simply handicapped by age. They cannot do necessary shopping, prepare their meals, or keep their homes in order; but they are up and about, are able to enjoy pleasant surroundings, desire some light occupation, and want to keep in contact with the outer world.

The relative number of old people in this situation may vary somewhat from country to country, but the problem of their accommodation and care is equally important in all five countries. In a sense the issue is, of course, age-old but its importance has increased with the gradual urbanization of the population and the general trend away from the former three-generation household.

See Chapter V, Housing, pp. 302-303.
A partial solution may be offered by the low-rent housing provided for aged persons in modern and specially adapted blocks of flats erected or subsidized by the public in several of the Northern countries.

However, the main answer to the problem has been the establishment throughout the five countries of *old people's homes* (homes for the aged). Although the pace of progress varies considerably from country to country, the main line of development within the past two generations has been the same: In the first place, the former poorhouses have gradually been transformed into homes exclusively catering to old people in need of daily care; in the second place, the last few decades, and particularly post-war years, have witnessed the erection of a very considerable number of modern old people's homes. The improved conditions of care have had for their corollary a simultaneous change in the status of residents, who – thanks to the introduction of national old age pensions – have gradually exchanged their former role of costly relief cases to become boarders who pay for their upkeep.

Denmark has taken the lead among the Northern countries in the development of modern old people's homes. Ever since 1891 it has been a statutory municipal responsibility to establish and operate such homes intended exclusively for old age pensioners who, because of age or infirmity, cannot live alone or be placed in private care. The accommodation and care in the home takes the place of the pension,

The Danish old people's homes serve as a model for the Northern countries. Here is "Solhjem" in Gentofte, outside Copenhagen. The blocks in the foreground above are low-rent pensioners' dwellings. The integrated layout makes possible more economical use of common facilities and also renders it easier for the aging pensioner to exchange individual housekeeping for life in the old people's home.

although a modest sum for pocket money is granted. As for financing, the central government refunds somewhat more than one-half of the operating costs to local authorities.

Today some 17,000 old people in Denmark are residents of about 550 old people's homes, more than half of which have been erected since 1930. Total capacity corresponds to 30 places per 1,000 population of pensionable age. In recent years there has been extensive construction of new homes, particularly in the rural districts where a shortage has long been felt. In this connection it should be recalled that low-rent dwellings for pensioners are predominantly confined to the towns and larger urban settlements.

As for the character of the Danish homes, main emphasis is placed upon the desirability of establishing dwellings which, while adapted to the special requirements of old people, are as "non-institutional" as in any way possible. The situation is rapidly being approached where each resident is assured a room to himself and married couples two rooms. Moreover, there is a general tendency to permit the aged persons to have their own furniture. Urban homes usually have all modern installations while the technical equipment in some rural districts is less up-to-date. On the other hand, the rural homes possess the advantage of being smaller, averaging 15–20 places as against 65–70 for urban homes; 93 per cent of all residents are single, married couples comprising only 7 per cent. More than half of the homes are equipped with special wards or infirmaries for residents who are in need of sick-care but not of treatment in a hospital or an institution for the chronically sick.

Plans for the reconditioning of existing homes or construction of new ones are subject to approval by the central authorities which have set up standard regulations and recommendations concerning the construction, equipment, and general character of old people's homes. While large institutions are not recommended, economic considerations speak for the establishment of a certain minimum size. Today a capacity of 20–40 persons is favoured as being generally the most desirable. The installation of modern conveniences is an obvious requirement. Moreover, accommodation of several persons in one room is specifically ruled out in new institutions. Detailed blueprints for various types of homes are placed at the disposal of local authorities who – since 1951 – have been able to obtain cheap State loans for such construction under the Building Aid Act.

See Chapter V, Housing, pp. 294–295.

464

Steady progress is being made in building and modernizing old people's homes in Sweden. The above home, of very recent construction, is designed to create the proper atmosphere of peace and quiet.

The situation in the other Northern countries is somewhat different since it has not yet been possible to achieve fully specialized care under public auspices of otherwise normal, aged persons in need of institutional accommodation. The main obstacle has been, and is still, the shortage of special institutions for the chronically sick, mentally ill, feeble-minded, etc., and a major expansion in these fields is thus a prerequisite to the establishment of genuine homes for the aged.

The statutory so-called municipal homes in *Finland*, successors to the old poorhouses, are intended for needy persons who cannot be properly cared for in their own homes or by placement with a private family. There are at present about 350 such institutions accommodating a total of 28,000 persons, of whom only slightly more than half are normal old people. Local authorities are under obligation to take, *inter alia*, the health and age of applicants into consideration when arranging for their accommodation. Also, every home is required to make special provision for sick residents; this is of particular importance since many chronically sick, for lack of other accommodation, have to be placed in these homes. About half of them have infirmaries or sick-wards. A somewhat smaller proportion maintain separate wards for those cases of mild insanity that cannot be provided for in hospitals.

This state of affairs is, however, in process of amelioration. Vigorous efforts have been made in recent years to transform the municipal homes into old people's homes proper and to separate the care of the chronically ill and the mentally ill from these institutions.

Until some years ago the situation in *Sweden* was practically the same as in Finland. Already in the 'twenties the municipal poorhouses and related institutions were renamed and henceforth termed old people's homes, but it was only slowly that their general character changed to conform with the new name. Just as in Finland, the main problem is the mixed clientele, some 25 per cent of whom are placed in the homes solely due to the shortage of special hospitals, etc.

In the last few years, however, considerable progress has been recorded. An increasing number of homes today measure up fully to the general directives adopted by the Swedish parliament in 1947, according to which old people's institutions should become boarding homes accommodating and caring for aged and disabled persons as paying guests. In compliance with a State recommendation the local authorities normally fix the rate to be paid by residents at amounts equal to their pensions (except for a minor sum for pocket money).

According to legislation enacted in 1953 the central government contributes a capital subsidy of up to 50 per cent of construction costs for new old people's homes. Moreover, as in Denmark, the State offers guidance and advice to local authorities contemplating such projects.

At the present time there are in Sweden approximately 1,400 old people's homes accommodating about 32,000 persons. Of this total about 21,000, or 25 per 1,000 population above 65 years of age, are old age pensioners. Although only 83 per cent of total capacity are utilized there are local differences, numerous homes being overcrowded. Single rooms are available for about one-fifth of the aged persons. As for the size of the homes, the situation is comparable to that in Denmark.

Norwegian and Icelandic conditions are particularly characterized by the absence of any legislative provisions governing the statutory establishment of homes for the aged and by the important role still played by voluntary organizations.

In *Norway* there are at present about 550 old people's homes with accommodation for more than 15,000. Most of them are operated by parishes, religious institutions, and professional organizations. However, in recent decades an increasing number of local authorities, particularly in towns, have established their own homes. The costs

Though retired, many old people still cherish the idea of doing creative work, of making a positive contribution. At the "Old People's Village", the principal old people's home in Copenhagen, residents are given the opportunity to pursue their hobbies.

are primarily covered out of the old age pensions of residents, but most local authorities make supplementary contributions.

The modern municipal homes are of high standard but – as in Finland and Sweden – many older institutions suffer from the mingling of normal elderly people with various categories of persons in need of special treatment, a result of the shortage of specialized accommodation for the chronically sick, mentally ill, feeble-minded, etc. Moreover, many of the homes are obsolete and do not satisfy present-day requirements with respect to modern conveniences and rational operation. A serious drawback is the pronounced lack of single rooms.

Although the overall capacity of the old people's homes corresponds to almost 50 places per 1,000 inhabitants above pensionable age – which is considerably more than in Denmark and Sweden – an acute shortage is experienced. In this connection it should be recalled, however, that the building of low-rent dwellings for the able-bodied elderly has not as yet gained appreciable magnitude in Norway.

467

In *Iceland*, finally, there are ten old people's homes, some of them public, others private. The latter receive annual subsidies from the local and central governments. Here, too, the homes are generally also utilized to provide shelter and care for certain categories of elderly sick persons. The homes are financed much the same way as in Norway.

It may be added that since 1946 the Icelandic National Insurance Institution has been entrusted with the task of preparing proposals for a network of new homes for the aged throughout the country. Although no proposals have been submitted as yet, the location of a number of new homes established during the last few years was chosen in consultation with the Institution which is also authorized to grant loans for the construction of such dwellings.

Old people's homes form an important part of welfare programmes for the aged. Still, only a slight minority are provided for in this way. Even when fully developed, these homes will remain a refuge for the few. As previously stated the vast majority of old people continue to live in their accustomed environment. This is as it should be and it is also in the public interest to assist the elderly in their efforts to live independent lives in their own homes. The old age pensions and special low-rent housing (or rental allowances) are means to this end.

Supplementary *welfare services* include the provision of domestic help, home visiting, hot meals, out-patient counselling services, and recreational activities.

See Chapter IV, Family Welfare, pp. 276–277.

Thus, in recent years increasing interest has been paid to the provision of attendance in the home to old people who, temporarily or permanently, are in need of a limited amount of care. In Denmark and Sweden the services of the municipal home helps have proved valuable in this respect although there is still a shortage of personnel. Similar services are offered to a varying extent by numerous voluntary organizations in all five countries. Moreover, many such organizations as well as an increasing number of local authorities have introduced regular home visiting and distribution of hot meals to lonely old people. Some Swedish towns have also appointed "social welfare doctors" to assist the authorities in finding the proper solution to individual problems encountered, *inter alia*, in the case of elderly persons; likewise, a number of geriatric clinics have been established in the last few years. However, viewing the Northern countries as a whole it would appear correct to say that these activities as yet are in the first stages of development.

CARE OF CHILDREN
General Features

The manifold programmes previously surveyed under the common heading of Family Welfare share two main characteristics: In the first place, they are universal in scope, generally covering all or the large majority of children regardless of their living conditions; second, they are essentially supplementary in character, assuming the day-to-day existence of the child to be provided for, materially and otherwise, within the framework of normal family life. Contrariwise, the measures reviewed in this section are restricted in scope, dealing with the small minority of children who for various reasons are *deprived of a normal home life* or in danger of being so deprived; moreover, they are to a large extent compensatory in character, aiming to replace – fully or in part – the normal educators, the basic consideration being to assure these children an existence as close to the normal as possible.

See Chapter IV, Family Welfare, pp. 235–280.

These measures are brought into action where one or both natural parents are missing, where the parents are unable or unwilling to take proper care of their offspring, or where the child shows serious social maladjustment indicating the failure of the family group to function because of internal conflict. This includes orphans and abandoned children, children born out of wedlock, children from homes that are broken due to desertion, separation, or divorce, and to a certain extent children of widows and widowers. It further includes children suffering from neglect or ill-treatment as well as delinquent children – the borderline between these groups being frequently very vague. There are differences as regards the age-range covered by the various statutes applying to different aspects of the subject, but in principle the legislative provisions for public care of children in all the Northern countries comprehend all minors up to the age of 21 years.

Here, as in other social welfare fields, the means adopted include preventive measures as well as remedial ones. Moreover, it is in keeping with present-day trends in social thinking and action that the preventive aspect has acquired ever increasing importance, though the nature of the problems involved in many cases imposes obvious limitations in this respect.

Before entering upon the provisions specifically relating to the care of children deprived of a normal home life mention should be made, first, of the profound general influence exercised by the comprehensive programmes in the fields of *family welfare, housing, and health* previ-

469

ously described. By improving the living conditions of families with children they contribute essentially to the prevention of the disruption of normal family life for large sections of the population.

To this must be added the financial protection afforded by the *special children's allowances* included in most social insurance schemes.

See above, p. 437. In this connection it is of particular interest to recall the children's allowances granted to widows, in Iceland and Sweden as a supplement to survivors' pensions authorized under the national pension schemes, in the other countries as a separate benefit.

The children's allowances just mentioned are in several of the countries supplemented by *maintenance advances* payable for children who are born out of wedlock or whose parents are separated, divorced, etc., in cases where the father (or, in those rare instances where the father has custody of the child, the mother) defaults upon the duty of maintenance. In Denmark the provisions apply up to the age of 18, in Iceland and Sweden up to 16 years.

In Denmark, where this scheme has been in operation ever since 1888, the advance is paid at the same rate as the so-called normal contribution, i. e. three-fifths of what the decent upkeep of the child would cost in a good home in the locality where the child is living, the mother being assumed to provide the remaining two-fifths. The normal contribution, which is automatically adjusted to changes in the cost-of-living index, is in the large majority of cases equal to the amount which the father is required by the authorities to pay for the maintenance of his child. As from April 1953 it amounts annually to 840 kroner in Copenhagen, 732 kroner in provincial towns, and 624 kroner in rural districts. Payment of the maintenance advance is subject to an income test but entails no legal effects for the recipient; by contrast, it is reckoned as municipal relief with accompanying disabilities to the negligent parent from whom the assistance committee will claim recovery of the sum advanced. At the present time advances are paid for about 60,000 children or 4.5 per cent of all children under 18 years of age – half of them born out of wedlock. It should be added that the same rules apply to the childbirth allowance which the father must provide for the unmarried mother. – An almost identical scheme has long existed in Iceland.

Sweden introduced a similar arrangement in 1938, a minor modification being that a father is not eligible for maintenance advances. Moreover, these may be claimed by the mother regardless of her economic circumstances. In recent years the advances have been paid in respect of nearly 40,000 children or almost 2.5 per cent of all children under 16 years of age. As from July 1953 the standard advance has been raised from 324 to 600 kronor for the entire country.

Finnish provisions of this kind are more restricted in scope. They entitle the mother only to advance payment from the local authority of the childbirth allowance due from the father and of the maintenance contribution for the child for the first nine months of its life.

The essential legislation pertaining specifically to the *protection and care of children* is in Denmark contained in the Public Assistance Act of 1933 and in Sweden, Finland, Iceland, and Norway in special Care of Children Acts dating from 1924, 1936, 1947, and 1953, respectively.

Their basic provisions are much alike in all five countries. While national legislation lays down the general directives, main responsibility for child welfare work is entrusted to the local authorities. Contrary to many other countries, where important decisions are referred to the ordinary or special courts, the administration of the law in the Northern countries rests exclusively with administrative organs. As previously noted, the child welfare committee is the responsible organ at the local level everywhere except in Finland where the social welfare committee is competent also in these cases; however, the difference is more formal than real. For convenience the term "child welfare committee" is used below in all cases to denote the local organ responsible for the programme in question.

These child welfare committees are a special Northern feature. They originate with the local boards of guardians which were originally developed in Norway and subsequently emulated in the other countries. While the functions of the boards were rather narrowly defined, the child welfare committees of today are charged with the general responsibility of ensuring adequate protection and care for the various groups of children deprived of a normal home life. In Finland, Iceland, Norway, and Sweden, it may be added, their terms of reference are even wider, covering the promotion of the welfare of all children and young persons within their area of jurisdiction.

While emphasizing the central role of the child welfare committees, it is equally important to stress that nowhere else within the broad sphere of social welfare has voluntary initiative contributed more decisively. Idealistic individuals and philanthropic organizations have been pioneers in the development of present-day programmes for the

471

care of children and the legislatures have largely built upon their experience. Even today, when everywhere the community has taken over main responsibility, these organizations perform vital functions within the general framework of national legislation and remain in direct charge of important branches of child care activities.

The governing ideal pervading all child welfare activities has been the same since the first children acts were promulgated some fifty years ago: All public intervention is considered primarily upon its merit as promoter of the welfare of the child. However, the practical content of this ideal has changed with the gradual re-orientation of the outlook upon childhood. The results of scientific research in child psychology have occasioned many decisive revisions of the methods applied, and this development has by no means run its course as yet. The new trend of thought has been characterized first and foremost by the abandonment of the old moralistic attitude in favour of more discerning and practical methods designed to assist the young public ward in becoming a well-adjusted and useful member of the community; and, second, by an increased understanding of the desirability of keeping the child in his own home if at all feasible and, where this is not the case, by substituting an environment which resembles the normal home as much as possible.

The lines along which the Northern countries have striven to implement this philosophy are almost identical. Nevertheless, there are numerous differences of detail between present-day programmes in the five countries, particularly with respect to the differentiation attained. An attempt is made here to give a brief survey of the main components of these programmes.

Supervision

The present-day rules governing supervision derive from the legislation enacted in several of the countries around the turn of the century on behalf of foster children, many of whom were then living under miserable conditions of neglect and ill-treatment. Subsequent decades have witnessed the introduction of such legislation in all the five countries and the gradual improvement of supervisory services which were long manifestly inadequate. Moreover, general supervision has been extended to other groups, notably children born out of wedlock.

Regulations pertaining to *foster children*, i. e. children brought up in private homes other than those of their parents, vary somewhat

Institutions can never fully replace a child's own home as the natural environment for growth and adjustment, but they may at least be made as pleasant as possible to live in. The picture shows a reception home for small children near Copenhagen, accommodated – as is very frequently the case – in a converted private dwelling.

in scope. In Finland, Iceland, and Sweden the child welfare committees are charged with the supervision of all such children up to the age of (usually) 16 years, in Norway 18 years. In Denmark, on the other hand, supervision is mandatory only for children under 14 years placed in foster homes against payment, although it may also be instituted in other cases.

In Denmark, Iceland, and Norway permission of the child welfare committee is required for the placement of a child in foster care. In

473

Finland and Sweden, on the other hand, this is not the case (except for Swedish infants under one year of age), but rules of notification establish the duty of the committee to ascertain the suitability of the proposed foster home and, if necessary, to lay down its veto.

Supervision is carried out along practically the same lines in all five countries. It is entrusted to specially appointed inspectors who may be public servants or other suitable persons, e.g. representatives of voluntary child welfare agencies. The inspector visits the foster home at intervals to ensure that the child is properly cared for and assists the foster parents with advice and guidance. If the inspector points out any shortcomings and these are not rectified by the home, the child welfare committee can issue a formal request for remedial action. Failing results, this is followed up by a warning, appointment of a special supervising guardian (in Denmark), and – ultimately – the removal of the child.

The supervision of *children born out of wedlock* is almost identical in character. Danish legislation provides for mandatory supervision of all such children below seven years of age under the same rules that apply to foster care. In Finland and Sweden, on the other hand, this group is dealt with under separate legislation which requires the appointment, for each child born out of wedlock, of a special child welfare guardian, supervision lasting until the age of 17 and 18, respectively. In Iceland and Norway there is no special supervision of this group of children.

In addition to the above-mentioned groups, supervision is also undertaken for certain other categories. Thus, in Denmark it is mandatory for children under 18 years living with parents in permanent receipt of Municipal or Poor Relief as well as for children for whom advance payments of maintenance contributions are being made; however, supervision may be waived when warranted by circumstances in the individual case and this is very frequently done. The total number of Danish children supervised by the child welfare committees today runs to about 43,000 or almost 4 per cent of all children under 18 years of age. The comparable Finnish figures are 50,000 and 5 per cent. In Sweden child welfare guardians are also appointed for numerous children born in wedlock, mostly children of divorced parents. Swedish supervision of foster children in 1951 comprised 34,000 while child welfare guardians had been appointed for about 106,000 children.

Preventive Services

The basic conception that children should be brought up in their own homes whenever possible has quite naturally placed considerable emphasis upon preventive measures. The child welfare committees carry more or less sweeping responsibility for those measures of a general preventive character – particularly institutions for the day-time care of children – which have already been described. In addition, however, legislative provisions call for supplementary preventive measures in cases where the situation, due to circumstances relating either to the parents or to the child, is such that the question arises whether the child should remain in its home or be removed.

See Chapter IV, Family Welfare, pp. 259–264.

These measures, which aim at extending moral support as well as, under certain conditions, economic assistance, may include warnings and admonitions to parents and/or children as well as specific directives, frequently combined with supervision along lines similar to those described above. The directives will instruct parents as to the general welfare, training, education, or work of their offspring. In many cases they will require a child to attend a day-time children's institution, e.g. a nursery school or leisure centre, or a secondary school; in other cases they will stipulate that a young person be given proper training or employment. Where compliance with such instructions involves the parents in extra cost, the child welfare committee may grant economic assistance, if needed.

It is probably correct to say that, on the whole, these measures have not yet attained a fully satisfactory level of development in any of the Northern countries. All-round therapeutic services, which may prove of great value in helping parents and children to overcome their difficulties, are as yet found only to a limited extent. In this connection considerable interest attaches to the child guidance clinics and family-counselling services which have been established in the last few years in a number of Danish, Finnish, and Swedish towns. Children who are a source of trouble in one way or another are here subjected to a thorough physical, mental, and social investigation by expert personnel (psychiatrists, psychologists, and social workers), the findings serving as a basis for directives and recommendations concerning remedial measures on behalf of the child. A related development is the appointment by a growing number of Danish local authorities of special school psychologists. However, on the whole, integrated programmes of this kind are as yet in their infancy.

The preventive measures outlined above are of rather modest numerical importance. Thus, in 1951 they were applied to only 6,000 Swedish children. Returns for the other four countries are on a corresponding scale. However, in evaluating these figures it should be stressed again that these measures are but a supplement to those comprehensive preventive services that are maintained within the general framework of family welfare programmes, the significance of which is not statistically demonstrable.

Placement of Children

Where preventive measures are inapplicable or have proved insufficient, the child welfare committee may, as a last resort, remove the child from its own home and provide for its proper care and upbringing elsewhere. Disregarding minor national differences of formulation, the children dealt with under these provisions may be grouped in .the following main categories:

1) Dependent children in need of support and care because there is no one to provide for them (most frequently due to the death or desertion of parents) or because the parents are temporarily or permanently unable to do so (due to illness or other incapacity).

2) Children exposed to physical or mental danger by neglect or ill-treatment and in need of protection.

3) Children and young persons who show particularly serious maladjustment, including delinquency, and who are in need of corrective educational measures.

4) Physically and mentally handicapped children who are in need of special care outside the home and whose parents do not undertake the necessary steps to ensure such care.

With respect to the first group, *dependent children*, the committee will intervene only upon the request of and in agreement with the parents or, where they are dead or otherwise missing, if the child is not properly provided for otherwise, e.g. by relatives. Such care is usually limited to children below the age of 16 (in Finland, Iceland, and Sweden) or 18 (in Denmark and Norway).

As for the next two categories, *neglected or ill-treated children* and *refractory or delinquent children and young persons*, the committee may take action even against the will of the parents. However, its decisions to this effect must be confirmed by or may be appealed to higher authorities under provisions which vary somewhat from country to

country. Generally, protective or corrective care will terminate at the latest at the age of 18, but in special cases it may be prolonged to the 21st year or (in Sweden) even beyond that age.

In this connection great significance attaches to the special rules concerning juvenile offenders contained in the penal codes. The minimum criminal age is 15 years in all the Northern countries, except Norway where it is 14 years. This means that no child below that age can be brought before a court for trial for a crime. As for offences committed by young persons between 15 (in Norway 14) and 18 years of age, it has become increasingly common to waive prosecution. Instead, the youngster will be handed over to the child welfare committee for treatment, either corrective upbringing or supervision, or placing in training or employment, depending upon the circumstances. In illustration of the importance of this practice it may be mentioned that the number of young offenders aged 15–18 years brought before the Danish courts in 1951 was roughly 1,200 and that in 97 per cent of all cases the charge was withdrawn. An alternative method, frequently applied in Norway and Sweden but more seldom in the other countries, is for the court to pass a conditional sentence, often combined with specified requirements as enumerated above. To a certain extent these measures may also be applied to offenders between 18 and 21 years (in Norway even beyond that age).

In other cases where persons in this age-group are convicted for crimes which normally entail imprisonment or penal servitude they may be committed to special juvenile prisons or (in Norway) to training schools which are equipped to give education and vocational training adapted to individual requirements.

Although decisions concerning the compulsory removal of children from their own homes are taken solely by the child welfare committees without any recourse to special or ordinary courts, committee procedure in these cases lacks nothing of the thoroughness associated with the judicial system. Exhaustive inquiries are made to obtain the fullest possible picture of the special circumstances of each child: Conditions in the home, school record, health, etc. A special Danish and Norwegian feature is that decisions require the presence of the local civil judge; the same applies in Iceland if there is no lawyer among the members of the committee. Moreover, the parents are entitled to appear before the committee and make a statement. In most cases the parents concur in the decision to remove the child and only relatively few decisions – in Denmark, Finland, and Norway as little as 6–8 per cent – are appealed to higher authority.

The sharp distinction drawn between the courts and the organs for the care of children was originally meant to accentuate the positive, non-condemnatory approach to the problems of maladjusted youths as opposed to that prevailing toward adult offenders. With the progressive transformation of general penal policies in a similar direction many may be inclined today to view this distinction as less obviously desirable than formerly. Also, the present system with its emphasis upon local self-government does not provide the same opportunities for utilizing the services of experts as would a more centralized scheme. Still, the existing set-up, which has by now – in most of the countries – a fifty-year tradition behind it, has functioned reasonably well and the Northern countries would appear determined upon its preservation.

As for *mentally and physically handicapped children* in need of special care outside their own homes, they are in most of the Northern countries subject to the same rules for compulsory removal as have just been described. In all five countries this group accounts only for an insignificant proportion of all children placed outside their homes. The measures on behalf of handicapped persons, including children, have been surveyed elsewhere in this book.

See Chapter VI, Health and Rehabilitation, pp. 359–377.

478

Although statistics in this field do not permit full comparability, the following figures still convey a rough impression of the *numerical scope* of the provisions reviewed above. In Denmark and Finland the total number of children under public care outside their own homes comprise about one per cent of all inhabitants below 21 years; in Iceland and Norway, on the other hand, the figure drops to about one-half of this level, while in Sweden it rises one-half above it.

Foster-home Care

Mentally and physically handicapped children apart, it is the clear intent of all Northern statutes bearing on this issue that, wherever practicable, the child deprived of a normal home life should be placed with a foster family. This usually applies to all dependent children in need of support and care, but in many cases it will also be considered the most desirable solution for children in need of protective upbringing, provided they have not shown particularly difficult character or bad behaviour.

If the child welfare committee has decided upon this form of placement, it will conclude the necessary arrangements with the prospective foster home or it will entrust this task to one of the approved voluntary agencies which in all five countries have fulfilled a valuable function in this regard for generations. In all cases the suitability of the home in question is investigated beforehand by the committee (or agency) with a view to ascertaining that the personal qualities and general circumstances of the foster parents are such as to promise satisfactory care and education of the child. As previously noted, the child remains under the supervision and guardianship of the committee but otherwise the relations between foster parents and children are meant to approach those of a normal family as much as possible.

See above, pp. 472–474.

While in Denmark only 30 per cent of all children under the care of the child welfare committees are placed with private families, this is the case with 50–55 per cent of such children in Finland, Norway, and Sweden. These figures compare with 30 per cent in the United Kingdom and 40 per cent in the USA. Quite apart from the obvious limitation resulting from the character of the children for whom placement is sought, it has in recent years proved increasingly difficult to obtain a sufficient "supply" of suitable foster homes. As the above figures show, this applies with particular force in Denmark.

"Freedom and responsibility" is the ideal of Northern schools for young offenders – an ideal which involves many problems in workaday application. The above welfare school is located outside Stockholm.

Institutional Care

Children for whom it is not practicable to provide foster-home care, or where such care has not yet been decided upon, are placed with one of a variety of institutions, differentiated according to the needs of the various categories of children. As indicated by the figures cited in the preceding section concerning foster-home care such placement applies to a large proportion of children deprived of a normal home life.

Roughly, a two-way distinction may be drawn between the various categories of institutions according to whether they are intended for temporary or long-term care and whether they provide for dependent children in need of support and care or for children needing protective or corrective upbringing and training.

Temporary care is furnished primarily by *reception* or *observation homes* which serve the double purpose of accommodating children in need of support and care during emergencies (illness of parents, etc.) as well as children for whom final placement has not yet been settled. As indicated by their name the length of stay is generally rather brief, thus in Denmark averaging five months; upon discharge the large majority of children return to their own homes. In Sweden the reception homes account for about forty per cent of the aggregate number and capacity of all children's institutions, while the corresponding figure for Denmark and Iceland is about thirty per cent; in Finland and Norway this type of homes is of smaller importance. They are supplemented by homes for infants and by maternity homes for the care of (usually single) mothers and their babies.

Normal children (including cases of less seriously maladjusted children) who are in need of permanent care outside their own homes and for whom foster-home care is found impracticable are brought up in *children's homes*. Placement here will usually be for an extended period (in Denmark averaging four years) and may last until the age of 14 or 15 (in Sweden frequently 16), whereupon the child will usually be placed in outside training or employment. Wherever possible the children attend the ordinary elementary school, although in certain cases instruction may be given at the home itself. Moreover, special homes are maintained for mentally retarded children and for young persons who do not require treatment under the special provisions concerning mentally handicapped persons. Children's homes comprise a second large group among the institutions, in Denmark and Sweden accounting for 55 per cent and 45 per cent, respectively, of the total number as well as total capacity. As a rule they accommodate less than 30 children, thus avoiding the impersonal character of larger institutions.

Sports and leisure activities in pleasant surroundings are important parts of the curriculum. Outside scene from a home for maladjusted girls near Copenhagen.

481

Maladjusted and delinquent children and young persons will usually be admitted to *educational homes or welfare schools* (names varying from country to country), differentiated according to sex, age, and mental characteristics. These institutions comprise school homes for the age group below 14 or 15 years and vocational homes for young persons above that age. Since in these cases it is considered necessary to keep the pupils apart from other children, instruction will here be given in the homes. While instruction in the school homes corresponds to that of the normal elementary school, the vocational homes aim to provide the young person with suitable training for a future occupation. This may include training for a skilled profession, e.g. tailoring, engineering, etc., in special workshops attached to the institution or instruction in agricultural work or gardening on the grounds of the home. School homes and vocational homes in all five countries account for 10–15 per cent of the total capacity of children's institutions. They are usually somewhat larger than children's homes, capacity ranging from 30 to 80 persons.

These main groups of homes are supplemented by specialized institutions for certain limited categories of children and young persons. Particular mention may thus be made of the Swedish homes for psychopathic boys and girls, which have as yet no adequate counterpart in the other Northern countries. Another example is provided by the apprentices' hostels, found especially in Denmark, one type of which provides both training and accommodation, while the other type accommodates young persons who work with a master craftsman outside the home.

The preceding paragraphs have aimed at giving a general survey of the diversity of Northern institutions for the care of children. However, there are considerable differences among the five countries with respect to the extent to which they have as yet been able to develop a balanced and adequate institutional system. The widest differentiation has probably been achieved in Sweden where a number of reforms undertaken in recent years – notably the taking over by the State of all school- and vocational homes – have led to marked improvements. Also in Denmark the situation may be considered relatively satisfactory in this respect. In Iceland it is only quite recently that a beginning has been made in the development of differentiated institutions for the care of children. In Finland and Norway some regions suffer from an unbalanced distribution of institutions among the various types. Moreover, in Norway there is an acute need for overall expansion of institutional capacity.

The approximate figures given below indicate the numerical scope of the main categories of institutions for children under the care of the child welfare committees.

CHILDREN UNDER INSTITUTIONAL CARE

	Reception or observation homes	Children's homes (incl. infants' and maternity homes)	Other institutions	Total
Denmark (1953)	2,200	5,700	1,900	9,800
Finland (1952)	800	4,500	2,800	8,100
Iceland (1951)	60	120	20	180
Norway (1949)		2,200	600	2,800
Sweden (1951)	2,800	3,300	900	7,000

In Denmark and Norway the large majority of institutions are owned by religious, philanthropic, or other voluntary organizations which traditionally have shouldered a main part of this important branch of child welfare work. Still, in recent years the local authorities have themselves established a growing number of such institutions. By contrast, most Finnish and Swedish institutions are today operated under public auspices. In Sweden a new phase was inaugurated in 1936 when the State decided to take charge of the operation of all child and youth welfare schools (school homes and vocational homes), the last private school being finally taken over in 1950. In 1945 this reform was followed up by the enactment of legislation which placed upon the provincial councils the general responsibility for the overall planning of all other children's institutions within their jurisdiction; it may be added that this did not free the local child welfare committees from their direct obligations in this respect. Also in Denmark, Finland, and Norway the State operates many of the school- and vocational homes.

All institutions are subject to control and supervision – national provisions varying somewhat. As a rule no institution may receive children under care by the child welfare committee unless it has been approved by the provincial or central authorities; these have also drawn up general rules concerning the proper layout, management, and operation of the various types of homes.

Although in some cases assured fairly large incomes from endowments, etc., most private institutions have traditionally laboured under rather strained financial conditions. However, recent years have witnessed a considerable improvement in this respect, particularly in Denmark, Finland, and Sweden, where substantial State subsidies are today granted for the establishment and/or operation of such institutions. At the present time the community – local and central governments – defray by far the larger part (in Denmark as much as 90 per cent) of the costs of institutional care for children, the contributions from parents or philanthropic sources accounting only for a minor share.

CHAPTER VIII

CO-OPERATION IN SOCIAL AFFAIRS

Regional Co-operation

The feeling of basic kinship and solidarity between the Northern peoples has quite naturally led to close co-operation in practically every sphere of activity, be it economic, social, cultural, technical, administrative, or political. A large and ever-expanding network of arrangements for collaboration has gradually been developed, both on the governmental and the non-governmental level.

By frequent exchanges of views the countries have been able to profit from each other's experience, the initiative of one country in undertaking some new programme very frequently serving as a pattern for measures subsequently undertaken in one or several of the other countries. In many cases co-operation has been organized by the establishment of inter-Northern bodies of varying character for joint discussion, study, and action. Special mention might here be made of the non-governmental "Norden" societies; the declared aim of these societies, which have exercised considerable and enduring influence, is "to deepen the feeling of relationship between the Northern countries, to extend their cultural and economic connections, and to promote collaboration among them".

Also, a considerable number of agreements have been concluded which, while preserving the full sovereignty of each participating country, have called for the co-ordination of legislative and other provisions to form a more harmonious whole. Thus, in important branches of statutory legislation, particularly commercial and civil law, a large degree of uniformity has been achieved by the enactment of parallel legislation. Among the most recent undertakings of this character is the reciprocal agreement of 1951 between Denmark, Norway, and Sweden, facilitating the naturalization of nationals from one of these countries in both the other countries; in this connection it is also natural to mention that, as from July 1952, no pass-

485

port is required for travel between Denmark, Norway, and Sweden by nationals of these countries.

In the social field efforts have largely concentrated upon reciprocal agreements ensuring all Northern citizens equality of treatment under the varying national provisions. These agreements are of considerable practical significance since quite large numbers of persons from each of the five countries have taken up residence in another Northern country. Thus about 30,000 Danes and a slightly larger number of Finns are today residents of one of the other four countries (mainly Sweden), while the comparable number of Norwegians and Swedes totals 15,000 and 10,000, respectively.

The absence of any serious language difficulties has clearly facilitated these activities very considerably. Although Finnish is the everyday language of the large majority in Finland, Swedish is second official language and is used in intercourse with the other countries; similarly, the knowledge of Danish is widespread in Iceland. Numerous Northern periodicals, mainly within specialized professional fields, present contributions in Danish, Norwegian, or Swedish according to the nationality of the author.

Generally speaking, collaboration has developed first and gone farthest among the three Scandinavian countries while Finland and Iceland have followed more remotely, due in part to their later economic and social development. In recent years, however, Northern co-operation has increasingly come to include all five countries – the present publication being but one manifestation of this trend.

The main vehicle of these efforts has been a multitude of formal and informal meetings and conferences called by government authorities as well as by non-governmental organizations and attended varyingly by political leaders, administrators at higher and lower levels, social workers, employers, and workers. Of special importance are the meetings of the Northern Ministers of Social Affairs which have been held frequently since the early 'twenties and, beginning in 1945, now take place every two years in one of the Northern capitals.

The conferences of Ministers of Social Affairs are supplemented by *ad hoc* expert committees which are entrusted with the detailed study and preparation of proposals on the issues currently dealt with. A further link in this organizational set-up is a permanent coordination committee comprising top officials from the departments involved and having for its purpose to streamline the various schemes

of co-operation and to study additional possibilities for fruitful collaboration. Among the most recent undertakings on the administrative
level are the proposals put forward by expert committees in 1951
and 1953 for the co-ordination of Northern social statistics with a
view to ensuring the highest possible degree of comparability.

It should be added that the newly established Northern Council
provides a general forum for the discussion among parliamentarians
of questions pertaining to Northern co-operation, including social
affairs. Thus, at its first session in February 1953 the Council *inter
alia* adopted a recommendation calling for the establishment of one
comprehensive social security convention covering all reciprocal agreements in the sphere of social insurance.

Apart from their general stimulating effects, these intimate relations
have led to the conclusion of a considerable number of conventions
and other instruments, sometimes bilateral, sometimes including all
five members of the group. The goal striven for has not so much been
that of full uniformity – although the desirability of establishing,
where appropriate, a higher degree of co-ordination and harmoniza-
tion of programmes is certainly not ignored – but rather a state of
affairs where, for practical purposes, the Northern countries constitute
an integrated area within which their citizens may move and live
and work while enjoying equal treatment regardless of nationality.

SOCIAL SECURITY
Social Insurance

Beginning already in 1907, Northern social insurance conferences have been held frequently, having programmes of insurance against employment injuries, sickness, disablement, old age, and unemployment on their agenda.

Among the most important results growing out of these and other periodic meetings has been a long series of reciprocal agreements by which each signatory has extended the benefits of its social programmes to residents who are citizens of one of the other countries. At the inception of these arrangements social insurance systems were as yet only partly established and there were very considerable differences in the scope of national programmes. Developments have, therefore, proceeded at a relatively modest pace, often starting on a bilateral basis, and it is only within rather recent years, when social insurance approached its present comprehensive character, that agreements covering most insurance branches and counting all or most Northern countries as participants have been concluded.

The first undertaking of this kind dates from 1911 when Danish and Swedish *health insurance societies* agreed that their members could transfer to a society in the other country without first having to prove their fulfilment of the usual conditions of admission (especially waiting periods). Efforts during the following decades to enlarge this machinery were climaxed by the conclusion in July 1953 of an agreement between Denmark, Iceland, Norway, and Sweden according to which all persons insured against sickness and taking up residence, permanent or temporary, in one of the other countries are henceforth entitled to full health insurance facilities. Permanent residents become ordinary members of the local health insurance unit while temporary residents will be entitled to benefits if only they are insured in their home country. Since Finland does not yet have any comprehensive health insurance, that country is not at present a party to this form of co-operation.

Also in the field of *public health* the Northern countries collaborate, partly with a view to the co-ordination of various health schemes, partly with a view to their participation in the World Health Organization where the advantages of a common Northern attitude have often been evident. The continuous day-to-day exchange of knowledge and experience is highlighted by periodic expert meetings for detailed discussion of selected topics. Not only have these close relations had a general stimulating influence, but in certain special fields – particularly food control and foodstuff legislation – they have led to considerable positive results.

Employment injuries insurance has usually applied to both nationals and foreigners, but there were certain exceptions concerning payment of benefits to persons leaving the country and concerning compensation to survivors living abroad. Consequently, in 1919 Denmark, Norway, and Sweden agreed reciprocally to grant full equality of treatment to citizens of the other countries. The adoption in 1925 by the International Labour Organization of a convention containing similar provisions made this agreement largely superfluous although a number of administrative clauses are still of practical interest. Moreover, in 1937 all five Northern countries signed a special convention regulating the cases where employers from one country employ labour in one of the other countries.

On the basis of a more limited arrangement dating from 1934 the Danish and Swedish *unemployment insurance societies* entered in 1946 upon a general agreement entitling members in one country to transfer membership to the societies of the other country. The practical importance of this was primarily that Danish workers employed in Sweden and Swedish workers employed in Denmark were hereafter entitled to unemployment benefits almost immediately, provided that they fulfilled the ordinary conditions laid down for the granting of such assistance. Implementation of the agreement was contingent upon the approval of each society involved, but at the present time practically all of them have acceded to it. While Norway has recently joined the arrangement, it has not yet been possible to establish these provisions on an all-Northern basis due to the fact that neither Finland nor Iceland has any extensive scheme in this field.

Perhaps the most far-reaching of these various instruments of cooperation is the convention on *old age pensions* concluded in 1949, with all Northern countries signing up. A citizen of any of these countries who has resided for not less than five years in another of the countries is henceforth entitled to an old age pension on the same terms as those applying to nationals of that country, despite the differences existing as regards payment of contributions and pensionable age. Danish and Swedish pensions are higher than in the

489

other countries, which implies an advantage for nationals of the latter. It is worthy of note that there is no refunding of costs, each signatory defraying the expenses falling upon it under the convention.

Comparable provisions regarding *disablement pensions* were agreed upon by the five countries as recently as July 1953. The new convention covers not only pensions but also medical treatment, retraining, and rehabilitation.

Social Assistance

In the broad and varied field of social assistance a similar pattern of collaboration, by means of conferences and meetings, consultation and agreements, obtains.

With respect to *general assistance* organized co-operation dates back to 1914. A convention of 1928 between Denmark, Finland, Norway, and Sweden follows the general line of approach characteristic of social insurance in providing for reciprocal treatment of all Northern citizens on a par with nationals of the country of residence. The former common practice of returning a person who has received general assistance to his home country has thus on the whole been eliminated within these countries. Until recently costs were still cleared between the respective treasuries, but with the adoption of a new convention in 1951 among all five countries it was stipulated that also in this field each signatory should defray the costs incurred without any refunding procedure. Mention may appropriately be made that the legislative clauses under which the Northern countries have extended reciprocal treatment to each other permit the negotiation of similar agreements with other countries as well.

Northern co-operation in the field of child welfare was initiated already in 1905. Since 1919 the Northern Association for the Protection of Children and Young Persons has held frequent conferences which have predominantly served as a forum of discussion and exchange of experience for staff employed in the child welfare institutions of all five countries.

Since 1931 an important Northern convention has applied to the collection of *maintenance contributions*. Any person who neglects his maintenance duty towards spouse or child (this is particularly relevant in the case of children born out of wedlock) and moves to another Northern country will consequently there be subject to practically the same strict rules as in his home country.

FAMILY WELFARE

Until recently no formal agreements existed with respect to family welfare services, but it would seem to have been general practice to accord Northern citizens the same treatment as home nationals. However, a convention signed by all five countries in July 1953 specifically established full reciprocity as regards all existing facilities and benefits for mothers and infants.

The *general children's allowances* introduced in recent years are in Denmark and Sweden payable to all permanent residents, thus including not only citizens of the Northern countries but other foreigners as well. In Finland, Iceland, and Norway it is, on the other hand, a condition that one of the parents be a citizen although the relevant legislation holds out the possibility of concluding reciprocal agreements with other countries for the mutual granting of such allowances. A convention providing for full reciprocity between Finland, Iceland, Norway, and Sweden in this field was signed in August 1951.

LABOUR

Legislative provisions regarding *labour protection*, particularly industrial safety, apply automatically to all employees regardless of nationality. The competent authorities, however, maintain close liaison not only through frequent meetings, but also by continuous exchange of information and consultation concerning safety regulations and safety devices. This day-to-day co-operation also extends to the work of medical and technical experts engaging in the prevention and treatment of occupational diseases.

As all the Northern countries are seafaring nations, it is only natural that the desirability of collaboration in the special field of *seamen's legislation* should have been early recognized. The basic enactments concerning the status of seafarers – the Seamen's Acts – have all been preceded by comprehensive joint discussions and show a high degree of uniformity today. Also existing legislation concerning hours of work on board ships, particularly in Finland, Norway, and Sweden, is largely the result of such joint consultation. A similar pattern of collaboration prevails with respect to welfare work for seamen when in ports. One example hereof is the Scandinavian office for registration and hiring of seamen in New York.

Recent efforts to create an integrated Northern *labour market* are also of considerable significance, both from economic and social points of view. Negotiations in 1945 at the conference of the Northern Ministers of Social Affairs resulted in the ratification of a convention on this subject by Denmark and Sweden the following year. Since 1947 working permits are thus no longer required by either of these countries for citizens from the other country. Furthermore, certain rules were laid down providing for the close collaboration of the public employment exchanges; one of the stipulations being that these organs should assist each other in procuring manpower that is required by one and available in the other country. The remaining three countries have not yet become parties to the convention. In practice, however, Finland and Norway participate in the programme and direct co-operation between the employment services of all four countries already goes far beyond the stipulations of the convention. Reference may also be made to the exchange programmes for trainees – young farmers and workers – which have been developed in recent years.

It remains to mention that *labour market organizations* in the Northern countries have for decades maintained very close relations. Collaboration among the trade unions of Denmark, Norway, and Sweden dates back to their establishment in the last quarter of the 19th century. Developments, in which the Finnish and Icelandic unions have participated in recent years, have followed two main lines. In the first place, there has been an intimate liaison between the national federations of trade unions on general matters of union policy; in the second place, the various trade unions have collaborated directly. Starting as far back as 1901 with the formation of a Scandinavian Committee of Factory Workers, a large number of Northern trade union alliances have been established. Their objectives include support to national organizations in times of labour conflicts, but they also provide a permanent framework for practical collaboration in the daily work of the trade unions with respect to labour legislation, wages, statistics, educational work, etc. Similar relations are maintained between the large organizations of salaried employees and public servants formed outside the central federations of trade unions.

Likewise, the employers' organizations have long maintained close relations. Northern conferences are held every second year and a standing committee ensures continuous liaison in all matters of mutual interest to employers.

Gradually a system of very intimate co-operation among the five countries has come into being. Within the various branches of legislation concerning social security, family welfare, and labour problems the general line of advance has been towards the establishment of equality of treatment of all Northerners under the different national provisions. To this should be added their continuous co-operation in practical administration and the unceasing exchange of views and information by means of meetings, standing committees, publications, etc.

By itself the considerable similarity in economic and social conditions has clearly tended towards greater uniformity in social legislation. And the many and varied forms of co-operation have obviously served as a further contributory factor in this respect. However, underlying conditions in the five countries, although similar, are by no means identical and since each country is after all a sovereign state the various programmes in the social field are quite naturally based first and foremost upon national considerations. It would therefore appear realistic not to anticipate any far-reaching developments in the direction of more uniform legislation within the near future.

To strike this note of reserve is not an expression of pessimism. Co-operation among the Northern countries has developed gradually, not out of any preconceived master plan, but on the basis of a sober appraisal of prevailing circumstances which have rendered such co-operation advantageous to the participating parties, governmental and non-governmental alike.

The preceding brief review will have illustrated the steadily expanding width and depth of the relations established. Rapidly the time approaches when the more ambitious conception of a common Northern social citizenship, long considered a Utopia, is coming within the bounds of practical policy. If realized – and there are still difficulties to be overcome – it would indeed represent a milestone in Northern history. It would, however, come naturally as a logical climax to those unobtrusive but persistent efforts of working together to solve problems of mutual interest to which must be awarded a large share of the credit if within the last few decades the five Northern countries have come to stand before the world as a homogeneous whole.

493

Co-operation on the International Level

The field of Northern activities outlined above should be viewed also against the wider background of international co-operation in social affairs. Although a large part of their efforts has been devoted to inter-Northern relationships, the Northern countries are eager to stress that this is the result of rather exceptional circumstances and not due to any deliberate policy of seclusion. Indeed, these nations have always participated very actively in international work in the social field.

When participating in such activities the Northern countries generally collaborate. More important issues are discussed beforehand, in recent years usually at the periodic meetings of the Northern Ministers of Social Affairs, with a view to exploring the possibilities of concerted action.

The result has been to lend added weight to the influence of the five countries. Obviously, it is not possible for each of these small nations to be represented on all of the multitudinous councils, functional commissions, and similar organs established in recent years, mainly under the United Nations and its Specialized Agencies; Finland, it should be noted, is a member of the International Labour Organization (ILO), the Food and Agriculture Organization (FAO), and the World Health Organization (WHO), but not of the United Nations proper, her application for membership having not been finally decided upon as yet. Due to their intimate co-operation this disadvantage is, however, of no great moment as long as one representative of the group is able to participate. In the ILO the Northern governments have always been represented by one member on the Governing Body of that Organization, as have also generally the employers' and workers' organizations of these countries. Similarly, at least one of the Scandinavian countries is usually represented on the United Nations Economic and Social Council and its various functional commissions.

While the influence of this group of small nations on the larger political issues is obviously very limited, their relatively well-developed economic and social institutions have given them a position in international relations in this sphere far exceeding their numerical importance. Much of the experience gathered in the North on economic and social problems has been, and may continue to be, suggestive to other nations also. On their hand, the Northern countries have always been receptive to what could be learnt from other countries.

Recent examples of both may easily be quoted: The Northern countries have contributed within their means to the programmes of Technical Assistance of the United Nations and its Specialized Agencies by placing experts within various fields at the disposal of the governments of under-developed countries and by receiving a considerable number of fellows who have come from these countries to study economic and social institutions in Northern Europe; the central direction of these fellowship programmes, under which the Northern countries are considered an entity, is undertaken in turn by each of the countries. On the other hand, the introduction after the war of joint labour-management production committees was framed largely on a British model, the same applying to the social security scheme established in 1946 by Iceland; similarly, the experience and techniques of American social casework have influenced social work practice in all Northern countries during the last years.

To the countries of Northern Europe it has appeared a matter of course to lend all possible support to international co-operation in humanitarian work. Such support has included the ratification of the conventions on Human Rights, Traffic in Women and Children, Opium and other Narcotica, the Red Cross, etc., as well as the practical organization of relief work in the field. Thus, in the years immediately after 1945 extensive feeding, clothing and medical relief programmes have been undertaken to alleviate the plight of war-devastated countries. Financed by voluntary and State contributions, these activities were carried out predominantly by the large voluntary associations existing in all of the Northern countries (Red Cross, Save the Children Fund, etc.). The anti-tuberculosis campaign waged during recent years in many countries by the Scandinavian Red Cross Societies working in co-operation under the auspices of the United Nations International Children's Emergency Fund has become particularly well-known.

Among the various international agencies special interest has been devoted by the Northern countries to the ILO. Of the some 100 conventions adopted by the ILO and actually in force the Northern countries have ratified about 25–35; 20 out of 36 conventions which bear directly on labour protection have been ratified by one or more of the Northern countries. In some instances legislative measures have been enacted to conform to conventions, in other cases such legislation was in force prior to their adoption and may have been instrumental in guiding the drafting of international standards. The fact that many conventions have been ratified by only a few or none of the Northern countries does not necessarily imply that these countries maintain a lower standard. For technical reasons some of the conventions are irrelevant in the North. In other cases solutions to labour problems – sometimes representing even higher standards – have been found along lines differing so much from those suggested by the conventions that ratification has not been possible.

Within the broad framework of the various programmes for the realization of a higher degree of European integration, numerous countries, among them particularly France, the Benelux countries, and the United Kingdom, have concluded mutual agreements providing bilaterally for the extension of social security facilities to each other's nationals. Also the Northern countries are increasingly becoming contracting parties to such agreements. Simultaneously, all five countries have participated under the auspices of the ILO in the establishment of the universal social security convention adopted in 1952. It goes without saying that the Northern countries take a very positive attitude toward the general idea of social security across the national boundaries. In the first place, they have a direct interest in being partners to such mutual agreements also with countries outside Northern Europe. In the second place, they feel that their long experience with these forms of international co-operation may prove useful also when applied to other countries which only now are beginning to enter upon this sphere of activity.

CHAPTER IX

SOCIAL POLICY IN PERSPECTIVE

Introduction

In the preceding chapters an attempt has been made to picture that wide range of activities which, today, the peoples of the Northern countries consider as more or less definitely a part of the social or socio-economic field. No precise definition of the subject-matter reviewed has been ventured and, indeed, to judge from the results of the numerous previous efforts to do so, it is questionable whether it is at all possible to establish an explicit and still useful definition. The compass of those aspects of community life that are viewed mainly in the light of social considerations has been constantly changing – the trend of development having usually been one of expansion. That which today is considered as being within the orbit of social policy is thus mainly a product of historical tradition and is not easily expressed in any single formula.

This is all the more true inasmuch as the term "social", which not so very long ago was almost identical with "charitable", has undergone a gradual and almost imperceptible transformation, reverting more and more to its original meaning of relations in general among members of a community. Today, social considerations in the sense of a desire to promote the general welfare of the population – or its majority – influence a vastly greater range of activities than that of nineteenth-century social welfare proper. This broadening concept has tended particularly to blur the traditional dividing line between social and economic policies, the distinction today being only of limited importance from the viewpoint of community welfare. For obvious reasons of expediency, however, it has been largely necessary to maintain the distinction in the present volume which would otherwise have become quite unmanageable.

Simply stated, this book has dealt with the way in which the Northern peoples have grappled with a number of basic problems of com-

497

munity life, problems relating to the existence of all or most of the members of these communitites, both as workers for a living and as human beings trying to satisfy their daily needs. The solutions to these problems have been sought along two main roads: By government action and by direct collaboration among individuals in large and small organizations. But regardless of the technique employed or whether directed at the interest of the population as producer or consumer, the common denominator of all of these activities has been the conviction that society should be organized in such a way as to ensure every member a reasonable measure of security and well-being.

Following the perhaps somewhat bewildering host of details previously given, an attempt will now be made to give a more general survey of the status of present-day social policy in the Northern countries, and to illuminate some of the more salient points offering themselves for discussion in this connection.

General Review

The traditional function of social welfare has been to come to the rescue of those in need of help, material or otherwise. This function obviously remains of key importance and one of the outstanding features of recent years has indeed been the continuous trend toward more adequate standards of assistance. But increasing emphasis has come to be placed upon efforts directed at the prevention of distress. Or to put it in another way: While formerly dealing primarily with the symptoms of social ills, welfare policy in our time attempts to grapple directly with the causes of poverty and other manifestations of social maladjustment. As a logical consequence of this new approach, which the Northern countries share with numerous other nations, social welfare policy is being gradually transformed into a policy of social planning having for its pivotal points the programmes for full and productive employment, family welfare and housing, prophylactic health and rehabilitation of handicapped persons.

The sum and substance of this general trend may be briefly formulated: The community has assumed main responsibility for ensuring a decent minimum standard in certain fields of vital importance to the life of every citizen, the scope of this responsibility as well as the order of priority being decided by ordinary democratic procedure. And, in keeping with the general advancement in national wealth and the steady development in social thinking the standard applied, though modest enough as yet in many cases, has been constantly increasing. Behind this process lies, first of all, the obvious fact that modern economic developments have made the position of the individual highly insecure and have enhanced his dependence upon his fellow-men. But there lies also a growing realization of the value of joint action as a principal means not only of overcoming difficulties but also of obtaining positive improvements in general welfare, tasks which but for solidarity put to practical use would remain wholly or partly unsolved.

It goes without saying that this policy has been directed primarily towards the improvement of living conditions for the masses and unquestionably it has to no small extent contributed to soften the glaring contrast of former days between the "haves" and the "have nots". Fundamentally, however, social policy can no longer be adequately defined in the simple terms of redistribution of income – the taking away from the rich in order to give to the poor. Social measures, especially those introduced within the last two decades, have increasingly taken the form of public services and facilities which are in principle at the disposal of the entire population, irrespective of economic means. Compared to this basic transformation it is of minor significance that, mainly as a result of the progressivity of income taxes, the well-to-do pay a higher proportion of costs than corresponds to their number. The same applies to all other government activities due to the general principle that everyone should be taxed according to his paying ability. Feelings of humanitarianism and of social justice are still important as driving forces for many social innovations in special fields. But the main motive power behind social progress will be found rather in a more rationalistic conviction that numerous improvements in living conditions for the whole or the major part of the population may be obtained in the most expedient manner through community action.

In the Northern countries the upper classes have never in modern times been so numerous nor so extremely rich as in some other countries – and, it may be added, also here their wealth and the possibilities of tapping it for the benefit of those less fortunately situated have frequently been overestimated. The expansion of public activities under the welfare policies outlined above has therefore had for its inevitable and by now fully recognized consequence that the majority of beneficiaries under the various schemes themselves have to contribute a considerable part of the costs involved, a situation which clearly illustrates the point made about this policy as being today primarily motivated by considerations of expediency. Another essential feature is that, since public programmes to a very considerable extent provide for the direct satisfaction of various human needs, a rather high degree of standardization is inevitable. The result might appropriately be described as the socialization of certain clearly defined needs or, rather, of their satisfaction.

It should be added that to the Northern peoples as a whole these developments do not suggest any extreme radicalism. In the first place, they largely originated with the "grass roots" – and not with the "blades" – and were undertaken gradually and in conformity with western democratic procedure. Second, they essentially imply that the same general conception of the role of the community which led to the early assumption by public authorities of main responsibility for hospitals, railways, postal and telegraph services, and other public utilities, has finally encompassed also the field of social welfare.

The idea of undertaking in common what the individual cannot master alone, so as to obtain for all a measure of security and well-being, has been emphasized as fundamental in the framing of modern social policy. Its application has, however, by no means been confined to government action. The instinct for team-work, which throughout this publication has been stressed as a characteristic trait of the Northern peoples, today finds its most articulate illustration in the multitude of organizations devoted to a host of different causes. Within the framework of this presentation main emphasis has naturally been placed upon the great labour and co-operative organizations which have been established to safeguard and promote the vital economic interests of broad population groups and which in these countries have risen to an eminence and exert an influence upon the daily life of the community which is probably unsurpassed anywhere else. We find the labour market dominated by vast trade union federations for the protection of wage earners' interests vis-à-vis similarly organized employers. And we find a large part of the population affiliated with the far-flung co-operative movement where consumers on the one hand and farmers on the other have united to better their economic lot.

These organizations are today as integral a part of the economic and social structure, as are the social welfare programmes. Without venturing any precise comparative evaluation it appears safe to say that in any attempt to account for the relatively stable development and steady economic and social progress experienced in the Northern countries during the last two or three generations the contribution made by the great organizations measures well up to that made through social legislation.

Status

The Northern countries have frequently been likened to a social laboratory, a place of experiments and research. In a sense this illustration is rather apt. Some experiments are successful while others fail – but work is continuous and the solution of one problem often serves to shed light upon others still unsolved. There is no such thing as a terminus for social policy. Conditions change, as do ideas, and social problems and requirements change with them. In this connection it may be appropriate to mention the important role of social research as a basis for the initiation of reform work. The submission of major legislative proposals is usually preceded by the establishment of *ad hoc* commissions which frequently comprise representatives of the political parties as well as experts from the competent authorities and organizations. Prominent examples from the last two decades are the population commissions, established in the 'thirties in Sweden, Denmark, and Norway, which undertook extensive enquiries into the problems in question and drew up the main proposals subsequently embodied in the family welfare schemes of these countries; furthermore, the three Swedish commissions on unemployment, on housing and on social security, and the Danish post-war commission on youth problems.

Now, a main justification for the preparation of this publication is the indubitable fact that the peoples under review have made quite a number of reasonably successful experiments. At the same time this is a proper place to emphasize that they have by no means found a ready and full answer to all the baffling problems of community living posed by our industrial age. The conception of the Northern countries as an oasis in a troubled world is a truth with severe modifications.

501

ACCOMPLISHMENTS

In viewing the contribution which social reform has rendered to the improvement of general living conditions within the last 50–60 years it is essential to recall that the spectacular development of welfare programmes has taken place against the background of a unique, concurrent increase in national wealth. It is too easy to forget that the impressive increase in living standards of the Northern peoples within the present century is overwhelmingly due to the expansion of their capacity to produce, where the early attainment of a high level of general education has been a driving factor of key importance. By comparison, the material effects of social legislation, although more important to some groups than to others, can in all honesty be accorded secondary rank only, its net contribution consisting partly in a certain redistribution of incomes, partly – and increasingly – in the improved organization for the satisfaction of selected human needs.

Two observations should, however, be added. First, the increase in general welfare made possible by social reform is hardly capable of being sized up solely by any quantitative yardstick. Its importance must to an equal extent be found on the plane of social psychology, in the reduction of social tensions and in the promotion of social solidarity; its profound influence in these respects would appear an incontestable fact. Second, it is worth recalling what has already previously been stated, that with the gradual development of social planning on a wide front, social policy is itself striking out upon a productive line, aiming – directly and indirectly – at broadening the basis for a further increase in national production and thus in general living standards.

The above remarks are intended to place the much heralded social advances as a whole in their proper perspective. This done, the ground is clear for a more concrete answer to the question: What has been accomplished by social policy?

Historically among the first developed and of necessity occupying a place of basic importance within the welfare structure of any modern society, the nation-wide social security programmes provide a rock bottom below which the standard of living of no one, whatever his identity or predicament, is permitted to fall. Techniques vary, the main risks of human life being dealt with by social insurance, other cases of distress by social assistance. But the principal line of approach has everywhere been that help should be effective and, although many shortcomings may still be pointed out, the Northern peoples take justifiable pride in the fact that today these programmes have been developed to a point where no one need go without at least the bare necessities of life. Hunger and similar evidence of extreme need have disappeared as social phenomena.

Social security has aimed at and largely succeeded in establishing a bulwark against the worst effects of the many situations where the ordinary basis of existence of the individual is placed in jeopardy. It is thus essentially defensive in character. Other activities and programmes, some of them long established but most of them developed only within recent years, have had for their main purpose to improve conditions in a number of fields of essential importance to the everyday life of the ordinary citizen. Their emphasis is upon the offensive, upon the planning and realization of a better and more satisfying existence for the broad population. What is the record?

In his daily labours the working man is today protected by a comprehensive network of regulations aimed to protect his health and safety; work hours have been shortened and annual holidays with pay have become his legal right. By joining with his fellows the wage earner has found a powerful means not only of furthering his economic interests but also of enhancing his general status and dignity as a useful member of the community. The downtrodden labourer of former days standing in wooden shoes and cap in hand before his employer is now but a memory from the bygone past. And last, but not least, the full employment policies of recent years have largely put an end to the appalling waste of human labour that was characteristic especially of the inter-war period, with results which have on balance proved immensely beneficial not only to the individuals concerned, but to Society as a whole.

The birth and raising of children in our industrialized age impose heavy burdens upon the average home. Society has a vital interest not only in maintaining the birth rate at a satisfactory level, but also in providing the new generation with the best possible opportunities for development. Consequently, comprehensive family welfare programmes have gradually come into being. These programmes have by no means implied the taking over by the public of full responsibility for the raising of a family. One of the ideas behind them has been, however, that to have more children should not imply a serious lowering of the living standard of the family; on the other hand, parents should not be awarded prizes for having children. The family welfare programmes have resulted in a considerable equalization of living standards between those with and those without children, at the same time as they have been utilized as a vehicle for the introduction of numerous reforms considered desirable for other reasons, viz. health, hygiene, education, etc.

Intimately connected with these measures we find the public as a large-scale promoter of housing construction for the purpose of providing decent accommodation within the economic reach of the ordinary man. If housing standards in the Northern countries have shown a truly spectacular improvement within the last two or three decades, this must largely be credited to the very active non-profit housing associations and the generous support offered by the government not only to such organizations but also to other building enterprises.

Health and medical services belong in the same category. Care and treatment of the sick have long been a public responsibility, and the Northern peoples today enjoy standards of hospital and medical care probably unequalled anywhere else. But although the curative side of health programmes has undergone quick and continuous development there has here, as everywhere, been a gradual shift of emphasis towards preventive action, and measures designed to promote health conditions in general have gained increasing importance.

GAPS AND INADEQUACIES

Without belittling the high importance of the results achieved, it is essential to recall the many issues which are as yet only partly solved or not solved at all.

Present social welfare structures in all five countries show many gaps and inadequacies, and a long series of reforms are still due to come. Social security systems are nowhere fully adequate. In several countries one or more branches, notably health and disablement insurance, but also survivors' insurance, are conspicuous by their absence or insufficiency. And in all countries, with the exception of Iceland, there is strong need for improved co-ordination between the various components of the system. Assistance for special groups has lagged behind in many cases and especially the problem of rehabilitating the handicapped largely remains to be dealt with effectively. Moreover, many allowances in scattered parts of the system need upward adjustment.

An important point which has hitherto received only rather scant attention remains to be mentioned. Social welfare programmes in the Northern countries have traditionally placed main emphasis upon methods providing for standardized services to meet certain basic material needs which are, by and large, the same for all members of the community. With the increasing complexity of human relationships the need for an individual psychological approach, somewhat along the lines followed by social casework in the USA is, however, making itself felt with increasing acuteness. An interesting illustration of this trend is found in the lively discussion within the last few years, particularly in Denmark and Sweden, regarding industrial wage earners in their relation to their work. This discussion has broadened into a general debate on the situation of the individual in, and his adjustment to, our modern industrialized society. These problems may be met in accentuated form within the framework of social security programmes, particularly when dealing with the needs of low-income families by means of general assistance, but the broad implications of environmental factors to human well-being are increasingly recognized also in the more recently developed fields of social planning, perhaps most markedly in housing policy. As yet only the surface of this important field has been scratched.

These defects are numerous and important, but their proportions are still such that· they may confidently be expected to find their satisfactory settlement within the relatively near future. From a broader welfare angle, however, the Northern peoples still confront enormous tasks. The raising of the standard of the broad masses, especially of families with many children, will require a continued and major expansion of family welfare programmes, which in some of the countries are as yet only partly developed. This applies also to the preventive aspects of health services. The improvement of housing conditions, which are still unsatisfactory for large population groups, will necessitate not only a sustained high level of building of decent dwellings, but also measures to ensure that the common man is enabled financially to obtain shelter. The lengthening of annual holidays as well as any further reduction of working hours will also call for a tremendous expansion of recreational facilities, which are only in their first stages of development.

Finally, those aspects of community life which have been dealt with under the heading of Labour present a similar picture. In spite of all preventive measures, employment injuries and diseases remain a problem of serious proportions. The impressive edifice of labour-management collaborative machinery has not altogether freed the Northern countries from intermittent comprehensive work stoppages, although most of the countries have in the last few years been fortunate in avoiding major conflicts. The question of how to settle such differences between workers and employers without undue hardship to the community at large still awaits its answer. Similarly, the critical issue of how to maintain a full employment policy without constantly begging the risk of inflation may, without exaggeration, be characterized as a chronic headache of legislators and organization leaders within the last few years.

The above may suffice to refute the contention sometimes met with, that the period of social reform may be considered by and large completed. The fact that the Northern countries today stand up rather well in international comparisons does not provide any excuse for leaving things as they are. If other nations of similar structure and background still exhibit serious shortcomings in the social field, this gives no justification to slow down the pace of advancement. Moreover, the lead which the Northern countries may still enjoy is not so very impressive, a number of other countries having in recent years made great progress – developments which the Northern peoples may not always have given the attention they deserve.

Costs

The preceding section has centered on the substance of social advances (and defects). To obtain a full picture of developments up to our time as well as a platform for the evaluation of future prospects it is, however, necessary to throw a glance at the immediate economic and financial implications of social policy.

The headlong pace at which social legislation has developed within the last two generations has obviously entailed a vast increase of expenditures, not only in absolute terms – a considerable increase was to be expected in any case as a result of rising prices and population numbers – but also relatively – measured in proportion to national income. Around the turn of the century social expenditures administered through public channels corresponded to 1–2 per cent of national income, varying somewhat between the five countries. Excluding those spheres which are not generally included in the specification of social expenditures, viz. public works and general subsidies for food and house-building, we find that this proportion has today risen to about 8 per cent of the national income in Norway, 9 per cent in Iceland, 10 per cent in Denmark, and 11 per cent in Finland and Sweden. By way of comparison it may be mentioned that a similar compilation of social service costs in the United Kingdom results in a 1950-figure of 10 per cent.

The following table illustrates the distribution of social welfare expenditures among the main programmes.

It will be seen that there is everywhere a heavy concentration upon the three items of Health, Old age and disablement, and Family and child welfare, which together account for 70–80 per cent of the

PERCENTAGE DISTRIBUTION OF SOCIAL EXPENDITURE
IN THE NORTHERN COUNTRIES (1950)

	Denmark	Finland	Iceland	Norway	Sweden
1. Health	28.4	19.6	36.2	38.2	27.3
2. Employment injuries and labour protection . . .	2.8	3.9	3.6	3.3	4.9
3. Unemployment	13.3	9.8	0.4	4.8	2.8
4. Old age, disablement, etc.	32.0	14.8	30.7	22.9	32.4
5. Family and child welfare	12.9	28.2	14.4	11.2	24.6
6. General unspecified assistance	3.0	7.4	2.5	3.5	4.7
7. War and other military disabled	0.4	11.0	–	2.0	0.4
Total 1–7	92.8	94.7	87.8	85.9	97.1
8. Central administration . .	1.8	0.4	1.2	0.4	1.2
9. Computed tax reductions in respect of children	5.4	4.9	11.0	13.7	1.7
Total 1–9	100.0	100.0	100.0	100.0	100.0
Total social expenditure . . (in millions)	1,848 Da. kr.	49,156 Fmk.	122 Icel. kr.	1,061 No. kr.	2,669 Sw. kr.

total (only in Finland somewhat less, partly due to the great part played by the assistance to disabled ex-servicemen). But this broad conformity still covers considerable differences, expressing the varying stage of development and the varying emphasis laid upon different programmes in each of the Northern countries. While old age and disablement schemes in Denmark, Iceland, and Sweden are the most important single item, accounting for almost one-third of total expenditures, the corresponding figures for Norway and (especially) Finland are considerably smaller. And while family and child welfare (including computed tax reductions in respect of children) in Denmark requires only 18 per cent of total expenditures, the corresponding percentage in Finland exceeds 33.

Social expenditures as related to national income provide the most adequate picture of the weight of the "social sector" in the national economy. But the question of how social welfare is financed is also of considerable importance, not only because of its fiscal and political implications, but also because it largely reflects the basic change in the character of social policy.

The long-term trend has been towards an increasing proportion of social expenditures to be financed over the public purse out of ordinary taxes, while direct contributions from the population have been steadily declining in importance. In part this is due to the decreasing role played by contributions from insured members in the social security systems, in part it is a result of the emergence of comprehensive new programmes, especially within the family welfare field, which from the start have had the character of public services. Developments have gone farthest in this direction in Denmark and Sweden, where today almost six-sevenths of all social welfare expenditures are directly financed by the State and local authorities, while the remainder is contributed mainly by the insured and a tiny fraction by employers. In Finland, Iceland, and Norway the public pays about two-thirds of the total; the employers in Finland and the insured members in Norway are responsible for most of the remaining one-third, while in Iceland each of the two groups shoulder about the same percentage. A natural consequence has been that social expenditures have come to carry very considerable weight in public budgets. In Denmark and Sweden they account for about one-third of all central and local government outlays, while in Finland, Iceland, and Norway the proportion lies around one-fifth.

Attention has here been drawn to the economic and financial implications of social policy as reflected in the public accounts. But it is worth noting that this illustration does not provide a full picture of the economic significance of social programmes, to say nothing of their contribution to the general well-being of the population. The shortening of working hours or the lengthening of annual holidays exemplifies numerous reforms which do not involve public expenditure and which cannot be evaluated in cash, although they are clearly of value to the beneficiary and of importance also from the broader point of view of the national economy.

Responsibility

Surveying the various fields covered by this publication, it is probably correct to say that in the Northern countries a large majority today considers the community as the final carrier of responsibility for the broad welfare of the population. And it may be added that there has been a growing conviction that this responsibility should be shouldered in an active way, implying that the public should not only intervene to avert serious distress to smaller or larger groups of citizens, but should also take positive steps to improve upon the existing state of affairs where such improvements are considered of sufficient importance to justify intervention. A significant corollary to this widening of public responsibility has been the marked long-term trend towards centralization, the State coming to occupy an ever more dominating position as against local authorities. This trend has followed inevitably from the development of an increasing number of national schemes which entail uniform rules for the whole population and where the central government carries the main part of the financial burden; local autonomy has been retained to a far higher degree in fields where local authorities still defray most of the costs.

It is within the broad framework of this umbrella of "welfarism" that the division of labour between the great organizations and the public agencies must be viewed.

The labour market organizations and the co-operatives, which have undergone a similar process of centralization, are in immediate charge of certain vital spheres, bound up mainly with the promotion of broad economic interests. Here the role of the community, although of increasing importance, has been limited to influencing the general climate under which these organizations operate and to intervention in certain critical situations. On the whole, experience has so far shown this "arrangement" to work rather effectively. Nevertheless, the vastly increased measure of State intervention in the last two decades has actualized the issue of how to synchronize the interests of these powerful organizations with those of Society as a whole. This applies with particular force to the labour market organizations where recent developments have repeatedly highlighted the inherent danger of conflicts arising between governments pledged to policies of full employment and price stability, and organizations pledged to promote the more narrow economic interests of their members.

On the other hand, the public is directly responsible for the vast majority of the many programmes which are traditionally considered as belonging to the social field proper. But also in this field private initiative plays its part, although under widely divergent forms. This is particularly apparent with respect to housing where public programmes to a considerable extent, and most so in Denmark, rely for their execution upon co-operative or other non-profit housing associations. But it applies also, albeit in varying degrees, to all other branches of social welfare. A distinction must here be made between activities where prospective beneficiaries have pooled their resources under the classical motto "help for self-help" and activities undertaken by philanthropic organizations and individuals.

As for the former category, which has served as the basis for numerous branches of social security, the non-governmental element is still prominent in some of the present social insurance schemes. Thus, in several of the Northern countries the administration of health insurance and unemployment insurance to this very day remains the responsibility of elected representatives of the insured. Another matter is that the State, as a natural consequence of the heavy financial subsidies granted, has assumed a large measure of general control over these schemes.

With respect to philanthropic undertakings it is clear that the assumption by the public of the bulk of social welfare responsibilities has shifted a main part of the burdens formerly devolving upon individual or privately organized charity. This development has undeniably sharply curtailed the range of private social work, which at present occupies a far more modest position in the Northern countries than, for instance, in the United States. In illustration it may be mentioned that while private charity expenditures in the latter country are estimated to amount to 2 per cent of national income, the proportion is in Denmark only 0.2 per cent.

Nevertheless, the importance of voluntary action in the Northern countries should not be minimized. It is true that under present-day conditions comprehensive programmes embodying financial assistance to large groups are necessarily outside the scope of philanthropic organizations and a proper concern of the legislative authorities only. The situation is, however, rather different as regards other types of measures which provide benefits and services of a more individual character. Such measures are found within all branches of social welfare, whether family welfare, health or general social assistance, and private organizations, which have in many cases been their original sponsors, frequently retain active direction or participation in schemes which have subsequently obtained legislative approval and financial support from the public. This particularly applies to the field of child welfare.

Such fields, furthermore, also today furnish ample scope for private initiative in its traditional role of pioneer. For instance, there is no doubt that in these countries the employment problem of the handicapped as well as the development of social casework services, to mention just two examples, offer great opportunities for voluntary action in the future. Historically, such experimenting in new social territory would correspond to the role which has always been played by private charity at its best. Also, it would not require excessive financial resources, a fact of no small importance since the long-term increase in taxation has undeniably brought about a severe stringency in the means available for voluntary social activities.

It is, however, essential that private interest in social work should not wane. For one thing, it has always proved less difficult to obtain public appropriations for measures which have already been tried out successfully in practice, and philanthropic enterprises with their inherently greater freedom of action unquestionably possess considerable advantages over public agencies in the undertaking of pilot projects. Similarly, it is of great significance to preserve contact and collaboration between the public authorities and that "grass-roots" initiative which has formed so important an element in the shaping of the present social structure of the Northern countries.

But, while such private initiative should be given all possible encouragement and credit, it must still be remembered that there are limits, perhaps even rather narrow limits, to the kind of tasks it may be expected to undertake with profit. The wider aspects of promoting social welfare must perforce be referred for public action, primarily because of the far-flung ramifications of modern social programmes, which call for the co-ordination of economic, fiscal, and social policies; furthermore, such programmes would never, in the same way as alleviation of individual distress, appeal to the sentiments inspiring philanthropic action.

Social Policy and Standards of Living

It has been stated above that within the last 10–20 years social policy in the Northern countries has entered upon a new phase, that of social planning, although it must be admitted that such planning is as yet incomplete and the implementation of plans even more so. This development, welcomed by virtue of the ensuing re-orientation of efforts in a more constructive direction, has also augmented the number of factors with which the social planner has to reckon. Issues of major social significance can no longer be dealt with separately but must be tackled by an integrated approach which evaluates these issues, as well as the solutions contemplated, against the total stream of national life and the general policies pursued.

In this connection the most important single fact to bear in mind is that social policy is not the only, and probably not even the most important, means of increasing the general welfare of the population. As previously emphasized, the relatively high standards of living enjoyed by the Northern peoples are primarily due to their relatively well developed productive capacity. For a long time, and particularly within the last two or three generations, a main characteristic of the Northern countries has been the general trend of expanding economy. An annual increase in national production and wealth of about three per cent (as against an annual increase in population numbers of only one per cent) seems to be an approximately correct appraisal of the average rate of progress. Although it is, of course, fully realized that this rate of progress is no natural law to be relied upon at all times, experience is nevertheless felt to provide some justification for the optimistic extrapolation of this trend into the not too far distant future. Where, as in Norway and Sweden, long-term programmes have been prepared, they are, in fact, based upon the assumption that this expanding line will be continued under conditions calling for the full utilization of all available productive resources. Such a development would permit further advances in the general standards of living and provide a favourable basis for the undertaking also of further social reforms. It is, however, of fundamental importance that plans for such social reforms be related to the general economic situation and that a balanced estimate be undertaken of the proper role to be played by social policy within the framework of a sustained expansion of the national economy.

In the first place, continued expansion may be dependent upon a more than proportionate increase in investments and exports. Where this is the case and where a sustained rate of expansion is considered a primary objective, the volume of consumption, in the broad sense of the word, cannot be allowed to grow with the full rate of progress. This general stipulation also determines the upper limits to social welfare reforms. True, a number of measures, which by tradition fall within the field of social policy, are privileged to rank among those investments which are of high relevance to the drive for higher production, but many of the programmes envisaged would certainly increase consumption without having any significant positive influence upon future productivity or, at any rate, without any immediate effects in this direction.

Moreover, it is by no means a foregone conclusion that the population (or its majority) in the Northern countries should wish the increase in wealth to be channelled through the government in the form of social welfare measures or, for that matter, other public services. People may wish to retain the increase in their purchasing power so as to be able to decide individually on its utilization. Undoubtedly there are still many improvements in living conditions which may be obtained only, or at least in the most effective way, through community action. The first step is, however, to ascertain which possible improvements are considered of such importance that public action, with its ensuing costs, is preferred to private management of the cash involved. The second step will be that of weighing any finally selected project against other items of the public budget which may be given priority over social expenditures.

The considerable level to which social services have been developed and the relatively high degree of political unity with respect to the broad lines of social policies may be taken as evidence that on the whole the peoples of the Northern countries have found it in their interest to safeguard a rather large number of human needs through community action, although this has involved giving up an increasing share of their private incomes. During its process of development social policy has itself contributed importantly to the strengthening of this attitude. It has largely dispelled original misgivings and through changing conditions it has proved an effective instrument in dealing with a variety of issues of essential importance to the broad mass of the population. Once the concept of public responsibility for social welfare has been accepted, the ideological ground has been prepared also for the future widening and deepening of programmes. Not only has each new step extended the circle of beneficiaries, but throughout the peoples, regardless of party affiliations, there has been a growing understanding and appreciation of social measures.

This obviously implies a rather favourable climate for the continued development of social policy along a positive line. Yet, the range of political unity should not be exaggerated. There may be general acceptance of the idea that common action, whether on the governmental or the organizational level, is necessary or desirable in important sectors of community life. But when it comes down to practical measures, considerable disagreement will be found to exist more frequently than not.

The effects of social policy upon productivity have been the subject of perennial discussion. During the last few years this discussion has turned particularly around the effects of changes in the labour market, including first of all the advent of full or almost full employment. Without here attempting any evaluation of the pros and cons, a few general comments may be pertinent.

It has previously been stated that modern social planning, by contrast with older social welfare programmes, largely pursues a "productive" line aimed to broaden the basis for a further increase in production and thus in living standards. It would, however, be an obvious fallacy to infer from this that social policy today should have adopted the continued rise in productivity for its one and all-important goal. An increased measure of social welfare may be found desirable even at the price of a slower growth in productivity – and methods for increasing the national product may inversely be opposed by social welfare considerations. Thus, major undertakings in the social field, e.g. shorter working hours, longer holidays, etc., find their justification on grounds which may, at least in the short run, imply a slowing down of productive expansion, while others, e.g. maintenance of the aged and helpless, are motivated by entirely different considerations and cannot at all be viewed as productive in the usual sense of the word. It is consequently not possible to lay down any categoric one-way relationship between social reforms and increased productivity, both of which must be viewed against the more general background of a concerted striving towards such future goals as may have been formulated in the various countries.

A second issue which time and again comes to the fore as a source of heated controversy pertains to the financial implications of welfare programmes.

Quite generally it may be stated that a continued increase in incomes, such as envisaged in the coming years, will automatically increase public revenues from taxation, assuming rates to remain unchanged. Insofar as expenditures do not rise automatically to the same extent, this development will in itself leave "space" for such innovations or expansions of existing public activities as may be preferred to a reduction of taxes. In this connection it is worth noting, however, that social welfare is only one of the potential fields of expansion.

Schemes which cannot be implemented within these limits pose a more intricate problem from the point of view of practical politics. At the present time government budgets in the Northern countries account for about 25 per cent or more of the national income; while this percentage is, of course, no absolute maximum, it is at least doubtful whether any major expansion beyond this limit will be considered acceptable under existing political conditions. This amounts to a tentative assertion that, as matters stand today, following several decades of sweeping reforms and under the current pressure of intensified defence requirements, there would appear to be a widespread feeling that some restraint should be shown with respect to the embarkation upon new and massive programmes.

A discussion along these lines assumes that social welfare measures are costly, and even very costly. This notion, admittedly based on solid experience, notably with such reforms as old age pensions, children's allowances, etc., should not be accepted, however, as a matter of course where future undertakings are under consideration.

515

That many social welfare expenditures are in effect productive investments, has already been stressed. Numerous measures, e.g. for the prevention of occupational injuries and diseases, and for the rehabilitation of handicapped persons, may even be expected to contribute to a lowering of social expenditures in the long run. It is of even greater significance in this connection, however, that although the aggressive, constructive approach to social problems unquestionably implies quite far-reaching changes in the very structure of society, it does not follow with equal certainty that the measures by which this reorganization is effected involve heavy public expenditures. The enormous increase of social expenditures within the present century, measured as a proportion of national income, should not of necessity continue at the same pace. The most expensive components of a modern social welfare programme, viz. old age and disablement pensions, medical and hospital services, and family welfare schemes, have already attained a fair degree of development in most of the countries reviewed here. Although considerable improvements may still be called for, there is consequently no compelling reason to expect expenditures in these fields to go on expanding at the high rate obtaining during the formative period. Moreover, employment and housing policies may well involve quite radical intervention with respect to the utilization of national resources but will not necessarily result in any spectacular expansion of public expenditures.

Turning from the general to the more detailed aspects of social welfare financing, we find the problem of repartitioning the taxes occupying the centre of the stage. To a certain extent the enormous increase in expenditures during the past half century has been financed by progressive taxation of persons in the higher income brackets. But as social welfare has more and more taken the form of programmes benefitting the whole population – rather than a minor group – it has to an increasing extent also proved necessary for the broad population itself to contribute to its financing.

Today probably all the Northern countries find themselves rather close to the practical limit of income equalization by taxation. Any expansion of broad welfare programmes which exceeds the margin provided by rising national income will consequently have to be financed predominantly by the large majority of beneficiaries themselves (although the higher incomes will obviously still be the most severely taxed).

With this development income equalization is taking on an expanded meaning. It no longer applies only as between persons belonging to different income brackets but also as between the healthy and the sick, the employed and the unemployed, the families with and those without children – who may all be within the same income brackets. What happens may be simply characterized by saying that the sense of solidarity and community of interest, which was the main motive force behind the early voluntary social insurance societies, is now being applied on a vastly widened front. But it should be added that the efficiency of resulting programmes largely derives from the degree of coercion which follows from public financing.

The living standard of any nation depends primarily upon the volume of goods and services which it produces. Social benefits, whatever their description may be, are part of this living standard. To a certain extent social policy implies a redistribution of goods and services in favour of less fortunately situated citizens. But to an increasing extent it stands forth as the result of a series of decisions, democratically arrived at, which have for their common denominator a conviction that certain important improvements in the living standard of the population as a whole are most practically obtained by authorizing the community to administer a share of the national income which would otherwise have been spent by the individual citizens according to their own judgment.

To ponder over what may be the ultimate limit to this trend is hardly a rewarding pastime. The Northern countries are democracies and future social welfare developments must, as they have in the past, depend upon the preference of citizens as expressed at the polls. It will be for the majority to estimate whether their well-being will be enhanced by any further expansion of community programmes in the social field or not.

Freedom and Welfare

The above heading serves also as a title for this book. It does so because in three words it summarizes the central theme underlying the multifarious programmes surveyed. The theme is a belief that freedom and welfare are but two sides of one great movement, the striving of the common man to obtain for himself and his fellows a more secure and more satisfying life. A variety of terms have been used to characterize the sort of community which is gradually emerging under the combined impact of this conviction and changing material conditions. Some, including many of the more sceptically minded, see it as the modern Welfare State, thus emphasizing the role of the government as against that of individual members of the community. A majority of the Northern peoples probably find their feelings better covered by the Swedish-coined characterization of this, as yet only partly realized community, as a "Home for the People".

To what extent have actual developments during the last generations borne out the belief that love of freedom and the pursuit of welfare along lines of organizational and governmental action have been in essential harmony? No evaluation of welfare programmes, in their broadest sense, can ignore this crucial question, much less so since in any argument over the pros and cons of welfarism and laissez-faire it never fails that loss of individual freedom is charged to the debit side of the former.

Accepting this view for a starting point one would look for remnants of the Liberalist epoch in order to find what freedoms have been left to the Northern peoples. And one finds those essential freedoms, notably universal suffrage, freedom of thought, religion and speech, freedom from censorship, etc., which these peoples obtained under Liberalist impulses and which are fundamental pillars of the present order of Society. Far from being curtailed, these freedoms have been guarded against encroachments and widened with every generation, the most spectacular advance of late being perhaps the emancipation of women. Political democracy thus remains the unchallenged heritage from our Liberalist fathers; it is as parliamentary democracies that the Northern nations have striven, and strive today, to make their countries into "Homes for the People". It is, consequently, not on this score that our modern community is open to criticism from Liberalist quarters.

But political democracy, however fundamental, represents only one main aspect of human freedom. Freedom to dispose of one's income and property at will, freedom of contract, freedom of employment, including the free choice of pursuing any trade, were the essential economic rights associated with Liberalism. Their attainment, it might be added, was probably the primary aspiration of this school of thought, political democracy only following somewhat later and not always supported by an equal show of enthusiasm on the part of

Liberals. The ideal, here as elsewhere, was a community in harmonious equilibrium with free competition as main regulator and propelling force, a concept which obviously implied that only a minimum of interference with individual freedom of action should be tolerated.

In this respect there can be no doubt that subsequent decades have involved a steady and by now quite considerable restriction of individual freedom, partly by governmental action, partly by the activities of organizations, including particularly the trade unions and the various associations on the employers' side. Still, the extent of this movement should not be exaggerated. In the first place, complete laissez-faire was never practiced – the Northern countries have never permitted economic liberalism to go to such extremes as in some other countries. And in the second place, any restrictions imposed still represent only modifications of a basic liberty of action. What has happened may perhaps best be characterized as a narrowing of the scope within which the free interplay of economic forces takes place, accompanied by the institution of certain rules for this interplay of forces.

The general background for this development has been the same in the Northern countries as in other industrialized parts of the world and may therefore be disposed of briefly. The freedom enjoyed in the "jungle", even in its Liberalist version, is essentially a freedom for the few and strong, the many and weak faring less well. The advent of political democracy combined with sweeping advances in popular enlightenment, however, gave the less favoured majority their opportunity, and by using it to the full they have gradually succeeded in building a community offering decent living conditions, not only for the few but also for the large masses.

A state of law and order has come to reign over practically all major aspects of community life. A network of regulations and agreements have replaced the near vacuum left by the Liberalist epoch. And social welfare programmes not only ensure that those in need are assisted but also seek, in a number of vital fields, to improve the standards of the broad population.

Some might feel inclined to call this a return to the paternalistic days of the absolute monarchy. Such a comparison would, however, rest upon a false analogy. It is no longer the King and his men who undertake one activity or another for the benefit of subjects; it is the people, themselves, who take the initiative through their own elected representatives – organizational leaders or legislators. If resulting action means abandoning a measure of individual freedom of action in the Liberalist sense, it will therefore be in accordance with the will of the people itself, as expressed in a community with democratic rules of government. That this process, although in itself natural enough, involves dangers should be freely admitted. There is, first, a risk that majority rule may lead to discrimination against smaller or larger minorities. And there is, second, a risk that the leadership may lose touch with the rank and file with the result that measures undertaken appear as dictates imposed upon the population.

In this connection it may be relevant to stress the important relationship between the origins of initiative in social policy and the degree to which proper consideration is given to the balancing of individual rights against the interests of the community as a whole. While those measures which are initiated from "below", i.e. by resourceful "common" men and women, and which receive popular response, will usually be in accordance with this balance, the same may not always be the case with reforms which are initiated from "above", i.e. by the government or by governmental agencies.

As has repeatedly been pointed out, the "grass-roots" initiative has been a decisive influence in shaping the present social structure of the Northern countries. However, there is no denying that many among the more recent programmes have not emerged in this way but are primarily the result of top-level deliberations between legislators, administrators, and other experts. To a certain extent this trend may be due to the growing complexity of our community and its problems which renders this procedure the only practicable one. But it does entail a danger of bureaucratization, including the loss of contact with the thoughts and opinion of the broad masses for whose benefit these measures are after all intended.

It has seemed important, especially with a view to developments in other parts of the world, to draw attention to these more controversial aspects of Northern welfare policies. This done, it appears fair to say, however, that there is quite widespread agreement among the Northern peoples that it has so far been possible to strike a fair balance between a fundamental respect for the rights of the individual and a considerable degree of mutual responsibility and solidarity.

Increased welfare may have involved numerous infringements upon individual freedom as conceived of by Liberalism. But freedom from want, and from the fear of want, are also essential freedoms, and on balance the average citizen of the Northern countries has come to enjoy a greater measure of actual freedom with greater opportunities for a satisfying life.

The goal pursued by the Northern peoples is simple. They want to make their countries a place worth living in for free men and women. This includes political freedom with all that this term implies by way of civic rights; but it includes also social democracy with all that this implies by way of broad economic and social welfare. To realize this goal requires work and increased production; and it requires co-operation in a spirit of practical solidarity. Against the record of half a century's efforts along these lines it is, perhaps, permissible to express confidence that these five countries will stand up reasonably well also in the future.

SELECTED BIBLIOGRAPHY
Publications in English, French and German

Note: * also available in French ** also available in German *** also available in French and German

GENERAL SOCIAL WELFARE LITERATURE AND BIBLIOGRAPHICAL WORKS

Afzelius, Nils. *Books in English on Sweden. A Bibliographical List.* Stockholm: The Swedish Institute, 1951.

American-Scandinavian Foundation, The. *A List of Books by Scandinavians and about Scandinavia.* New York: 1946.

Hedin, Naboth. *Guide to Information about Sweden.* (N.Y.: 1947); supplemented by *Books about Sweden 1946–1949.* The American-Swedish News Exchange, 630 Fifth Avenue, New York 20, N.Y., 1949.

Höjer, Karl J. *Social Welfare in Sweden.* Stockholm: The Swedish Institute, 1949.

** Jensen, Orla. *Social Services in Denmark.* Danish Information Handbooks. Copenhagen: Det Danske Selskab, 1948.

Ministry of Social Affairs, The. *Labour Legislation and Social Service in Iceland.* Reykjavik: 1949.

Nelson, George R. *Social Welfare in Scandinavia.* Copenhagen: The Danish Ministry of Labour and Social Affairs, 1953.

Norwegian Joint Committee on International Social Policy, The. *Norwegian Social and Labour Legislation. A Collection of Laws and Regulations.* Second Edition. Oslo: January 1953.'   •

* Salomaa, Niilo, ed. *Social Legislation and Work in Finland.* Helsinki: Ministry of Social Affairs, 1953.

** *Social Denmark. A Survey of Danish Social Legislation.* Copenhagen: Socialt Tidsskrift, 1945. 2nd Impression, 1947.

Social Sweden. Stockholm: The Social Welfare Board, 1952.

Tegner, Göran. *La Sécurité Sociale en Suède.* Stockholm: Institut Suédois, 1951.

CHAPTER I. THE NORTHERN COUNTRIES

Arneson, Ben A. *The Democratic Monarchies of Scandinavia.* New York: Van Nostrand, 1939; revised edition, 1949.

Bukdahl, Jørgen. *The North and Europe.* Copenhagen: Aschehoug, 1947.

Foreign Ministries of Denmark, Finland, Iceland, Norway, and Sweden, The. *The Northern Countries.* Stockholm: 1951.

Friis, Henning, ed. *Scandinavia between East and West.* (With an English bibliography). Ithaca and New York: Cornell University Press, 1950.

Gathorne-Hardy, G. M. and others. *The Scandinavian States and Finland. A Political and Economic Survey.* (With an English bibliography). London and New York: Royal Institute of International Affairs, 1951.

Hovde, Bryn J. *The Scandinavian Countries, 1720–1865.* 2 vols. Boston: Chapman and Grimes, 1943. Ithaca, N.Y.: Cornell University Press, 1948.

Maré, Eric de. *Scandinavia. Sweden, Denmark and Norway*. London: B.T. Batsford, Ltd., 1952.

Scott, Franklin D. *The United States and Scandinavia*. (With a list of suggested reading). Cambridge, Mass.: Harvard University Press, 1950.

Sutton, P. W. and others, ed. *The Scandinavian Year Book 1953. A Comprehensive Guide to Commerce, Industry & Tourism in Denmark, Norway & Sweden*. London: Wm. Dawson & Sons, Ltd., 1953.

Toyne, S. M. *The Scandinavians in History*. New York: Longmans, 1949.

DENMARK

Begtrup, H. and others. *The Folk High Schools of Denmark and the Development of a Farming Community*. With an introduction by Michael Sadler. Copenhagen: 4th popular ed., 1948.

Bure, Kristjan, ed. *Greenland*. Copenhagen: The Royal Danish Ministry for Foreign Affairs, 1951.

Danstrup, John. *A History of Denmark*. Copenhagen: Wivel, 1948.

Gedde, K. and K. B. Andersen, eds. *This is Denmark*. Copenhagen: Gjellerup, 1948.

Manniche, Peter. *Living Democracy in Denmark*. Copenhagen: G. E. C. Gad, 1952.

* Royal Danish Ministry for Foreign Affairs, The, and the Danish Statistical Department. *Denmark 1952*. (With a list of selected works in English and French). Copenhagen: 1952.

** Skrubbeltrang, F. *The Danish Folk High Schools*. Copenhagen: Det danske Selskab, 1952.

FINLAND

Alenius, S. *Finland between the Armistice and the Peace*. Helsinki: Söderström & Co., 1947.

Hall, Wendy. *Green Gold and Granite. A Background to Finland*. London: Max Parrish and Co., Ltd., 1953.

Hinshaw, David. *Heroic Finland*. New York: G. P. Putnam's Sons, 1952.

Lounasmeri, Olavi. *Finnish War Reparations*. Reprinted from The Bank of Finland Monthly Bulletin, nos. 11–12, 1952. Helsinki: 1953.

Ministry for Foreign Affairs, The. *Form of Government Act and Diet Act of Finland*. Helsinki: 1947.

Scott-Laing, J. M. *Finland: Economic and Commercial Conditions*. London: H.M.S.O., 1948.

Shearman, Hugh. *Finland. The Adventures of a Small Power*. London: Stevens & Sons, Ltd., 1950.

Strode, H. *Finland Forever*. New Edition. New York: Harcourt Brace & Co., 1952.

Suviranta, Bruno. *The Completion of Finland's War Indemnity*. Reprinted from Unitas. Quarterly Review of the Pohjoismaiden Yhdyspankki (Nordiska Föreningsbanken). Helsinki: 1952.

Toivola, Urho, ed. *The Finland Year Book 1947*. Helsinki: Mercatorin Kirjapaino ja Kustannus, O.Y., 1947.

Wuorinen, John H. *Finland and World War II*. New York: The Ronald Press, 1948.

ICELAND

Johnson, S., ed. *Iceland's Thousand Years*. Winnipeg: Icelandic Canadian Club, 1946.

Thorsteinsson, Th., ed. *Iceland*. Reykjavik: The National Bank of Iceland, 1946.

NORWAY

Adamson, Olge J., ed. *Industries of Norway*. Oslo: Dreyer, 1952.

Hölaas, Odd. *The World of the Norseman*. London: The Bond Publishing Co., 1949.

Larsen, Karen. *History of Norway*. Princeton and Oxford, for the American-Scandinavian Foundation, 1948.

Martin. *Norwegian Life and Landscape*. London: Booles, 1952.

Mortensen, Sverre and A. Sköien. *The Norway Year Book*. Oslo: Tanum, 1951.

SWEDEN

Andersson, I., a. o. *Introduction to Sweden*. Second Edition. Stockholm: Forum, 1951.

Andersson, Ingvar. *L'histoire de la Suède*. Stockholm: Institut Suédois, 1951.

Childs, Marquis. *Sweden, the Middle Way*. London: Cambridge University Press, 1936. New York: Pelican Books, 1948 (revised edition).

Elshult, Alv, Erik Höök and Hans Risberg. *La Vie Economique de la Suède*. Stockholm: Institut Suédois, 1952.

Gehnich, K. G. *Schweden. Eine Einführung*. Stockholm: Schwedisches Institut, 1952.

Kastrup, Allan: *The Making of Sweden*. New York: American-Swedish News Exchange, 1953.

Lindbom, Tage. *Schweden Gestern und Heute*. Hamburg: Ernst Tessloff Verlag, 1949.

Nilsson, Arne. *Sweden's Way to a Balanced Economy*. Stockholm: The Swedish Institute, 1950.

Osvald, Hugo. *Swedish Agriculture*. Stockholm: The Swedish Institute, 1952.

Stockholm Chamber of Commerce. *Sweden's Mainspring – Private Enterprise*. Stockholm: 1952.

Strode, H. *Sweden. Model for a World*. New York: Harcourt, Brace & Co., 1949.

Swedish Institute, The, and AB Svenska Shell. *Graphic Sweden*. Stockholm: 1950.

Swedish Institute, The, and AB Svenska Shell. *Sweden in the World. A Comparative Graphic Survey*. Stockholm: 1951.

Swedish Tourist Traffic Association, The. *Sweden, Past and Present*. Stockholm: Förlags AB Svenska Samlingsverk, 1947.

CHAPTER II. LABOUR

DENMARK

Galenson, Walter. *The Danish System of Labor Relations*. Cambridge, Mass.: Harvard University Press, 1952.

Industrial Relations in Denmark. Edited and published by Socialt Tidsskrift, Copenhagen: 1947.

FINLAND

Niini, Aarno. *Vocational Education in Finland*. Helsinki: Ministry of Commerce and Industry, 1952.

NORWAY

Arbeidernes faglige Landsorganisation i Norge. *The Trade Union Movement in Norway*. Oslo: 1951.

Galenson, W. *Labor in Norway*. Cambridge, Mass.: Harvard University Press, 1949.

Norwegian Joint Committee on International Social Policy, The. *Employment Policy in Norway. A Survey*. Oslo: 1950.

Slaby, S. M. *The Labor Court in Norway*. Oslo: Norwegian Academic Press, 1952.

Andersson, Sven and Hilding Starland. *Problèmes et Législation du Travail en Suède*. Stockholm: Institut Suédois, 1952.

*** Landsorganisationen. *This is LO.* Stockholm: 1952.

Lindbom, Tage. *Sweden's Labor Program.* New York: League for Industrial Democracy. Pamphlet series, 1948.

Myers, Charles A. *Industrial Relations in Sweden.* Cambridge, Mass.: Massachusetts Institute of Technology, 1951.

* Neymark, Ejnar. *Vocational Guidance in Sweden.* International Labour Review. Vol. LVII. 1948. Pages 438–53.

Norgren, Paul H. *The Swedish Collective Bargaining System.* Cambridge, Mass.: Harvard University Press, 1941.

Robbins, J. J. *The Government and Labor Relations in Sweden.* Chapel Hill, N. C.: University of North Carolina Press, 1942.

Royal Board of Vocational Education, The. *Vocational Education in Sweden.* Stockholm: 1952.

Schmidt, Carl Christian. *Mediation in Sweden.* (In Elmore Jackson, *Meeting of Minds*). New York, Toronto & London: 1952.

Swedish Employers' Confederation, Confederation of Swedish Trade Unions, and Swedish Central Organization of Salaried Employees. *Agreement about Enterprise Councils.* Stockholm: 1947.

* Swedish Employers' Confederation, The. *A Survey of Social and Labour Conditions in Sweden.* Stockholm: 1947.

TCO. *The Central Organization of Salaried Employees. Facts and Figures about a New Movement in Sweden.* Stockholm: 1948.

CHAPTER III. THE CO-OPERATIVE MOVEMENT

D E N M A R K

Pedersen, Thor. *Urban Co-operation in Denmark.* Copenhagen: Det Kooperative Fællesforbund, 1950.

** Ravnholt, Henning. *The Danish Co-operative Movement.* Copenhagen: Det danske Selskab, 1950.

F I N L A N D

Central Union of Distributive Societies, The (KK). *Finland's Progressive Co-operative Movement.* Helsinki: 1950.

Agricultural Co-operation in Finland. Helsinki: Pellervo-Seura, 1949.

I C E L A N D

Jonsson, Hannes. *Co-operation in Iceland.* Reykjavik: 1950.

N O R W A Y

Grimley, O. B. *Consumers' Co-operation in Norway.* Oslo: NKL, 1950.

Grimley, O. B. *Co-operatives in Norway.* Oslo: NKL, 1950.

S W E D E N

Ames, J. *Co-operative Sweden Today.* Manchester: The Co-operative Union, 1952.

Co-operative Association. *Educational Work at Vår Gård.* Stockholm: KF, 1950.

Harris, Thomas. *Sweden's Unorthodox Co-operatives.* Stockholm: KF, 1949.

* Hedberg, Anders. *Consumers' Co-operation in Sweden.* Stockholm: KF, 1948.

Hedberg, Anders. *Co-operative Sweden.* Stockholm: KF, 1951.

Håkansson, Richard, ed. *Swedish Agricultural Administration, Education and Research. A Manual for Visitors in Sweden.* Stockholm: Sveriges Lantbruksförbund, 1950.

* Odhe, Thorsten. *Consumers' Co-operation in Sweden's Economic Life.* Stockholm: KF, 1949.

Stolpe, Herman. *Cog or Collaborator. Democracy in Co-operative Education.* Stockholm: KF, 1949.

*** Sveriges Lantbruksförbund and Riksförbundet Landsbygdens Folk. *Swedish Farmers' Organizations.* Stockholm: 1950.

CHAPTER IV. FAMILY WELFARE

Iliovici, Jean. *L'aide aux Familles en Scandinavie.* Paris: Collection Informations Sociales. Edité par l'Union Nationale des Caisses d'Allocations Familiales, 1953.

Lund, Ragnar, ed. *Scandinavian Adult Education.* 2nd edition. Stockholm: KF, 1952.

DENMARK

Dam, Poul and Jørgen Larsen, eds. *Danish Youth, Work and Leisure.* Copenhagen: The Joint Council of Danish Youth Organizations, 1948.

Gille, Halvor. *Family Welfare Measures in Denmark.* Population Studies, Vol. VI, no. 2. London: 1952.

Novrup, J. *Adult Education in Denmark.* Copenhagen: Det danske Forlag, 1952.

FINLAND

Kallio, Niilo. *The School System of Finland.* 2nd edition. Helsinki: 1949.

Lastensuojelun Keskusliitto-Centralförbundet för Barnskydd. *Statistical Survey of Child Welfare Work in the Communes of Finland in 1948.* Helsinki: 1951.

Ministry of Social Affairs, The. *The State's Gift to the Mothers of Finland.* Helsinki: 1948.

NORWAY

Norwegian Joint Committee on International Social Policy, The. *Family and Child Welfare in Norway. A Survey.* 2nd edition. Oslo: 1951.

*** Norwegian Joint Committee on International Social Policy, The. *Children of Norway.* Oslo: 1950.

SWEDEN

Arvidson, Stellan. *Education Suédoise.* Stockholm: Institut Suédois, 1951.

Düring, Ingemar. *The Swedish School-Reform 1950. A Summary of the Government Bill at the Request of the 1946 School Commission.* Uppsala: 1951.

Gille, Halvor. *Recent Developments in Swedish Population Policy.* Population Studies, Vol. II, nos. 1 and 2. London: 1948.

Myrdal, Alva. *Nation and Family. The Swedish Experiment in Democratic Family and Population Policy.* 2. ed. London: Kegan Paul, 1945.

Swedish Institute, The. *Social Services for Children and Young People in Sweden.* Stockholm: 1948.

* Åkerman-Johansson, Brita. *Domestic Workers in Sweden.* International Labour Review. Vol. LXVII, April 1953, pp. 356–366. Geneva: 1953.

Östergren, B., ed. *Higher Education in Sweden.* Stockholm: The Swedish Institute, 1952.

527

CHAPTER V. HOUSING

DENMARK

Hiort, Esbjørn. *Housing in Denmark since 1930.* London: The Architectural Press. Copenhagen: Jul. Gjellerup, 1952.

Thorsteinsson, Th. *Mortgaging of Real Estate in Denmark.* Copenhagen: 1949.

FINLAND

Apartment Houses. Post-War Housing Problems in Finland and the ARAVA Scheme. Reprinted from Arkkitehti no. 6–7. Helsinki: 1951.

NORWAY

Comité Tripartite pour les Relations Internationales concernant la Politique Sociale, Le. *La Lutte en Norvège contre la Crise du Logement.* Oslo: 1952.

Norwegian Joint Committee on International Social Policy, The. *Housing in Norway. A Survey.* Oslo: 1951.

Norwegian Joint Committee on International Social Policy, The. *Building Practices and Housing Standards in Norway. A Statistical Survey.* (Supplement to *Housing in Norway*). Oslo: 1950.

Royal Norwegian Council for Scientific and Industrial Research, The. *Building Research in Norway.* Oslo: 1950.

SWEDEN

Dickson, Harald. *The Housing Market in USA and Sweden.* Land Economics, May 1950. Supplement.

Hald, A., P. Holm and G. Johansson, eds. *Swedish Housing.* Stockholm: The Swedish Institute and others, 1949.

HSB. (Tenants' Savings and Building Society). *Co-operative Housing.* Stockholm: 1952.

Hultén, Bertil. *Building Modern Sweden.* London: Pelican Books, 1951.

Larsson, Yngve and Göran Tegner. *Community Facilities and Services in Sweden.* United Nations. Housing and town and country planning. Bulletin no. 5. 1951.

National Association of Swedish Architects, The. *Swedish Housing of the Forties.* Stockholm: 1950.

National Association of Swedish Architects, The. *Ten Lectures on Swedish Architecture.* Stockholm: 1949.

Silk, Leonard. *Sweden Plans for Better Housing.* Durham, N. C.: Duke University Press, 1948.

Smith, E. H. *Sweden is Modern.* Stockholm: The Architectural Forum, 1947.

Smith, G. E. Kidder. *Sweden Builds.* New York and Stockholm: Bonniers, 1950.

CHAPTER VI. HEALTH AND REHABILITATION

DENMARK

National Association for the Fight against Tuberculosis, The. *The Fight Against Tuberculosis in Denmark.* Copenhagen: Nyt Nordisk Forlag, 1950.

National Health Service, The. *The Combating of Venereal Diseases in Denmark.* Copenhagen: 1949.

FINLAND

Jansson, Kurt. *The Care of Disabled Ex-Service Men in Finland.* Helsinki: The Disabled Ex-Service Men's Association, 1949.

Jansson, Kurt. *The Vocational Rehabilitation of Disabled Ex-Service Men in Finland.* Helsinki: The Disabled Ex-Service Men's Association, 1949.

Virtanen, Paavo, and others. *Return to Work. Vocational Rehabilitation of the Physically Handicapped in Finland.* Helsinki: 1953.

Savonen, Severi. *BCG Vaccination in Finland.* Helsinki: The Finnish National Anti-Tuberculosis Association, 1949.

Savonen, Severi. *The Battle against Tuberculosis in Finland.* Helsinki: The Finnish National Anti-Tuberculosis Association, 1947.

ICELAND

Jonsson, Vilmundur. *Health in Iceland.* Reykjavik: 1940.

Sigurdsson, Sigurdur. *Tuberculosis in Iceland. Epidemiological Studies.* Public Health Service Publication No. 21. Washington, D.C.: Federal Security Agency, 1950.

SWEDEN

Birch-Lindgren, Gustaf. *Modern Hospital Planning in Sweden and other Countries.* With a foreword by Marshall A. Shaffer. Stockholm: The Swedish Institute, 1951.

Maunsbach, A. B. *The Public Dental Service in Sweden.* The Dental Magazine and Oral Topics. London: Oct. 1948.

Myrgård, Arvid. *Sweden's Public Health System.* American-Scandinavian Review, Dec. 1947. New York: The American-Scandinavian Foundation.

Sjöhagen, A. *How a Swedish Temperance Board Works.* Quarterly Journal of Studies on Alcohol. Vol. 14, pp. 69–77. New Haven, Conn.: March 1953.

Ström, J. and H. Johansson. *Maternity and Child Welfare Work in Sweden.* Stockholm: The Medical Board of Sweden, 1950.

Swedish Institute, The. *Public Health and Medicine in Sweden.* Stockholm: Forum, 1949.

CHAPTER VII. SOCIAL SECURITY

FINLAND

National Pension Institution. *National Pension Insurance in Finland.* Helsinki: 1950.

NORWAY

Norwegian Joint Committee on International Social Policy, The. *Social Insurance in Norway. A Survey.* (With a supplement issued in 1952). Oslo: 1950.

** Norwegian Joint Committee on International Social Policy, The. *New Universal Social Security Plan for Norway. »Folketrygden«.* Oslo: 1949.

SWEDEN

Bexelius, Ernst. *Die Sozialversicherung in Schweden.* Berlin: Sonderdruck aus Berliner medizinische Zeitschrift, 1950.

CHAPTER VIII. CO-OPERATION IN SOCIAL AFFAIRS

* *Scandinavian Co-operation. A Report to the Council of Europe.* Prepared by the delegates of Denmark, Iceland, Norway, and Sweden. Stockholm: 1951.

INDEX

Explanatory Note.

Italics denote names of individuals, institutions, and geographical locations. – Entries which refer only to one or two of the five Northern countries are accompanied by a (D) for Denmark, (F) for Finland, (I) for Iceland, (N) for Norway, or (S) for Sweden. – Organs whose names begin with such words as "National", "Council", or the like, are entered under the subject or subjects with which they deal.

530

534

538

539

PHOTOGRAPHS

The photographs appearing on the preceding pages have been contributed by a large number of photographers, institutions, firms, and individuals. In the following enumeration C indicates Copenhagen, H: Helsinki, O: Oslo, R: Reykjavik, and S: Stockholm.

Aero Luftfoto (C), 9 (bottom), 373; AKA film (S), 323; Aktuell A/S (O), 188, 265, 356; Aluminia A/S (C), 91; Andelsudvalget (C), 215; Andersen, A. E. (C), 19; Andersen, Knut (O), 331; Andersson, Yngve (S), 197, 339; Arbeiderbladet (O), 129; Brødrene Andersen A/S (C), 85; Bøgh Christensen, W. (C), 481; Carrebye, J. E. (C), 223, 309 (top); Centralförbundet för barnskydd (H), 253, 254; Dansk Folkeferie (C), 97; Dansk Medicinsk-historisk Museum (C), 336, 341 (bottom); De Gamles By (C), 467; Det kgl. Bibliotek (C), 31; Dittmer, H. (S), 27; Eriksson, L. M. (S), 73, 82; Fennia-Kuva (H), 2; Foto Fritz (C), 159; Foto Hernried (S), 77, 79, 145, 213, 241, 242, 250, 269, 274, 277, 285, 315, 333, 347, 461, 465, 480; Foto Roos (H), 24, 203, 287; Foto Service (C), 3, 83; Gjørling, S. (C), 98; Gleie, E. (C), 341 (top), 402, 403, 455; Gullers, K. W. (S), 11, 21, 67, 149, 247; Gunnar Wangel Film A/S (C), 189, 375; Götaverken (Gothenburg, Sweden), 80; Göth, S. (S), 367; Hansen, Gerner (C), 324; Hansen, Vagn (C), 208, 303; Hauerslev (C), 477; Henriksen & Steen A/S (O), 94; I.F.A. (S), 358; Jonals Co. (C), 301; Jósepsson, Thorsteinn (R), 7, 29, 69, 194, 273, 292, 317, 343; Järlås, S. (Sweden), 323, 447; Kalmio AB. (H), 252; Karlskrona Klichéanstalt (Sweden), 381; Kidder Smith, G. E. (New York), 205; Knudsen, Erik (Ålborg, Denmark), 365; Larsson, Carl (Gävle, Sweden), 260, 261; Maarbjerg, J. (C), 473; Mødrehjælpen (C), 255; Nilsen, Ulf (C), 262; Nilsson, Lennart (S), 5, 62, 71, 357; Nordberg, B. (S), 199, 305, 327; Olsson, E. H. (Åkeshov, Sweden), 81; Osuuskassojen Keskuslutto (Finland), 226; Petersen, Erik (C), 59; Petersen, Poul (C), 263; Petersen, Max (C), 463; Pietinen, A. (H), 349, 422; Politiken (C), 321; Pressens Bild AB. (S), 51; Rasmussen, Carl (C), 35, 63, 264, 266, 427; Ravn, K. (Holte, Denmark), 33; Sjögren, F. (S), 431; SKF-foto (Gothenburg, Sweden), 25; Soldan, T. L. (H), 361; Staf, E. M. (Tampere, Finland), 55, 259, 411; Strüwing (C), 283, 291, 311, 463; Sundahl (Nacka, Sweden), 309 (bottom); Suomen Kuvalehden (H), 439; Teigen, K. (O), 297; Teknisk Foto (C), 318; Thomsen, Pétur (R), 369, 487; Tvedt, L. (O), 4; Ulmerudh, T. (S), 23, 173; Weyl (Sweden), 258; Wilst (O), 9 (top), 224.